ЯazoR

ЯazoR

Revolutinary Art for Cultural Revolution

Amiri Baraka

TWP
THIRD WORLD PRESS
Progressive Black Publishing Since 1967

Chicago

Third World Press
Publishers since 1967
Chicago

First Edition
Printed in the United States of America

The production and printing of this book has been generously
supported by the Lomax Companies of Philadelphia.

Library of Congress Control Number: 2009938304
ISBN 13: 978-0-88378-300-9

16 15 14 13 12 11   6 5 4 3 2 1

Cover Design: Keir Thirus
Interior Layout: Relana Johnson

Contents

Sixties and Eighties

Nineties

Contents

The Millennium

Contents

Notes on Culture, Art and More

CONTENTS

Sixties
and
Eighties

Ritual Confrontation
Drama of the '60s & '70s

I first heard the term "ritual drama" when it came out of my white character's mouth in the play *The Slave* in 1964. The character, Easley, uses the term to put down Walker Vessels, the would-be Black revolutionary. Easley said of Vessels' literary work that it was just "ritual drama." Later, after he has been shot by Vessels, for attempting to jump him, and is dying, he also condemns Vessels' somewhat ambiguous revolutionary posturing as "ritual drama" as well.

So, from its conception in my mind, the term referred to a kind of literature, but could describe a life-style as well. Later on, in the late '60s, I came to be more conscious of actually utilizing elements of ritual in my own work. At this point, I was referring to an African derived ritual element, where chant and dance forms, plus aspects of African religious and cultural rites recur in a cultural symbolism which puts me, the writer, and the audience in touch with what I conceived to be an African theatrical experience.

Ritual drama should take form as recurring symbolic action which sought to reach deeper into an audience, especially a Black audience, than the shining surfaces of American response and produce deeper emotional recognition of self and nation—the Afro-American nation—self in nation, and cultural history as emotional response.

But the idea was never to rest on surfaces, as merely dance,

3

or chanting, repeated quai-religious symbolist act. The ritual was to, as ritual always most legitimately does, reach down and back, to raise consciousness in the entire action, speaking for the past, present, and future. The wordless mimed *Resurrection* was one level of ritual—a communication history, viz., how we got here like this. There were short chants like *Black Power, Ritual*, and in 1967 the historical pageant *Slave Ship* in which I tried to extend the ritual, the repeated symbolic acts, to express the metaphor and literal reality of our enslavement and its ultimate destruction.

But even in more abstract works like *Bloodrites*, I always tried to connect repeated symbolic action to literal reality. My motive was always to make reality more understandable! At heart, the Black Liberation Movement (BLM) itself was my subject and catalyst. And it is interesting that the development of Black drama during the late '60s and early '70s can best be understood by investigating the social context of its creation.

Malcolm X's assassination is a real turning point in the Black Liberation Movement. Malcolm X was the most articulate spokesman for the Black masses, particularly their working class. When he defined the BLM as a struggle for self-determination, self-respect, and self-defense, we were moved because he was saying back to us what was really in our hearts. When he called for Black unity and Black Power we echoed his thunder, because we recognized it as our own!

Malcolm's murder, by the same forces killing our people in Atlanta, Buffalo, Mobile, and all over this society, by the same forces that killed Evers, Hampton, Featherstone, and Dr. King, left the movement with a deep void.

By 1964, Martin Luther King's middleclass leadership had been called into question. The March on Washington in 1963 had been the high point of the Civil Rights Movement, but the Birmingham bombing and the lack of real change was its repudiation. James Baldwin's *Blues for Mr. Charlie* in March 1964 questions non-violence. Hansberry's *Raisin In The Sun* is *the* civil rights play, *Blues* is actually post-civil rights and even has the clear element of class struggle in the confrontation between the King-like preacher Meridian (a border line) and his militant son Richard (Baldwin even related to sexual symbolism within). In fact, Baldwin even has Richard murdered by the white racist because Richard has given his gun to his father in an attempt to live the father's non-violent philosophy.

4

Blues, a great play in my estimation, also has distinct elements of ritual and ritualized action in it, by way of the disordering of time and space. We move backward and forward as if order is willed!

History and dreams collide with reality and extend it, yet all of what we see and feel is connected with a literal and social reality of the United States, even right now! The lynching of a young boy a few weeks ago in Mobile, Ala should attest clearly to this.

The next month after *Blues* opened on Broadway (an event that caused James Baldwin to be negatively review by white critics) *Dutchman* had a different type of opening off Broadway. Basing itself in the Black skin white mask schizophrenia of a sector of the black middle class. It told of that groups confrontation with America. It showed the seduction (carrot) aspect of the United States (a white woman) but also the violent repression (the stick).

Where *Blues* deeply questioned the civil rights approach to Black Liberation, i.e., non-violence, *Dutchman* dismissed it, but showed a black middle class individualistic intellectual who, isolated from the black masses, is quickly slaughtered. And the threat of the endless repetition of the slaughter is certainly ritualistic, as another young black man appears, apparently, to be murdered by the same white murderers.

The long hot summer of '64 showed decisively that the Black masses had gone beyond the civil rights thrust of Black middle class leadership-rebellions in Jacksonville, Harlem, Jersey City, Keansburg, New Jersey, Dixmoor, Illinois (a suburb of Chicago), demonstrated that the Black masses had the will to carry the revolution through to the end!

Malcolm's assassination cut off his rise as maximum leader of the BLM who would be functioning as head of a largely independent working class organization. Within the BLM, militant sectors of the Black petty bourgeoisie became more visible and without the leadership that a working class leader like Malcolm could provide, and in the absence of a real revolutionary party, middle class intellectuals in some cases swept past reality into various areas of metaphysics. For example, the Nation of Islam, which catapulted Malcolm to national prominence, was itself a creature of great contradiction. One, on the positive side, it had revolutionary nationalism — a resistance to white supremacy and Black national oppression. Plus, it had a distinct call for self-determination, including the demand for land and political power!

On the other hand, the Nation of Islam was based in metaphysics, religion and the ideology of the small producer. When Malcolm was murdered, the metaphysical aspect of the Nation of Islam that also existed in the BLM went extreme within the whole movement. Many people simply missed the significance of Malcolm's split with the Nation and how revolutionary nationalism and anti-imperialism were no longer compatible with cultural nationalism and metaphysics.

Malcolm's important teaching of the significance of Africa in our consciousness as Afro-Americans struggling for self-determination in North America was distorted in sectors of the BLM.

The Black Arts Movement of the '60s used Malcolm as its fundamental reference of Black responses toward America. The woefully integrated black intellectuals of the '50s were slapped awake by Malcolm's fire words and the torrent of events that forced change in the real world. But without the constant of black working class activist focus to guide the movement, both the BLM itself and the Black Arts Movement that showed it to itself (and the world) also turned more abstract and metaphysical.

Attention to Africa is important to the BLM because it is part of the restoration of historical identity to the Black masses and one aspect of the growth of Black national consciousness, which is necessary to make the cry of self-determination for the Afro-American nation more than just a revolutionary democratic slogan. The Black Arts Movement reflected this necessary refocusing on Africa. But Malcolm meant a living Africa, a fighting Africa, an Africa fighting against Imperialism.

Too often post-Malcolm attention to Africa in sectors of the BLM and in the BAM became abstract and metaphysical. It was a never-never-land — Africa. The Africa of "Roots." In fact, I was chairman of a cultural nationalist organization that not only tried to partially impose African feudalism on Afro-Americans in the name of Black values, but even justified male chauvinism on the grounds that this upheld African tradition!

The trend in the so-called ritual drama and in Black literature in general during this period shows this shameful shift in emphasis. Atavism and metaphysics abound under the banner of African tradition and culture. And many people during the period of the early '70s began to utilize the African Ritual form as an end in itself or to justify African traditions the African masses are trying to transcend or the rituals became little more than religious "trips" as useful to real life change as the average church service!

But the fundamental role of Black theater as an Afro-American Revolutionary Theater must be the same as any conscious element of Black life—resistant to national oppression and racism and project practicable alternatives politically and aesthetically.

The most conscious and active Black Theater must be tied to the Afro-American Nation's historical struggle to liberate itself. The main tradition of Black Artists has been this resistance and struggle, and while Black theater has suffered terribly because of the lack of resources needed to fully project its products, it has existed honorably and powerfully. Part of this problem, of resources will only be solved by forming Black artists organizations and commercial and educational institutions, including theaters and publishing houses. We have *never* been citizens of this country, only its slaves—even today—and as long as we resist this intelligence the reward for our confusion will be minimally frustration and in many cases death! Either we fight for self-determination and begin to create those real institutions that will carry and develop our ideas and our own traditions in art and scholarship, commerce and communication, and politics, and so forth—all with sound self-controlled economic bases or we will go on in slavery.

In essence, the most powerful ritual animating our real lives has been the centuries old struggle for Black liberation. And the Black artist, as Langston Hughes said in his great essay, "The Negro Artist and The Racial Mountain," must base himself or herself in the actual life and emotional power of the Black masses if moving and meaningful Black art is to be created. The ritual of Black life is confrontation with the horrifying monster, white racist monopoly capitalist America. It is worse and more deadly than any demon or devil or evil spirit, so that our artistic rituals must also reflect that confrontation.

Today, all over this society, an absolutely reactionary trend has been consolidated, legitimated and now even legalized. The murders of twenty-one Black children in Atlanta; Buffalo Blacks with hearts ripped out; lynchings in Mobile; the Klan and Nazis freed after assassinating five people on national TV; police murders of Blacks and Latinos going wild-and add to these things budget

7

cuts to the tune of 37 billion dollars, which will hit Blacks and other oppressed nationalities first and worst, and the rising danger of nuclear war and you have a picture of a nation whose white racist bourgeois rulers are lurching toward fascism. The rise of racist violence is a clear calling card of fascism. And even the attack on president Reagan must be seen as Malcolm X saw the assassination of Kennedy as merely "Chickens coming home to roost." In a climate of racism and violence, some of that hate might even spill over on its initiators.

For Black Theater, like the BLM, this is a critical and dangerous time. But no matter what these racists do—we are not intimidated. By the end of the '80s they will be wishing the '60s would return! For Black Theater, like Black people, adversity will only make us stronger and finally invincible.

(1981)

Amiri Baraka on Langston Hughes

*New York Center for Visual History
October 17, 1985, Small's Paradise New York City
Director: St. Clair Bourne Interview
(Amiri Baraka opens reading four of Langston Hughes' poems.)*

AMIRI BARAKA: **"Let America Be America Again"**
Let America be America again.
Let it be the dream it used to be.
Let it be the pioneer on the plain
Seeking a home where he himself is free.

(America never was America to me.)

Let America be the dream the dreamers dreamed—
Let it be that great strong land of love
Where never kings connive nor tyrants scheme
That any man be crushed by one above.

(It never was America to me.)

O, let my land be a land where Liberty
Is crowned with no false patriotic wreath,
But opportunity is real, and life is free,
Equality is in the air we breathe.

(There's never been equality for me,
Nor freedom in this "homeland of the free.")

Say, who are you that mumbles in the dark?
And who are you that draws your veil across the stars?

I am the poor white, fooled and pushed apart,
I am the Negro bearing slavery's scars.
I am the red man driven from the land,
I am the immigrant clutching the hope I seek —
And finding only the same old stupid plan
Of dog eat dog, of mighty crush the weak.

I am the young man, full of strength and hope,
Tangled in that ancient endless chain
Of profit, power, gain, of grab the land!
Of grab the gold! Of grab the ways of satisfying need!
Of work the men! Of take the pay!
Of owning everything for one's own greed!

I am the farmer, bondsman to the soil.
I am the worker sold to the machine.
I am the Negro, servant to you all.
I am the people, humble, hungry, mean —
Hungry yet today despite the dream.
Beaten yet today — O, Pioneers!
I am the man who never got ahead,
The poorest worker bartered through the years.

Yet I'm the one who dreamt our basic dream
In the Old World while still a serf of kings,
Who dreamt a dream so strong, so brave, so true,
That even yet its mighty daring sings
In every brick and stone, in every furrow turned
That's made America the land it has become.
O, I'm the man who sailed those early seas
In search of what I meant to be my home —
For I'm the one who left dark Ireland's shore,
And Poland's plain, and England's grassy lea,
And torn from Black Africa's strand I came

To build a "homeland of the free."

The free?

Who said the free? Not me?
Surely not me? The millions on relief today?
The millions shot down when we strike?
The millions who have nothing for our pay?
For all the dreams we've dreamed
And all the songs we've sung
And all the hopes we've held
And all the flags we've hung,
The millions who have nothing for our pay —
Except the dream that's almost dead today.

O, let America be America again —
The land that never has been yet —
And yet must be — the land where every man is free.
The land that's mine — the poor man's, Indian's, Negro's, ME —
Who made America,
Whose sweat and blood, whose faith and pain,
Whose hand at the foundry, whose plow in the rain,
Must bring back our mighty dream again.

Sure, call me any ugly name you choose —
The steel of freedom does not stain.
From those who live like leeches on the people's lives,
We must take back our land again,
America!

O, yes,
I say it plain,
America never was America to me,
And yet I swear this oath —
America will be!

Out of the rack and ruin of our gangster death,
The rape and rot of graft, and stealth, and lies,
We, the people, must redeem
The land, the mines, the plants, the rivers.

The mountains and the endless plain—
All, all the stretch of these great green states—
And make America again!

*****

"Dream Boogie" "Dream Boogie"
Good Morning, daddy!
Ain't you heard
The boogie-woogie rumble
Of a dream deferred?

Listen closely:

You'll hear their feet

Beating out and beating out a -

You think

It's a happy beat?

Listen to it closely:

Ain't you heard

something underneath

like a -

What did I say?

Sure,

I'm happy!

Take it away!

Hey, pop!

Re-bop!

Mop!

Y-e-a-h!

******

"Madrid"

*Damaged by shells, many of the clocks
on the public buildings in Madrid have
stopped. At night, the streets are pitch
dark.*
   — News Item

Put out the lights and stop the clocks.
Let time stand still.
Again man mocks himself
And all his human will to build and grow
Madrid!
The fact and symbol of man's woe.
Madrid!
Time's end and throw-back,
Birth of darkness,
Years of light reduced:
The ever minus of the brute,
The nothingness of barren land
And stone and metal
Emptyness of gold,
The dullness of a bill of sale:
BOUGHT AND PAID FOR! SOLD!
Stupidity of hours that do not move
Because all clocks are stopped.
Blackness of nights that do not see
Because all lights are out.
Madrid!
Beneath the bullets!
Madrid!
Beneath the bombing planes!
Madrid!
In the fearful dark!

"Johannesburg Mines"

In the Johannesburg mines
There are 240,000 natives working.

What kind of poem
Would you make out of that?

240,000 natives working
In the Johannesburg mines.

***

BARAKA: As far as the question you asked about Langston being a torch-bearer..."In the Johannesburg mines," yes, I think that Langston was a kind of torch-bearer of Black literature. And I think you can see that from his piece called, "The Artist and the Racial Mountain," or "The Negro Artist and the Racial Mountain," which I think came out about what — 1925, 1926 in the *Nation* Magazine, as an answer to George Schuyler. George Schuyler had written a piece called, "The Negro Art Hokum," in which he said — you know, he drew the brilliant conclusion that there couldn't be really such a thing as Black art. And for Langston laying out really the kind of the basis for that kind of definition in his mind, really laid out a kind of — I guess a kind of stance for the Black artist in terms of dealing with white supremacy on one hand, the whole question of the relationship of the artist to say, culture and politics. And I think he laid — I mean that's like a manifesto for the Harlem Renaissance.

Q: Did he in fact follow it in his work in the '30s, and can you kind of give us an example of some of the stuff that he did?

BARAKA: Well, in the '30s Langston I think went further because he took the kind of "Black is Beautiful" and the African history, Black consciousness writing that he was doing in the '20s, and in the '30s he began to expand that to deal with the concept of pan-Africanism, for instance. You knowing, showing that not only were the Afro-American people exploited, that Black people were exploited all over the world, whether it was Johannesburg, or Trinidad or Jamaica. And then later he, as the '30s progressed, you know, the heavy influence of socialism on American intellectuals, and Black

14

intellectuals particularly. And I think that Langston is much more profound than people realize, for the obvious reason that Black literature is low-rated anyway, but Langston Hughes is not only a great poet, but a fantastic short story writer. There is no finer book of short stories written in the '40s than *The Ways Of White Folks*. He's also a brilliant playwright. He still was the playwright who had, as far as a Black playwright, who was on Broadway longer, and with more plays, than anybody else, starting with MULATTO. And plus Langston was a great translator. I've been thinking about trying to do a book called *The Translations of Langston Hughes*, because when I first read Garcia Lorca, it was Langston Hughes' translation. Nicolas Guillen was Langston Hughes' translation. Aimé Césaire, Leopold Senghor, Dumas, you know, Jacques Romain's great novel, *Masters Of The Dew*. All these are Hughes' translations, you see, and when I read García Lorca, for instance, I stopped because I saw Langston Hughes under it as the translator, you know, and such a beautiful poem. But I'm saying that it was Langston who was sort publicist for the whole Black arts movement in the '20s.

Q: Well, when he did *The Weary Blues*, for example, why do you think there was such an uproar by the Black press and certain critics, in using blues as a basis for his poems, and why do you think they didn't like that?

BARAKA: Well, see because Langston and... (Q: petty bourgeois Negroes?) Yeah, Langston and "The Weary Blues," why there was criticism of that. Well, it's because there were—many of the so-called—very conservative Negro critics who thought that because Langston and people like Claude McKay focused on working people—you know what I mean, the kind of mass of Black prototypes. A lot of those people thought that well, why are you, talking about those kind of Black folk? The Black folks we want you to talk about is the kind who are like socially mobile and aspiring to move up into the middle class, and so forth and so on. And interestingly enough even somebody as progressive as DuBois, who, you know, was going through his constant transition, made that kind of criticism, saying, you should be showing, you know, a different kind of Black people. Same criticism as Claude McKay. But like Langston said in the "The Negro Artist and the Racial Mountain," he said, this is the strength, he said, this is the strength that the Black artist can claim, to actually be able to perceive the world the way the Black masses do, with the additional clarity, you know, and the additional kind of, let's say power, artistic power and political clarity that the artist can provide.

Q: Okay, so there's blues, and there's that. Let's say twenty, thirty years later he dealt with be-bop in a series of poems. Now, was he also in the vanguard there, or was he taking his lead from somewhere else?

BARAKA: Langston has always been in the vanguard. See this is what I'm saying, this is why people sleep on Langston. The first poet I saw in the '50s after I had come home-from the service, you know, looking for the intelligentsia, you know, the modern intelligentsia. The first poet I saw reading poetry with jazz was Langston Hughes, with Charlie Mingus, you see. And that was when a whole lot of people walking around who didn't even understand what that was, who later then had to catch up with that and try to claim it. But Langston was doing that. The only other person I knew who was doing that at the time, who could even be remotely compared to Langston was Kenneth Rexroth. But all the people who were like advertised as being the great P & J folks, they don't come along dealing with that until later. But it was Langston. And Langston again in his writing, "The Negro Artist and the Racial Mountain," says, and it's very important, says
that, the Black poet has to write, and create poetry as powerful as Bessie Smith and Duke Ellington. And, that's clear. I mean that's the deal. Has to create work that is like Afro-America, that is a creation, just like you can listen to Bessie Smith and say, that is a creation, of the African-American people, you understand. And with that kind of high consciousness.

Q: Okay, Amiri, in terms of his music and poems of the '50s, is that Afro-American music tells conditions, right? What was his poetry?

BARAKA: Well, it depends on when you want to, analyze it. Well, in the '50s what Langston did was try to return to some of the kind of militancy and intensity, I mean after the McCarthy bust, after he was humiliated before, Eastland and H.U.A.C., when the sort of Black Arts Movement began to rise with the civil rights movement

16

and the Black Liberation Movement, Langston then began to take another fresh look—and began to write poems fully as important as some of the poems he wrote in the '20s and the '30s. I'm talking about the book called *The Panther And The Lash*, or *Ask Your Mama*, the jazz sequence. So I think that what Langston did is took strength from the kind of rekindling of the movement after the Cold War, McCarthyism, and so forth. And his last poems show, a kind of return to the kind of intensity and grace of his earlier work.

Q: Now you were on the scene then. What was your reaction to him—well you and other poets—I mean, was he sort of like, did they consider him as a guy who was past his prime, or did they consider him like a, you know, a tribal elder who was no longer relevant, or was he still.

BARAKA: Well, I think most of the people that I knew—I guess you'd have to divide according to who you're talking about, because if you're talking about most of the, I think, the Black poets, there is a kind of, I think, a respect for Langston, but for a generation—when they're very young people, they really don't know Langston's works, you know. I remember reading his works to one young poet who said, oh wow, I always thought his works were just funny. I mean it's a complete distortion of Langston's work, but you see, Langston, like I said, was such a great publicist of poetry and such a great person and so on, when I first came to New York, when I first published a poem, he was one of the first people to actually recognize me. He sent me a letter, and I'd never talked to him before in my life. He sent me a letter and said, he liked the poem, and you know, we began a correspondence.

Q: Did you think that his—as a critic—did you think that his poems were technically that cool, or were you...

BARAKA: About Langston? No, see what I thought about Langston was that Langston was very glib and facile. That he could write you know as easily as breathing, and it's true. What I didn't understand is that the consistently high quality of all that he did write because Langston has a tremendous kind of output that I don't think people really realize. I mean he wrote books on the N.A.A.C.P. He wrote a children's book about jazz and a children's book about Africa. I mean he wrote a book about Black entertainment. You know what I mean? He's written at least about twenty-five songs, television scripts, novels, short stories, autobiographies, those kind of things — so I mean, when you really check out the enormous amount of work that Langston has done, and the high level that most of it's at, then you can begin to understand who he is.

Q: Why do you think he has not been played up? Like you said people think he's just funny. Why do you think, Why do you think...

BARAKA: Well, that's true for all Black art. No Black art is played up, except momentarily to be pimped off of.

Q: Okay, give it a full sentence. In other words, I think that....

BARAKA: Oh, no—I think that Langston was never really recognized at the level that he deserved to be because there are no Black people recognized at that level. I mean if you have to recognize who Langston Hughes is, then what does that make you if you're part of that force that's oppressing him, and that he's talking about in his plays. If you have to admit who Duke Ellington is, what does that make American Music and American culture. If you have to admit that of all the composers in the United States there are not many that can even be spoken of in the same sentence with Duke Ellington, certainly not the ones that they think of in these, you know, these academies. But so then you say, well if that's true, if Duke Ellington is, perhaps, the greatest composer that America has produced, a man who registered two thousand pieces of music, then you have to say, well, if this country has been given to harassing, insulting, exploiting-well, if this country has been given to, like, harassing, insulting, exploiting, and oppressing Black people, and in the name of white supremacy diminishing everything we do, (make it seem) childish, primitive, late, backward, stupid, you know, over-emotional, corny, of no value, academically unsound, you know, or whatever. Then if you have to admit Langston Hughes is Langston Hughes or Duke Ellington is Duke Ellington, then where does that throw the rest of your white supremacy constructs?

Q: And you're saying that's been institutionalized and therefore...

BARAKA: Sure. I mean, it's perfectly normal for people to admit that Duke Ellington, until the last days of his life was working one-night stands, and ditto Count Basie, who was working one-night stands in a wheelchair until the day he died. Now I was at a forum in town and the people told me the Count wanted to do that. That he really wanted to play one-night stands while he was like paralyzed until the day he died. You know, well maybe they believed that.

Q: If you had to have an overview, what would you say was Langston Hughes' greater contribution to Black literature?

BARAKA: That he was (Q: I think that...) Langston Hughes greatest contribution to literature is that he was an author, that he was principally a very skilled intellectual with a great deal of energy and optimism, and if you go to other countries, you can really begin to get Langston's greatness when you go to other countries and ask. When I went to Cuba, the first person Nicolás Guillén, who is now the president of the whole Cuban Artists association, asked me, where is Langston? If you read the signatories to the petitions in the '30s about the Spanish Civil War, the anti-Fascist group, it's Langston Hughes. Any thing of value that he could find in Spanish, you know, or French, he translated. And there's an enormous amount of his translation that we have to be familiar with. But he was an unrelenting publicist for Black art and Black people. And I think that's his greatest gift.

Q: Now, this might be a separate subject, but in terms of the quality of the craft of his poetry, aside from the effects and the...quality and the craft, and I know you can't talk about those outside of the effect, but in a sense you can. How do you rate him?

BARAKA: Well, see, Langston, and this is the problem with I think a lot of Black intellectuals — we tend to be semi-literate because we go to these colleges and we study other, to be other, for other. You know. So the question is that when we come upon the original, like Langston Hughes, who is an original, who tells you in his essay that what he wanted to do was write using the form and content of Afro-American music, that's what he's done all his life, and he's been imminently successfully. And I think what you see, the whole thing about Langston—if you read *The Ways Of White Folks*, there's no better book of short stories written in the '40s, and I'm talking about the period of the Harlem Renaissance as contemporary with Anglo-American modernism. So you have to talk about, you know, F. Scott Fitzgerald, you know, William Carlos William, the writers of short stories, then Issac Babel, Cheever, or whoever you want to lay out as the writer of short stories. *The Ways Of White Folks* is constructed at a level equal to any of that. So I think that it's important—you see because if you don't understand the whole of the movement from the '20s to '40s, it's like you're talking about Allen Ginsberg's work and leaving me out, in terms of a discussion of American poetry. Well, that might suit some chauvinist principles, but it's not accurate. So it's the same thing in terms of, if you talk about Stravinsky, you must talk Duke Ellington, since Duke Ellington influenced Stravinsky. You can talk about William Carlos Williams, but you must talk about Langston Hughes, otherwise people will think you're ignorant. You can talk about Gertrude Stein but you must talk about Zora Neale Hurston, whose concerns about feminism are much more relevant than Gertrude Stein's are today— I mean in terms of the real deal, I mean in terms of studying it. In terms of the handling of literature, check out Zora Neale. The problem is that in these colleges, they're only taught a very narrow kind of national chauvinist view. So you never really get to understand the kind of richness and diversity of Afro-American literature.

Q: Last question. What kind of price do you think Langston paid? Okay, what was the kind of stuff that Langston wrote in the '30s?

BARAKA: Well, see, the kind of development that Langston went through in the '20s, his poetry was what you call, "Black is beautiful," Black consciousness, you know, African history. In the '30s he began to take on more of an internationalist content. First, a kind of pan-Africanist view that identified Black people all over the world as being oppressed, and from a common source. That is, he began to identify imperialism. And then, finally, more and more socialist ideas are incorporated into his work, and you know, he went to the Soviet Union and so forth, and he was published a few times during the '30s by Marxist Leninst organizations. There were a couple of books that were put out by the International Workers Order. One was *Scottsboro Limited*, which was really avant-garde, a kind of revolutionary play that was never done. In fact, it's never ever put into the bibliography. And he wrote poems like "Good Morning Revolution," you know, "Goodbye, Christ," a poem to Lenin, a poem to the Chinese revolution. These were really some very heavy things. Plus, some poems about the Spanish Civil war, and his continued a kind of analysis of the national oppression of the Afro-American people. Now, he paid for this in a sense, because Langston wanted to be a writer. I'm saying that he wanted to be a writer, because a lot of writers understand that they have to do something else if they want to write. Langston said he wanted to be a professional writer, and so that's why he set out to write all kinds of things to keep himself afloat, financially.

What happened is, as he began to take more and more of these left positions, the state, a lot of right wing individuals, like for instance, Aimee Semple McPherson, actually they began to demonstrate against Langston. He would show up in the city to read and people would have picket lines out in front of the place. Or, hotels would not let him stay because he was a Red poet. They went so far as to, when he went to Spain, a newspaper published an account that the anti-Franco forces had actually killed him in Spain. I saw that up at the Yale University Library. There was his handwriting on the headlines that he'd sent to a friend that said, "I'm dead." So, they put pressure on him leading up to the House Un-American Activities thing, when they tried to actually purge the kind of left and progressive ideas from American intelligentsia. And I mean that's the whole — when the Hollywood Ten — that's when Reagan rises to try to sterilize and absolutely commercialize American film. American film has never been the same after McCarthyism. All you have to do is check the films that they make today, and check out the complete works of Henry Fonda, John Garfield, Humphrey Bogart, or for that matter, you know, Joan Crawford, Barbara Stanwyck, and those people are more progressive than any women that they have playing now, even those who are supposed to have a feminist consciousness. Those women were much more politically conscious, you know, *Stella Dallas*, for instance. Barbara Stanwyck, is much more conscious politically than women in film today who call themselves feminists.

This means that the whole culture itself is being destroyed.

American popular culture is being destroyed because they are now straitjacketing the culture and making it serve imperialism. I mean American film was like classically liberal, Democrat, you know whether it was Frank Capra, you understand, it was still liberal Democrat. That was the kind of projection that it wanted, but after McCarthyism, that's when you begin to get police as heroes, you see. And Langston actually was hammered down in the H.U.A.C. thing, because they made him "confess" to Eastland that he was sorry he had written "Good Morning Revolution," that actually "Goodbye, Christ" wasn't his point of view, that was some unnamed person's point of view, that he just was repeating which he had license to do as an author. But I think, even though Langston said those things, it's unfortunate — still he had the sense to bounce back, and we have to understand, that was a period when they attacked Black intellectuals. You know they ran Richard Wright out of the country into exile. They indicted W.E.B. DuBois as an agent of a foreign power. He was ninety years old, you know, a little old man with round glasses and a three piece suit, they said, this is the most dangerous man in America. Or somebody like Paul Robeson they actually destroyed. They took his passport, they would not let him perform on stage and screen. So it was an attack on Black intellectuals to get rid of the whole left ideology that came out of the '20s and the '30s and the influence of the Communist Party. And Langston got beat up a little bit, but I think he came back.

Q: Is there anything?

BARAKA: No, except that I think that it's really important for people who think of themselves as intellectuals to know Langston Hughes' work.

Q: Okay, Amiri, why did he write what he wrote in the '30s — what did he write in the '30s and why did he do that?

BARAKA: Well, by the '30s Langston's poetry had moved from the early kind of "Black is beautiful," Black consciousness, African consciousness phase, to a kind of pan-Africanism where he began to see that Black people all over the planet were suffering from the same kinds of exploitation and oppression. And then, I think, based also on the fact of the influence of socialist ideas during that period,

22

you know, the Russian Revolution had been in 1917. By 1929, the Depression came, a lot of people were disillusioned with capitalism. And the ideas coming out of the Communist Party U.S.A. had a great deal of influence on American intellectuals in general, and Black intellectuals specifically — for obvious reasons. And by the '50s the leading Black intellectuals were almost run out of this country by McCarthy and company; I mean, Langston was brought down to H.U.A.C. and chastised...Langston began to write poems as a pan-Africanist, identifying the exploitation and oppression of Black people everywhere. There's a poem called "The Same," and it says, "whether you're in Johannesburg or Harlem, whether you're in Jamaica, or Trinidad, it is all the same." He identifies a kind of Afro-American national oppression. By the '30s, with the intensification of Marxist ideas, he becomes first a Pan-Africanist, and then you can see very clearly socialist thought, you know, beginning to influence his work a great deal. I mean, poems like "Good Morning Revolution," or "Goodbye, Christ" and things like that. Those are all poems that are heavily influenced by Marxist-Leninist theory and ideology.

Q: At a much slower pace, tell me what was the price he paid for this sort of career. What happened — what's your analysis of what happened?

BARAKA: Well, Langston did have to pay for that, you know, his progressive ideas, as early as the late '40s then right wing groups, the state, began to harass him about being on the left. For instance, even people like Aimee Semple McPherson, the evangelist. She picketed Langston Hughes' readings and certain hotels refused him admittance. Certain places where he was supposed to speak, at the last minute the hall would close up. So, since he wanted to make it as a writer, this was very detrimental to his career. And I think essentially that's why Langston said the things he said: I'm sorry I wrote "Good Morning Revolution," and "Goodbye, Christ:" these are not my sentiments, these are somebody else's sentiments. I'm just using them in the poem. He really had to pay for that, even as late as the writing of the whole "Simple" series, because Langston's work was not simple. What he did was focus on the masses, the working class Black and draw a very profound kind of analysis out of that. But by the end of his life, with that column he had in in the

Post, to talk about Black life he had to quote "make it simple," when Langston himself knew that it was not simple, but that it was very complex. But after a time he knew a revolutionary statement had to be made. So I think that by the '50s and the '60s, he had sort of reintegrated himself to his previous revolutionary stance. Because I think he was encouraged by the whole Black Arts Movement and the young writers who seemed to be taking, a kind of militant stance and understanding the need for that.

Q: Give me another statement.

BARAKA: Well when he went to the H.U.A.C. Well, first he went there and the irony was that what's the guy's name, the great Democrat? Eastland, from Mississippi, was the one that challenged Langston on "Good Morning Revolution." During the '50s, H.U.A.C. was harassing all the Black intellectuals. DuBois was indicted as an agent of foreign power, Richard Wright was run off into exile, Paul Robeson's passport was seized — he was put under virtual house arrest by Harry Truman, etcetera. And Langston had to appear before H.U.A.C. and actually confess his "crimes." They let him know that if he wanted to continue to make it as a writer, if he wanted to read, if he wanted to make these appearances, then he not only had to appear, but this kind of line had to be put out there, about how America had changed, and when he was young and wild he had written these things, but now he had changed up, and so forth and so on. This was the same era that they took the Hollywood Ten to jail, the same era that they trashed American film. But I think Langston recovered marvelously from that, I think by the end of the '50s, he had gotten back that kind of militancy, broad commitment. I think during the '50s, there was a kind of chaos along with a lack of organization especially with the communist party under attacked and in disarray because of F.B.I. infiltration. We have to remember because all those times are back again. I mean, our boy Ronald Reagan began his career by trashing the movie industry. That's how he got big, you know, as president of the Screen Actors Guild and an FBI informant. After he did that then they sent him to California as the Governor, where he killed up a lot of the Panthers, so I guess he showed that if he could deal with the Reds and the Blacks he had dealt with the two most problematic colors in the United States. (Laughs)

24

Q: Anything else you'd like to say?

BARAKA: No, that'll hold it till the next time. (Laughs)

(10/1985)

Protest and Progress
(Toni Morrison's *Dreaming Emmett*)

First what should be understood before this explication is that, to me, Toni Morrison is one of the finest writers this country has produced. At this point she is the usually somewhat mythological "state of the art." Mainly because she has taken the Black liberation spirit of the '60s and brought it forward, specifically shaped to dig deep into the fundamental relations of the strugglers themselves.

This is important because in the present epoch of what is called the women's movement, Toni has not only raised very clearly the question of Black women's oppression (and the triple chain of class, national and sexual oppression Black working women bear), but she has had the deeper insight and understanding to, at the same time, continually raise the basic question of Black national oppression and the ever more destructive values on all the citizens of the American white supremacy capitalist society!

This is critical because it is clear that Toni understands that at base it is the society itself which is at fault and so casually murderous with its fiendish social, political, and economic structure, which rests historically and in the present on the slavery of the African, the economic exploitation of workers, and the genocide of Native Americans. The essence of all this is a fundamental denial of democracy, in an all around non-illusory way, to all but a few wealthy white men.

The struggle against women's oppression is a struggle for

democracy, equality, in much the same way that the Black liberation struggle is or the Chicano national struggle or the struggle of workers to make a living from their labor. It is in the villain's interest only that these struggles are made to seem isolated and unrelated or mutually exclusive or contradictory.

In fact, they are part of the same national democratic struggle that all of us, but the owners and their trustees, must wage to survive and develop. For instance, the present use the owners are making of the general women's liberation movement is that they are constantly trying to assert that the struggle for women's rights and the broad struggle to eliminate imperialism are at odds with each other. Even the bucks that publishers and the media are making now off the women's movement come in the main from putting out a steady stream of garbage that separate the various democratic struggles or puts them in confrontation with each others. Yet some works of real value get through.

Remember the publishing wave that came as a result of the Black wave of fire in the '60s Black Liberation Movement (now it is extremely difficult for Black writers to publish, even those with names in the '60s). In a few years the woman's movement will be like that. The johns will have scraped all the bucks out of it. The only women who will be published on a regular basis will be those who oppose the most profound aspects of the movement itself. But Toni's vision, if you will, is grounded in the whole life of the people not just some faddish distortion of the democratic movement that reactionary publishers will pay for. One of the most consistent distortions that the licensed robbers and killers that run this society put out in literature, stage, screen, and radio, is that the contradictions between the Black man and Black woman are more severe and deadly than the contradictions between the African American nation and white supremacy monopoly capitalism. They are willing to put *effects* on the great white way, give Pulitzer and other prizes, but they will not stand for *causes* to be mentioned. So that we now have a body of woman's literature, or I should say, a great deal of what gets published or produced tends to deal with what is happening or has happened, but not why! The rulers say either you all hate each other more than you hate me, because I'm neutral; I give everybody a chance. Its just that your own men or your own women hate you and hold you back, or else entail the equally untrue tact that women's oppression is a joke, more evidence of the glorious scattered braininess of women.

What Toni has been doing that is so profound is that she has raised the question of women's liberation, particularly B lack women's liberation, from within the context of a continuing struggle against the major source of everyone's agony, the white supremacy capitalist system itself. So that, in one sense, Toni's work is or forms a continuum from the Black fire '60s to the Woman fire '80s. *The Bluest Eye* is one of the most brilliant books I have read. The repression and degradation of Black woman as woman and as one aspect of the Black nation, crushed psychologically and socially by sick racist America is laid out at such a high level of art that all the questions get asked, and all the villains get fingered.

Is there a more innovative and searching, emotionally free form work than *Sula*? Is there one in this epoch that explores the promise and contradictions of "sisterhood" more deeply? *Song of Solomon* is a work of 19th century classicism reshaped by the harmonic and imagistic traditions of the 20th century. The language is at such a high plane it should be mandatory reading for persons posing as contemporary novelists. And *Tar Baby*, where Toni has given us the two, actually four sides of Black man, Black woman adrift from themselves and each other, desperately in love with and in need of each other but at terminal odds. DuBois's "double consciousness" i.e., what is it to be Black and American? What is it like to be a problem? What is it like to be judged by people who hate you? What is the life behind the dark side of the veil? The problem of the 20th century is the color line. DuBois runs through Zora and Mary Lou Williams.

The work *Dreaming Emmett* makes my case — Emmett Till the Black northern youth lynched one summer in Mississippi. In truth Till's hideously murdered face in that issue of *Jet* that first carried it might have been the first shots of the Civil Rights movement! So horrible was it, and so widely circulated. At 12-million copies per week, it means almost every black eye and hand gets a chance to mash it at one time or another. I know that *Jet* photo stayed with me. My southern emigrant parents and grandparents had told me stories before about the fascist madness of southern white rule. My grandmother told me when I was about twelve about a young Black man who supposedly had raped a white woman, who was caught and murdered by having his genitals ripped out. And then how the supermen who killed this boy gathered all the young black women they could find and made them watch as they stuffed his "privates," my grandmother called them, into the dying boy's mouth! Yes, more than anything she wanted me to know what this world really was and how dangerous it was for me in it!

The brilliance of Toni's retelling of the Till story is that she brings the Civil Rights and Black Liberation movements back into the light, as cause and effect. She also shows some of the most damning contradictions in that movement, as people struggled for equality; the self hate and male chauvinism that are the masters' teaching and which benefit only the master. But we must know why these sicknesses, these flaws in our struggle exist. We must also know from whence they come! Ms. Morrison's analysis always comes with the caveat "resist or die." We must understand that our enemies are not invincible. So often we see ourselves as our own worst enemies while the White House, Hollywood and Broadway cheer, "Right on!"

The play posits our existence on several levels, which is the bench mark of contemporary art. It is polyrhythmic like Black music, like Eisenstein's creation of the montage in film — recognizing the multiple levels of what is the total breadth of the real. She wants to investigate the object as well as subject so that the truth will appear and the hypocrisy and beastiality of America is exposed every which way possible.

Black art meets resistance in the society for the same reason that the cries of the oppressed are either dismissed or silenced by the oppressor. One reason is that they are not just "cries" — they are, according to the consciousness of the crier, specific accusations. They are demands; they are information and instruction. They are not just cries of pain, they are also battle cries. That's why you can't get published or get your plays produced, they tell us. This is not art, it complains. Art doesn't complain. Sartre said, if you accuse and don't name the villain that is art. If you name the mo fo, that is social protest.

Toni raises Emmett Till not just to cry, but to re-experience that horrible pain and soul nausea his mutilated corpse threw into our hearts. Yet there are still unanswered questions that Till's murder raised then and raises now. Till has been "forgotten," like the shadows lowered around the '60s liberation movement by lack of Black institutions and the murderers' media.

She raised Emmett so that he can raise his dream, his life,

29

and murder, who he was and what he wanted and what was it in the society and in him that created his butchering. The classic question, "What is Death?" is presented in this vile context so that we can face what is a stopped life. It is not coincidental to me that by raising Emmett's dream we can dig into the Black psyche in a way that Dr. King's more famous dream could not do. But the commonality of the oppression, the fact that both King and Till were murdered by the same forces, and their dreams did touch each other, were in fact parts of the larger whole of the African American nation, the oppressed Black nation, itself.

In returning, Emmett thinks he can "revise" his life, that perhaps he can win out over (the evil forces, since he now, he thinks, has control over) his dream. But it is life that shapes the dreamer and the dream. The dream is merely the dreamer's projection. And finally, we have no more control over our dreams than our lives.

What did Emmett want and who was he really? The trapped Black boys (and girls) in today's ghettoes — do they have any greater chance than Till, even if we acknowledge the changes made since he was murdered. But already much of what was "changed" has been changed back, led by the right wing ideologue in the caucasian crib. Emmett, as play, and as character, wants to evaluate what real changes have gone down. "Am I the last Emmett" he asks? We remember Michael Stewart in liberated Manhattan, with his murderers freed just a few weeks ago, and we know the answer. "You a dead nigger "he is told," can't no Black mayors change *that*.

But Emmett, like the Black liberation movement itself, refuses to be dead. He will not disappear even with benign neglect or the lies of the famously ignorant. Reagan says he never knew there was a racial problem, which is why I guess he gave the opening speech of his first electoral campaign in Philadelphia, Miss. where civil rights workers Chaney, Goodman, and Schwerner had been butchered like Emmett Till!

It is a character called "Major" who answers Till, that there are no changes and he should know: he is in charge of seeing that there are none. Toni wants us to see that even in the brutish national chauvinism that white supremacy is, there are class store keepers, the social base for organizations like the infamous murder gang the Ku Klux Klan and the rulers. As payment for Major's maintenance of white supremacy he is run out of town by the real rulers, the banks and companies, who use white supremacy to keep poor whites looking at blacks as their enemies rather than the wealthy tyrants who kick all of our asses.

And even "Princess" Major's wife, the white woman who was whistled at by Till, supposedly, is constantly battered by the blows of male chauvinism. It is Major's contention that Princess must be watched. Hell, Major knows all the "poontang" he done got, so he figures blackie must have an eye on some white leg, and damn, who knows what Princess's thinks. Major can never bring himself to dealing with that reality except by establishing his manhood as white supremacy using his bloody brutality as Princess' chastity belt. For when we talk about rape, the white male south must without a doubt be in the *Guinness Book of Records* as world champions. And everybody knows—payback is hard.

The arguments between Emmett, his mother, friends and the white folks are an impassioned analysis of racial life in the United States. After hearing this for awhile, Emmett can say, returned from his tragic grave, "I'm up to date, now."

Emmett comes back angry and resentful. He hates his murderers and resents the fact that no one in the Black community could save him from the murderers. He hates the fact that he has never lived past fourteen, that he does not even know what manhood is. He was cut down before he found out: He wants to get back at everybody. His dream is to be his reworking of his life, his molding of an existence in which he can survive and even, in his own way of looking, triumph. But there are no individual triumphs, no individual paybacks that answer the substance of our deepest unknowing and social insecurity. And as it develops, we find that Emmett, just like the rest of us, though he returns from the dead, does not even control his dream.

Plus Emmett is still a boy and even his paybacks are childish and shallow—symbolic rather that substantial. The rest of us have grown older as we continued to try to live our lives past Emmett's murder. But he cannot re-dream his life unless we are, his mother and friends, the white folks, "the same" and that can never be. It is a dream of unreality which wants us to come face to face with subjective and objective reality: Act two involves us with the present period of one principal American social intercourse and struggle: the democratic struggle against woman's oppression, and while Toni obviously is looking to hold up in relief the problem of Black women's oppression, as I said, this is done within the context of the whole social structure and its terrifying contradictions. In the white woman, "Princess," repression by the society is raised as well with both compassion and criticism, which is honesty of the dialectical method.

The focal point of this section of the play is the appearance of a young Black woman, Tamara (like *tomorrow*, though she says and is *today* as well). Just before the first act ends, we see signs that Emmett is losing control over his dream: It is my dream he protests. It is to be a movie. But the dream merely comes through us; it is shaped and focused as it is by our lives, but our lives are in society. We are not ever really alone.

Emmett chides his murderers because they didn't do a good enough job. They didn't cut off his feet and hands or put sand in his mouth so that he and all the other murdered Blacks can haunt them with dreams of murder, because not even the murderers have control over their dreams. They have dreamed us "niggers" which is why they can kill us with impunity. We try to dream ourselves free, which is our resistance in real life society. Our lives and our dreams are in conflict, because they are both shaped by the actual societies we live in and are shaped by.

So now a Black woman appears and comes from out of the "audience." Emmett screams, "You ain't in my dream." Tamara answers, "Maybe that's the trouble with it." And we know it is. The split, the separation, the self belittlement that removes half ourselves from our own minds, that distorts our dreams into fragments of the oppressors. One of Emmett's "crimes" in real life and in the play is that he carried photos of white girls in his wallet. This Emmett has Maria Montez and Dorothy Lamour from off the silver screen. He has succumbed to some of the same psychosis that bludgeons Pecola Breedlove into insanity in *The Bluest Eye*. She actually enters the world of the oppressors and becomes their loving servant. Her own family are oppressive obstructive shadows getting in the way of her total absorption into fake white life. Fake because, face it, the real oppressors are not even straight with most white people. What is shown on tv and in the flicks ain't them either. It's just that too many go for it, just like a lot of people think Reagan is correct simply because he looks like them.

Somehow Emmett Till's vision of manhood involved walking around with white women's pictures in his wallet, whistling at and making suggestive motions at a white woman.

Tamara wants him to face this. Tomorrow vs. Yesterday. So that now we are brought with full force into one of the most powerful themes of the recent Black women's literature, and as a variation on and further investigation of the criteria for our own total liberation. How can you defeat our main oppressor if you gonna be a small time version of him, a little oppressor? Too often it is the oppressed, acceptance, even unconsciously, of the oppressor's values that makes it more difficult to end the oppression. Malcolm said, without self respect, for instance, you can't beat your enemies because you half way think they're right.

Toni can also deal with the contradiction of the Black woman's just criticism of Emmett for leaving her out of the dream. Her speech to Emmett contains the sharp essential probing that the drama turns on.

"You don't want much do you? Just make me a kite" and then you kill why you ain't published or produced, brothers and sisters, oppressed and exploited people of all nationalities, races, and sexes, "*your mouth.*" It's too big, too constant in its descriptions of reality and consequent criticism of the oppressors oppression. "If I was quiet," says Tamara, "I could be in your dream? If I just wouldn't say anything?"

Yes, we can be part of the American dream, at least by inference and advertisement, if we would just be quiet. It is the talking, the mouth pushing out those words of description, criticism, challenge and inspiration that keeps Tamara and the rest of us breathing. The words are our humanity, and we refuse, like Tamara, to have them stripped from us, finally making us inhuman because then we will be dead, on the real side.

So the woman motivated by the struggle for equality cannot be silent. But it is her words that alone can add the living dimension to our travails, that can make life alive. Life is not a one dimensional artifact created by males, without another human sound (the woman's). We are a dream dreamed by something already dead. Yet, is this not a constant complaint of the males about women they do not like or can not get along with, their mouths. It could be the employer at a factory, a dean at a university, an officer in "the man's" army, an emotionally crippled policeman, and they will tell you, they will threaten you, just like the militant male chauvinist, they will threaten you because of your mouth. To create equality, which is our fundamental struggle, you must believe in equality, otherwise you just masturbating on a treadmill. It is in the act of creating ourselves as democratic that intensify the general struggle for democracy. The fools that demonstrated against *The Color Purple* were opposed to *The Bluest Eye* — as if the things that Toni and Alice presented in their works were truly fiction. The B lack male chauvinist wants positive black (male) images but refuses to begin with himself. Why don't you picket *DC Cab* or *Rambo*? I object most to the mouths of Reagan, Meese, Jean Kirkpatrick and Clarence Pendleton. Unless we breathe and talk and reason together we can't really love together, and one another. We remain in separate worlds of oppressed and oppressor. And being oppressed by a big ugly is no excuse for you oppressing as a little ugly. Yours might not be the worst but it is the base upon which the worst is built and it stinks just like the worst because it's part of it.

Emmett lost control of his dream because he can only control it if he can control the real world. To control the real world, one must adapt one's self to live the most beautiful and productive life possible, and this can only bring peace with real struggle in the real world — not, finally, dreams. Though our dreams will reflect this and our victory, just as they reflect our projections of victory or our memory of defeat. Toni's thoroughness in this play is impressive. She deals as well with the contradiction in the woman's movement that the national struggle brings into sharp relief. "Your husband touched me on the behind, should I have him shot?" Tamara asks. They should be sisters, Black and white woman, are turned into enemies by the large contradiction of class antagonism. (Blacks are a "lower class," because of white supremacy, than even white workers. It has worked so well that Hitler used it against Jewish and foreign workers in the 3rd Reich).

Emmett keeps shooting and shooting his enemies, but he is dead. He cannot kill anyone directly, though he will keep rising up in whatever venue to haunt his murderers and those who collaborate with them. ("A nigger come up out the cotton field told me," Major says, after his wife has told him first. "I had to keep my reputation.") Toni also shows us how Major and Princess's "support" of Tamara's just criticism of Emmett is only self serving. They are in support of the woman's movement only to the extent that they feel it weakens the whole fabric of resistance to their racist rule. We have to be dialectical enough in our thinking so that we criticize in ourselves and in the society what is incorrect and at the same time uphold what is correct.

The image the rulers create of the women's movement being against men is self serving nonsense — the real women's movement is against the oppression of women. Just as some of us mistakenly thought the Black Liberation Movement was a movement against white people, when it is a movement against national oppression, racism — and both the women's movement (which includes Black women in its mass character) and the Black Liberation Movement are joined together at their most effective and profound point, as a struggle for democracy and against national and sexual oppression. In fact they both have common enemies, but we cannot defeat them by becoming them. The women's movement cannot do without men just as the Black Liberation Movement cannot do without progressive allies, of all nationalities.

Emmett's kite, or the kite some Black boy was killed for stealing, is his projection or living dream that is held only by strings, but when released will be "what it really wants" whooosh, the author says. Our traditional dreams of freedom have always taken the form of flying. *Solomon* digs deep into that. "Swing Low Sweet Chariot," we sing. What do you see, a band of angels coming after me. The African dream, the Ashanti of our Tomorrow, must have our real desire on its face. As if all our faces could blend into one face, or perhaps two faces, what the two aspects of the life sign, the ankh, really are, man and woman, embraced, and whooshing at the speed of new light into what human life one day can be: freed from the sickness of animal rule. It is not Captain Marvel we want on our kites (souls). He is just another overly hyped cover for real strength and beauty. It is ourselves, together, that we want, our souls the collective creation of our entire history. The cross bars that hold the kite together is our national soul. It is us together, embracing and struggling, together with the wind — which is the only way the beautiful thing can fly.
(1/1986)

The Poetry of Urgent Necessity

A discussion of form and its meaning seems useful today because there are facts and arguments that need to be consistently restated, particularly in this period of rabid right conservatism or rising fascism, depending on your access to reality.

Art, for the billionth time, is merely one reflection of a time, a society, a people, a world, &c. It is subject to the same contradictions and influences as everything else.

In the halls of the Academe, the inmates stuff the bottoms of the doors, cover the windows, electrify the fences, to posture that art creates the world. But in truth it is the opposite.

It is the world that creates life, among that humans and it is humans that create what we are discussing.

A particular aesthetic or way of seeing the world which manifests as some artifact is as specific in its philosophical reference, as measureable in its aesthetic, hence socio-ideological stance as an organizational manifesto. The sharp and deadly drift, nay, push, of US society toward a Reagan led Rightism should be obvious by now to anyone calling themselves "intellectual."

Economically, the continuing contraction of the US economy, through national liberation struggles, decolonization, new economic competition with Europe and Japan, and sharp political and economic competition with the USSR are important contributors to this situation. The fact also that the U.S. can not sell its products abroad because they are too expensive, all help account for the economic desperation which caused the old line North East economic establishment to be eclipsed politically and brought on the far right Jingoism of the Sun Belt and Western nouveaus.

Reagan's cover, for the neo-fascist essence of his tenure has been Americanism, "Tradition" (really Kinder, Kirche, Kuche). It is interesting as well, that it has been Reagan, who has presided over the attack on and trashing of the U.S. film industry. (See V. Navasky's *Naming Names*.) Just check the pre-McCarthy and post-McCarthy social ethic of American films. The American film industry today is a disgusting and disgraceful swamp of vulgar commercialism, pornography, teen age fantasy and neo-fascist garbage. Are *Rambo, D.C. Cab, Rocky, Indiana Jones, Star Wars*, and the myriad and various horrible ghoulish (fascist) monsters all that is left of the once inspirational and mainly democratic themes of the U.S. film industry? Just compare the work of Henry Fonda, Muni, Capra, Welles, Hitchcock, Bogart, Bette Davis, Joan Crawford, Barbara Stanwyck with today's stars and themes and films.

A cop could not possibly be a big hero in pre-McCarthy U.S. films. Now U.S. films and television are bloated with all kinds of cop heroes. A sign of the times. So in U.S. academic and literary (and general Art) culture now, this same backward wind is blowing in its own more boring context.

We are now to be harkened back to poison caves of McCarthy era "literary criticism." "The New Critics," who were probably more liberal than fascists, hooked up with Allen Tate and his *Reactionary Essays*, the sub-English Tory Southern Agrarians, Penn Warren, Ransome and them.

The *Kenyon, Sewanee, Hudson*/Pound boys and churls. Worshippers of T.S. Eliot and Yeats, their backward politics and starched or frocked

>   white witchdoctor — ism
>   & stiffness
>   & deadness
>   & worship
>   Of
>   The
>   Dead!

The Agrarians as a fading economic class (south land slave genteel) worshippers and un-American imitators of Queen Victoria's booty/banditry. A fat hairy carnival cool ugly lady who ruled most niggers the Americans didn't.

"Fade-ism" equal love of the past. Lotion scented Gothic-eg., Faulkner, one of their projections. The "English" cover, (French spice, or Russian, Italian, &c) is a "respectability" get up. Really, a Tory Feudalism obsession, because American slavery expanded and maintained, with psycho-social economic-political implications, "maintains" a black slavery based, pretentiously "Attic" South African styled culture.

One fundamental "betrayal" of the American revolution was the continued domination by English culture (worldview, &c.) upon the wealthy & powerful Americans and their rising institutions, form " style" as a reflection of economic ties, maintenance of the status quo, and the dream of the American bourgeoisie to be "wealthy as kings." Which means the society must be frozen to raise this ransom, which we are still unwillingly paying!

Wealth, "breeding," power, intelligence can all be suggested in this society by an English accent. (Even the teenyboppers of a more democratic era go for the cockney which the Beatles brought in.)

English Departments are powerful. American Studies are fledgling on average. Black Studies is under attack, and they just got here in 1967.

The old feudal (Kings and them) land owning wealth still remains intact in the rich and powerful families and relationships of the modern capitalist world: now as mineral or energy wealth, now as cartels and prestigious mammoth trillion dollar a day multinationals — into every thing they can think of. This binding is cultural and it is political and economic. Of course it is manifested even in dance or song.

The narrowness of what is regarded by U.S. official culture makers as "tradition" is called Greek, Roman, Jewish, Christian, though all these are derived from an older culture. Anglo Saxon Law. A big French statue (as indication of the advanced struggles for social progress therein) played off as "bohemianism" or bizarre sexuality.

History changes as the present changes. For instance, even those churches, religions, connoted by the cultural matrix of Western capitalism, cover political power and cultural hegemony.

Where, after all, is Jerusalem? Right now, it's in Israel. Christ then, was an Israeli?

A form is a philosophical construct, reflecting a variety of disciplines and influences, but it is more or less specific as to its origins and use.

The same rightward shift of U.S. politics animates the new formalism (as well as the contrived "old" formalism we see on the march again today). The fact that *New Directions* James Laughlin (of Jones & Laughlin Steel) his eminence of the grey "avant" should step out in *The NY Times* just recently hoisting "ol Ez" colors back up into the light. Should tell you something about Bitburg.

And then artists in capitalist society are still hooked up (depending on their consciousness) with feudal court socio-aesthetic. What other small producers, for instance, would accept 10 percent of their own product and still think of themselves as some kind of elite?

But the important point is that the forms being raised now are the forms of reaction in general. The attempted resurgence of sestinas, sonnets, &c; the emergence of new generations of formalists now called structuralists, confirms the obvious influence and catalytic role of social life to art and even academic conjecture.

The so-called "New Critics" of the '50s were "new" only in the sense that they demonstrated the post World War II reaction. Western, particularly U.S., ruling circles brought in with their "Red Scare" and "Cold War," McCarthyist anti-Soviet politics. This was caused by their need then to contend sharply with the Soviet Union for a world market, now that the World War II United Front with the USSR against fascism was no longer necessary!

The McCarthyist Auto Da Fe marked A QUALITATIVE CHANGE in American films, with suspected radicals either fired, scandalized or actually locked up (eg. Hollywood Ten writers and directors sent to jail on Smith Act "contempt" charges). The American film industry has never recovered, losing, among other things, its populist democratic character.

More generally it marked a qualitative change in American Culture, stripped of its populist democratic idealism: it is more blatantly, principally, an imperialist culture! So that domestic expressions of the political power focus are openly fake, hypocritical, neo-fascist, sexually pathological, racist, male chauvinist, given to horror (its fascist consciousness strengthening—murdering horribly, murdering, murdering, murdering) counter-historical, self congratulatory reactionary, fostering teen age pornography and fantasy as adult concerns. The establishment aesthetic is openly Tarzanic—ignorant, brutal, drooling, square, banal, insipid, sick.

The existence of Ronald Reagan as head of this is so juicily precise; the plastic butchery of his hair sums up so much of what middle America wants. Ronald Reagan had a lot to do with this attack on film progressives, as he recently bragged at a press conference.

As California Governor, Reagan helped lead the systematic murders of the Black Panther Party. This is obviously the key to 666's political hegemony at present. Some of the far Right must have shrieked, Egad, he dealt with the Reds and the Blacks, the most dangerous duo within U.S. social tendencies!

McCarthyism was an attempt to purge artistic and academic and intellectual circles of the ideas of the revolutionary '30s and the United Front '40s.

The so-called New Criticism sought to separate form from (and even deny the existence of) content. Formalism is the official aesthetic of the repressive rulers. The art must be lifted from its real life, social, context. They must from uber allies, because art can only exist, fully valorized, in bourgeois society as decoration. (That's why artists have to be viewed as frivolous.)

This is the reason *Birth of A Nation*, a Ku Klux Klan recruitment film and one of the vilest anti-Black films made, can be celebrated by establishment "critics." *Triumph of the Will* is a Nazi recruitment film. But formalism says look at the camera angles, the close ups, the panoramic sweep of the action, the characterization, i.e., the "style" and this is supposed to cover the animal content. So that they can say, the poem means nothing, it is! Is what?

Bertolt Brecht's essay, "On Non-Objective Painting" signifies (in the African American usage) that the abstract red is safer than the red seeping out of slaughtered workers' bodies. Humanistic (i.e., realist, naturalist, social realist, critical realist &c.) art must "take sides" blocks and circles and squares on zoot suit Tranes full of bubbling color dis connects is safer. Is it any wonder, that once the villains got over their normal, less sophisticated response to abstraction, they finally dug it as a good thing. The banks and brokerage firms and a myriad other of the Killer institutions now are swamped with abstractions. So much for the "far out."

Diego Rivera's mural sent up to Rockefeller was so "far out with the green snake image of *Rocky I*, they removed it. It was declared ob-scene (i.e. Greek for kept off the scene)!

Formalism always evades the substance of art. Finally Content is more important than Form. The question how to deliver the *feeling* of it, which is its only life, is seriously to address the question of form. Obviously, without a form that enhances, extends, "suits" that content, any content will suffer by being obscured or illy served.

It should be equally obvious why the formalist-academic stance dominates U.S. art circles, universities and official intellectuals because "successful" American art must hide much more than it shows. Such art is to preserve the status quo not transform it. So the rising tide of formalism in the U.S. is simply confirmation of a social retrenchment and continuing wave of reaction.

The 1960's art, indeed from the Beatnik '50s, was in open opposition to existent academic impotence and traditional formalism. The Black Arts Movement wanted its creations to exist as attacks on white supremacy and Black national oppression. The leading figures openly and consciously took revolutionary social stances and their works were confirmations of those positions.

The forms most popular in the Black Arts Movement were close to how Langston Hughes described the kind of poetry he wrote… "using the forms and meaning of (Black) music" which carries the fire storm of Black life! So that given the African American classic musical forms, Spiritual, Blues, Jazz, Gospel &c. Not only are these forms, "in themselves," very different from Anglo-European couched academic verse, but the content is consciously shaped most times in opposition to the values expressed by such verse. The Beats (AG &c) wanted most of all, in my reading, an open poetry, that could tell all and would indeed seek to tell all.

Charles Olson's *Projective Verse* set forth an important text declaring the profound difference between *Open* (i.e, "New American") and *Closed* (traditional bourgeois European and U.S. Academy) verse. The poem was defined as a process that the poet arrived at by writing, and *form*, therefore, was a verb, not a noun, and most definitely not an adjective!

The Black Mountain (Creeley &c) folks, NY Poets (O'Hara, Koch, Ashbery, &c.) all called for a repudiation of the deathly grip of formalism and European addicted academia.

This was part of a wave of the world wide progressive social transformation. The '50s is the beginning of the end of Colonialism-

India (47), China (49). The African independence movement and revolutionary struggles of the '50s. The U.S. civil rights movement, its Martin Luther King petty bourgeois nonviolent sector and its working class self determination, self respect, self defense, Malcolm X sector. The *motion of history* is what the Arts do reflect, both in changing forms and content. The recent so called structuralists are open standard bearers of conservatism. Henry L. Gates holds, in my estimation, the record for flakiest statement of structuralism award. He wrote an essay on Fred Douglass called, "The Recurrence of Reflexive Pronouns in the Speeches of Frederick Douglass." Not what Fred said, but how many what names he dropped. Such scholarship obviously can get you shot up through the establishment like a helicopter jet. What is most creepy is that the structuralists try to perform the robbery they philosophically advocate even to describe the proposed theft. What Frederic Jameson, among other critics of these folks has pointed out is that Lukacs, Benjamin, Adorno, of some of the easily dropped names of "Struc" literary references, all claim some affinity with Marxism.

Marxism points out that the world is "both hidden and open." So that an artist, as Mao said in "Yenan Forum On Literature," expressed in his work the stance (which side they're on) attitude (what they see as beautiful, ugly &c.). The artist expresses for whom they create, as well as the work and study they do. Real life is being expressed. Literature is a reflection of the ideology of society in the artist and vice versa, splayed from aesthetic to social relationships. in the world.

The artist has no choice but to be the structuralists who want to use a kind of Marxist originated analysis ("close reading") that seeks to penetrate appearances (e.g., the illusion of real democracy that allows bourgeois democracy to fool people) and reveal the real meanings of things. The "Causal Connections" in society Brecht called them. The obsession with symbols, mythology, semiotics and the like are all meant to revitalize a dead status quo formalism. The main intention is to pretend that literature points only to literature, not life and society.

Content of literature is myth, dreams, obscure references — laughably deviant psychology, word games, grammar. They insist symbols are unconnected to real life and only exist as parts of their personally or Ph.D. sanctioned code glossary.

It is a dull religion or arty kind of accounting that is sought, with a whirl or sprinkle of mysticism to keep the matter immaterial. Black Art has always existed as an alternative version of the world than its oppressors genuinely celebrated. Its forms are an expression of its creator's lives. Those creators' lives, as are any creators not in-tune with the past, backwardness, male and national chauvinism or who attempt to reflect the lives of the American or world majority are kept behind the veil. They are "covered" as the big record boys would say. In the '60s, a mass upsurge of democratic struggle even affected the literary art and academic world. Their sadness and world weary boring artifacts were literally shouted down with the shrill finality of the Black Panthers walking into the Sacramento State house in 67 with drawn weapons. The stodgy dead forms were dismissed as the Maginot line of dying bourgeois aesthetics. The Black Arts Movement called for Art that was *African American* as Bessie or Billie or Duke; Oral, accessible, and *mass oriented*, and finally, an art that would help in social transformation, i.e. *revolutionary*. But just as reaction has hopped back upon us with a vengeance, the little roach personality cultural hit persons of the dead, the elite, the unintelligible, the thoroughly despicable, have also eased back into view. As scholarships to oppressed nationalities and working class youths get cut back in favor of exploding rocket ships, trips to Bitburg, threats to Nicaragua, the invasion of Grenada, open support for South African fascists, &c. The very presence of the Black Liberation Movement as it created first a Black student movement then a progressive multinational student movement, and then after nationalism stunted that development, a largely white war student movement in the '60s altered even blunted the reactionary academic "norms" in all areas. Black Studies came in 67 with the BPP, Detroit and Newark rebellions. This was a profound challenge to white supremacy curricula. But just as affirmative action is under attack, so too the revolutionary spirit and gains of the revolutionary '60s.

Latino studies, Chicano studies, Urban studies, Woman's studies, all proceed from that catalyst and all these thrusts bent the force of racist university and academic and "scholarly" status quo-dom. The larger numbers of oppressed nationalities and their rising productive-forces allowed to circulate in the "art world" had a similar impact. Just as the movement itself was attacked and the '60s now is a dirty word in all directions according to the bourgeoisie, so now an attack on the liberating forms and telling content of the art

of that period. The NEA now has a Reagan appointed director who says he will oppose funding "welfare disguised as scholarship" or art. But as a closing example, take two of the most important Black writers from the Harlem Renaissance, McKay and Hughes. McKay's poetry, fit into the Miltonic sonnet form and is still powerful, but the form stiffens and makes less impacting the hot content (Winston Churchill recited "If We Must Die" in Parliament during the Nazi bombings and raids called "The Battle of Britain." Though he did not, of course, identify the writer.) McKay's great novels; on the other hand, still sing with the living accent. *Home To Harlem, Banjo, Banana Bottom,* live so intensely because their dialogue issues directly from the real life of the time and the characters. Hughes' works are so gigantic because he always understood what Mao said later, that it is the speech of the people that lives longest and strongest. Wm Carlos Williams made this same discovery, in contradistinction to Ez's icy elitism. The strength of their forms is the strength of social life precisely reflected (and summed up) even in the language, which itself is part of the form and content of the works. So that the struggle in art between formalism and open expression is in essence the struggle between the dying and what's just coming into being. The arts struggle cannot be resolved, independent of the struggle in society itself. The "order" we live in is a dying barbarism, its lacy skeletons, the racists want to run up the flag pole again as *traditional forms.* But these are costumes for the new national holiday, Halloween, which will soon replace Xmas. The explosion of the shuttle Challenger is the kind of fireworks such holidays generate!
(1986)

Langston, DuBois & McKay: Contradictions Between Art & Politics During The Harlem Renaissance

As the Harlem Renaissance comes again under the attention of the various apologists for imperialism, it is important to define exactly what the Renaissance was, what were the laws of its development, and the most dynamic of contradictory forces embodying it. This is because our enemies are constantly defining and redefining us and our history and future in ways injurious to our sacred goal of self-determination!

The Harlem Renaissance was actually part of a worldwide insurgence against imperialism. The Russian Revolution (1917) was the chief blow, and from this blow a million vibrations in all directions helped shake imperialism, the worldwide rule of monopoly capitalism and white supremacy, to its foundations.

Russia, a semi-Asian country (as far as nationalities found within its borders and the kind of eastern feudalism that had characterized the Asian world), was a dying absolutism defined as both feudal and capitalist simultaneously. It was the weakest link in the worldwide chain of imperialism. Previously, Marxists had thought revolution would come in the most industrially developed European society, but imperialism's rise carried with it an incredible opportunism developing among European workers, outright bribes to a smaller sector, white supremacy being one of the most highly developed legitimizers of both!

In fact, it was just this third world resembling aspect of the Soviet Union that made its revolution shatter earlier anti-capitalist scientific speculation when it erupted with such force and changed the character of the world.

The nations and peoples of the third world now were drawn into the main-stream of world wide revolutionary motion. Imperialism itself had divided the world into a handful of industrialized pretenders to civilization. Those pretenders enslaved and underdeveloped the masses of the world and described them as "savages," although the pretenders were the savages.

The United States was the most developed capitalist country of the early part of the 20th century. World War I had brought it full up onto the central stage of world exploitation. The Mexican War (1848) and The Spanish American War (1898) had given it new territory to exploit. The Civil War 1861–65 had given the bankers and industrialists of the north outright control of the U.S. economy which had moved from competitive capitalism(including slavery) to the domination of the economy by the large banks and their ability to combine their capital with the big industries creating finance capital.

The Hayes-Tilden Compromise of 1876 corresponds to the Economic Panic of 1875. The re-enslaving of the Afro-American people, using the Southern Planter class as a loyal comprador of the northern bankers, was the betrayal of democracy that contrasts earlier U.S. competitive capitalism and slavery with later (end of the 19th century) U.S. imperialism and Black national oppression (which the compromise signaled).

The prototype of European Fascism is the overthrow and destruction of the southern reconstruction governments spearheaded by the Klan and southern planter class, completely supported by the new northern rulers! Even Hitler's racial laws, he took directly from the Black Codes which were put in place after slavery was supposedly ended. Fascism finally is about slave labor — the surplus value (profits, &c.) of which are used to empower a racist corporate state. It's principal industry is warfare!

DuBois developed and emerged publically during the post-slavery epic which should have been the triumphant rise of the African American people to equality and full citizenship in the U.S. But the mass Black disenfranchisement was in force by the time DuBois was eight years old. By the time he was twenty-seven years old, 1895, Booker T. Washington, the most powerful Negro of the period, backed by imperialist philanthropy, had publically accepted the disenfranchisement for all of us saying, "The wisest among my race understand that the agitation of questions of social equality is the extremist folly." And just as in the summer of 1988 Atlanta was the site of this re-Exposition of Betrayal, because Atlanta is the home of the Black Bourgeoisie in the Black Belt south (Chicago is the American capital!)

So that DuBois, in his great classic *The Souls of Black Folk*, must oppose Washington, though he masterfully lays out in a completely dialectical way Washington's positives as well as the negatives. But DuBois concludes "Mr. Washington represents in Negro thought the old attitude of adjustment and submission." And again, "Mr. Washington's program practically accepts the alleged inferiority of the Negro races." Further, "Mr. Washington distinctly asks that Black people give up...three things, First, Political power, Second, insistence on civil rights, Third, higher education of Negro Youth."

Quoting Douglass, DuBois supported "Ultimate assimilation through Self-Assertion." And it is this call for democratic rights and equality which was always at the base of DuBois's political stance. He had made these basic determinations before the 19th century ended and had begun to sound them. Some important changes in DuBois' philosophy in the 20th century was first that he is able to move past his early projection of the Black bourgeoisie and petty bourgeoisie, the "Talented Tenth" as the catalysts for Black development, fundamentally, I think, because he could see now, certainly by 1915 and *The Negro* that racism and white supremacy were not just caused by ignorance, as he had previously imagined. But that ignorance was one favorite product of white supremacy and that white supremacy, racism &c. were abiding and systemic elements of the world economic system of imperialism! He also came to understand the sharp class struggle between the Black bourgeois classes and the Black masses.

DuBois' confrontation with Garvey in the '20s also made a deep impression on DuBois, so that he could see that at its best Garveyism spoke to Black Self-Determination. And although DuBois never altered his call for democracy and equality, i.e., assimilation through self-assertion, he came to understand by the '30s and the publication of *Black Reconstruction* the national

47

liberation aspect of Black struggle, even in the U.S.! DuBois's call for Black economic networking and methods of circulating dollars through the Black communities before they exited, he saw as ways to strengthen and intensify the struggle for democracy, because after all without Black self-determination (i.e., self-assertion) there could be no democracy!

DuBois also moved from bourgeois democrat to social democrat to Marxist in the 20th century. DuBois's world-gripping statement on his 90th birthday that he had fought for democracy all his life and that he would fight for democracy and communism as long as he lived, ending by saying, "And I still live!" sent chills around the world; chills of happiness for many and chills of terror for the rulers!

And in 1961, when DuBois became a member of the Communist Party by saying "Capitalism cannot reform itself, it is doomed to self-destruction. No universal selfishness can bring social good to all. Communism — the effort to give all men what they need and to ask of each the best they can contribute — this is the only way of human life!" This statement among many others sent the bourgeoisie scrambling in all directions to make DuBois forever obscure. As he said, after defeating the government's attempt to characterize him as an agent of a foreign power, "Now the children will no longer hear my name." So DuBois in his long and heroic life, which has yet to be properly analyzed, celebrated and systematically taught as part of the requirements of our revolution must be understood to be one of the classic petty bourgeois democratic intellectuals, a social scientist who found that truth cannot be discovered or presented without earthshaking struggle. Who, by dint of his lifelong commitment to scientific truth, is pressed into active political combat. His passion for his subject, humanity, connects him to the lives of people in a way there could be no betrayal. The People, themselves, were the truth. And it is this recognition of the passion inside himself that makes his politics and his scholarship the tip of a deep, deep love for the people themselves!

The main baggage that DuBois carried with him that had to be cast aside, bag by bag, at each juncture of his political developments was the idealist notion that America wanted democracy. This flawed predicate of the middle class democrats' commitment to the American capitalist system was shattered for

DuBois by the obvious and continued torture of the African American people and the parallel of such torture all over the Pan-African world. As the Father of Pan-Africanism, DuBois not only studied African civilization, its glories and its decline to slavery and colonialism very closely, but he became an early and outspoken activist on behalf of Pan-African Unity.

America could not want democracy since America was part of a world system of imperialism. *The Negro* is the preface written twenty years before the appearance of *Black Reconstruction*, which is the major piece of American Historical Investigation in a proto-Marxist genre. With his early misunderstanding of American society as essentially democratic came not only his belief that American Blacks must somehow qualify for citizenship, by showing themselves worthy, if only by the correct educational and moral preparation, there was also an identification (vouchsafed by his Harvard and University of Berlin Sociological training) with the "glories" of Euro-American Culture! Including the education and class security of the bourgeois intelligentsia.

DuBois's "respectability" is part bourgeois baggage, but it is also and this should be understood, part of his defense against the stereotypes imperialism makes to justify its oppression of the Pan-African people! His impeccable dress and New England accent were curve balls he kept as his arsenal against imperialist lies and stereotypes. It was the seriousness of his commitment to understanding and change that vindicated him, that kept him developing and growing ever more clear and ever more fierce in the struggle.

When DuBois addressed one million people in China's Tienamen Square with Mao Tse Tsung on the podium as well, he said, "I come to speak to you not as a celebrated scholar or distinguished scientist, I speak to you as a Nigger" (1962). This meant no matter the education, the clothes, the accent, or the prominence, this is who I represent, this is who I am!

******

Claude McKay's famous clash with DuBois came to a head around the publication of McKay's first novel, *Home to Harlem*. Both men had come to New York around the same period...DuBois 1910, McKay around 1912. Garvey had also reached New York around the same time, 1916. But DuBois and Garvey had met earlier in Jamaica in 1914.

The convergence of these men representing converging forces in New York should be obvious. Yet it was not just a Harlem Renaissance, as Sterling Brown so emphatically maintains. The insurgence against imperialism, and its particularity, colonialism in the third world, was obvious. The Russian Revolution represented the most intense convergence of those forces at imperialism's weakest link hence the revolution. But neither the Russian Revolution nor the Harlem Renaissance were exclusive or qualitatively unique. They were both part of the rising tide of anti-imperialist resistance worldwide!

The clarity I am trying to indicate in this essay is that as in all phenomena the process of class formation and development and struggle is natural. The Harlem Renaissance is no more a socio-political monolith than any other factor of human existence. Our blackness is defined by class and nationality, experience and ideology.

The Harlem Renaissance, fundamentally, was a socio-political upsurge by the African American people against imperialism, including white supremacy and the artistic and cultural reflection of this development. This upsurge was called Negritude in Europe particularly France by the West Indians and Africans gathered there, e.g., Aime Cesaire, Leopold Senghor, Leon Damas. It was called Indigisme in Haiti, led by revolutionary intellectuals like Price-Mars, Jacques Roumain and Jacques Alexis. In the Spanish-speaking Caribbean it was called Negrissmo, and identified people like the great Afro-Cuban poet, Nicolas Guillen.

In all of these movements, the fundamental dynamic was the struggle against imperialism and white supremacy. Cesaire's *Return To My Native Land* or Damas' *Pigments* or Roumain's *Masters of the Dew* or Guillen's *Songoso* poems are dazzling weapons both opposing the enslavers of Black Life and redefining the Pan-African people according to their true history, exact conditions, and will to transform reality. These are the "Black Is Beautiful" movements of the period, just as the Harlem Renaissance was the "Black Is Beautiful" period of the early 20th century.

The celebration of Blackness was a weapon to attack the denigration of Blackness which imperialism had codified. DuBois's *The Negro* in 1915 is a work of historical scholarship which states in the preface its aim at fighting against the imperialist racial stereotypes it used to legitimatize its exploitation and oppression of the Pan-African people. (Just as today the whole "war against drugs" so-called is being used more and more to justify the building of fascist repression in Black communities all over the United States, co-signed by some of our most famous Negro "leaders"!)

What is predictable, but effective, has been the de-politicization of the Harlem Renaissance, by the apologists for imperialism and their Black and white and sycophants, and bankrupt non-scholars. We have seen books come out recently in which most of the persons celebrated as the movers and shakers of the Harlem Renaissance were the Negro petty bourgeois heads of social agencies, and the middle class pretenders to so-called high art and middle class upward mobility. The watchword of the Harlem Renaissance is fast becoming culture in its most static and comprador aspects, while the actual ties of the Renaissance to Struggle and Social Redefinition are being covered, Art itself being conveniently deconstructed to suggest that literature for instance is at best a tired word game for people who refuse to watch "Jeopardy" on television!

DuBois, McKay and Langston are so critical to understanding the movement of class forces and the insistence of political definition on the art of the Renaissance. McKay, the son of a Jamaican middle peasant was also a self admitted early worshipper of Britain and the empire, despite being its vassal. He had early sought a place for himself within the framework of British imperialism. He even became, for a short period, a Jamaican Constable, or policeman.

His earliest published works in *Songs of Jamaica* and *Constab Ballads* bear an uncanny resemblance to Paul Laurence Dunbar's dialect verse, except he celebrates "Old England" often, e.g., of a visit to England he says, he visits, "de lone spot where in peaceful solitude/rests de body of our miss is Queen, Victoria the Good."

As McKay grows older his earlier unbridled love for England and things English gives way to Black nationalism that can develop in a state where power had to be delegated, neocolonial fashion among the largely Black population, unlike the U.S. where African-Americans are a distinct minority!

In this fashion, McKay's Jamaican nationalism had a great deal in common with Garvey's. But where Garvey pursued nationalism and raised it to organizational significance around the world—though much modified in the end, McKay's nationalism became organized by white bohemianism and a worship for the "primitive" and the noble savage that flirted for a time with Marxism but finally dismissed it as a further limitation on man's "natural freedom!"

Garvey first fought with DuBois about DuBois's lack of an economic program for Black people, though in truth, the first disagreement Garvey had with DuBois is the number of white people shuffling around the New York offices of the NAACP.

DuBois always had an economic aspect to his program, but it was first defined by its intention to be a vehicle for the Black bourgeoisie. Garvey and other Black nationalists and the Left too criticized the NAACP increasingly for its lack of an economic program. And it was these forces who had also put a damper and a silencer on DuBois's attempts at economic planning, calling it Black nationalist, when DuBois spoke of Black people as "a nation within a nation."

But certainly Garvey's UNIA had an impact, as far as economic planning on DuBois, as well as the depression which made discussion of "integration" overtly futile, since just like today, when the imperialist economy goes into a tailspin Blacks are the first to feel it, and jobs they had struggled to get yesterday now revert to being jobs for white men.

The liberalism of imperialism exists only in times of high profit; it is then they can hold out (but only in the face of the increased struggle that can exist during periods of "more democracy"), the olive leaf of gradual integration for the oppressed nationalities. In times of economic downturn segregation is put back on the front burner, now!

McKay's separatism was positive earlier in the sense that he wanted Black self-determination in the same way Garvey did. Although, after 1921 and Hoover's threat to Garvey while he was in Jamaica, the UNIA policies lessened the call for outright resistance in favor of a Black separatism that could co-exist with rising fascism. (See Robert Hill and Manning Marable and Shirley Graham DuBois.) McKay incurred DuBois's wrath with *Home to Harlem* because DuBois charged that McKay was writing an essentially apolitical book that sought merely to titillate the sensibilities of white bohemia, and was not a weapon in the struggle for democracy!

McKay's rejoinder was that DuBois knew nothing about aesthetics. "Certainly, I sympathize with you and even pity you for not understanding my motive, because you have been forced from a normal career to enter a special field of racial propaganda, and honorable though that field may be, it has precluded you from contact with real life, for propaganda is fundamentally but a one-sided idea of life."

Langston defended McKay, and called *Home to Harlem* the greatest of McKay's works. And true to the spirit in which Langston evaluated this work, the imagery and narrative description of the book are passionate and moving. But DuBois had said previously, "I don't give a damn for any work of art that is not propaganda...and consciously so." And if we look closely at art as the ideological reflection of human life, we must see that all art is propaganda — i.e., it is pushing some version of human life. Even if it is some perception given bogus rationale by opportunism of one sort or another.

McKay's later embrace of Marxism, when he left the U.S. and went to the Soviet Union as a guest...I was an "Ikon" he reports...was short-lived. He left the states in 1919 and did not really return until 1934. In effect, he spent the most important years of the Renaissance abroad. And when he returned to the U.S. he had already tired of Marxism and disassociated himself with it, in the same fashion as the other petty bourgeois intellectuals he admired in Greenwich Village, chief of whom was the anti-Marxist one time Trotskyite, Max Eastman.

Essentially, McKay came to see Blackness as a Bohemian quality. Something that removed him and Black people from the straight out bourgeois life. In his letters to Eastman, McKay celebrated the freedom that each sought in the most striking petty bourgeois fashion from the social responsibility that thought should enforce.

Ray, the intellectual in *Home to Harlem*, unlike the working class, cannot settle down to dull life. He takes off to sail the seas leaving the Black woman, Felice, happiness, in NYC, longing for him.

The fact that even in McKay's strongest poetry he never moved past English sonnet form, and by the end of his life had joined the Catholic Church—speaks the parallel of bourgeois attention his concerns manifest no matter what they are called.

******

When Langston published "The Negro Artist and The Racial Mountain," there are two very striking indications of his place in the pantheon of Black intellectual life that are important to this discussion. First, Langston said repeatedly that the most important book to him had been DuBois's *Souls of Black Folk*. (See DuBois Letters) One critical theme in *Souls* was the concept of the "double consciousness" (how to be Black and American at the same time.) Two selves warring was how he described it. What is it like to see yourself through the eyes of people that hate you?!

DuBois's lifelong struggle for democracy and self-determination and communism was the fuel that made him transcend this double consciousness. What amounted to imperialism's opportunism for the Negro, in fact, it is the creation of the Negro. The house servant as loyal citizen, screwed up beyond belief, the thing described by E. Franklin Frazier; the Sowells, Walter Williams, Ann Worhams, Pendleton, and their literary and journalistic equivalents.

"In Racial Mountain," Langston first takes on the Negro who does not want to be Black but merely the nonexistent existent. I don't want to be a Negro poet but a poet. Langston says, "You'll be no poet at all, you are not true to your own experience."

Langston jumps on the middle class Negroes and their embrace of white bourgeois culture as entrance into U.S. society. Now the Negroes voice their pathology as "high art" which, I imagine, is an aesthetic narcotic. He castigates them for fleeing Bessie Smith, and "Of The Sorrow Songs" (it was DuBois in *Souls* who did the first heavy research on the Spirituals and their African origins and the Black aesthetic as demonstrated by Black Religion and Music).

"Mountain" is a cry for self-determination, a cry for democracy. But there is a curious scratch on it that puzzled me until recently. When Langston says, "If White People Don't Like It, We Don't Care"...we can understand that justifiable defiance. But when he says, "If Colored People Don't Like It, We Don't Care," this is a nick in the slick. Because it is here that a purely petty bourgeois individualism emerges. And it is this individualism that DuBois wearied of and grew depressed by in the Renaissance, that the most publicized of the Black artists veered away from the clear responsibilities of political warfare for the vague gesturing of McKay's "Art;" Hughes' "individualism" especially against the attacks he, DuBois, suffered from all quarters. He was fired from the NAACP twice, also from Atlanta University. And even the early "Black is Beautiful" phase of Langston's thought could find easy alliance with McKay's Bohemian Primitivism.

What is interesting is that on the positive side, Langston lays to rest the conundrum. The "double consciousness" spelled out for DuBois, "The Racial Mountain" could be scaled, we're gonna be true to our dark-skinned selves sung Langston. Hail Sorrow Songs, Hail Blues, Hail Jazz, Hail Black Us. And get out the way, here we come!

But at the same time, we must see DuBois, though vilified by the social democrats posing as Marxists like Owen and Randolph, and castigated by the nationalists like Garvey, struggling in a real world, with the real problems of the Pan-African people, like a statesman, like an artist, but always as a scientist! It is no surprise then, that by the '50s when DuBois was under fire as a "red" from the state department he could call Langston to task for leaving Paul Robeson out of his book on music. (Or that during the HUAC hearings Langston could be bullied by Eastland &c., into denying his earlier socialist influenced poetry. His repudiation of his Communist poems in order to remain unobstructed in his literary career is the apotheosis of petty bourgeois submission.

But the denial of a concrete relationship to working people and the concrete necessities of real world revolution characterized the white bohemian world of Claude McKay and the Black petty individualism of the Harlem "Niggerati." And Hughes, unable to carry out his words into real world action! Of course, when the Blacks of the '60s after the Civil Rights upsurge of the '50s brought new life to the Movement, Langston Hughes wrote *The Panther & the Lash*, and returned to the fold of full out anti-imperialist struggle.) Who knew that soon Claude McKay would be a Catholic, or that at DuBois's trial for "being an agent of a foreign power," after days of government lies, the sole witness brought forward by WEB's attorney, Vito Marc Antonio, should be Albert Einstein.
(11/1988)

Transformations of Ethnic Content in Contemporary Art

Once we get beyond the slightly academic gloss of the title there are some important questions this topic must include. First, Ethnic means literally pagan or goyim, i.e., the tribes outside the more developed civilizations, i.e., the non Israelites who did not uphold the Israelite civilization and by that to mean primarily the belief in one God and the original culture of the pseudo ancient world.

So that from the outset, Ethnic is a term of disparagement, like pagan (meaning literally "country" i.e., unsophisticated). The use of these kinds of terms in relationship to art is to consciously or unconsciously set the standard as American (i.e., Bourgeois usually Euro-American, white bourgeois art) with all the other expressions of peoples' lives on the planet being, by definition, second rate.

This is the reason that we should speak of African or African American art, if that's what we're discussing. The art of specific nationalities, cultures, even Third World is a political term embracing mainly the nations and peoples of Africa, Asia and Latin America.

Art, according to Mao in his Yenan Forum on Art and Literature, is an ideological reflection of human life. It reflects that life in various ways, with various forms and contents depends on what kind of life is being lived. Ideas, for instance, do not drop out of the sky, to paraphrase Mao again, but from our social practice, how we live.

The sustenance of food, clothing and shelter are the basic concerns of human life, without obtaining these there is no reproduction of life in the 1st place. So that society is formed primarily on the basis of how these are obtained — the mode of reproducing real life — so that these concerns are the parameters of our ideas, the catalyst and the shaper.

But even though it is true that it is the economic factors that have the fundamental role in shaping our lives, there are also ideas reflecting those economic factors that have influence on society, even help shape it, as well. This is the dialectical aspect of nature, objects, ideas, so that the economic base creates ideas and institutions to maintain and legitimatize that base, and as if that base changes, so too do the ideas reflected in the superstructure (ideas, institutions, &c.)

So we are saying that the economic base has the principal effect on us, but also the ideas and institutions erected on that base have one on us in dialectical fashion. Certainly as the base changes the ideas and institutions, the art, aesthetics, and even the reasons and uses for the art change.

For the sake of this forum to be brief, WWI brought specific economic and with it social and political advance to the African American people. The move north for jobs and to escape repression before World War I was one such boost, and then 40 years later the same conditions corresponded to the buildup for World War II. After the WWI ex-soldiers came home to be lynched and to resist and the Red Summer and race riots and rebellions were the response. The same kind of thing happened after WWII. After the Korean War the same kind of thing happened. Black soldiers indoctrinated to "fight for democracy" return to find there is none where they came from. In order to fight in these wars, Imperialism had to advance the economic and social base of the slaves. Political consolidation was the result many times and it is these developments that even the arts of the time reflect.

The McCarthyism after the Korean War is meant to fight against these progressive tendencies in the U.S. The increase of lynchings after Korea were aimed at doing the same thing in the AA community. But the raising of the productive forces, the instruments and education of the workers to work these more advanced instruments, even for Blacks, produced ideas in the society that led to the civil rights movement.

The struggle content of much African American art is historically continuous. This generation is no more political in a generation than the last except as conditions change. My generation, coming to full expression in the '60s, expressed the full out struggle of the civil rights movement with its expressed or indirect plea to the American Establishment for justice being transformed into a revolutionary movement that saw the government as an enemy instrument of suppression. So the poetry and art of the '60s expressed this, even to the extreme of cultural nationalism and anti white chauvinism.

The Black Arts Movement, The Black Theater Movement, The Wall of Respect in Chicago or the Mural movement all saw this emphasis on a content that desired Black self determination, self respect and self defense, quoting Malcolm X. It was an art a poetry that wanted to be Malcolm poetry, Black Panther poetry, peoples' art, Black art, militant art, all in reflection of what was happening in the real world.

By the late '70s, the movement itself was shot and beat and exiled and assassinated into temporary quiescence on one hand, and mainly the Negro bourgeoisie and petty bourgeoisie got those few handouts which signaled to them that the revolution was over and that they had won (if they had their name on the office door and a 30 or 40 thousand dollar job.)

This change in the society itself, developing with Jimmy Carter to its full expression in the Raygun, wrought a change in the arts of the masses as well and particularly the petty bourgeois who are the largest percentage of artists.

We saw and see now the emergence of the retrograde trend, in keeping with neo colonial style of political organization that is needed by imperialism all over the world. Anti Colonial movements world wide meant that imperialism had to rule with native agents. As it was in the large cities of the U.S. with Black pluralities and majorities or Africa or the rest of the third world. So in the last ten years there has been a distinct buppie yuppie sector of the population (the fruits of neo colonialism) in the main a retrograde trend that reflects the manipulation, quiescence, cooptation of progressive forces.

Many so called black films, dramas, paintings and other media now carry an anti-'60s, anti-struggle line. So-called militants can now call our leaders bugged out, revolutionary historians —

spastic uncommunicative pests, interested in making a buck, and worse tell us first that our struggle is no more profound than putting some black folks pictures in a pizza parlor, and that Yusef Hawkins and the other Black youth slain by racists (police or civilians) were murdered for playing their radio too loud. And this can be acclaimed because it coheres with the retrograde trend, which basically wears the Black superficial mass culture symbols but whose analysis is a confirmation of what imperialism tells us is wrong with us.

This is one reason we must have a cultural revolution, a political struggle to oppose the imperialist attack on the values and principles the images, and philosophy of struggle to replace them with submission, neo colonialism and individualism viz the cry. The content of art changes as society changes and as the ideas reflected by the economic base of society and with that the politics since economics is the most concentrated statement of politics.

But we also should understand that this is not Europe, it never has been. And that if we are called ethnic or pagan or outlanders, we must know that imperialism is the standard by which such a value system measures us. We must resist this, continue to make cultural revolution, understanding that we want to create art that is aesthetically powerful and politically revolutionary, we want art not aren't.
(10/1989)

Jacques Alexis

Jacques Alexis, the great Haitian writer murdered in 1961 by "Papa Doc" Duvalier, was both a powerful artist and revolutionary activist. Along with Jacques Roumain, he led a generation of young Haitian intellectuals to arm themselves with Marxism, the ideology of revolution, and make a concrete analysis of the concrete conditions of making revolutionary social transformation in Haiti.

Both Alexis and Roumain were trapped and victimized by the bourgeois cultural nationalism of Duvalier and his followers and like many of the other sincere revolutionaries, Marxist or otherwise, who were exiled like Roumain or slaughtered like Alexis.

The fact that Alexis was *stoned* to death reminds us that this same biblical era style of execution was the fate of another revolutionary intellectual and artist recently, when the American fed dogs of Edward Seaga murdered Jamaican poet, Michael Smith in the same brutal fashion!

The true revolutionary intellectuals of any society are always a threat to the imperialist status quo — of colonialism, apartheid, neo-colonialism.

And when we see how Duvalier and his so called "Griots" used "Black Talk" and "Folklore" to take Haiti to Black Fascism and the murder and exile of some of Haiti's best minds, then we also should be instructed that revolution first is a political task, an expression of *class struggle* and that unless the politics of the working class and the class struggle itself are in the lead of our liberation and revolutionary movements, they will not only fail, but strengthen the diverse enemies of the working and peasant masses.

For instance, when we say Cultural Revolution, we mean an instrument of political and class struggle led by the working class and its revolutionary politics to oppose the counter attack and tendency toward fascism of imperialism today, and the necessity to continue our political struggle, our revolutionary class struggle in the superstructure, i.e., the education system, the arts, in institutions that effect our lives, to see that these ideological factors all serve to continue revolution not oppose it.

The *retrograde trend* that exists today of so called Buppies and Yuppies, uses nationality, age, the fascist tendency itself to tell us our struggles, our struggle for revolutionary consciousness are old hat and passé. But Self Determination, Self Respect and Self Defense are never passé – they are the requirements for evolution!

This retrograde trend tells us that our leaders are "bugged out" that the police kill our children for playing their radios too loud, that our progressive historians and scholars are spastic misfits who the people regard as pests. Such slander is the twisted rationale of our enemies, of imperialism itself.

We need a mass political party independent of both wings of the dying vulture of bourgeois politics, Democrats or Republicans. We need the Decriminalization of Drugs instead of the War on Youth. We need Cultural Revolution: Continuation of the revolutionary political struggle in the arts and education, in the realm of ideas and institutions that effects our lives, whether the police department or the church.

Jacques Alexis was killed for the same reason Jesus was: Resistance to Imperialism! For saying that the wealth of the world must be shared by all the people of the world. This is still a very dangerous statement. And the imperialists, whether Caesar or Duvalier or Bush still murder revolutionaries.
(10/1989)

Nineties

Chinua, Brother

Chinua, Brother, when the news reached me of your, our, tragedy. (He was paralyzed in an automobile accident.) I was shaken to the marrow, and probably stood fix-eyed staring at words inside my head. There is a wind of senseful response to something like this. The "Why?" is always paramount. And then, with us, since we are under fire, since our monstrous enemy is continuously wounding or killing us, you pause very deeply to look around, even to consider, is this something again of theirs? Like Marley, or Harold Washington, one never knows, do one? Not really. The ending of the year that saw Washington, John Killens and Jimmy (Baldwin) go out set up the panic of air carried Hooverism. Perhaps.

Especially since we were together the last time at a conference "Art & The Political Crisis." At Stony Brook. At the Schomburg. At fascist Rutgers. Earnestly, with Nurrudin and J.P. Clarke and Amina and Jayne Cortez and Duma, Louise Merriweather, Rashidah, Richard Wesley, Louis Rivera, Sizwe Ngafua, Abdul al Kalimat, Abby Busia, Nathan Heard, Claude Brown and some others, still putting together the necessary connections of our Pan Africanist destiny. That we are, all of us, Pan Africans struggling to rid ourselves of Imperialism and White Supremacy and achieve, as Malcolm called for, Self Determination, Self Respect and Self Defense.

Seeing the magazine, *African Commentary*, come out under your editorship just after you left was another one of those make you pause images to ponder the exact nature of our vulnerability. We understand oppression, only too well. But bad luck, naw, I can't never get with no bad luck. Yet here it is again.

Not to mention Sassy, Dexter, Woody, Buhainia who just went out of here. Or our many family members chemicaled into submission. Or sucked up in the Christmas turning into Halloween success ghoulo phone and advertised as transformed 'mericans. Or the made to order Frankenstein Negroes coming out of Stanford and places like that who tell us our nigger shadows is the real enema, that the founding fathers crossed their eyes as symbol of promise yet to was.

What I mean brother is that I fear for all of us, especially those of us who are exposed, those of us on the front line who are pointing out who do d evil and whoever do d evil is devil. I fear for those of us committed, the advanced, the artist/intellectual/scholar activists among us for whom Bush latest rebuke is just more fuel on the fire of the giant firestorm of mass retribution to come. I fear for us like I fear for the people, because I know, come rain or come shine, we are in for it. I fear for us, for you now lying fixed to your ideas as the sole mobility in your life, because I know it is always about hard times, always about the frustration of what we understand as the easy progress and advance of the mind opposed by the real and material blocking of our lives by these murderers.

I fear for us like I fear for Amina and my youngest son, Ahi, who was shot in the head this summer by an even less conscious victim of animal rule. Because in this year, in this world of continuous tragedy we expect the worst. But then like Ahi rose not on miracle but on strength, his motion was the marvelous.

I fear for us just as clearly as I grow strong thinking of our collective strength. No matter our respective countries' mindless lurch toward Fascism! The collapse of Social Fascism; the restoration of Mitsubishi and Farben, Krupp, the new order alright, the new military-industrial international money-Reich. While we who fought for democracy still have nothing! I fear for us but I am like you are, not afraid! Though they land themselves in Saudi-Black to oversee the oil crookery directly. They will come back looking like Brothers and understanding why Africans worship the sun.

I fear for you but I am, like you, full of a dangerous and subversive strength! The ominous muscularity and power of the Big We Self! Though they set us killing each other in Liberia and

Capetown, the ever lying incredibly real creditor predators who have enslaved us now for hundreds of years.

Then I know why I fear for us but I also understand why I know we will win. And that that fear is the rationalism of dealing with the mindless savage of race and money freaks. Just as I know you will prevail, I feel we will prevail, and that is a knowing like no other. Chinua, Brother, let us be each others' strength.

(10/1990)

God, Revolution, Rhythm

The God "Monotheist" dualism is the ideology of oppression and slavery.
God is what is and Christ asked for consciousness as the Am light "perceived" as evolution!

If there is God there are subjects. But Life is the subject and the object.
What it is is the total existent. "Allah" suggests that.

But it is "Lord" of the whirls, motion not "worlds," except as "punctuation" for the total expression of what exists. "Lowered Motion"
Laird
      Layered
           Lard
               Greece
                   Gris
                       Grey
The class development from communion to slavery brings God as "supreme" rather than omniscient—which is what "Allah" signifies.

The old religion sprang from real life perceptions. In a transitional society moving from animal high to human low. The communication of the early society reinforced the perception of nature as a collective of forces, each perceived as a process or phenomenon but all connected.

It was the whole (0) and the source as both itself and its origin. Its direction and motion, since it was not resolvable but only changed.

It was is, the equation IsIs signifies the reproducing endless motion! It is the all manifest existent is that is awesome. The whole not the do
nut.

The change in phases of class defined social transformation is what results in what's called monotheism. But the worship of "one god" is ultimately less sophisticated and less natural than the original animism: all is alive alive is all is is.

This "worship" (continued by the word) was sensitivity to the total manifestation of the beating, the is.

Religion is a priest word. The law of life actually, but the priest in inserting himself or herself between nature and nature (between humans and every thing else) begins class differentiation.

It was science and learning as wealth that developing society identified as a special source of power. It was the provider, priest, the scientist-artist, in their rise as a specific recognizable phenomenon which becomes formalized and eventually empowered.

This is the 1st "God," a person of celebrated specialization. The continued empowerment, separation and elevation of this (group of) person(s) seems to me the 1st class differentiation. Or at least what prepared the way to the consolidation of this class which could only be based on the emergence of surplus wealth (slavery!) and the priest group wd obviously be the first recipients of this surplus. (As tribute, sacrifice, gift, &c.) When Western Europhiles pontificate about Europe being the originators of monotheism. (Actually, that is a claim of official Judaism as in Judeo-Xtian Civilization. Dah Dah!)We should ice this by mentioning that the Romans worshipped idols polytheistically until 300 B.C. (It was they that killed Jesus, 'member?)We should also drop a dime on the Attic Greeks and their pantheon of rock and roll stars, ie African Orishas, forces of nature, spirits, &c., given the Elvis treatment as Zeus, Apollo &c.

But monotheism is a base corruption of animism and the replacement of the communal force of the is with a personality (actually a personal ie, individual "God") such as the Greeks for whom each household had their own personal God! For the Greeks the Gods were Greeks and solely theirs! Even the Greek city state is a similarly restricted social construct based on a kind of isolation (or "individualism" or elitism), much less workable than the southern (ie, south of the Mediterranean) notion of the nation-state.

The Supreme Being (as noun rather than verb) is the metaphysics of slavery! The "Call & Response" traditional form of African music should be looked at to see how its change over time through social transformation relates to the form of society it reflected. E.g., leading from Excellent Practice vs Leading as a function of formal office!

The Call was first available to all as a practice of being. The Response, the confirmation that I exist because we exist. The later "confining" of Call to the priest is the result of class stratification borne of economic hence social change, and the rise of the priest class as a politically powerful group.

So religion, the "law of (a) God" was the first separately held wealth! The God was the class power, as bestowed upon the priests, by themselves with the collaboration of (the changing social status of) the people. Ignorance's greatest ally is itself. It is like the unmanifest manifest as not. It is revealed as what it is not.

Yet if we understand the all, the everything as everything, the animist principle, then we understand all is rhythm, a beating a motion, and matter is what is moving, and moving is what is matter. Then we could understand the devilishness, the ignorance and delusion of hierarchies. The Pharonic period already had destroyed the animist power of ancient African religion and culture. The constant struggles between upper and lower Egypt, the final domination by the sedentary, what is rising to fall, which replaces what had risen, to be carried further, higher and lower at the same time, in the dialectic of "giving up to get."

So that communism must seek to understand that the world is connected totally, that everything is everything. And that it is not the alternative hierarchy that will replace slavery but the non hierarchical, the polyrhythmic consciousness, the animist restoration, as social life based on a nuclear age communal economy, where to all from all, and the whole of our collective soul is reconstructed so that our language and prayer coincides as everyday speech, and science replaces religion and art is a description of how we live.

(1/1991)

Paul Robeson & the Theater

Paul Robeson was unique, yet part of a great ugly pattern of American life. Robeson, one should know, was an immensely talented, broadly intelligent man, one whose dynamic persona was always animated to the fullest by the still ongoing struggle for democracy. He was an Afro-American, the son of escaped slaves, so that this democratic struggle which he saw as multi-national and revolutionary, was always projected most directly from the stance of the oppressed Afro American people. Paul said, "Two things my enemies don't like about me — my nationality and my opinions."

Though he did perceive the struggle as a "racial" struggle, particularly earlier in his life, he quickly came to understand that, at base, the racial question was a class question and that the slavery of any people limits the freedom of all people, in one way or another. He understood that the only way to measure the "racial oppression" was in terms of its class nature, i.e., if one people are imprisoned in a socio-economic dungeon painted in racial terms, nevertheless, the only way to measure the oppression, robbery, deprivation of democratic rights, and violent repression, is by the factor of class. That one people is forced to live a *lower* more depressed and uncertain marginal existence, that other people "live better" than they, and this is the ultimate disposition of class. They are, a "lower class" as an entire nationality. Racism, which is persecution because of physical characteristics, simply makes the fundamental national oppression more demonic, since the oppressed nationality can be attacked "on sight." This is why the Nazis made the Jews wear the infamous Yellow Stars so that they could be singled out from the rest of the population, since they were all "white."

Robeson's own family had suffered the inhumane existence of chattel slavery and this was impressed deeply in his mind. And even though he did perceive of the need for a broad multinational united front to be in the front line of the struggle for democracy, Robeson knew, as DuBois pointed out in "Black Reconstruction" that there had been many other peoples who suffered similar exploitation and repression, workers and farmers in Asia and Europe, but the difference was that "none of them was real estate!" Actually, The U.S. is the society that asks the question, as yet unanswered and still lied about, "Can property become a citizen?" Because up until this very second, the U.S. has never been a democracy and Afro Americans have never had equal citizenship rights!

It is this last factor that confronted Robeson, like all Black people, whether they are fully aware of it or not. But Robeson was keenly aware of this fact all his life, and it was a catalyst for his historic life's work, as well as the basis for the vicious attacks that the U.S. government and various anti democratic forces waged against him for decades.

Robeson was so remarkable a person, physically, mentally, morally, ideologically, that he was through most of his early life constantly being "honored" even by "White America" (the racist media fiction, The U.S. has always been multinational!) Born in Princeton, New Jersey, which was very much a "southern" small town, he attended school in nearby Somervllie, when the family had to move because his father, a minister, lost his Princeton Church.

Robeson's father, although an escaped slave, educated himself and later graduated from Lincoln University. The same Black university Langston Hughes and Kwame Nkrumah were graduates of. And when his wife, Paul's mother, died in a tragic accident, Rev Robeson raised Paul and the rest of the family by himself.

Paul graduated from Somerville High with honors and won an academic scholarship in 1915 to Rutgers. He was the third Black person to attend Rutgers after it began to promulgate the fairly recent fiction that it was "a state university." But during his stay at Rutgers he was the only Black at the School. He won the major oratorical contests four years in a row; he was Phi Beta Kappa in his third year and was twice named to the All-American team, the first Black All-American in Rutgers history. (I wonder have there been any other All Americans named from Rutgers?)

He was also the outstanding catcher for Rutgers' baseball team, the star center on the basket ball team, as well as a member of the Rutgers Choral society, even though he was limited and belittled by the deeply racist atmosphere of the place. He was barred from most of the social activities on the campus. Still, he was graduated from Rutgers as Valedictorian of his class! What is amazing is that every time racist America pats itself on the back saying, "So and So is the first Black...to whatever, or first Chicano or first woman (usually, white) they take the tac that somehow this shows what a great place the U.S. is. When it is exactly the reverse. They are actually showing you how old and deep is the backwardness of anti-democracy in this society. It's like someone who thinks this is really "1996," which is like attesting to the lateness of one's grasp of civilization!

When he graduated in 1919 (the same year as the infamous Red Summer and Palmer Raids) he moved to Harlem and graduated from Columbia Law school. Working his way through Law school, he played professional football, as well as coaching basketball. Robeson thought that Law would be an important post from which to fight for Black Liberation. But when he graduated and got a job with one of the city's most prestigious white Law firms, the racism and petty apartheid made him rethink what he would do with his life. It was during these years that he married Eslanda Goode, the first Black analytical chemist to work at Columbia Medical Center.

Robeson never aspired to be in the theater, though during law school he did perform in two plays. He was Simon in Ridgely Torrence's play "Simon The Cyrenian" (1917) performed at the Harlem YMCA. Torrence, who was white, did several plays at the beginning of the century with "Black Themes." Robeson played the title role, the Black figure who carried Christ's cross. The play gained small notice, but Eslanda Robeson had gotten people associated with the Provincetown Theater to come to the performances and as a result of this, Robeson was offered the starring role in O'Neil's "The Emperor Jones," but he turned it down! Still uncertain what he wanted to do with his life, particularly from the stance which he outlined in his Rutgers' Valedictory address.

Nineteen

"We of the younger generation especially must feel sacred call to that which lies before us. I go out to do my little part in helping my untutored brother. We of this less-favored race realized that our future lies chiefly in our own hands."

Robeson, at this point, did not see the theater as a vehicle for this quest he had set for himself. Interestingly, this address has much of the same thrust that DuBois had made years before in his famous "Credo" in which he also pledged himself to the same task, raising the level of Black life, struggling for democracy. But the brother of Isadora Duncan, the internationally acclaimed dancer, was also part of the audience at the Harlem Y, and he convinced Robeson to take a part in a play he was directing in London called "Taboo" later called "Voodoo." So in the summer of 1922, Robeson went to England and toured in the role, which was opposite the English actress, Margaret Wycherly. In the play, the Black character, a slave, falls asleep on a plantation and returns to Africa in his dreams. As he falls asleep he sings, the spiritual, "Go Down Moses." Because of the heavy audience response, the director, now Mrs. Patrick Campbell, beseeched Robeson (on stage while the play was going on) to sing more songs. The audience rose and called for more songs.

It was probably at this point, that Robeson realized that the theater was a way to reach the people, not only Black people but anyone sensitive enough to hear his voice without prejudice. Certainly, when he returned from this tour and joined the law firm he found that the deepest characteristic of that context was bigotry, insult and the stunning ignorance of racism. So this time he went looking for O'Neil and got a part in one of O'Neils ground breaking plays "All God's Chillan."

What is important to understand about O'Neil's theater is that until he bursts on the scene there was almost no theater that featured working people. Certainly, not any with Black people on the "Great White Way." (Ridgely Torrence and Paul Green were two white playwrights who did write on Black themes, with varying results.

The theater, internationally (at least in the small group of industrial mostly European nations who live off the rest of the world), has moved through the centuries from the drama of the Gods, to the drama of Kings, to the drama of the Bourgeoisie and the petty bourgeoisie, until finally just before the Russian revolution there was a theater emerging, particularly in those centers of social ferment, that consciously began to focus on working people, their lives and struggles.

O'Neils' early drama is deeply influenced by the revolutionary naturalism and expressionism of the German and Russian theater of the revolutionary period. Particularly, a great play like "The Hairy Ape" shows this influence, of the most advanced expressionistic theater of his time. Likewise, "The Long Voyage Home," "Anna Christie," the wealth of naturalistic and social realist theater using the expressionist percussion of image and new form, many which focused on the working class and the wild vagaries of the life at sea, from the common seaman's point of view are a much grander legacy from O'Neil for the American theater than the later overblown "autobiographical" meditations.

Both O'Neil and Robeson came to maturity during this revolutionary period leading through the Russian revolution. The German and Russian experimental, revolutionary, proletarian, work in theater and in film influenced the world. Erwin Piscator even performed O'Neil's "Moon of The Caribees" at his Volksbuhne Theater quite often. As well, not only the work of Strindberg and Ibsen from the 19th century but the work of Stanislavski and lesser known writers (for O'Neil) like George Kaiser plus Eisenstein's great revolutionary film work are part of it. The incredible outburst of world art as a reflection of this period of social revolution is obvious. Whether in the output known as Anglo- American "Modernism" or the still to be fully documented expressions of "The Harlem Renaissance." It was a period rich with political sweep and artistic projection of this. A period of intensified class struggle as well as the struggle of experimentation with new forms and bringing "new content" to traditional forms.

The arrival of W.E.B. DuBois (1910) and Marcus Garvey (1916) in New York city, and with the hosts of young artists and seekers of new direction, like Langston Hughes, Zora Neale Hurston, Jean Toomer, Duke Ellington, all from some where in the boondocks of regular America, together with the mass of white American youth, many from the same places, seeking similar release and expression, was the essential social force redefining American contradictions at the beginning of the 20th century.

What is lacking in summing up this period is the objectivity and all sidedness that U.S. racism prohibits. The separateness of "white" Modernism and The Harlem Renaissance, exists only because of the still virulent segregation that existed in the U.S. at the time, but also the continuing tendency to "cover" Black anything and report what is of significance through the opaque glass of "White American" social dishonesty. That's why Paul Whiteman was "The King Of Jazz," Benny Goodman, "The King Of Swing," Elvis Presley is "The King" and talentless Mick Jagger named leader of "The Greatest Rock & Roll Band In The World."

But the tenor of the time, place and condition of that world Robeson grew in shaped him in a fashion generally unknown widely in the U.S., Robeson was a product of the 20th century, in a way that no one before him, obviously could be. DuBois, perhaps, was the closest thing to Robeson in terms of the intellectual vigor and activist focus with which he surveyed his accursed homeland. But DuBois could never gain the broad popularity that Robeson did. It is not overstatement to say that during Robeson's day he was the equivalent to Muhammad Ali in international popularity.

Robeson's sojourn in the world of theater and film not only exposed him to vast millions across the world, but was a distinct factor in his continuing education to the evils of that world, as manifest in what DuBois called "The Color Line." Robeson came to see that that Color Line was simply the cover story for the general exploitation of working people by the rich and the powerful, "race" allowing an extra, super exploitation, of those exploited under the foul rubric of "inferiority." Hitler came right out with what the American slave masters had institutionalized centuries before with slavery, calling himself from "the jump," a member of "The Master Race."

Certainly, given the class nature of national oppression, Robeson could have isolated himself from the mainstream of Black life, and lived out his life in relative distance from the ugly heart of Black national oppression, but he was, by his home training, and by his intellectual and moral focus, committed to destroying oppression not kowtowing to it. The fact that finally he chose the role of a cultural worker, one of the best known, ever, in the world, to bring this fight to the enemy and inspiration and information on how to destroy this enemy to his own people and to progressive and freedom loving people all over the world, is a tribute to his sincerity, his knowledge, his essential correctness and his energy.

It is basic to any understanding of Paul Robeson, his life, it's development, his public ideological stance, his wonderful cultural work and the opposition and vicious attacks he drew from the slave master continuum of U.S. governmental and official quarters, to really grasp the fact that Robeson was a 20th century Afro American. A 20th century American intellectual, in the deepest sense of the word.

When Robeson performed in Eugene O'Neils, *All God's Chillun*, the Klan threatened to picket DuBois, in "Black Reconstruction," points out that after the civil war, for sixty five years, the slavery addicted U.S. superstructure depicted the Afro American people as Sambo, Buckwheat, Step 'n Fechit, Sleep & Eat, Birmingham, culminating with the dishonest Klan recruitment film, *Birth of A Nation* which a film critic at the Village Voice said was the greatest film of all times.

The fabled "Jazz Age," "Roaring Twenties," "Harlem Renaissance" and "Anglo American Modernism," appeared at the same time crazed white lynch mobs (like those in Europe that murdered Jews, called "Pogroms") wantonly slaughtered Black people in East St. Louis and lynchings rose across the south. The summer of 1919 was called "Red Summer" to immortalize this barbarism. The Ku Klux Klan reemerged dracula style, as well as a myriad other racist rabble-rousers, everywhere in the U.S., from the backwoods of Georgia, to the congress of the United States. Bilbo, Vardarman, &c., daily spit out their murderous backwardness.

But just as DuBois really was the harbinger and first voice of the 20th century Afro American intellectual, no longer able to be sweetly patronized by so called friends or immediately strangled by sworn enemies, based on the formal educational subtraction created by slavery. DuBois fought from his youth to raise Black people to full citizenship and social equality, Robeson was the next issue of that more fully independent trend of Black intellectual consciousness.

Robeson came out swinging, so to speak, He could never be made to feel inadequate by the mindless savagery and profitable mediocrity of U.S. social mores. He knew they were backward, from the jump. Robeson says in *Here I Stand*, that as he graduated Rutgers he thought, "As I went out into life, one thing loomed above all else, I was my father's son, a Negro in America. That was the challenge." Both men answered that challenge with every ounce of determination they could muster. Both were leaders of great stature, but we all stand on the previous generations' shoulders if we are at all conscious, and this is where Robeson, in the context of his time, place, and condition, placed himself. "Equality might be denied, but I knew I was not inferior" (ITMS).

What is interesting is that even with the advance of the times and his own petty bourgeois highly educated background, Robeson could not abide in the standard professions of his class. Just as Fletcher Henderson and Jimmie Lunceford, two consummate orchestra leaders in the pantheon of Afro American music, took up the music professionally because they were opposed everywhere else. Henderson in chemical engineering and Lunceford in the academy, so too Robeson was rebuffed, by the outrageous racist repression that existed so openly in the field of Law. Not that he couldn't by this time, have pushed his way through (which wasn't even possible in the earlier post slavery world). But Robeson would not put up with it, so in that sense, he had a wider narrowness to choose from.

Robeson had been heavily exposed to music and singing before his school days. Growing up in and around his father's church, the Black religious music was a constant aspect of his environmental consciousness. "I heard my people singing in the flow of parlor coal stove and on summer porches sweet with lilac air, from choir loft and Sunday morning pews — and my soul was filled with their harmonies. Then too, I heard these songs in the very sermons of my father, for in the Negro's speech there is much of the phrasing and rhythms of folk-song. The great, soaring gospels we love are merely sermons that are sung; and as we thrill to such gifted gospel singers as Mahalia Jackson, we hear the rhythmic eloquence of our preachers, so many of whom, like my father, are masters of poetic speech."

It was DuBois *Souls*, which gives the first comprehensive analysis of these "Sorrow Songs," as the spirituals were first called. Robeson was the first concert singer to give programs of songs comprised completely of songs composed and arranged by Afro Americans. He sang these spirituals in concerts all over the world.

Robeson was interested in drama, casually, even in high school, but he never thought it would be his career. Both the singing and acting crossed his mind, but then so did taking up the ministry like his father. As he moved through U.S. society he could more clearly measure the densest areas of resistance to social equality and his drive to be as free as he could, to speak out, to "take a stand" pressed on him. Even, later, when he made the decision to become a "cultural worker," he is not immediately clear on how to approach it and still be true to his earlier pronouncements.

"In the early days of my career as an actor, I shared what was then the prevailing attitude of Negro performers — that the content and form of a play or film scenario was of little or no importance to us" (And though this attitude was sharply opposed in the militant Black Arts '60s, it is clearly back with us again, e.g. the Wayans, "Living Color" and the other sad Negro saps "jeffing" for their supper!)

He goes on, "What mattered was the opportunity, which came so seldom to our folks, of having a part — any part — to play on the stage or in the movies; and for a Negro actor to be offered a starring role — well, that was a rare stroke of fortune indeed! Later I came to understand that the Negro artist could not view the matter simply in terms of his individual interests, and that he had a responsibility to his people who rightfully resented the traditional stereotyped portrayals on stage and screen."

It seems apparent that part of this growing awareness was due to the entire spectrum of national consciousness focused through Afro American artists during the Harlem Renaissance. Just as during the 1960's Black Arts period, when there is a sharp political upsurge, the artists and cultural workers who are most sensitive and in tune with the people, produce an art that reflects this intensified struggle. Langston Hughes' virtual "manifesto" of the Harlem Renaissance (which was actually a national even an international Renaissance, fueled by the world wide intellectual explosion caused by Russian revolution and the sharpening of the anti colonial struggle in Africa and the West Indies and internationally) "The Negro Artist and The Racial Mountain," speaks to the ideological repositioning of a whole generation! So there was a global political radicalism to the period that infected that whole generation.

For Afro Americans, not only among the younger artists and intellectuals, but also as a result of the violent attacks by the Klan and the police, particularly when Black people tried to move from the south into some of the northern cities, there was a clear consciousness of resistance that developed among the Black masses. DuBois led a march of 10,000 down Fifth Avenue to protest the East St. Louis racial massacre. He had also sat in front of his house, during the Atlanta anti-Black "pogrom" with a shot gun. Black soldiers had gone to WWI to "make the world safe for democracy" and came back to the same neo-slavery and blatant inequality. By 1915, Black people could not vote anywhere in the south, *Plessy v. Ferguson* had brought American apartheid into the world in 1896 so instead of the "brotherhood of man" the U.S. had become an imperialist empire. Between the years 1891 to 1945 there was only one Afro American in the U.S. Senate. From 1901 to 1929 there were no Blacks in the Congress at all!

As Robeson came to consciousness, DuBois had formed the Niagara movement, which became the NAACP, Marcus Garvey had headquartered his Black mass Universal Negro Improvement Association, in New York as well. There was also The African Blood Brotherhood, a left bloc in the UNIA who formed later as an independent organization and finally joined the CPUSA. DuBois's *Crisis* magazine gave new voice, to Afro American artists and a razor sharp "radical" political analysis of U.S. society, so "radical" the attorney general seized one of its issues. There was a broad and multidimensional assault on the racist superstructure of the U.S., an attempt to create an alternative set of ideas and institutions that could hammer out Black mass resistance to national oppression and educate both Blacks and anybody else, not only to Black national oppression but to the historical and contemporary distortions of Black life the rulers pushed, across the whole dimension of U.S. Culture.

The political struggle of the people vs. national oppression, racism, white supremacy, robbery and lack of democracy was the underlying theme of this renaissance, in song and story, poetry and drama. What DuBois called "The Gifts of Black Folks" (to the U.S.) "Labor, Song & Story, Spirit," were being used as part of the whole struggle for liberation. The Renaissance brought a more focused national consciousness among the people and the most advanced Afro American artists reflected this.

Robeson also became deeply interested in Africa, another ideological focus that emerged at the beginning of the 20th century. DuBois' valedictorian address at Harvard, "The Suppression Of The African Slave Trade" is still in print. Ironically, it was not until Robeson went to England to appear in "Voodoo," that he began to realize the critical relationship of the Afro American people to Africa, their motherland. "Like most of Africa's children in America,

I had known little about the land of our fathers, but in England I came to know many Africans. Some of the names are now known to the world—Nkrumah and Azikiwe and Kenyatta" (leaders of the first African nations to emerge from European colonialism).

He met many of the regular African seamen as well. And listening to tales of their lives made him delve even deeper into Africa, it would be a touchstone of his general scholarly, artistic and political work for the remainder of his life. It colored how he would approach roles given him, it also made him aggressively seek to act in works related to Africa. In "Voodoo," he went back to Africa in his dreams, in *The Emperor Jones*, he goes to a West Indian isle to "rule," as an escaped convict, "Brutus Jones," but the essential geopolitical mood is something African. In Eugene O'Neil's mixed portrait of Black "individual" rebellion there is a continuing naiveté and even savagery the playwright projects, though Robeson does try to surmount it. Ironically, there is an element of truth to the portrayal, if we understand who Mobutu, Abacha, Butelezi, Savimbi and similar creations of neo-colonialism really are. In fact there was one nut who did declare himself Emperor, although his primitivism did not allow him to murder as many people as Nixon or Bush.

This was one of the contradictions Robeson faced throughout his acting career, dealing with outright racist or imperialist-sympathetic scripts. Sometimes, especially in films, the producers would just lie, and put in their ugly after Robeson had shot his part. (This happened in "Sanders of The River," which after Robeson finished his work, a more colonialist-sympathetic political line was added to the film.)

American art at the beginning of the 20th century, like European art, and what was called Anglo American "Modernism" was heavily impacted by the disappearance of the old Victorian world in a torrent of fire and blood that marked WWI. The shallow hypocrisy of the 19th century's supposed article of faith, "The Brotherhood Of Man," which was always a sham vis a vis European Colonialism, shook European intellectuals who had to come to grips with the "Wasteland" of Bourgeois life and philosophy, now that those same colonial ambitions had driven these "civilized" European nations to spill each others' blood in the struggle to redivide colonial spoils. But as DuBois pointed out, this is what they had been doing to Africa and Asia and Latin America for years. Colonialism also brought Africa and the 3rd world into the

European psyche more directly just as annexation and cultural aggression passing as "Missionary" work of Christianity and Humanism was imposed on the colonized people. Picasso and the Cubists used Africa as the resource for their innovations, as did Stravinsky or Paul Whiteman or Rimbaud. Bourgeois "Primitivism" was the trendy aesthetic reflective of this forced relationship, Dada, Artaud.

The U.S. was now "opened" by the very thrust of its rulers' economic expansion. The parochialism of pre-civil war "Uncle Sam" was gone and the destruction of chattel slavery was itself a historic and characterizing profile of the society that had to be reshaped by its ruling profiteers so the same super exploitation could be maintained and even deepened in its "revised" political and economic "use." This reshaping had a socio-psychological impact confirmed across the broad spectrum of human life.

Robeson had to deal with his own "opening" as maturing intellectual consciousness, particularized and given social dimension by his Afro American experience. Ultimately Robeson developed into one of the most astute and nationally conscious artists Afro America and the world has ever seen. (Despite the dishonesty and/or ignorance of some commentators, that as Robeson moved further to the Left he moved away from Black people. Quite the contrary, what Robeson did, that can be confirmed by even a cursory reading of his works, is become more internationally oriented, but still at base, he was an Afro American patriot, with an openly militant national consciousness...though he certainly moved away from Nationalism!) The very tumult and revolutionary sweep of those times, like all revolutionary periods, provided Robeson with a more rapid process of militant political consciousness. His commitment and focus on democracy predictably brought him to socialist positions. Robeson's very emergence as a well educated focused artist as well as political activist was the result of the advance possible by the civil war and the end of chattel slavery. But also, as he developed his consciousness, his advance, at base fueled by his emotional and intellectual closeness to all the dimensions of Black life, these were all pushed forward sharply and continuously, dialectically, by the daily destruction of Black peoples hope for equality as a formal achievement of U.S. society. So that the struggle for this equality was increasingly defined as "outside" the mainstream of the U.S. body politic.

The Afro American pursuit of democracy and social equality has *always* been radical, even revolutionary, in the U.S. Hence, from that under girding provided by everyday conditions, Afro American Culture, by definition, has an aspect of "disruption" vis a vis the U.S. mainstream. Even Robeson's lifelong research into music, for instance, why he arrived at the universality of the Pentatonic scale, showing how the many seeming diverse musics on the planet have related and associated antiquities, was itself subject to constant racist rebuttal and controversy.

As Robeson understood more clearly the vicious contradictions that the continuing slave kingdom of "white America" presented to Black people, the more he was transformed by this impacting clarity. He developed cutting social analysis but also profound aesthetic theories on the role of the imperialist nations in relationship to art and culture that are controversial and still true today.

As Robeson saw it, especially as he got more deeply involved in the mainstream of American arts, the industrial west was on the road to forfeiting any spiritual values for the commercialism that the much trumpeted "western rationalism" had produced. In a "money uber allies" world, art was marginal and eviscerated, at best. He could see that the anti Black bias of U.S. art was but a surface emptiness that really covered a deeper spiritual emptiness produced by denying reality and mass social development for the sake of profit and power.

Robeson's comments on "Othello" show how he traced the socio aesthetic production of the west, "Othello in the Venice of that time was in practically the same position as a colored man in America today" (London 1930). This to a so called critical establishment that wanted to deny that Shakespeare was even concerned with racism. Just as these same analytical ostriches would say that "The Merchant of Venice" had nothing to do with anti-Semitism.

Robeson's continually deepening social activism brought him face to face with aesthetic questions that the mainstream American artists never confronted or understood. His career as a concert artist allowed him to understand the commonality of human expression as well as what distorted and covered it or reduced it to commercial simplification and stereotyping. His studies of Africa and African culture gave him self-consciousness, of his roots, his responsibilities as an Afro American intellectual and the grand historic achievements of the enslaved African civilizations, that the mediocre bureaucrats soiling American arts culture found hard to deal with.

Robeson's singing and his studies in anthropology gave him liberated approaches to the creation of art. "My ancestors in Africa regarded sound of major importance, they were great talkers and orators and story tellers. "Hence Paul Robeson Jr., tells a story of how when the celebrated Harlem gangster (one of Robeson's close friends!) Bumpy Johnson was holed up at Camp Unity with a couple of bullets in him, he and Paul Sr. spent the time of Bumpy's recuperation playing chess and discussing the differences between Chaucerian English and Shakespearean English. This is while Robeson was preparing to do "Othello" and wanted to "speak the speech" precisely.

He did *Show Boat* in 1928 in London, with the blues singer, Alberta Hunter. His version of "Old Man River" has remained the great classic rendition. And with characteristic social consciousness Paul changed the lines "You get a little drunk / and you land in jail" to "You show a little spunk...&c." He was to change the words to this song many times. England, for Robeson, was always a more productive venue than the U.S., and he lived there with his family for over a decade. In the twenties, this virtual émigré life was popular among U.S. artists. But for every Pound or Eliot or Henry Miller or Richard Wright, who stayed, most were brief observers and then returned. Spring 1917 was the first time Black actors had been on Broadway. This was in Ridgely Torrence's plays; they also had been at Madison Square Garden and The Ziegfield Follies and Carnegie Hall. Charles Gilpin played "Emperor Jones" in 1920 at Provincetown. "Shuffle Along," which revolutionized American musical theater, transforming it from the earlier standard European Operetta form appeared in 1921. It was not until 1929 that Garland Anderson's "Appearances" appeared on Broadway, the first play written by an Afro American on the Great White Way.

The first production of "Emperor Jones" starred Charles Gilpin in Greenwich Village. But O'Neil's next play, "All God's Chillun" opened in 1924 at the Provincetown, and it caused a sizeable race—quake. It featured Mary Blair, a white actress, and the theme was interracial marriage. WHAT? Plus Robeson actually kissed the woman...a few times. Which brought not only the Klan out of their garbage can, but even a few upstanding open minded Americans thought the play should be closed and banned because it "would cause riots." What it did cause was Eugene O'Neil and Paul Robeson to become instantly recognizable internationally.

But it was not until "Emperor Jones," later in 1924, that Robeson received floods of accolades for his powerful performance, drawing standing room ovations at most of the performances. This recognition by audiences of Robeson's incredible power as an actor and performer spread quickly and internationally. The Renaissance period did bring more recognition to the Black artist, as a reflection of the victories of oppressed people all over the world. After the Russian revolution, workers and the poor and even Black folks, became momentarily trendy among bored petty bourgeois poseurs and the more expressively idealist. Even so, it was a space made intolerably narrow by national oppression and racism.

Paul had gained some measure of recognition as early as 1922 as he began to tour and perform as a concert artist. He even got a part in the seminal "Shuffle Along" at the Cotton Club. For three years he crisscrossed the country with his repertoire of folk and workers' songs, and always he featured the Black sorrow songs or spirituals. He said, "All that breaks the heart and oppresses the soul will one day give place to peace and understanding, and every man will be free. That is the interpretation of a true Negro spiritual." He also remarked that when he first suggested taking the spirituals to perform in England, he was laughed at!

Kern's music in *Show Boat* in 1928, brought Robeson even greater recognition. The major song of the work, "Old Man River," was actually written with Robeson in mind, and it remained one of his most formidable vehicles. First performed in London, it made Robeson an overnight "star" with the English audiences waxing ecstatic over his performance. The American embassy, however, ignored the event.

Robeson settled in England at this point, feeling there was more freedom of expression than in the U.S. with its continuing expression of chattel slavery, Black national oppression. It was here that his interest in Africa took its deepest roots, where he studied and mastered African languages. His national consciousness took on a deeper and more thorough form as he continued to study. He was not a nationalist, because nationalism carries a bourgeois narrowness to it that denies the equality and beauty of all peoples.

Rather, national consciousness, is the development of the "true self consciousness" that DuBois spoke of in *Souls*. So that the oppressed no longer see themselves through the eyes of people that hate them.

Contrary to Negro nationalists immune to investigation, Robeson was one of the deepest theoreticians on the place of Black national consciousness in Art and politics. He understood that the imitation of oppressor aesthetics had less to do with Art than ideological and political submission and more generally that the Afro American people could only find their artistic or political voice by understanding and utilizing their own broad social and emotional experience. But this was to communicate and broaden human solidarity, not to exclude or create some metaphysical relationship to the other peoples of the world. But he also constantly explained that the abandoning of the cultural and political expression of Afro American life could only bring a destructive alienation and soul withering submission to the oppressor's will. In this he is similar to DuBois ("The Double Consciousness"), of course, also to modern African revolutionaries like Amilcar Cabral of Guinea-Bissau (See *Return to The Source*) and Hughes' "The Negro Artist And The Racial Mountain."

Robeson's stage appearances were generally the most positive aspect of his dramatic career. Hollywood, on the other hand, was horse manure of a totally different odor. As he came to more clarity ideologically, Robeson became more and more horrified at how his image was being used and Black people demeaned by the corrupt and racist Hollywood moguls. Robeson was the first Black actor to get "final cut." How many others have gotten that, even until this very moment? Many wouldn't even understand why Robeson needed this. Certainly he felt almost alone in that cardboard nightmare factory, particularly in his insistence on a "defense" against the racist image makers. And for that reason, he was a solitary figure among the "skinners and grinners...the Toms and the Jeffs" tap-dancing for massa in tinsel town.

Robeson made *Body and Soul* in 1922 for Black filmmaker Oscar Micheaux, who himself had a vacillating self consciousness. Here, Robeson was a quixotic contradictory preacher, oppressive and slippery, yet flashing a muted integrity and sympathy for sincerity, even if he wasn't up to it. Only one copy of this print remains.

Borderline, 1930, was a Swiss "experimental" film that

wanted to "treat Blacks as humans," arriving at a deeply confused scramble of images and perceptions, and very unclear statements. "Emperor Jones" was made for the screen in 1933 (the same year Auschwitz opened). Du Bose Hayward, a white writer on Black themes ("Porgy & Bess," "Mamba's Daughters") was commissioned to adapt the play. J. Rosamond Johnson, James Weldon Johnson's brother, with whom he co-authored the Afro American National Anthem, "Lift Every Voice and Sing," wrote the music.

The film could not be as sharp and cutting as the stage production, not because of any weakening of the acting and general plot, but because Hollywood cut out some of the most intense and meaningful parts of the script. One scene cut after it was shot was of Robeson's Brutus Jones, who while escaping a U.S. chain gang, defied then killed one of the white prison guards. The Hollywood version is intent to make Brutus Jones even more the ignorant brutish dupe than O'Neil's original. But contrasted to *Birth of A Nation* (1915), Hollwood's justification for the destruction of the Reconstruction and the betrayal of Black democracy, the film with a Black star, and intimating the possibility of Black self determination, even independence, though, of course, doomed, was clearly a forward step.

Sanders of The River (1934), was the film that caused Robeson to come to full arms against Hollywood treachery, though it was not until *Tales of Manhattan* (with Ethel Waters intentionally "fattened" so she could project the Black "mammy" image, although Ms. Waters was one of the most glamorous Afro American singers) that he acted finally upon his declaration not to make anymore Hollywood films.

In *Sanders*, Robeson is an African possessed of the sensibility to challenge and manipulate British colonialism. His persona carries that resistance to absolute submission, implying a developing political self consciousness among the colonial peoples that was unwanted in the imperialist metropolis. It is a colonial world in which Robeson's character exists and far from opposing colonialism outright, he ingratiates himself to its *Colonel Blimp* straw bosses and is even held valuable by them, as a modern African, ready to breakaway from the old tribal prejudices and metaphysics. He is depicted as a kind of stabilizing presence, almost a role model for the other less advanced colonial peoples.

Less rapacious and backward than the "old chief," he inserts himself as chief over some village of Ocoli peoples (though he is from Liberia!), unsanctioned by the colonialists. Yet his "manipulation" of these ultimately oppressive forces is quite frank and open. Accompanied with some light hearted ironies which make it clear that indeed he is the "new" smart expressive slave, who is useful to the rulers by virtue of these qualities, which earlier would be seen as defiant. Though, if we look at it closely, we can see that even depictions of chattel slavery always had the crafty house slave able to speak frankly about something the master or mistress might be unclear on. We think immediately of Hattie McDaniel in *Gone With The Wind*. In this context, there is, as well, the implication that this should be the role of the Afro American "trustee" vis a vis Africa.

Robeson said, after the film was released, that an ugly pro-colonial temper was added after the shooting. He never forgot or forgave this dishonesty and subversion of his humanity. Hollywood thus gave final public shape to the film. However, Robeson's young chief was, by virtue of his own persona, a strong figure, abiding British colonialism and adapting himself to it, by his sophisticated manipulation of it, as opposed to absolute submission to the ignorance of the old king, i.e., the "savagery" of pre-colonial Africa. Some might wonder naively how European imperialism could represent itself as the civilizers of Africa and the Third World, covered with blood as they were. But this is going on at this very hour, if we think about events in Zaire, Somali, Burundi, &c. *Song of Freedom* (1936), was one of Robeson's best film appearances.

He plays a Black dock worker whose singing attracts opera producers. Again, he has a revelatory connection to Africa. Even his name, Zing, conjures Nzinga, the heroic Queen of Ngola who resisted colonialism. Robeson says of this film, "I wanted to disillusion the world of the idea that the Negro is either a stupid fellow or, as the Hollywood superfilms show him, a superstitious witch doctor under the spell of witch doctors." He thought it was, "the first film to give a true picture of many aspects of the life of the colored man in the west. Hitherto, on the screen, he has been caricatured or presented as a comedy character. This film shows him as a real man." Twenty years later Kwame Nkrumah, about to become prime minister of the first post colonial African state, modern Ghana, celebrated Robeson for this film. Robeson's dramatic output again and again touches on Black peoples' relationship to Africa, which is neither atavistic nor romantic, but actually part of his intentional educational thrust to make Afro Americans more conscious and aid the African liberation movement which had begun to gather steam parallel to DuBois's calls for Pan Africanism and his Pan Africanist congresses. Robeson would later bring DuBois into his National Council on Africa, which continued to do direct political work around African liberation, until attacks by the U.S. government forced it to close.

Roles in this like *King Solomon's Mines* in 1937, offered limited direct focus on the anti-colonial theme that Robeson harbored, but at that time Robeson felt just the portrayal of Africa as a real place, with real people, or at least as real as Hollywood national chauvinism would allow, was positive. Robeson's character here is an Afro American who does not understand his historic relationship to Africa, as if mirroring Robeson's own earlier lack of clarity on Black American heritage and history. His anthropological studies, which his wife, Essie, herself an outstanding anthropologist, obviously furthered, especially in the area of world musics and the antiquities from which they sprang, for instance, convinced him of the similarity of much of Chinese and African culture. Later, he saw a general commonality in the antiquities of African and European folk music.

Jericho (1937), is a forceful film in terms of the underlying political imagery Robeson tried to project. Not only is Africa, again, the focus, there is also a strong statement on the need for African-Arab unity. He rejects the "Negro subservient" image as a courageous intelligent self sacrificing "brother" who carries freedom in his heart. One reason for this was that Robeson opposed the weakness and moral chicanery of the film's original ending, where Jericho is caught by military police who are tracking him to return him to the U.S. because, during World War I, he had accidentally killed a cowardly officer who orders him to abandon his men below deck when their ship is torpedoed. Robeson's ending has Jericho remaining in Africa pardoned by his pursuer, because of the good works he has accomplished for the African people.

Big Fella (1937), was an adaptation of Claude McKay's, *Banjo*. Robeson is the title character, who is the émigré leader of a Pan African group of seamen in Marseilles. McKay's novel is the personification of the bourgeois theories of "Primitivism" that were rampant in Europe and The U.S. at the beginning of the century, especially after the first world war. Banjo is a sort of "noble savage," who cannot fit in with the inhuman industrial west, because he is too rooted in the fundamentals of nature and primordial human feeling. McKay seemed to be saying, like many of the Euro-American intellectuals, that the childlike primitives of the Third World would always be out of tune with western rationalism because they were rooted in a timeless "Blackness" and related to the world by instinct and spontaneity, not intellectually.

But isn't that what the religious missionaries and colonial exploiters say, perhaps in different words with different intentions, but how different, finally, if we are told that Expressionism, Cubism and Dada are European movements, very rarely being informed that the aesthetic catalyst for these are Africa and the Third World. McKay's non-scientific non-materialist bourgeois romanticism is perfect for imperialism. Blacks cannot ever get into the modern world, not because of oppression but because of their heritage which renders them outside the precincts of "modern" rational industrial society. Shortly after this, Robeson was moved to say, "One man cant face the film companies. They represent about the biggest aggregate of finance capital in the world. That's why they make the films that way. So no more films for me." This from an interview in London in 1937.

Proud Valley (1939), was made in Wales. Robeson had refused major roles in Hollywood films for two years. Then he agreed to appear in an independent film made in Wales about Welsh coalminers. This film, is my own personal favorite. Not only does it completely avoid the loathsome denigration of Black people that Hollywood still persists in and still denies, it cast Paul as a heroic figure in complete unity with white working men. He is David Goliath, who is at the center of this film, and who magnetizes the struggling Welsh miners with his magnificent songs and learns their heritage and even helps them organize a movement among the miners for better working conditions. Goliath dies in the mines, sacrificing his life in a deeply heroic and moving scene, to save his fellow miners. The film is clearly the most successfully wrought and emotionally satisfying of all Robeson's films. It is a greater film than most American made films. The solidarity of a Black worker struggling alongside white miners against the repressive mine owners was a genuinely revolutionary aspect of the film.

Robeson's last Hollywood film, *Tales of Manhattan* depressed

Robeson on its release to the extent that he tried to buy up all the prints of the film to take it out of circulation. He had tried to do the same thing with "Sanders of the River." Robeson had come back to the U.S. as World War II began to ravage Europe. Still, he refused offers from Hollywood and Broadway with some producers offering "to make him rich," if he would just let them shape and control his public image.

Added to his general disgust with commercial American oppression, was his own consolidation more and more of socio-political aesthetic analysis that moved him even further away from the mainstream. He now "perceived art as such a direct instrument of revolutionary change that any dichotomy between the cultural and political would be meaningless and false before his system of thought" (Stuckey, *Going Through The Storm*). Even before the later attacks by the state, Robeson had begun to see that his agents scaled down ticket prices for his concerts "so that working people would have access to them" (ibid.) He began to openly express his resolve to bring art more directly to the people and not just the well to do concert hall audiences. He said in one interview, during this period, things have gotten worse for my people, "My personal success as an artist has not helped them." (ibid) He began to give more and more concerts not only for working people, but also for the African Liberation Movements and various West Indian causes. In 1941, he sang for 23,000 people in Newark, N.J. He was deeply involved in the cultural thrust of the Afro American liberation movement and helped bring a stronger influence of socialist ideas through his art to Black people. He was directly involved with Langston Hughes' Suitcase Theater and helped with the founding of the Negro Playwright's Company, by a group of Black writers, playwrights and actors, "to serve as outlet for the creative works of race dramatists." The first work they produced was Theodore Ward's powerful "Big White Fog." In a statement summing up this company's approach to the theater they said, "Only through portrayal of the deepest tragedy of the Negro people, their oppression at the hands of American rulers, can a Negro culture be truthful and strong. Robeson was shoulder to shoulder with Black writers expressing socialist sentiments at the time, Richard Wright, Langston Hughes, and of course, W.E.B. DuBois.

Robeson's singing of songs like "Ballad for Americans," his participation in programs such as the musical pageant, *The Negro In*

American Life (1941), sponsored by the International Workers' Order and his charge to the audience to "make America a real land of Freedom and Democracy" had great impact not only on the increasing mass Black and white audiences, but even helped shape the focus of the most relevant part of the U.S. left, including the Communist Party itself.

When he did agree to make another Hollywood film, *Tales*, he was then utterly convinced of the hopelessness of dealing with the deeply ingrained commercially sanctioned distortion and racist attacks that accompanied anything "Black" from a morally bankrupt Hollywood. *Tales* is a series of short stories woven together around an overcoat with millions of dollars stuffed inside, that has passed through the hands of Henry Fonda, Ginger Rogers, Cesar Romero, Edward G. Robinson. In the tradition of the "sophisticated" comedies Hollywood had begun to make during the depression '30s, Robeson, Waters and Rochester are confronted with the coat when it drops out of an airplane. Predictably, Robeson wants the money shared within the entire community in a communal development for economic self reliance, while the preacher, Rochester, is the comic foil for Robeson, bringing an overarching mood of childish ignorance to the whole scene.

Robeson had wanted to do the film because presumably it focused on Black sharecroppers, in realistic contrast to the suave bourgeois nincompoops the rest of the film centered around. But in the end, Robeson said the film was outright "offensive" to Black people, and that he "wouldn't blame any Negro for picketing it."

So much (and so little) for Robeson's Hollywood travails, but in truth, he had summed it up when he said how could one person change Hollywood — especially, when Hollywood was going down to the local Black musicians union and signing up some of the finest musicians in the United States to run through fake African jungles as savages, at the same time hiring white musicians to play these savages' music and eventually even claim it.

Othello was the peak of Robeson's dramatic presence internationally. He had performed it first in 1930. Ira Aldridge had performed it one hundred years before in his African Grove Theater in Greenwich Village, NYC's first Black community. The theater was later destroyed by "white ruffians." White actors had played the role since Aldridge. Robeson took a pre Edmund Kean approach, as he said, and played "Othello" as it had originally been played, by and as a Black man. "Shakespeare meant *Othello* to be a Black Moor from Africa, an African of the highest nobility of heritage. From Kean on, *Othello* was made a light skinned Moor because the West had since made Africa a slave center and the African was pictured only as a slave."

He goes on. "English critics seeing a Black Othello were likely to take a colonial point of view and regard him offhand as low and ignoble. Shakespeare's play has deep social meaning today. Shakespeare saw his era in human terms, an era of change from the feudal to higher forms of social relationships. In *Othello*, he anticipated the rape of Africa and some of the subsequent racial problems."

Othello' opened in the U.S. in 1942 with Uta Hagen as Desdemona and Jose Ferrer as Iago. The production broke all records for Shakespearean productions on Broadway, 296 performances. It then toured for 10 months across the U.S....except the South. Robeson refused to play before segregated audiences. A half a million people saw *Othello* by 1945. Robeson himself, as do advanced contemporary cultural workers, saw the production as a weapon against the backward racist ideas that dominate the institutions and ideology of the reactionary U.S. superstructure. It was now that Robeson was faced with even more intensifying opposition and the rise of "red baiting," as the anti-democratic spirit projected by the Banker-Corporate-Military-Industrial rulers of the U.S. superstructure. It was now that Robeson was faced with even more intensifying opposition and the rise of "red baiting," as the democratic spirit projected by the Banker Corporate-Military-Industrial rulers of the U.S. when the people had to be roused to oppose out and out fascism began to be opposed. But there has always been in the U.S. nation-state from its inception, a contending anti-democratic essence, flowing directly from the settler colony, imperialist and slave relations. It has had with the native, Chicano and Afro American peoples.

The bankers and corporate rulers now openly changed their relationships with the socialist states whom they had just recently been in a United Front with fighting against Germany and Japan. They moved to dam up the flood of democratic ideas that had been raised very sharply by the anti-fascist war as well as by the higher level of productive forces arising from their surface posture as "Leader of The Democracies" and the various programs that saw whole new sectors of the population return from the war to go to college and buy houses with the G.I Bill.

This gesturing with democracy was dangerous for the 6/10ths of one percent of the population who own the land, the factories, the media, the transport, &c. With too much democracy, the next thing you know the people might want to get rid of capitalism itself. Especially after such enforced fraternization with commie Russia and China.

Robeson's "worldwide" image as a consummate artist was now to be dismissed gradually replaced by the rulers' scribes, and his career itself, as a world popular artist, obstructed, attacked, under fusillades of character assassination and witch hunt scapegoating. Ultimately, it was destroyed.

A 1946 meeting with President Truman at which Robeson urged Truman to oppose lynching (some 15 known that year alone, registered in the presentation to the United Nations by DuBois, William Patterson and then called "We Charge Genocide"). But this meeting turned into virulent hostility and confrontation. Reporters at one point besieged Robeson with questions like, "Are you a communist?" Robeson told them of his general pro-socialist views but told them as well they had no business asking.

To another question, Robeson answered that..."he would not turn the other cheek," if attacked. But instead, he would "tear (his assailant) head off, before he could hit me on the other..." The most shocking statement of Robeson's to Truman was that, "if the government did not do something about lynching, Negroes would!" Truman, no slouch as an intellectual, said, "It sounded like a threat..."

From this moment on, the press declared war on Robeson and concerts all over the country were canceled, 85 in 1948 alone. He was now widely called, "a Communist sympathizer." Yet, Truman would not even issue a statement condemning lynching. Robeson was further labeled, "an avowed and active propagandist for Un-American Ideologies" From then on it was open war. The anti Democratic U.S. Government as the repressive armed power of capital, its various Lieutenants and flunkies vs. Paul Robeson, Revolutionary Afro American artist.

At root, it was not just Robeson that the most backward forces in the U.S. began to attack ruthlessly. As the cold war propaganda began to poison the American people ubiquitously and

McCarthyism moved fully out into the open, the entire "Left" radical, revolutionary and of course, Communist presence in the U.S. would be assaulted by every sector of the state and corporate power. The ideological unmasking of the U.S. ruling class and the shrill frenzy with which "Communism and the Communist conspiracy" were sounded throughout the nation, signaled that now that the war against the Nazis was won, the U.S. rulers could attack their most dangerous enemy, socialism.

By 1950, the U.S. was in a war in Korea to install its military occupation of South Korea while attempting to destroy North Korea, encircle the Chinese and threaten the Russians. By 1951, DuBois was indicted by the U.S. government as "an agent of a foreign power" (a case which made the government look ridiculous before the whole world, as they lost, with Albert Einstein standing by as WEB's lone "character witness"). The backward Negroes at the NAACP had moved first, firing DuBois, for the second time, in 1948. In 1949, Robeson was brought before the Un-Americans for stating at the Paris Peace Conference that Black people would not fight in a war against the Soviet Union, no matter the anti anti-war antics of the Charlie McCarthy political hustlers working and speaking for the U.S. corporate kings.

The "integration" of the Negro baseball leagues at the same time was simply Monopoly as imperialism snatching a national market, pretending to push democratic reform and using the small group of the "integrated" as their mouthpieces. This is the way Jackie Robinson became the first Black in corporate baseball, not because he was the best player, but because he fit the class and ideological/psychological requirements for "the first Negro." The rulers promptly used him to denounce Robeson! So too, the willing requirement the rulers had for the NAACP's new "leaders," Walter White and Roy Wilkins and the other kneeling Negroes of the slavish house boy sector of the Black petty bourgeoisie, was that they denounce Robeson and DuBois, which they did smilingly with tongues made of newspapers.

WWII was the last "just war" the U.S. could be involved in. The U.S. "power elite," as Eisenhower had mealy mouthed (Woodrow Wilson had as well many years before) could now oppose both the peoples' former allies, already redefining the U.S. bourgeoisie and petty bourgeoisie benefit, explains, for instance, the clamor around Jackie Robinson. And as the U.S. becomes increasingly more racist, such ersatz examples of "democracy" will be celebrated, while genuine Afro American patriots like Robeson are still "covered" by U.S. censorship.

Robeson's career, as a dramatic and concert artist, in the end, was savaged by the same forces that profited from the chattel slavery of his parents and the whole of the Afro American people. And though the years of struggle, the rise and fall of the Sisyphus syndrome, have continued, and given old content new form, the ugliest opposition to human freedom remains in power. So that, even today, the most ferociously anti-democratic forces in the world still hold the ultimate power of life and death, being or "nothingness." Robeson's pitiless harassment, character assassination, career destruction, ultimate physical sickness and death, are another legacy of American slavery and the continuing rule of money.

(1991)

The Blues Aesthetic & The Black Aesthetic

The term "Blues Aesthetic," which has been put forward by certain academics recently, is useful only if it is not de-politicization of reference. So we can claim an aesthetic for Blues, but at the same time, disconnect the historical continuum of the blues from its national and international source, the lives and history of the African, Pan African and specifically Afro American people. The Blues Aesthetic is one aspect of the overall African American aesthetic. This seems obvious because the blues is one vector expressing the material historical and psychological source.

Culture is the result of "a common psychological development." But the common psychological development is based on experiencing common material conditions which are defined ultimately, politically and economically.

The African American culture comes to exist as the living historical experience and development of the African American people, a Western hemisphere people! whose history and heritage are African and The Americas. By the 19th century, this new people had become consolidated and Back To Africa no longer represented the escape of captives and was replaced by either the psychological and political submission of a small sector of that people or the mass main stream ideology of Stay & Fight.

The Blues arises as a late 19th century early 20th century secular thrust of the African American musical culture, whose oldest musical and lyrical heritage was Africa but whose changing contemporary expression summed up their' lives and history in the West! The B lues reflects earlier developments of an African American speech and continuing musical experience now given new forms as reflection of the post Civil War African American culture that was no longer limited as severely to religious reference or the social restraints of slavery. The Blues is secular: it is also post chattel slavery.

The drumless African choir sound of the Sorrow Songs (much like Black Ladysmith Mambazo) gives way to a sassier actually "more" African and more contemporary American. The later Gospel style reflects this as well. By the 19th century the diverse Africans had become African Americans and the Blues, from spiritual and work song, through Hollers and Shouts and Arwhoolies, jumped out to celebrate Black entrance into a less repressive, less specialized world, less harsh more uncertain but still tragic and depriving in too many ways.

The blues as a verse and musical form is one thing, but what needs to be gotten to here is the whole, the aesthetic overview, the cultural matrix that the Blues is but one expression of. Particularly the Blues is African American secular-country or city. The former is older, relating even into chattel slave society. The various city and other urban forms reflect that social and historical motion. Black people 1st moving from plantations to southern cities from civil war on and then by the late 1880s beginning to go up north, fleeing the destroyed reconstruction, the KKK, and looking for the new world.

The Blues aesthetic must emotionally and historically carry the heart and soul of the African Antiquity, but it is also a *Western Aesthetic*, i.e., expressing a western people, though African American. (Finally, Europe is not the West, the Americas are! Head west from Europe you come to Jersey! West of the Americas is the East!)

So the Blues itself must express the human revelation of life outside, or "post" the plantation—though I guess we ain't got very much "post" that bad boy yet! It is regional, or southern, or urban, &c. Its instrumentation changes to reflect the level of the people's productive forces and the social, political and economic structure of those peoples' lives.

But that is the particularized yet constantly altering changing form of the Blues qua blues. Yet it is deeper and older than itself as this self. If we study Equiano, DuBois, Douglass, Diop,

Robert Thompson and LeRoi Jones we will see that the single yet endlessly diverse African cultural matrix is the basis not only of what's called the Blues Aesthetic, but any Black Aesthetic.

First, the Africans are the oldest humans on the planet and all aesthetics on the planet, relating to human society, must use them at least as a point of departure! Even the European so called Appollonian Aesthetic mode (formalism and restraint) that characterized the Athenian Attic culture is so significant because it emerges not only in contradiction to the older, once world dominating Dionysian (expressionist, emotion characterized humanistic) philosophical and aesthetic mode.

It is a re-division of human sensibilities and priorities as epoch creating as the flood that divided the world as the Mediterranean. We are still dominated by those tribes that emerged north of this biblically referenced waterway. In capsule, the African Aesthetic in its seemingly most ancient projection, first is an expression of the Animist world view of our earliest ancestors. That is, to the classic African sensibility, everything in the world was alive. but even more important, everything that exists (as present — because both the past and the future only exist in the present and as speculative continuum of the is — the African "Goddess" Is/Is) is part of, connected as, the same thing!

Everything is one thing, one living thing. In this case you can see how even so called Monotheism is like "Rock & Roll" (my term for the Bourgeois culture north of the middle of the world). The ideas of "One God" is already jive decrepitude of the philosophy of the antiquity. It is not "One God," as opposed to many, the qualification for savagery — but that every thing is one — All is All, everything is everything! Allah means literally All/everything is part of the same thing. Like the donut and the hole are both space!

So the continuity, the endlessness, the myriad multiformed expressiveness of "The One" what is is/is. The continuity of even later African religion carried a fundamental relationship as in its continuing Call & Response form. That is Priest to Congregation. The One & The Many, are one thing. Like the heart beat-beating is sound & not sound (where be is at — at least now then, when). They are not disconnectable as existent.

Evidence, Monk says (scat) the African celebrates. His life is meant, consciously, as evidence — it is in that sense *material*. (E.g.

natural evidence, like it is, rather than artifactions, i.e. formalism. Everything is in it, can be used, is then, dual — reflecting the earliest economic and social form, *communalism*. Above the Mediterranean what it looked like was more important than what it was or what it did. In the southern Cradle what it did, its practice, its content was principal.

The African religion (See DuBois on "The Sorrow Songs" and "The Faith of The Fathers" in The SOBF) had their Priest and Congregation as Call and Response ("Two is One" says Monk and Marx). Dialectical character of what is, negation of the negation, the unity of opposites. The religion must also have music. Since "The spirit could not descend without song."

Spirit is literally *breath* as in in/spire or ex. Where you aspire is where you (go be at) headed, like the church spire. No breath No life. But the drum replicating the 1st human instrument keeps life, the sun replicating itself inside us. Its beat. Night & Day. In and out, the breath. Coming and Going, the everything. The Pulse, the flow, the rhythm carrier. (Time is formal, it is the reverse of expressionist sensibility i.e., emit vs. time.)

So, as DuBois explains, Priest, Congregation, Music; which brings the Spirit down (from where? the soul is the invisible influence of the Solar — what life means, the smallest I, the largest Eye).

It is the *Frenzy*, the soul possession, that the African thought scientifically and as a result of historical cultural perception, rationale and use, that the re-combining of the two, (the single with the all) the atonement, the Gettin Happy, which is the music's use. A way into consciousness of the whole, transcending the partial understanding of the single self.

The ecstasy is the being, the is/life. So Jazz, is Jism, Come music, creating music. Coming is the spiritual presence of the all existent one focused we can see, inhaling. The northern aesthetic has never assimilated sexuality, to it sex is dirty or embarrassing. But the sexual experience is as explicit a reflection of the One is Two dialectic as well. This is also a reflection of the overthrow of Mother right (the matrilineal social relations of ancient Africa) and the enslaving of women. The anti-woman character of the northern cradle, whether Salem witch burning (specifically to totally eliminate Dionysian survivals) or anti-ERA is historically consistent.

So the revelation, the Going out, quality of African American culture as music or anything else is constant and evident. From religion to social relations, the polyrhythms of African music are a further reflection of this animist base of the culture. But not only music, also in the clothes—body or hair adornment, graphic or verbal arts of the people, as a consistent means of characterizing the Pan African culture and its international significance. The bright colors of the Pan African culture are reflection of those same polyrhythms. Acknowledgment of several levels or sectors or "places" of life *existing simultaneously*.

So the historically traceable *Cosmopolitanism* of the African people. Open and welcoming, intrigued by diversity and the "other." Ironically, in this sense, Diop points out the essentially non-African essence of Nationalism. Again, the recognition of all as All—everything is everything. The attempt to denigrate Pan African people with the stereotypes of racialism by claiming that the only things Pan Africans can do is sing and dance (Okay w/me—just let us be in charge of it! How many people can we house and educate just with Michael J's 93,000,000 albums sold?) Equiano points out in his narrative "We are almost a nation of singers and dancers." The socialization of the people was song and dance. As expressions of being. On all occasions. (Like America's stereotype as sports fans.) The Africans were socialized around song and dance and the participation, contribution by everyone in that. Art itself was a collective and communal expression. It was also functional and social.

Even the Blue, the color, from our own proto-Krishna faces, so black they blue. Diop says people in Southern India are the blackest people on the planet—like Krishna they blue. But also Equiano tells us that "Blue"—that beautiful Guinea Blue was "our favorite color." The Italians, though dark, didn't like to be called Black Slaves. We, of course, are the *real* Guineas, our head was on the English gold coin of that name gotten from the old "Gold" or Guinea Coast. The Blues as the expression of sorrow, should be obvious a reference to our sad African slave lives here as well. It is also, after Black Mama is/night a sign that the sun gonna be at our door directly. So a poem of mine says, "Blues came/even before Day/Got here."

So the Blues Aesthetic is not only historical and carrying all the qualities that characterize the African American people, but social in the same way. It must be how and what Black life is and

102

how it reflects on itself. It is style and form but it is the continuum of the content, the ideas, the feelings' articulation that is critical as well as the how of the form. Yet form and content are expressions of each other.

As verse form, the typical AAB Blues form is by its structure and dynamic, given to emphasis (repeated 1st lines) as well as change and balance (the new rime line, the AA BB rime scheme).

The flatted 3rds and 5ths, the slurs or bending of notes of singer or instrumentalist, is the Kamite antiquity cultural character and summation of reality. KA — or HAM means change, (the changes, the chemistry — the Chemists or Kamists) Hamites were the first chemists. The change from one quality or element to another. The dialectic of life itself. One is two as Lenin said explaining the dialectic in The Philosophical Notebooks. Everything is itself and something else, at the same time i.e., what is or becoming.

Twelve bars are the four quarters of the 360 (4 arcs i.e., seasons) of the trinity — past, present, future — the pyramid of dimension and motion itself, rhythm *not* time — dancing, those Arthur Murray footprints which is advertising finally and money, not dancing at all.

And the blues is not even 12 necessarily, the insistence on that forms formalism (as say Martin Smithsonian is guilty of when he says that Billie Holiday wasn't a blues singer because her songs weren't 12 bars!) But Blues is first a feeling a sense — Knowledge. A being not a theory — the feeling is the form and vice versa.

John Coltrane could turn Julie Andrews "My Favorite Things" into our real lives. The CAMIST — going through changes — rhythm & changes rhythm and blues — about feeling not counting. (Goin thru Changes is the Blues.) Rollover, Beethoven, we cry and relate it to us over and under any way. We blues or jazz up, syncopate any and every. We are incumaters and syncopaters. One is Two. One Breaks into Two.

The Black woman is everyone's mother and the domesticator of the human being from the animal, the black man is the second domesticated animal. His wife done it! The key to the distortion of the so called xtian trinity is there is no woman in it, so it is a cross sign. The ankh indicates. The head and nuts are missing from the Christian cross, hence neither reproduction or creativity — a death sign. So the northern culture hangs on to the memory of the old blue black church with fragments of the black madonna. But Roman church is rock and roll. Jesus (Jesse-I am) evolves (Christ) crosses to higher ground, re birth or continuum of human development.

I am hip is what Jesus Christ means—I am become Hip. As Fred said, "No progress w/o struggle." It is not the flattened distortion of Betty Wright and Negro politicians "No pain no gain." It is not *pain* indicated but *struggle*. As in "the sun's gonna shine in my back door one day." The past (black night's your mother) is also the future (What is nigh is coming—Eve before *AM*. The Present was here before it was the past and after it was the future. The world is a tragedy i.e., it is a carrying, the weight, the changes—not time, rhythm, not counting, feeling.

Any and Every—All are related as the *one*. part of a whole, whole of a part. The hole and what goes in and out, the creating (as it was in the beginning and ever shall be, world w/o end, &c). What is funky is history, what comes goes.

The Blues is the first come from Black—Red, the last, going out to re-come. The cycle the circle. The Red what reading did re adding reproducing revolution, red, old going out into black and coming back through blue Mood Indigo.

So blues is the past, the blown all what got blew; the expressive i.e., the blowing; the loss, the blown, the blowing. The known gone, the unknown coming all the non time.

We are sad about what was that is not and about what is that should not. And we are glad just to be feeling. G the name of expression, La the sixth birth, joy the reaffirmation and are is out is Dee is worth what everything exists as a whole holy.

Being and Changes Coming and Going Happy and Sad. It is life's feeling, and the rising restay of revelation, evolution, raise on up, rah rah rah we say to our sol above the first cheer leader Rah Rah Rah alive is holy the—consciousness which ultimately combines KNOW & HOW is Conscious perception, rationale, use, as Mao laid out explicating the marxist theory of knowledge.

Love ultimately we feel (the upgrading of the fuck mode—Anglo saxon word "fuck" means to hit, imagine then what "fucked up" i.e. pregnant, implies for this culture). Love is the necessity even as sex for our continuation. When Love is the Law and The Consciousness—The Holy Family will be what it is anyway like Every thing is Every thing.

The Holy Family of human world, not exclusive but inclusive no separation eg, form and content or form and feeling. Hamlet is the northern opposite to be or not — the liberal — not even sure life is worth while. We seek Wholeness. Atonement.

Not Nietzsche saying feeling made it hard for him to think. For us what cannot feel cannot think. They say Dr. J., Magic, Michael Air are "instinctive." Boston Larry B, &c "intelligent." The highest intelligence is dancing not the Arthur Murray footsteps advertising! The highest Thought is a doing a being not an abstraction.

Hence the *improvised*. the spontaneous, the intuitive, the felt are so valued like the B line AAB — that rising B is the recognition of form but the primacy of content — like the revealed ecstasy of the congregation, enraptured, gettin happy, funky, high, moved, what is and what will, what was is where we coming from, our story, our tail just like that snake crawling into its own mouth.

Calling ourselves tale, we can admit of no Blues aesthetic that tries to hide from the politics of wholeness like the recent retrograde trend of Buppie/Yuppie trying to cop the "style" of w/o Black the substance, struggle, the changes. As Fred said, "they want the sea w/o its' awful roar." And for the Negro who is using this to side step the politics of liberation for the economic and social advancement of the Pimp. The people who make the authentic Blues *have* the blues, it is not something out of a school book — the vicious and laid back pimps of dawning compradorism can tout to enriching w/o endarkening.

It is Black life historically, politically and socially, the form and content of the Blues, as Langston says, the *signifying* is what revealed us as higher forms of animal, and yet as we were the *first* to raise up off all fours, it appears humanity is still some ways off. But w/o the signification, the meaning, the tale to swing, the story of the seeds. Where we come from and where we going loses its significance. The signification is what makes the monkey, man. Remove the words (past, pass that baton runner, run it beat it out on wood or skin, even your own, rapper) the signs Breath and Change and everything is a design w/o a key the Man Key he opened it up.

There is a current retrograde trend of black artists who see black life as caricature, there is another part of the same trend, the so called "new black aesthetic" which tries to disconnect black art from black life and make it simply "a style" (e.g., the *Village Voice* coven of young Negroes (sic) but this is certainly not the mainstream currently or historically. The black aesthetic is drawn from black life in the real world, just as any so-called blues aesthetic would necessarily be, as well.

Held in the forms and content of the black aesthetic, in any of its cultural or historical elements, there is the will the desire the evoked "name" of freedom. What Monk was talking about. Freedom! Bird. Trane. On Higher Ground. Duke. Count. Lady. Sassy. Bessie. Monk, &c., &c.

The retrograde Bup/Yup trend can't handle the African American Aesthetic because it signifies, it "talks shit" from Rap to Rap. From Fred to Big Red. The Black Aesthetic. As communal, revelational and ecstatic, expressionistic, content focused, first signifier signifies freedom (new life, revelation, evolution, revolution) always. Songs, dances, clothes. Freedom Now, Freedom Suite, Free Jazz!, &c., &c. Asked about Jazz Monk said, "It's about Freedom, more than that is complicated."

It can not be an authentic reflection of the main thrust of the African American aesthetic without dealing with the Question of Freedom. As person or as part of the One. It's Afro American symbols, contain the freedom expression whether Brer Rabbit, who lay on symbol and got over through guile (showing in American culture as Bugs Bunny) or the other side of the dialectic, e.g., Stagolee or John Henry or Jimmy Brown, who dealt with force and power. Our history is full of such dialectically contradictory heroes and heroines.

To depoliticize the African American Aesthetic is to disconnect it from the real lives of the Afro American people, and instead make an offering to the seizers—that is—we must understand that not only our history aesthetically is contradictory to the so called Northern cradle, but certainly as slaves and now an oppressed nation, the slave/slave master contradiction is the most serious of all.

Without the dissent, the struggle, the outside of the inside, the aesthetic is neither genuinely Black nor Blue—but the aesthetic of submission—whether for pay or out of ignorance or ideological turpitude.

(1991)

The Black Theater Movement &
The Black Consciousness Movement

Actually, this paper should be directed to the whole of the Black Arts Movement, historically and in all its dimensions, not just theater. But theater, as George Thompson said in *Marxism & Poetry* (1975, Wishart, Eng.), "new drama usually rises in periods of revolution." Because of all the arts, Drama is the most ambitious or pretentious, in that it seeks to put live people into "live experience" and as art. Or at least something purporting to be art. But since the '50s even art has been publicly marginalized & only tolerated as commerce, titillation & metaphysics.

Film & television have replaced live drama in the main and large audience theater is strictly commerce aimed at tourists as part of middle class vacations. It is an alienated entertainment like circuses. Whatever the most influential cultural expression in a society is also a portrait of that society. For the Afro American people, like any people, our cultural expression describes and speaks as part of us. Historically, whenever there has been a political upsurge among the Afro American people (& I'm sure this is universal) there is also an artistic outpouring reflecting and at the same time influencing that political and social advance in society.

The anti-slavery movement of the 19th century brought the Slave Narratives as well as the speeches and sermons and Appeals and Confessions of the Frederick Douglass, David Walker, Nat Turner, Linda Brent. The lives of Garnett, Tubman, Vesey, are part of the literature & art & social expression of the period. The classic works of history, as profound as the scattered Greek writings about the Peloponnesian Wars or Caesar's Commentaries, recreating a classic European period.

But by the forced end of Reconstruction, the revolutionary social period was destroyed and the cultural expressions of American life were transformed, had been changing according to the material life of society. What was actually *happening what* was most transforming (impacting, influential)! The revolutionary literature gives way to Chesnutt & Dunbar & the rhetoric of Booker T. In society itself, the consolidation of American Apartheid, the expression of the victory of U.S. fascism over democracy for the Afro American nation post Civil War.

Birth of A Nation & minstrelsy are imperialist America's characterization of Blacks after the war. Instead of U.S. citizens, we became, by force, an oppressed nation, excluded from the full U.S. franchise & democracy. Earlier, William Wells Brown's *The Escape* is called the "first play" by an Afro American, but Afro American culture uses its dramatic presence throughout its whole expression. Whether the church, the slave song, artifact, dance, oral, are dramatic. Yet the very experience which these express also confirm that it is slavery they are talking about, where you are not even credited with or legally allowed to think! Theater as a public expression required Freedom, Liberty. Citizenship! Democracy! Equality!

To fully express, as an entity of full artistic power, access to public resources is critical. Though the theater (& film) we should be trying to create today must perfect "the shorthand of poverty" and draw live human experience & reality from the maximum realization of our *actual* resources—beginning with the people, the cities and their institutions. The very absence of what the people need is our vibrant explosive stage!

The rise of the Harlem Renaissance in the U.S. paralleled & influenced the rise of *Negritude* in the French speaking Black world. & as *Negrissmo* in the Spanish & Portuguese speaking Black world. Haiti spoke again with *Indigisme*. A return to Black, African roots of the Black Consciousness & Pan Africanism expressed by DuBois & Garvey & the world Black Anti-Colonial movement.

The resistance to Booker T's apologia for Black national oppression was focused on by DuBois (*Souls of Black Folks*) & the young Black university trained intelligentsia, like Monroe Trotter. Ida B. Wells was one transforming social ideological catalyst expressing the people's rising level of productive forces and the strengthening of Black social & political organization. Minstrel shows moved in circuits. The Black dramatic (music, dance, verse, graphics) expression can be distributed publicly. Professional Black artists arise as a parallel to the emergence of a Black bourgeoisie. Segregation creates a need for an alternative entertainment industry, as the expression of the slaves' formal freedom. The cultural expression of the slave can now be legally objectified, described for public consumption.

But this is also an expression of near slavery. The Minstrel was the identity of Black culture to permit it any "freedom," e.g., to be allowed to be public expression, to have the self-determination, as person, so as to be able to choose playing the piano or singing rather than be forced to pick cotton as a slave or even as a share cropper.

After each revolutionary upsurge, the social as catalyst for the artistic, a period of minstrelsy is created describing the reactionary forces that dominate society. So that the victorious slave of the 1860s becomes the eye rolling coon of the 1890s. But let us dramatize Nat's *Confessions*, with the music and full expression of that explosive period, 1831. Wells Brown's *The Escape* had a similar effect even read aloud to audiences since he lacked equal access to resources and freedom of expression.

The reading of the Slave Narratives would galvanize Black audiences. Just as Douglass' or Garnett's speeches. As words are at the center of drama, setting the stage & expressing the action, the motion, the meaning! Hughes, Hurston, carry the fully expressed dramatic sensibility of the Harlem Renaissance. DuBois wrote of the dramatic heritage of the Afro American people, as a historic aesthetic of their culture. He also wrote a giant pageant, aimed at the churches, *Ethiopia Reaches Forth Her Hand*, and organized the Krigwa (Crisis Group of Working Artists) Theater. Toomer and McKay are dramatic writers. *Cane* or *Home to Harlem, Banana Bottom* and McKay's other novels are great theater. Part of the great treasure chest of Afro American Arts & Culture still rendered inert by our lack of Self Determination!

The period itself is a great drama. The telling of which, as theater, (See this author's *Remembering Weselves*) will be part of the democratic social transformation. DuBois' Krigwa theaters were proposed to use drama as a method of unifying a sector of the Afro American people through an artistic culture of liberation & self-determination.

Hughes' *Mulatto* dramatizes the American white supremacy Slave-Slave master relationship as a tragic domestic explosion that represents and envelops the whole town. Who are Americans? What is the American family? The lie of race. The slaughter of the slaves' humanity. All these questions roll throughout *Mulatto*.

The American culture itself is a composite of peoples. All the peoples of the world! Yet slavery, explained & justified by white supremacy, commands & oppresses most of the people in U.S. society (and now, ca. 2007, the world). The Eurocentric focus & nature of official U.S. culture is an expression of European colonialism and the slavery of the African peoples. Drama itself is a form of existing human society, however expressed. It characterizes & codifies, makes paradigm & particular the actual relationship and expression of real social life. Which is the fundamental resource of drama, as all life. Hughes' *Scottsboro Ltd*, not only presents as form a combining of poetry, movement, music & theatrical dimension that is wonderfully "avant garde!" He makes a Poetry & Jazz Drama of the most critical social oppression, the legal lynching of the Scottsboro Boys.

Mule Bone is the near legendary collaboration between Hurston & Hughes. It is a miracle of poetry, music, movement, artistically expressive pageant of Afro American folk culture. The work is as compelling & as unifying as a historical cultural presence whose politics are understood, if only by contrast to the social political culture of the American rulers. Even the underlying philosophy (the poetry & music tell it) the characters speak from the continuum of Black history. From the profundity of how Black life continues, carrying the sweet feeling of the laughter and lyric consciousness of the classic folk culture.

The Negritude of the Harlem Renaissance & The Pan African arts movements always acknowledged and raised the cultural history of the people as a source of consciousness! Africa, Black life & Culture, the drama of slavery & resistance. The revolution of Black expression, the playing out of the antagonistic forces at base in society. From the slave's eye and feeling. *The Sun Do Move* is Langston's history of the Afro American people. Langston opened several theaters, The Suitcase in LA, The Loft in Harlem.

The Lafayette Theater Players was one of the most visible expressions of a Black theater movement in the '20s, which even after the depression, continued in the Federal Theater Project productions of Black drama, including Ted Ward's *Big White Fog*, which is probably why the theater got removed from the FTP as "too far to the left."

Fog sums up a Black family's disintegration in the social and economic struggles of the '20s and '30s and their turning from Garveyism to Communism. Ward brought the play from Chicago to New York, producing it as a production of The Negro Playwrights' Company.

Only Hansberry's *Raisin In The Sun* characterizes Black ideological diversity within one family as sharply. Though there is no play that handles the explosiveness of class antagonism within the Black family and the extension that is a Black community as sharply as *Fog*! The Harlem Renaissance had been transformed by the 1929 Crash & depression – to the extent that Black cultural expression is tied to the general economic development of U.S. society.

The '30s show a sharp movement to the left inside the Black Liberation Movement. The Negritude & Black consciousness thrusts are transformed by time, place & condition and so become less speculations about Africa, Black culture & consciousness, the legacies of slavery and Black responsibility to resist it, reshaped into repeated characterizations of the U.S. social-economic system itself. The racism and national oppression are described, but finally as reflections of the general inhumanity of capital. *Scottsboro Ltd* & *Fog* are spectacular examples of this. The Black consciousness is expressed as an ideological stance toward the U.S. social system entirely, not just its enslaving of the Afro American people.

The ideological conflict that arises during the Renaissance between, for instance, DuBois, Langston & McKay, inside the Black consciousness stance particularly around the question of the function of Art in relationship to politics is the famous caustic exchange of letters between McKay & DuBois arising from DuBois criticism of McKay's novel, *Home to Harlem* as pandering to the white petty bourgeois. When attacked by McKay for confusing propaganda with art, DuBois declared that he did not "give a damn" for any art that wasn't propaganda. In essence saying there is no nobler pursuit than human liberty and self-determination and that art must be a means of seeking and securing and describing that quest, as an expression of its highest function. DuBois's grand pageant *Ethiopia* was designed to be acted, participated in, literally, by thousands as a mass public ritual expressing the historical consciousness of Black aspiration for human ascension from the chaos of ignorance and bondage. DuBois saw drama, particularly, as one continuing aspect of Pan African culture and art as the expression of culture.

Hence, when speaking of the "Gifts of Black Folk" to America, he lists the gift of labor, the gift of song & story, and the gift of spirit (i.e. the spirit of the struggle for democracy). Black Art is an expression of the people's lives & history. Played out as the contemporary materialization of memory & desire. Art is not an artifaction of extra human revelation, it is the elevation of humanity to become a grander thing.

The '30s & '40s plays of social consciousness characterize Black drama & U.S. serious theater generally. The concerns of race in *Mulatto* are replaced by the concerns of general social justice and class alliance. The Federal Theater Project gave public exposure to a new wave of Black playwrights, Ted Ward and the '30s Langston the most impressive. Paul Peters' *Stevedore*, & John Wesley's *They Shall Not Die*, both 1934, both white, demonstrate in parallel the emergence of a new left theater in the broader U.S. culture expressed by people like Odets and The Group Theater. Ted Ward's *Our Lan'*, a grave meditation on the betrayal of Reconstruction actually made it to Broadway, attesting to the social dynamism of the left in the '30s and the '40s, the continuing social progress World War II ironically made possible, because of its populist opposition to Fascism. This also meant expanded production and the increased hiring of Blacks into defense jobs made possible by A Philip Randolph's threat to March on Washington armed with the righteous anger and determination to end slavery times of the Black masses at the eve of World War II as the depression ended.

There is a continuing social thrust, a conspicuous commitment to struggle against discrimination & segregation in the socially conscious Black drama of the '40s, when Richard Wright's *Native Son* arrives on Broadway. Into the early '50s a whole host of Black playwrights, Louis Peterson, Alice Childress, William Branch tried to construct a relevant socially conscious Black theater, still largely unperformed in mainstream America.

What has always deterred Black theater is the denial of resources and access to the mainstream of public production — literally the low development of Afro American productive forces, repressed by slavery and national oppression. This is the replication of the place of the Afro American people in U.S. society. The U.S. has never been a democracy. It isn't now. Rodney King not only represents the Dred Scott decision in its 1992 form. This bit of drama still says that Afro Americans have no rights in the U.S. *because we are not citizens*!

In this sense the camcorder footage is only a preview, a coming attraction of the full drama, which was made fully possible with the help of "dramaturge" (Police Chief) Daryl Gates, a passion play with The Crips and The Bloods, a multi national, multi cultural cast of thousands. Fire City! "I Rise In Fire" cried the Phoenix! BA in Egyptian, the Black Soul Bird. And middle class Negroes & white Bush people complain. It is simply ghetto stereotypes The Yo! Boom Box! NWA style. Yet they accuse Sister Souljah or Public Enemy or Ice Cube or Ice T of cracking wack. Well check the fires. Bus dat home, some of LA is gone gone gone.

So the Hansberrys & Baldwins bring in the last part of the '50s raising that transitional post WWII concern into a deeper more impassioned expression. *Raisin* & *Blues for Mr. Charlie* are truly great works. They are key statements of high social art tracing the changing dimensions of Black Liberation consciousness and the human expression of Black life & concerns of the period, plus the weight & continuing legacy of slavery.

The 1960's Black Theater movement as an expression of the general Black Arts Cultural Revolution was further confirmation that out of each social political upsurge an artistic explosion emerges — shaped by the social political trend and in turn helping shape it. In each of the three main upsurges, 19th century anti-slavery movement, early 20th century Harlem Renaissance and the Civil Rights and Black Liberation Movement of the '50s, '60s and early '70s there was a vital efflorescence of related art movements.

Baldwin & Hansberry were the classic forces and voices that made a nexus to the older Afro American literary & social traditions to form the historic continuum of Afro American art & social concerns. *Raisin* is the ultimate civil rights drama, shaping in a single multi faceted sweep the day to day human concerns of a Black working class family in Chicago.

Blues raises the question of class struggle between Malcolm X & Martin Luther King, as representative of contradictory class forces within the Black Liberation Movement, even as it struggles against the white fascist south. Both plays were right out of the '50s and '60s headlines. In the Black Theater Movement that followed, revolutionary dissent from the status quo of Black national oppression. My essay "The Revolutionary Theater" tried to draw an emotional parallel between the concerns of Black revolution and the need for a truly expressive Afro American drama. It was the same function, the aesthetic ordering, the political organization, in different media.

Just as Cultural Revolution continues the political struggle in the superstructure, that area of ideology and institutions created by the material i.e., economic base of society. It is just such Cultural Revolution that Lenin & Mao called for to serve socialist construction. Counter revolution prevailed over Cultural Revolution in both cases (after Mao & Lenin's deaths). We called for three things in the Black Arts Movement. (1) An art that was demonstrably Afro American. (2) A mass art that would no longer be limited to the campuses and libraries, but enter and interact with the great masses of people. And (3) We wanted an art that was revolutionary. That would help transform the U.S. social system!

The Black Theater Movement openly sought to parallel Black political struggle & its creators saw themselves as revolutionary fighters. Larry Neal, Askia Toure, Ben Caldwell, Marvin X, Ed Bullins, Carol Freeman, Sonia Sanchez, Jimmy Garrett all saw theater as a form of revolutionary expression, purposely designed to raise Black Consciousness. And many times the issue was "Blackness" as a definition of our commitment to liberation. Yet Blackness is literally a quality of color not of ideology, and just as in other periods one breaks into two. The Black united front, any united front, is always given dimension by its own contradictions. Just as in the '20s, Black Consciousness became the 1930's class consciousness with those contradictions. Within the Black nation there is a bourgeoisie, a petty bourgeoisie and a working class. They all have voices. Every nation has two cultures. The culture of the oppressed & the culture of the oppressors.

So Blackness no longer held, after a time. The contradictory aspects of class identification, stance and struggle became more and more wide open. The longer the particular generation struggled, the

114

more openly would the class contradictions surface.

The Black bourgeoisie rose, by the middle of the '70s, into positions where they were able to co-opt the main stream of the Black Liberation Movement and turn the principal thrust of the BLM into electoral politics. So too did a new wave, a retrograde trend of "Buppies," Black upwardly mobile professionals, backward academics and artists who emerged as a totally reactionary antidote to the generally revolutionary democratic nature of the BLM.

As an expression of the counterrevolutionary down slope of the Sisyphus Syndrome, we have seen a whole movement of backward traitor Negroes, not only civil rights spokesmen but academics, artists, who mirror the oppressor nation's trying to belittle the quality and requirements for revolutionary art.

"Flash" Gordone was made the first Black Pulitzer in drama. Because his *No Place To Be Somebody* was literally the first wave of counter attack on Black Consciousness and the Black Arts Movement and Black liberation itself. They have since given another Pulitzer to Charlie Fuller for *A Soldier's Play*, which seemed to tell us and be uplifted by the fact that the best way to rise in the newly integrated U.S. army was turn in the Black militant to the authorities for killing the Black comprador who had murdered Black folk expression (a Mississippi peasant) because it made him "shame."

Since then a whole host of backward Negroes coughed up out of the Stanford University commode have been belched through the Pulitzer process, used to reward backwardness & attack the BLM. The irony of victory over U.S. apartheid is that it produced a superficial sector who are made important so that they can dispute the voices of national consciousness and self determination with backwardness, collaboration and cute Tomming.

There is a school of Buppies around the *Village Voice* who speak of the "New Black Culture." Close inspection reveals it to be Negro toms trying to eliminate social relevance from Black culture, reducing it to a "style." The U.S. stage has been filled with a wave of Negroes reflecting the dominance of reaction on U.S. society and open dismissal of the revolutionary ethic and commitment. Open embrace of white supremacy & U.S. imperialism as qualifications for full U.S. citizenship!

Plays like Fuller's *Zooman and the Sign, A Soldier's Play*, the wave of Negro Ensemble look-alikes all funded by the powers to replace Black revolutionary theater by Skin epics valorizing bourgeois & submissive Negro ideas. At base of all this work, like the essence of the sorry furniture music that commerce replaced authentic Jazz with in the same period, "Fusion," expresses social betrayal. The freezing of creative elements of Black music in commercial slavery. From "Afro Blue" improvisation to the dripping punk jerry curl of fusion. A whole sector of a generation has been brought to the stage carrying bought & paid for backwardness, like the collusion of Black Republicans with Southern Democrats and Northern corporate forces to objectively finish off Reconstruction.

Every day a new spokesperson or soi-disant (self-proclaimed/so-called) Negro artist pops out of the commode of reaction to valorize continued slavery. The Stanley Crouches, Playthell Benjamins, Walter Williams, Thomas Sowells, Clarence Thomas are the cutting edge of "Black": anti-Black commentary. These are the Roy Innises and Butelezis on stage and screen. On these campuses, in these books and galleries — a Negro African from Harvard told us in the *NY Times Sunday* that Africa only existed as a figment of white colonial imagination. That there was no such place as Africa! So these people not only want to submit to imperialism they want to make it responsible for thinking up Black people.

The Skip Gates' school of deconstruction wants us to know that Black art & expression is a function of classic mighty whiteness. A genius award & chair of Harvard Afro American studies is his reward for this "intelligent" calumny. The Spike Lee film vita is likewise fueled by a fundamental motion to collaborate with imperialism even while covering up class contradictions by co-opting the public style of Black youth. So Spike can make millions associating in ads with Michael Jordan, yet in person dismiss Jordan as unserious as a role model when compared with the white owners of the Chicago Bulls.

Even Malcolm's "X" has already been transformed into a commercial symbol, now it can be sold, for Spike that X is simply a multiplication sign, as Spike Lee's Joint opened this morning in NY City's Macys! One hopes the Malcolm film is not equally commodified. Spike says he has changed it, but early drafts of his script transformed Malcolm's life into a Spike Lee Joint, with more attention given to Malcolm's pimp & dope days. A whole wave of essentially middle class Negroes have been flushed out by the money and quite a few mindless anti-Black mass films appeared.

The *House Party* syndrome. The Yo/Boom Box surface rip off of Afro American urban culture.

Townsend's *Hollywood Shuffle* correctly (perhaps unintentionally) describes how the Black petty bourgeois comes into Hollywood to get the movie job as "street hoods." Having therefore to learn Black English, the ghetto strut &c., all excruciatingly corny and excruciatingly anti-Black mass culture. Townsend's next film was so positive (*5 Heartbeats*) it's hard to believe he made *Shuffle*. Damon Wayans probably had a great deal of influence on the project. In the same style as TV's *In Living Color*, but for all the mock integrity Wayans and Townsend express by having the hero, Townsend reject the Black caricature role in this film, looking at *In Living Color* or some later project like *The Last Boy Scout* lets you know its all a bitter joke. The Wayans are as hard working as the Toms and Stepin Fetchits ever was.

So that this period where the forces of reaction dominate U.S. society & the world, there is a Negro art, Negro academics & social spokespeople who reflect the stalled condition of U.S. social revolution. But this is one reason, not only cultural revolution is so crucial, but the entire area of contest must be altered.

It is stupid to attack imperialism & white supremacy yet sit around waiting for them to publish yr book or produce yr play! Where are the camcorder films? The Rodney King epic shows the real possibilities of this epic. We cannot & wd not spend 80 million dollars (for Batman).We must seize the creative initiative from Hollywood by force of our commitment to revolution. I would rather produce plays in my basement theater, seats fifty, & bring new & classical American music to this same site than be frustrated waiting for imperialism & white supremacy to do the right thing, discover you, which they will never do!

Where are our revolutionary publications, national periodicals, publishing companies, revolutionary newspapers? Instead, we wait for imperialism to transform itself. It will never do this. So too with education. The schools must be forcefully changed by revolutionaries. This is one key focus of the U.S. Cultural Revolution—the transformation of public education. The Literary Canon is the colonialism and slavery of the super structure of the status quo. We cannot wait until imperialism admits us into its reactionary canon, we must transform the curricula and methodology of education by organization & force. Where are our revolutionary schools & Institutes? Our training programs in Arts & Culture that we form and transform our youth into revolutionary fighting artists? Self Determination begins with the Act & is expanded by each successive act!

This present art that pretends to represent & speak for the Afro American people is, in truth, the expression of American reaction like the minstrelsy that arose as Reconstruction was beat down. Like the trends which bourgeois foundations & philanthropies build, like "Genius awards" to recruit poison house Negroes (of all nationalities) to do their bidding.

For one thing, America is multi-national and multi-cultural, like American culture. American drama is also retarded because Americans are disoriented about their culture. It is Brown (i.e. red, black, yellow) & they think they are "white." It is Pan American, they are Eurocentric. It speaks Latino everywhere, they speak English the way it is only spoken in Europe. Most Americans speak some form of American. So North Americans are illiterate in their own culture. This is why dead Eurocentric claptrap can pass for theater & music & art everyday. Because Americans, ignorant & arrogant, as they be, do not recognize or respond to their own culture, their own selves, except as distorted or twisted by corporate liars & white supremacists.

The U.S. theater on Broadway is simply proof that the Tories won the cultural counter-revolution. English Departments are bigger than any American Studies. British Theater, *Cats, Les Miserable, Ms Saigon* (ow!) British social democracy creates publicly funded theater to ship to Broadway as private enterprise. The Broadway real estate dealers get in the action so it's okay. But there is no American Theater. Sex Violence Money Reaction. The Big Four of our vapid stage. And now & then a fly in the buttermilk, a spook to sit by the door. A flurry of Pulitzers to disguise Def imperialism still in charge, even maintaining white supremacy, but got a "nigger" rapping. I check it out, its okay. "Niggers" deserved slavery & national oppression.

For every Public Enemy, X Clan, Souljah, Ice Cube, the corporations manufacture sets of poison rappers, The Fresh Princes, Two Live Crews, Naughty By Nature, Young Black Teenagers, Vanilla Ice to cover the real with the cultural distortions. PE and other progressive rappers want to sing about liberation, about self determination, while the children of 666 sing about OPP or Ho's & nigga street scams.

Instead of Jesse Jackson leading an independent Rainbow People's Party to Challenge the two parties of Imperialism, we get a Pierrot (a masked clown who will do anything for money!) As the art & social practice reflects the life & ideology of society in its diverse aspects, our lives must be self projected as examples of Self determination.

(1991, 2007)

Aesthetics of Afro American Theater

Aesthetics relates to the concept of Beauty. Which I connect with Passion in Form & Feeling. The trail of Emotion as sense and act.

Raymond Williams in *Poetry & Marxism* calls Theater the most ambitious of the arts because it tries to represent, literally, real life. He says also that during periods of revolutionary social activity is when new and innovative drama develops.

He cites Shakespeare, the bourgeois revolutionary whose chronicle of the dying class the feudal kings and queens he chronicles so well. *Macbeth, Richard III*, Hamlet's mother and uncle. &c., &c. Shakespeare also covers the major themes that will remain within society as long as capitalism remains—*Hamlet*, the liberal; *Othello*, racism; *The Merchant of Venice*, Anti-Semitism; *Taming of the Shrew*, Women's Oppression and Male Chauvinism; *Coriolanus*, relationship between people and leaders; *Julius Caesar*, democracy and idealism.

Even the Bourgeoisie seldom does Shakespeare straight up shorn of the jingling Elizabethan verse that too often puts us to sleep and covers the real meanings of the plays. Now even though they celebrate him they don't want you to know what he's talking about either.

If we wrote plays about the U.S. rulers. Richard the Nix, Ronnie the Rage, George The Reefer, we would not be called classical. The plays would not be done; just like they are not done now. (I've never had a play on Broadway. No play even in a major off-Broadway house in ten years.)

Feeling—emotion, the trail of form and feeling. What is most important. The content. So the content of our lives, whose form is also a part of the content is what is most important. What was produced and has been produced by feeling.

Slavery & White Supremacy have not only oppressed us (50,000,000 in the middle passage—how's that for a holocaust?—and we hadn't got here yet. They have also oppressed our culture (the entire entity of our lives and history).

William Wells Brown's "1st Afro American play" *The Escape* was about, you guessed it, escape from slavery. The abolitionists did it, read it. But there should not be too much question as to why Brown couldn't get it done on the great white way. It was has not changed very much in the 127 years since we got loose (Jan 1, 1863).

Our creations carry and speak from our lives. If we are sincere, and deliver the depth of our feelings, then obviously our enemies cannot abide what we say. Our observations are accusations. Our aesthetic, what is beautiful, must carry, in essence, our will to freedom, our will to self determination, self respect and self-defense.

Our songs and dances, our paintings and books, our entire cultural projections at base, in essence, speak constantly to the desire for freedom. Even our drums had to be banned because they spoke very functionally of freedom! (demonstrate).

So the aesthetic, our concept of beauty, must revolve around the concept of freedom and at the same time, dialectically, against the concept of slavery. Jazz, Monk said, is about Freedom, to say more is to complicate it. Free Jazz, Freedom Suite, BeBop, Improvisation, even the blind old funkateers in the recent slave south, always pushing freedom, "...the sun gonna shine on my back door one day. I may be wrong, but I wont be wrong always."

In the slave society, naturally, naturally our creations are always measured, by the slave master and their sycophants by the intentions and desires, the interests and Devil Reefer Bush whacks, of the slave master. As Douglass said, when the slave master stopped him from learning to read. What they hate we love, what we love they hate.

Like Devil Reefer Bush designating January 15 the birthday of our prince of peace, MLK, as the day of death and greedy murder in the middle east. DECLARING WAR ON DR. KING'S BIRTHDAY

IS A WAR CRIME! AN INSULT TO THE AFRICAN AMERICAN PEOPLE AND THE PEACE LOVING PEOPLES OF THE WORLD!

We are obstructed by a national oppression which includes, as WEB pointed out, a *Double Consciousness*, where even our so called intellectuals and artists too often see the world through the eyes of people that hate them. But if we look historically at our artists, people of the theater, say Brown, DuBois, Hughes, Childress, Hansberry, Baldwin, Ward, Peterson, Branch, we will see that the overriding emotional projection of the work, the aesthetic, the form and feeling of passion, ultimate concern from the work, is about freedom. Do Hughes' *Mulatto*, or *The Sun Do Move* (*Don't You want To Be Free?*) or *Raisin* or *Blues for Mr. Charlie*, or *Big White Fog*, check the concerns, the attention to both history and day to day life, and the bottom line of feeling, emotional registration about those lives?

Our theater, like our art, must strive to be emotionally powerful and politically revolutionary. To paraphrase Mao. We must be writing to change ourselves and the world, most particularly to free the people in the world, as part of the whole evolutionary process of human development.

The entire educational system in the slave society (and this is still part of it) teaches submission to slavery. That any action or idea opposed to slavery is terrible and backward. Certainly anything created carrying such ideas could not be art or scholarship.

The reason for the opposition to multicultural curricula is that our inclusion and most of the peoples of the world say, the native Americans — what does their art say, does it paint pretty pictures of the "white eyes" who committed genocide on them and banished them to reservations (plantations, bantustans, concentration camps). Panamanian and Grenadan art. Would they paint pretty pictures of white supremacy and imperialism?

In the Black Arts movement we said we wanted our art to do three things. (1) Be identifiably African American. (2) Be mass oriented; to come out the libraries and seminars and boogaloo out there with Malcolm and Dr. King, The Panthers, Rob Wms, Fannie Lou and The Deacons. (3) To Be revolutionary, to be a part of the world force of change.

We had dug that you did not have to be backward to be an artist. That we could create works that were artistically powerful and politically revolutionary. That is what we meant by Black Art! That was our aesthetic.

Where we made our mistake, being nationalists, was in not seeing clearly the class nature of society and oppression. We had known, of course, about niggero toms, but we were unprepared for the new wave of "backwardness neo colonialism" we would bring in. And that now we would see a black middleclass arise who were no longer even physically connected (living in the same neighborhood with other blacks) for whom black was an abstraction. Like the sinister creeps Stanford University keeps manufacturing and the other negro factories telling us we are our own worst enemies. Like Thomas Sowell, Shelby Steele, plus Walter Williams, Ann Wortham (the physically sick female slug who said on the Bill Moyers' show — "the founding fathers told us what to do") and the Stanley Crouches. Playtoy Benyesmens and Frankenstein monsters like this negro Michael Williams in the education department, who finishes Bush's one-two punch of not only vetoing the civil rights bill but now even taking away minority scholarships yet sending us in great numbers to Saudi Arabia to die in the sand!

There is even a small coterie of negroes, part of the retrograde trend that emerged after the revolutionary up surge of the '60s — from the first negro Pulitzer winner, (in drama), telling us black power (weeping in drag) was a drag. Now there has been developed a full fledged group of negro playwrongs and movie dismakers whose bottom line is not only to attack the revolutionary '60s, as if all black people were rebelling about is a handshake, a haircut, some African clothes and the right to put down white people.

These people tell us the '60s were ridiculous, especially any militance. They tell us money is what it be. That history and the real lives of the African American people don't matter. And they are made instant neon numbers in our consciousness. They tell us our women got to have it. That our schools are for copulation and rock and roll. That our struggle is to put photos in pizza parlors and that our leaders are bugged out, and that Yusef Hawkins and Phillip Patells and Eleanor Bumpers and Howard Beach victims were killed because they played their radios too loud.

They are *In Living Color*, or live at *The Negro Museum* or they think our children are *Zoomen* and urge us to have enough balls to kill them, they tells us we should become good soldiers in the mans' army and turn in the militants, because they're the reason we got troubles, besides if we bust them we can become negro officers.

But we can see from the youth, the Public Enemies, and KRS Ones and X-Clans, among rappers, and many more, and the USO's and Nia Forces, high school and college militant student groups that more and more of us are finding out, "What time it is." We used to say, "It's Nation Time!" in the '60s, but now it's InterNation Time, time for the world's people to self consciously tune in to their fundamental and instinctive aesthetic, freedom and creativity! Which is to say time to remobilize and reorganize against imperialism which is the most creative act there is.
(1/1992)

Eye to the Ground

"Poetry Institutions" is an expansive phrase. To say it is at once to conjure what exists that must be destroyed and at the same time to "Europe-DooDoo" the folk. Like we used to say, "Fool 'em, Devil!"

The main so-called poetry institutions are part of the devil' bi'ness, the superstructure of imperialism to be sure, what they raise to raise themselves in the material ritual of the continuance of evil.

Except we have to keep the eye to the ground, to the real basis of what poetry is in the first play. That is, motion E, continuance of what everything is born from and returns to. It's expressing of living.

The institutions that could be called Poetry Institutions, 1991 USA are like the priests of the inquisition. As this is the animal world right on, still on the pre-human tip behind not yet solving the problems of food, clothing and shelter. It was our tail that let us swing, our tale, &c. Yet we have stopped at the worship of minerals, where primates self hypnotized create a world, whose God is yellow and shiny, a mineral. Where they literally live in paradise but reduce it to hell and try to destroy it everyday. Where they have the brain-to-mind of the totality of all consciousness. but keep most of it closed. like rooms in old mansions its too expensive to heat.

Poetry Institutions would, in any circumstance, be part of a super structure. The complex of philosophy and the structures erected to continue to express that philosophy reflecting the economic base they have been built on. In an imperialist and white supremacist society like the U.S. with a monopoly capitalist economic base, the mainstream of formal art education, culture and consciousness, artifacts and structures reflect that economic base.

So that both the "official" poetry and its formal structures of forwarding in the U.S,, in the main. express the solipsistic, "unnatural," individualistic, greedy, superficial, reactionary, racist character of the society itself.

American "official," e.g. "prize winning" poetry is death on wheels. The big wheels that run the U.S. cultural establishment, and the bigger wheels that turn the whole political economic structure.

What is pushed in the schools is mainly Bourg eois, Eurocentric and dead. The nature of American higher education is still 18th century colonial, as if the Tories had won the American Revolutionary War and continue to rule the Yankees from New England (e.g. Harvard. Yale, the Ivies, &c).

English literature, and of course, English poetry are still foisted upon those thinking they are being educated. When neither of those hardies (with certain pointed qualifications) has existed for 100 years. (Oh, please, I don't mean Yeats, O'Casey, Beckett, Wilde, Joyce, Shaw (My God!), &c., you know, of course, they're the I.R.A. chaps not Thomas (naw, he Welsh) What about ... Eliot, Pound, no, for christ sakes, they were American hicks. That's why they never went back to the states like Williams, Hughes, &c because they were embarrassed by cracker hickishness, when it turns out they were the biggest hicks. Eliot from St. Louis, you know that Missouri twang? The "Show Me" state. Show you what? We don't have time to show you every thing! Pound was from goddam Idaho. He and potatoes and Joe Hill heaviest things outta there. Please! The U.S. university is the largest bastion of 18th century. European colonialism in the U.S. The double consciousness that DuBois analyzed in the black American petty bourgeoisie and as one aspect of the cross class" slave mentality" wherever it was found, i.e., looking at yourself through the eyes of people that hate you, has a somewhat analogous parallel to the American people generally. Taken from the perspective of their so called higher education, American bourgeois, formalist, "official" intellectuals have been taught that nothing American (or even alive!) can be classical.

The language, texts, cultural referencing of The American University and the American mainstream artist still are shaped and limited menacingly by the dead, the distant, the foreign, the bourgeois, the racist.

What is not understood by too many of us is that one of the reasons that "American speech" and "American poetry" were of such import in the '20s (e.g., Harlem Renaissance and American Modernism)in the most advanced aspect of U.S. culture was that they were sharp thrusts against the explicit European bourgeois colonial model that still serves as the paradigm for so called "H i g h Art." A term that in itself spells out the class perspective it seeks to describe.

Important works of Langston Hughes "The Negro Artist and Racial Mountain" and Williams on the "American Measure" (or the "variable foot") during the period were guides laying out a term of struggle against colonialism and slavery, implicitly and explicitly of the language arts and of the culture in general. The political relationship (the enabler of the economic base) is duplicated by all the others.

This is the importance of the Cultural Revolution that Mao projected from what Lenin said had to be done post October Revolution to see that the influence of the still existent bourgeois superstructure did not undo the political victory, even that gained by armed struggle.

Mao's call for Cultural Revolution in China, and as a tenet of continuing and historical Marxist-Leninist ideological development should be seen, certainly in the light of the tragedies going down at this very moment in the USSR and to a lesser extent the PRC. Both. to a great extent from the failure to mount or to continue the work of Cultural Revolution. (That is, Continuing the political struggle in the sphere of the superstructure.)

What this carries for us is that the courageous work of many young people in the '60s in the U.S. anti imperialist struggle includes the cultural work. Certainly the arts, and particularly poetry, and music, were at the center of the black liberation movement. In fact most of the U.S. oppressed nationalities developed arts weapons as part of their anti imperialist anti racist arsenal. There was certainly even a more general "Anti Academic" stance taken by some of the more "populist" "white" literary schools, (Beats, New York School, Black Mountain, San Francisco, &c.) which paralleled to some extent the anti-imperialist tenor of the period.

When we speak of "the state of poetry," we must understand that what the superstructure of this society pushes, on all levels, is the *poetry of the state*! The valorization of the imperialist white supremacist state.

So that it is critical for the whole *objective* united front, (the actual disposition of class forces who are tied to each other even independent of their will) so to speak, of cultural workers, artists, intellectuals, &c must be to create poetry institutions that represent and reflect the anti imperialist nature of the majority of the American people.

The counter attack of the New Criticism, for instance, under the guise of "deconstruction" (a good term if we understand what, say, Reconstruction proposed to be after the U.S. Civil War, and how it was "deconstructed" by the Counterrevolutionary old slavery forces (KKK, &c.) connected with the rising post competitive capitalist ie imperialist forces (Wall St., &c). So the destruction of the U.S. Reconstruction saw slavery turn into fascism (the U.S. slave plantations are the paradigm for the 20th century concentration camps).

The reactionary period we live in today a reflection of the *downward* aspect of the historical cycle of the "Sisyphus Syndrome" the Black Liberation Movement and indeed the entire struggle for American Peoples' Democracy and Communism. The torturous upward and downward — forward and backward development, e.g! Socialism abandoned in USSR, Social Fascism clearly dominating in China, just today the Albanian communists have been toppled, Nicaragua, Grenada! Bush's Desert Storm Troopers consolidating neo colonialism in the middle east and continuing colonial domination by Israeli imperialism and South African apartheid, the seemingly "low comic" maniacal ism of the Ray Gun replaced by the middle management no nonsense maniacalism of the Bush man. All as the extreme opposites of the '50s, '60s, early '70s world political trend that we summed up "Revolution is The main Trend In The World Today!"

So the counterattack of the formalists. the academics, of the '90s who carry the same backwardness. class domination and racism as the "Southern Agrarians" of the '40s. Tate! Ransome, et. al. who want to reestablish the primacy of the schoolmen "the critic" over the artist. Where the death worshipping academies define and refine art out of existence as part of the are not.

And part of that process is to always deny, dismiss, disqualify & hide (like Columbus, what they "discover" they cover with Dis, the real lives and expression of the people as disqualified)!

All these are carried in by the rush of political backwardness and counterrevolution that are sweeping the world today! Even though significant resistance internationally, still exists.

In fact, part of the whole destructive assault of political reaction carries with it as a focus and method of domination, the substitution of history by propaganda. Whole periods are eliminated or disguised, problematic persons routinely eliminated from history, contradictory philosophies caricatured and distorted, the ancient slave philosophy continuously revalorized.

So that the "statement" of poetry, as an expression of the context of its appearance, must, to be actual poetry, and not advertisement for irrelevance or the status quo of world torture, must be an expression of what exists and at the same time a "defining" of it by "showing" it, not only as image but as the body of what life? The "feelings" of the oppressors have long ago become technology and rules. The suppression and contradiction to reality is on basic form of greed sanctioned act which they pretend philosophy. The logos of feeding.

Poetry, as the expression of feeling, emotion, as a representation of what exists, is the Art (which form, is outlined, or outlines, the Ain't) and carries by that function a "Grandness" that is heavy as a real branch on a real tree. A real cry from a real person. That is, it connects, as an exclamation, as the cries of the worshippers, possessed, by what creates as an epiphanic consciousness of the created. Jazz replicates the self consciousness of creating as a body, newly born as the action "which is naming."

Poetry is the "Yeh," the confirmation. The call. A bridge between what is eternal. Is deathless, and the particular. Each soul before and beyond its "place," but as part everywhere.

Ja Is! Jazz! Coming like the "word" the "Big Bang" of which prayer is one formal reflection and ritual of memory. The seasons the year, day and night, time, the motion and continuous natural opposition and unity dialectic between quantity and quality, the pulse, the heartbeat, rhythm, the breath. So the worshippers leap in the air saying Yes, Yes, like the breath of a body as the body of something even finer. I feel the heat of the sun, yet I myself am a property of the sun.

To become everything's creator, Nothing, pregnant with for instance. the source of creation, the circle of origin and continuity. Coming in and Going out.

Just as the word created this world so the word will create and is another world. The present bulges with history and moves forward as will to will. The poet is the bridge of was is will, poetry the utterance of that peeped motion.

The reactionaries value form over content, because no one must know what is going on. Formalism hides content under the abstraction of motionlessness, "tradition" class denial, academic shallowness. Life is outlined and given form by what it is not. What surrounds it as the contradiction that gives dimension.

Poetry appears as the Griots proposed, as history culture recreated as art, as verb and noun. To inform—the town crier. That is what Griot means. to cry out, give the world the gift of self consciousness. To make soul aware of itself as a power of transcendence and revelation. The U Turn of light and seeing, of the mind's function, confirming itself by seeing itself see itself.

On the real streets of this world, poetry like all the things we need to live, must be created by understanding and consistent informed practice. The flash of perception confirmed as rationale (a name) and then used (practiced). From the mass perception, rationale and use comes the development of science and more advanced feeling. Our poetry institutions must begin exactly where we are, like our poetry. They must be formed by poets and those who need poetry, but a poetry of advancing humanity, of developing post imperialist society.

From where we are, the storefronts (just like those other congregations), the basements, public schools. playgrounds, bars & restaurants, hey. Even. What the hell. Try libraries and the other cultural institutions nominally controlled by the dead and the devilish. The life of our desire is its health and its commonality.

The Rappers have demonstrated much further than our own earlier defense how black poetry and black music are mated, as well as the lie that "politics" is separate from art!

The point is to take poetry away from the devil by being the mouth of good. Or the place of good. This is the desired state and institution of the mass poetry, that which makes good appear as the continuum of our feeling, deeply and ubiquitously. So that we are the doing as we are the being.

We need the poets focused on our real lives, and by the poetic act itself help transform those lives. The poetry and those institutions we create to foster this continuous, evolution to revolution, are whatever we have that can also be transformed, by a more intimate act ... a mimeograph sheet, a poetry reading in a playground, classes for youth, artists-in-residence in public schools because art is the teacher. Yet there are formalists who try to teach grammar or "English" without having the students read.

But even those more intimate or "smaller" acts must be linked as networks. An anti-imperialist poetry network for publications, readings, institutional development is what we need. This kind of network will give the mass prizes create the nitty gritty distribution being, tours. writers conferences. As long as the Yale Series of Younger Poets, The Pulitzer, Hearst Monster Publishing, Hollywood, Broadway and phony off Broadway twist our heads and arms through our continued loyalty to them, even measuring our lives by them, then Freedom is simply the name of another religion.
(1992)

Multinational, Multicultural America vs. White Supremacy

American culture, first of all, is Hemispheric. When we say America, we are really saying Pan America. Most of the people of Pan America are brown and speak a Latino Spanish. Moreover, the official "Western" culture — the rightist wags and academics speak of — is Europe. But Europe is not the West. I have a poem that says, "Leave England / headed West / you arrive in Newark."

The Europe "cover" to Pan American or even North American culture is merely the continuation of European colonialism and slavery. In fact, from its origins the term — the "Western World" — meant Europe in relationship to Asia and Africa. Pre-Columbus' "discovery" of El Mundo Nuevo. the New World. And that discovery. we know from experience☐certainly combines Dis and Cover. The Rappers let us know what "dissing" someone means. to disrespect them. The biggest "Dis" is that they can even make you Dis/appear.

Cover is a record company term meaning that. for instance. when Big Mama Thornton put out a record, or Big Joe Turner (or Duke Ellington for that matter). The white supremacist oriented record industry immediately put out a "cover" or a version of the song by a white performer. In the first two cases. Elvis Presley and Pat Boone. Just as Vanilla Ice or Young Black Teenagers (a white rap group) are beginning to do to Rap.

It is very important to these corporate/government powers that control American society always to keep the music lovers

segregated. Like Confucius said. "If the people hear the wrong —
music the Empire will fall." And for the broad multinational masses
of the American nation to take up the sentiments the content of Afro
American music, in this case, is to disrupt the racist national
oppression that is the fundamental super-structural philosophy of
the American social system reflecting its imperialist economic base.

When we say that American education must be as
multinational and multicultural as the reality of American society.
We are just saying that what is taught in the schools should be the
whole culture of the American people.   Americans are still
remarkably unconscious about the totality, the whole dimension, of
their own culture. But tha t is because the powers that is are
determined to maintain white supremacy, as the philosophical
justification for the exploitation and oppression of most of the
world's peoples. Certainly, in relationship to all the variety of people
inside the U.S., the Eurocentric construct of so-called official
"Western Culture" America is a racist fraud. A fraud that has held
the entire culture of the world. Certainly of the Pan American world
as hostage.

The assertion that the actually very brief period of European
hegemony In the world means that "European" culture (a term that
could be argued with even in the 19th century since neither
Germany nor Italy exist, as states, prior to this) is eternal and the
supreme measure and description of civilization is, of course, Nazi
diktat, there is no reality to it. Except as a reflection of the rise of
European hegemony in the world, along with the rise of capitalism,
the slave trade, colonialism and modern imperialism.

The Greek Attic, like any culture, can not be isolated from
the whole context of its emergence and development. It is the result
of what came before it, just as any other culture. But even more
repressive is that since the majority of the peoples in the world are
not European, then this kind of thinking is just neo-Goebbels/ism,
very fitting for our time which has all the earmarks of another
Weimar Republic, the last democratic government and period in
Germany before Hitler and fascism took power.

The very move to the right in the U.S., for instance,
particularly with the fall of the revisionist USSR, has seen the rise of
extreme nationalism, not only in the U.S. but around the world. The
attempt to maintain a mainly Eurocentric and blatantly racist
curriculum in public schools in the U.S. is an attempt to maintain

old slavery while calling for new slavery!

Part of the stunning development of the retrograde trend in the U.S. of backward negro academics, artists, politicians as part of the whole reactionary period emerging in the '80s shows how so-called integration into the racist academic and social curricula of these colleges has helped shape a whole new generation of Buppie Toms, who have profited by black struggle but who have been taught to disconnect themselves from the black majority, ideologically as well as socially.

One reason for the alienation of Black and Latino students from the schools is the curricula which they begin to understand by the 3rd grade has very little to do with their lives or history. The incorrectness of the teaching methodology comes from this as well, since these distortions and lies must be taught by *rote*, committed to memory rather than learned!

And even though, the rubric of the Blooms, Schlesingers, speaks of Western culture, and makes obeisance: to the ancient Greeks and Romans, in their modern cultural assessment, these same white supremacists dismiss both these modern peoples as "degenerate." (More Goebbels!)

In fact, in the modern world, "Western Culture" means mainly England, France and Germany. Spain and Italy are always neglected, and the rest of the world plunges into silent oblivion.

When you speak to upholders of the status quo of undemocratic education and the culture of inequity, they will tell you that multicultural curricula are impossible because it's "technically impossible" to include all people's cultures in the curricula, suggesting that only the distorted paper culture of national chauvinism is "normal" (a northern sickness).

It is simply that we want the real lives of the people of our world, the whole world. American culture is the creation, for instance of all Americans. It is the combining of all the nationalities and cultures here that is the actual national character of American culture. And no one is belittling the accomplishment of European Humanism. Actually an authentically multinational and multicultural curriculum would revalidate the authentic masterpieces of all cultures, highlight their fundamental unity and help diminish their conflicts.

The undeveloped material life of most Americans is justified by both their absence from U.S. school curricula or distortion of their lives in them. The racial chauvinism of the so called Literary Canon justifies the military cannon that enforced colonialism throughout the 3rd World yesterday or the invasion of Panama, Grenada, the destruction of Iraq today. The academic or artistic chauvinism explains the economic and social exploitation.

But the very underdevelopment of the Northern Colossus itself, in real terms, with millions of Americans living under the poverty line, including the majority of the Afro American nation's children, is tragic for Black people but it also is an economic deprivation, a lack of development of the larger U.S. itself. Since the lack of education and livelihood of the Black masses subtracts from the whole of the U.S. livelihood and economic development. Even though the old slavemaster continuum that Bush and U.S. imperialism favors generally has already been proven economically outmoded. The Black and minority aspects of the U.S. market detracts from the total U.S. prosperity, since Black Americans constitute an important part of even U.S. monopoly capitalist market, whose potential cannot be tapped because of the low level of productive forces, including marginal education and high unemployment rates.

In the case of the almost neo-colonial domination of English culture in the U.S. its as if the Tories at least won the cultural revolution, when you have huge English departments (even though "George Washington Won The War") and American studies is tiny where it exists and Black Studies &c are always under fire and in danger of being removed. And it is just this Eurocentric, white supremacist cover of the real American culture that issues like multicultural education seeks to eliminate. The Jeffries CCNY issue was not so much about what Jeffries said (since the influence of the Jewish bourgeoisie in Hollywood has been well documented already by Jews and the influence of organized crime, including the Mafia, has been equally publicly discussed. And no one of the slightest analytical capacity can doubt the caricature of Black lives in U.S. flicks. But then! – to paraphrase a writer in Cineaste, look at Hollywood's distortion of Jews and Italians anyway). Jeffries has been talking black cultural nationalism for years and nothing happened. It's just now. Since he was a leading member of the committee that put together New York's so-called Curriculum of Inclusion, by attacking him dirt could be thrown that would cover that proposed new curriculum with much dis.

135

Remember change of curriculum would lessen the domination and influence of many vested interests within the schools and even result in the expansion of certain curriculum and teaching jobs within the education system. The development of a really democratic educational curricula and "formal" U.S. culture would reflect a movement to create a more democratic U.S. and a more equitable relationship to the rest of the world.
(1992)

Revolutionary Art

Revolutionary poetry is poetry expressing — first as content and then most effectively as form — the ideology, stance and practice of revolution. Direct and complete social (and as political and economic and cultural change). That is to change society by changing human relations within the society and by so doing change the humans ourselves.

One factor of imperialism is that it has the capacity to absorb, coopt, distort or completely destroy almost anything. Except ultimate resistance to it, because like change, struggle is a constant.

But definition is sterile or critical. One class's Revolution is another class's Yeltsin i.e., abject and craven counter revolution.

Those artists who say their art has nothing to do with politics or society are simply retarded or winking at their own seduction as state and corporate prostitutes.

Art expresses the ideological essence and fundamental contradictions of society, of our human social relations. The vaunted "craft" by which this kept sector daunts the naive and the philosophically insecure is the same cry of the rulers who excuse the savage bloodiness of imperialism by claiming the formalism of technology is civilization.

Like those who praise the skill with which Jack The Ripper disemboweled his victims. "This man is a trained surgeon!"

The purpose of what Marx called The New Humanism is simply the transformation of society so that the majority of people wield the power to shape our lives according to the material and spiritual needs of the people. That the rulers of the world be the great mass of humanity themselves! Matter transformed by consciousness!

But the transformative power of Art (as opposed to Ain't) Life vs. Death, Creativity vs. Destruction is the essence of the dialectic which confronts us and informs our work. So that Mao asked first of the would be revolutionary artist, For Whom i.e., for whom do you write? Second, in the *Yenan Forum* Mao asked, "What do you celebrate and what do you attack?" From this we can tell whose side you're on, The oppressed or the oppressors.

In the same way what you think is good and what you think is beautiful, what you think is ugly also helps identify whether the work is revolutionary or counter.

The bourgeoisie tries to stifle the explosive transformative nature of art, it's magical properties, except as a correlative to religion or illusion or as "nifty" advertising.

Art is the human expression of endless birth and rebirth, the "big bang" of universal becoming for the poet (and the world), the hot eruption of world jism from which the living creature, e.g., egg & ego, the being produced manifest of ecstatic fire, space into speech. Vision as the science of motion, as the interior life of what will always exist—.

Revolutionary art insists on the whole world as its measure and the equality of being. It demands and forces into human consciousness the outline of the whole self of the world. Connects is & be, proves their materiality.

Revolution is the eternity of the world. The endless breath the endless heartbeat. To deny it is to lie and truth is the final reality.

For the poets, it is critical to reject and step away from the Death sellers and suave priests of savagery. Poetry lives as an expression of life. It is as strong as its life force, what it re-presents in and to and from the world.

We are taught to deny the power and force of art, except as elitist license. We do not believe that our poetry can function as a force of nature to transform and cleanse and destroy and resurrect. We settle for being "craftspersons," fashioning cunning little artifacts devils' use to drink blood. We are the good manners of vampires.

I am a communist, so I believe that the nuclear force of the poem must be used to unite revolutionaries and win the advanced

138

to communism. That it must be used as a weapon against the rule and domination of Heathens. To be cynical is not revolutionary. If you claim revolution, you must also claim science, as well as truth and beauty.

To be a revolutionary is to grasp the key link of our expression as a form of class struggle. A people's weapon to force the true Self Consciousness that DuBois wrote of and the human self realization, Marx & Lenin spoke of in their philosophical notebooks. And that the class struggle, the struggle for scientific truth and the struggle for production (even against so called writers' block) are revolutionary struggles and our poetry is an expression of our relationship to these, objectively, independent of our will.

In these times of rising fascism, and class betrayal, where one time and soi-disant (so-called or self-proclaimed) revolutionaries snore instead of speak and worship gibberish and obscure song, what revolutionary artists must do is enlist themselves and organize themselves in cultural revolution!

It is not possible to deny the incredible filth of U.S. "popular" read Commercial culture as pornograped by film, drama, music, painting, &c. We cry our defiance of the devil endlessly, yet wait impatiently to be discovered or rewarded by our declared enemies.

Where are the Camcorder, under $200 movies, the revolutionary awards that celebrate the Margaret Walkers, and Sembene Ousmanes or Ernesto Cardenals or Herbert Apthekers? We settle for cynical comments on the Nobel and Pulitzer, on the National Laureates and "genius awards," but create no DuBois or Brecht awards to raise revolutionary themes and lives!

When will we be able to call the poets and musicians and painters and dancers out of their studios and class rooms or "to hell with it" stylish hovels and lofts, to bring their art, their energy, their vision, into the streets and communities to disrupt the old society and point toward and help create the new?

Even those of us who claim revolutionary stances spend most of our time talking about our enemies. When even when we criticize them, we expend our energy and force on them, rather than on the creation of the new, the transformative, rather than with the creation of what does not yet exist, which we must swear to bring into being, if we are truly revolutionary.

One Hundred poets reading at population centers across this city on revolutionary themes in weekly or monthly consistent blasts could force a new consciousness, however modest, into being. But this idea is confused as bohemianism or "Politics" and remains as non-existent as the national revolutionary political circles we need to survive this present fascist onslaught. The commitment to revolution, to the complete overthrow of savage oppression and the spectrum of ignorant or disingenuous evil reaction is also a commitment to *Work* and *Study*. It is a commitment to *Organization* and *Mass Expression*.

Where are our revolutionary journals and newspapers and magazines? Where are our revolutionary movie houses and galleries and theaters? Instead we hear snoring or the fashionable cynicism of the "loyal opposition?" Loud with frustration till the big buck comes or the recognition by monsters as officials Ho's?

It is the Self-Determination, Self-Respect and Defense of life and it's revolutionary movement the poets must concern themselves with as intimately as their own personal lives.

It is a new world we want to create not an endowed chair in the concentration camp! It is form as well as content, science and vision. Art must be our magic weapon to create and recreate the world and ourselves as part of it!
(5/1994)

Language & Evolution

The word is a sign
   But also a sound
     if it is only a sign
      it is incomplete.
       Even on the flat silent
        page, it makes a sound
         in yr head, in itself
          to be got, as a living
            being. There is no word
            that is merely a sign.
            it is an enclosed sound
            Which uncovers as it is
            read (silent or loud).
            A word is also a content.
            A carrier of meaning.
            If it has no meaning
           as direct or implicit
        or connected or imagined
        it is not a word. Even a
         sign means. "Meaninglessness"
          means that or it wdn't
            be that. And outside of Whatever
            convention or "ready made" use
            it remains sound and sight.
             & being (verb & noun & adjective, &c.)

The dissociative, deconstructive,
"Wholly literary" i.e., "for its (own)
sake" distortion of art,
is a sham, a simple screen
& fraud extended by the
rulers of the world
into the very "individual"
psychological crevices
of humanity, to guarantee
their hegemony is
  unchallenged. Since
nothing is related to life
  (as material, social,
actual or real) except
the all embracing "results"
of their domination & power.
Religion is the dominant
essence of human interpretation
& "use" of life, as thought
theory or useful practice.
Except to submit & work
for their power & the domination
of ignorance. Good is controversial
God is universal.
The Churches are the tower of
Babel. The search for the
beautiful mysticism of
what does not exist.
Tragedy is high art to
legitimatize the reality of social
pain under universal oppression.
Co/ Me/ day, the ancient collective social relationship of
universal family.
(matter & motion, feeling and geography)
So religion is about the never, art cannot speak about the world,
everything is unresolved except your work day, Love is sex,
money is the reward
for being chosen by the mysterious, Goodness is replaced (the
living
verb of practice)

w/ a non-existent noun of submission, viz "God."
God was created to explain slavery. The Devil, likewise is a screen,
an "idol" to cover the actual existence and perpetrators of evil.
Humanity is stalled half animal like the sphinx because it cannot
understand itself as the world (nature).
Consciousness, Science and Conscience are the real trinity of post
animal development, Communism is necessary before humanity
actually appears. Since it is the basis for rational social
relationship which produces a human society.
The earth is ruled by half or pre-human predators. They are
predators and we are their prey. Pre date (pre human, pre
Knowledge (data) pre community).
"Rugged individualism" is the description of a jungle animal.
The rulers despise & distort & remove history, which represses
consciousness & social development. Because history's
comprehension is the
formulation of science, real knowledge.
The earth is Hell, a pre-human violent jungle ruled by predatory
were wolves, vampires (the "myths" are not myths) because it is
ruled by the King of the Beasts.
The 10 Commandments were a prescription for developing
Human
Society, scientifically. But the Pharaohs who created themselves as
"God" were already degenerated from early communal "Eden."
Even Social Collectivism.
And so spawned mad "European" Bull Shit.

Slavery, which begins with the overthrow (of mothers' rights) &
enslaving of women — the 1st class struggle — and the worship of
Things, Idols, idleness (idolatry, adultery) & the emergence
of money, the expressed and
ruling power of waste. Feces instead of fecit, to make, which
becomes fake it.
Prayer is Prey. Prophet is profit. Money, the exploiter of used
labor. Do Do instead of Do. Death is Powerful (encouraged,
spread, worshipped,
romanticized).
Death rules life. But death is like God & the devil, a lie. Not Matter
in Motion.

(Except as the power & force of ideas.) & Life "In & Out." Memory is the history inside the Black Hole. The Father is the visible clitoris. Now a dick tung, speech. The Poem. Which degenerates into The Male (Armor not amor) Ruler. (Who measures.)
The Heathens seize the church as a lie and religion as business. Judeo-Christian is the name of the cleaned up Barbarians whose rule is slavery since they are now Aryans (having shaved) and once untermensch now ubermensch.

The tower (to where, destination) of Babel.
The Vow wells disappear, headed north. The ancients indeed thought it Babble. We know its Ma Bell or Pa Bell. The tower is national slavery, national
and gender oppression, racism, imperialism, imperial
Rome. Romulus and Remus are Gog & Magog. Now in the U.S. (e.g., Supreme Ct. Scalia and Tom Ass).
Learning is suppressed. Beauty is suppressed. Wisdom despised. A collective Human Family is subversive. (To say "Fight Communism!" is like saying Fight for Animalism & the hegemony of slavery, torture, ignorance, disease). So that fat animals can "luxuriate" ignorant as lizards in their modern cave societies and pass expensive stools. Money doo doo from money the God of gold feces.
Fascism itself, the distortion of the farmers sheaves of wheat into "doo joby" (my family called it) the jewelry of feces (Shit. Love becomes Fuck, hit in the Anglo Saxon) Imperialism, capitalism, the herd animal traits. Commerce is the
aborting of the evolutionary process. So that low thought, low art, low religion, low beastial society is maintained by violence & fraud. (Animals that lie and trick to kill and steal.)

Only commerce is valuable, not art or philosophy. Everything sd to be those things to fill up the intestines, the bowels, the Colon rectum Wreck Them Pow! (Well)

The evolution of true humanity & human society is possible only with the conscious construction of the universal family, where all are "equal" (have equal access to resources and development).

Humanity cannot exist except as a body. A whole. This is what

144

Holy means. To make of the earth, the world,
one body conscious of its allness.
Growing into the sky as the expression of its total integration with
nature. So called individualism is the dysfunctionality of
disconnected (or diseased) organs. As if eyes, mouth, heart,
functioned separately and contradictorily, creating a frenzied
predator turning in circles, with certain parts grossly enlarged
through cannibalism.

Wisdom, Love, Truth, Joy, Ecstasy, Happiness, "Life w/o End" are
the real question and answer. The "Divine" To WHERE. The
Electric Search, the actual relevance of meditative prayers of
knowing — so that humanity merges, whole, from the
paradigmatic Sphinx, half human, (woman reproductive) the
womb, the Who, half animal and from the higher development
finally understands, connects, utilizes, consolidates (like
recreating fire) these qualities. And ultimately becomes them, and
thus the assumption of "life without end" as conscious being
(matter motion energy consciousness). We
learn to love and can even, further, become love.
(7/1994)

Writers, Critics & Social Consciousness
(National Black Arts Festival 8/94 Atlanta)

Writing, like all art, wrote Mao Tse Tung in the *Yenan Forum*, is an ideological reflection of real life. That is, writers express their lives and the life of the world through the ideological prism of class, nationality (i.e., what some call "race"), gender, sexual orientation, plus time, place and condition. But ultimately, class stand or point of view is principal, no matter where we might be coming from originally.

So that the writer's expression is "personal," to the degree it is specific, but at the same time the work's particularity also renders it a common paradigm, what they call "universal." But it is important to reemphasize that the universal consists of all the particulars and there is no universal without the particular.

We say class is primary because though class itself can be changed (rags to riches stories abound, though actually infrequent, just as riches to rags stories) no matter what class we are born into. The ultimate jammy is / as my wife Amina is always pointing out, "Who's side are you on?" The oppressed or the oppressor.

Here in the United States the Afro American people are an oppressed nation with the right therefore of Self Determination. As DuBois pointed out, the U.S. is not and has never been, a democracy and even most of us should know, by now, that the Afro American people have never been citizens. But though this history and the state of the oppressed Afro American people is objectively so, that does not mean that it must automatically be reflected either by those who attempt to write about us and/or themselves. As I said what writers write is what they think or feel or believe is happening, not necessarily what is really happening. What they think or feel or believe according to what is reflected through their class stand. That is, whose side they're on!

This is true, of course, for the critic just as it is for the artist. Actually, criticism is just another form of class struggle. Again, to paraphrase *Yenan*. What causes the writer, for instance, and the critic to conjoin or to conflict is the nature of their views, most frequently the content of their ideological orientation. Good and Bad, Beautiful and Ugly finally are matters of ideology, whose side you're on.

So that even with something that can be determined objectively, like for instance the status, the state of the Afro American people today, ie, there are facts and figures, graphs and statistics and whatnot, even that interpretation is a matter of ideology, whose side you're on. DuBois, in *Black Reconstruction*, also speaks of the Sisyphus Syndrome of Afro American history, where like the mythological character Sisyphus, who was the son of the wind — god, we are punished for tricking death. That is, when death came for Sisyphus, Sisyphus tricked him, so the Gods decided that he must then spend eternity rolling a huge rock up a mountain only to have it roll down on his head when he had gotten it to the top.

The good doctor says that the whip crackers (that's where that term comes from) speculated that we would be dead by the nineteenth century because of slavery, but when we put the Jimmy Brown/Dr. J move on them and in fact multiplied, that we had to be punished by pretending we had finally emancipated ourselves only to find that we were at the bottom of the mountain once again. Hence, the 1860s parallel the 1960s revolution; the 1870s the 1970s presumed reconstruction, and now the 1990s parallel the 1890s, the destruction of Reconstruction. Remember the so-called Redemption of the South? So that by 1895 the oppressor nation could bring in Booker T. (just as in the 1990s they bring on Clarence T.) and then shortly thereafter *Plessy v. Ferguson*, Separate But Evil became the law of the land. The 13th, 14th 15th Amendments and forty acres and a mule, just a trick of the whip gods.

Just as today, the anti-poverty program, the great society, affirmative action, are all in the wind. In fact, the voting rights act, civil rights act, all those good things, are just tricks the whip gods play on black Sisyphus everyday and the most visible results of our struggle to climb the mountain of the 1960s and 1970s is the fact that now we have even more Booker T's ubiquitous in America telling us that if we ain't got nuthin its our own fault, and that now separate and evil only applies to us backward majority of Black people who have not realized that we've already reached the top of the mountain and only believe we at the bottom of the mountain because...because...well, because we are, you know, niggers.

The bizarre irony of the civil rights struggle is that it created a whole sector of the black petty bourgeoisie whose gig it is to bullshit people that America is a democracy, that the civil rights movement is over and that they are proof. Some of these negroes are merely reactionary, that is, they are ideologically backward, they ain't running at speed. But some others of these new mouthpieces for imperialism are actually *compradors*, what the Latinos call Vende Patrias, (sellers of the nation). That is, they are speakers for the oppressor nation, the United Snakes, like the Tom Ass Clarences or Colon Powells (the Colon connects the lower intestine to the rectum, &c) their only connection to Black people is to help oppress them.

The relevance of this is the relevance of our lives to our lives. In the Black Arts Movement of the '60s we said we wanted an Afro American art that was mass oriented and revolutionary. This was our attempt to express the needs of the Afro American national liberation movement itself. To mobilize Black artists on the side of the struggle of the whole people for Self-Determination, Self-Respect and Self-Defense.

The Black Arts movement became broadly popular because objectively, no matter our errors and subjectivity, it expressed the real needs of the Black masses. To create an art that would fight for us as well as educate and entertain us. That is when we came up with the word Inner Attainment. You can see that even today, as bad as things are for Black people generally, there is still something called the National Black Arts Festival, which still does reflect, to some extent, that movement of Black artists for self determination and to aid in the liberation of the Afro American people of thirty years ago. Though now, certainly Black Arts is no longer viewed by our backward as a frightening aberration, since in practice, as we have seen throughout the land, in the last few years, the term can be not only put down with almost utter impunity but pimped like the church pimps religion.

We now have a whole section of new pimp buppie negroes

whose gig it is to be skin-black but ideologically aligned with our oppressors. Not only did '60s integration sprinkle a very light topping of chocolate here and there on the vanilla only of American apartheid. (The U.S., by the way, was the founder of fascism, when it raised the Klan to destroy the reconstruction governments. Hitler's racial laws are drawn directly from the south's post civil war Black Codes.) But many of the old line toms who couldn't get much play in the turbulent '60s have been raised from anonymity to infamy today.

Certainly, if we speak of Afro American art, with anything approaching objectivity, we will see that there is a revolutionary tradition. That the most famous of our writers have been at the point of Black struggle for equality and self determination. Douglass, William Wells Brown, Henry Highland Garnett, David Walker, The Slave Writings, The Black Convention speeches and sermons, Turner, Truth, Frances Ellen Watkins Harper, DuBois, McKay, Hughes, Hurston, Margaret Walker, Richard Wright, Ted Ward, Lorraine Hansberry, Jimmy Baldwin, The Black Arts Movement, &c.

We should also know that the critics of the oppressor nation have, in the main, continuously attacked these writers and other black artists like that nation has attacked black people. These critics have provided an ideological legitimacy for the main social repression of the slave and imperialist relations the U.S. has to the Afro American people. Even the idea of our being artists had to be rendered absurd. We had to be seen as less than human, so we could be passed over by the American civilization like fools pass by them pennies in the street (the only colored money. Three/fifths is what we were in the constitution, that's why when you speak up they tell you you're trying to put your two cents in...then you got five senses and turn in to a niggel, the lowest white money).

Remember, for instance, when *Down Beat* had to re-review the earliest records of Diz and Bird and Monk because when they first appeared they had been given no stars by the critics? But in the end, if you look at it, these publications even then only wanted to make these artists more "respectable," or at least better known, so that they could be stolen from more easily.

Didn't Herr Bone in his book on the novel determine that there was only one "negro novel" of any note and that was Ralph Ellison's, by inference to justify the national book award And certainly we know the "elegance" of Ellison's writing, but we must also remember that his ideological stance in Invisible Man, rejecting both black nationalism and marxism, is more attractive to the mainstream U.S. cultural police.

Didn't the literary supplement to the Encyclopedia Britannica just state that there was, no, none at all, repeat, no, none at all, black writers in the world who were worthy of inclusion in the canon. DuBois, they said, came closest, but even he didn't make it because, they inferred, he was writing about the world. Oh, one woman, white, Willa Cather, made that list. (See this author's *Cultural Revolution + The Literary Canon*.)

If you think about it for a minute, for instance, how many Afro American critics have the main writing gigs writing about the most advanced Afro American music in major American newspapers. I don't know of any. Certainly, there are none in New York. When Stanley Crouch was writing in *The Village Voice* about the music they kept him on the margins because Stanley does know something about that, on the real side. But when he got to something he knew absolutely nothing about, politics, and published his anti-black attacks in *The Hanging Judge*, they gave him a genius award!

Some of us might know about the recent removal of the progressive veteran Black journalist, Earl Caldwell, from the *New York Daily News*, for writing a column on the maniac NYC policeman who raped Black men. Caldwell was replaced by Playthell Benjamin, which says on the face of it that the *News* feels more comfortable with Benjamin. Again, his social consciousness coincides with the *Daily News*. That is, his class stand is more congruent with the *News* than Caldwell's.

Why? Well if you have read any of Benjamin's coverage of Farrakhan or Sharpton or the Rappers in *The Village Voice*, you will begin to understand. I am saying this not because I expect you to agree with any of these people I have mentioned, certainly I do not agree with Sharpton or Farrakhan in many areas, or the coopted Rap of the Two Live Crew, "B's & H's," gangsta, &c. (or the middle class Jazzy Jeffs and Fresh Princes, nor the Elvis Presley syndrome of Vanilla Ice, &c) but to me Sharpton and Farrakhan are part of a united front of Black struggle against Imperialism, even though I disagree with them on many things. But that is why such a united front is one of unity and struggle...unite to struggle and struggle to unite. But to dismiss these men and their organizations, or the rappers for that matter, categorically, and with such absolute contempt, is the work of the comprador, the paid spokesperson for

U.S. imperialism, even further away from the Black masses than the average backward petty bourgeois negro.

Even the backward negro businessman or preacher or artist is reflecting a largely erroneous and subjective view of the world, but is still a category of ideological development within view of the Afro American nation. The Black businessman's market is still Black people, but the comprador sells his booty to America.

The social consciousness of the writer is their class stand. As Mao said, we can look at their writing and tell For Whom they write. We can tell what they think is good, what they think is bad. That is, we can see what they celebrate and what they put down. We can tell what work they do and what they are studying. In other words we can tell what side they're on.

For some, the idea of equality for the Afro American people, the concept of Self Determination is absurd and we read it in their works especially in works of criticism, which are just class struggle. The stream of reactionary garbage appearing in this period of backwardness, the various *Fly Boys in The Buttermilk*, *Affirmative Action Babies, Colored People, Do The Right Thing*, the steady stream of anti-black soi-disant supposed to be artists and intellectuals raised up by the U.S. means we are right back in that period that DuBois describes in *Black Reconstruction*. When after Black people had fought for equality in the civil War, it was necessary for the Oppressor nation to vilify, caricature, attack Black people "for 60 years," culminating in *Birth of a Nation*, in order to convince the world that we were still slaves only because we were not qualified to be free human beings.

This is what is going on today, and the various Sowells, Gates, Walter & Juan Williams, Spikes, Playthells, assorted and sordid ass negro DE/CONSTRUCTIONISTS (dig?) the would be separators of art from politics, and other spokesmen for our enemies, Black or white, must be opposed not just with words, but deeds. That is, we must create our own self determining alternatives to the backward and the compradors. We must create the publishing companies, the theaters. We must give out the awards, build the networks of distributors and museums. We must create the arts institutions we need, otherwise we will continue to suffer from the double consciousness, and see our enemies raise up people to speak for us who really speak for them or who are not even clear enough to understand there is a *them*.
(8/1994)

Wordmusic

Halim Suliman is a poet (a say lore on the crew of the word ship, Blue Ark) a bout to be more widely known. Like most of this generation, they have been heard more widely, especially if they have something to say, than they have been read. So it is good these examples of his developing form and its effective expression of contrasting emotional content, be seen.

This is a poet, whose fullest realization is in his voice and its various contemporary and traditional rhythms. It's cargo of living experience, that raises these compositions into the whole feeling of their intent. Breathing human pictures.

For this reason the pieces whose form is a verb of deepest concerns are the most memorable. How those feelings, heart beats, revelations, come. Expressing them with that spontaneity of the mind improvising and free. This is the ~Djeli ya~ and Halim the ~Djali~.

We brings the Knews and the news. The Go Language!

Eternity of Truth. The Re-All. The body of going, the all
    ways.

Halim is at his heaviest as the moving body of thought.

I SEE! SAID The MUSE

    The Funky Truth.

    The boomalooma of O YeH!

    I Is   (JAZZ)

"The Line," "Be Bop~ particularly and ~Per/Verse," about your boy Tom Ass Clarence, are visible thought forms. Compositions which when played on the instrument of The Djali make "place~" animate.

It is also good that he is putting the book out. The presence of alternative voices to the kept trustee tee hee and reaction trumpeted by our fascist moving official voices is the basic necessity. Only self determination will bring a consistent and strengthening revolutionary art, the fundamental fuel for cultural revolution. *(3/1995)*

The Role of The Writer in Establishing a Unified Writers Organization
(South Africa)

The role of the "individual" writer is to reflect the Lives, History & Struggle of the great majority of the African working people, the workers and farmers, their democratic allies, as well as the revolutionaries. Also to be part of the overall political force for a democratic Africa in rapid transition to become socialist South Africa.

Likewise, for all of Africa, Pan Africa, the Third World, and ultimately across the world. A productive people's artist, energetically creating the living art of the South African workers and farmers. Not out of some isolated petty bourgeois elitist ebony tower, separate from and disdainful of the people. but linked indissolubly to them as part of their still suffering body and as a significant and necessary aspect of the continuing development of their revolutionary consciousness.

We artists, calling ourselves revolutionary or people's artists must strive to be as necessary to the people's intellectual and cultural development as food is to their physical development: We must created works which are educational, inspirational as well as fundamental to the continued dynamic of a revolutionary democratic people struggling for socialism.

But as one great writer, Mao Tse Tsung, has written, we must create works, which are both politically revolutionary as well as artistically powerful. One sidedness won't do. We must do both. We

154

cannot forsake the political for the artistic — whose art would that be? What class would that nourish? Who would it serve? No one but our former, though still living and still aspiring to be, masters. No, our works must serve the politics of the continuing democratic revolution and be part of the cultural revolution which must intensify as fuel for the coming of socialism!

But our works cannot be absent of artistic depth. We strive to create a people's art, a revolutionary art, a socialist art. An art that will help create the new socialist society here in South Africa. While we here are alive and yes, throughout the world.

But part of our problem, we would be people's artists, we would be revolutionary artists, is that most often we place our whole production, our lives's work in the hands of our acknowledged enemies or their faithful lackeys and ideological servants.

We revolutionaries must criticize the enemies of the people, both the slave masters and their agents (and they come in all colors, genders and nationalities) but we must not be content merely to criticize the people's enemies.

We must increasingly take up our time organizing alternative institutions, organizations, structures, networks, alliances, collectives, which can forward and develop and create ever more productive answers to the question of How Do We Liberate Ourselves from all Oppression and Oppressors? How Do We Do Away With All Pests? We must answer Lenin's question, "What Is To Be Done?" With answers of organization and system and concrete social development.

Our art must serve and be inextricably bound to our political and economic development, as well our cultural development. For certainly, they are different fundamental aspects of the same quest, democracy, self determination, socialism.

This writers organization that we seek to put together, and it is ironic that alas, we have not yet put such a critically necessary organization, union, structure, and network together in the other USA either, USA/USA, dig that. And let it be known, from the outset that I am proposing that there be some basic linkage between us, because we are spearheads of democratic and revolutionary development in societies with highly developed productive forces. Societies with large black working classes, the largest concentration black proletarians in the world. Most black people, we ought to know, are still on the land. They are still marginalized by industrial society. But we are squarely in the midst of these societies. And the significance of this must not be overlooked. It must be studied even more closely.

I have been raising this question of an Afro American national writers organization or union for some time. Just last year at the Black Arts Festival in Atlanta (where some 1,000,000 people attended) we raised these questions. We asked various assemblies and those who administrated (Black and white) "Shouldn't we set aside some portion of this festival, in which there has been much fun, much inspiration, much human, emotional and historical unity recalled. There were the actual great Pan African artists of the world present, and an impressive number of intellectuals and scholars. Together! And it was a wonderful, joyous, week. questions. We asked various assemblies and those who administrated (Black and white) "Shouldn't we set aside some portion of this festival, in which there has been much fun, much inspiration, much human, emotional and historical unity recalled. There were the actual great Pan African artists of the world present, and an impressive number of intellectuals and scholars. Together! And it was a wonderful, joyous, week.

My wife, Amina, and I went to see Maya Angelou at 7PM one evening, Cassandra Wilson and the great Abbey Lincoln later on the same evening! And then off to Miguel Algarin's NuYorican Café Theater party for the cast and author of *Life in Wartime*, Wesley Brown. Then back to the hotel where we talked to Abbey in the restaurant even further into the evening, and then talked in rapid succession, that night and later to David Murray the great tenor saxophonist, Quincy Troupe, Sonia Sanchez, Calvin Hernton, Don Pullen, Hattie Gossett, Linton Kwesi Johnson, Askia Toure, Haki Madhubuti, Ishmael Reed, Miguel Algarin, Toni Cade Bambara, Wesley Brown, Eugene Redmond, Butch Morris, David Henderson, and on and on. We went to see Thornton Dial's new works, heard Ras Baraka, my and Amina's very fine poet son read with Angela Jackson. We went to see Ruth Brown and Little Jimmy Scott made us cry with the blues. We even struggled with various conservatives. We were on panels and forums, held formal and informal gatherings. And on one joyous evening we had a beautiful surprise (to Amina) 27th wedding anniversary in which all these folks and more laughed and sang and read up in a penthouse ballroom overlooking downtown Atlanta. But still I raised the same question, shouldn't we put some time aside to discuss seriously and with concrete suggestions which could be implemented by us till next we met — some time to discuss Self Determination and Self Reliance for Afro American artists and arts? Shouldn't we spend some time trying to organize ourselves and indeed Afro American art and artists toward Self Determination? If we really believe that the Afro American people are an oppressed nation in the U.S. with the right of self determination. Shouldn't we be using this grand gathering of some of the finest artists in the world to begin to build the theaters and publishing companies, the art galleries and networks of performance venues and cultural centers so that we never have to rely on people who made us chattel slaves, and after the so called emancipation betrayed us again into the same thing with a different name. Who segregated us, discriminated against us, lynched us by the thousands, who destroyed Reconstruction and delivered us into the hands of the southern whip crackers whose ruling class we had just sent to hell in the civil war? Read next Patterson's *We Charge Genocide* and shudder at the bloody trace of our residency in the U.S. The United States has never been a democracy, to paraphrase DuBois, and we have never been citizens!

Why should we continue to play the vicious American game paper citizen and real slave? Why should, particularly our artists and intellectuals continue to function as if they were really integral parts of the U.S. social body politic? Why should they continue to hang around in pathetic double consciousness, seeing, as DuBois said, ourselves through the eyes of people that hate us.

DuBois called for true self consciousness and it is exactly this the revolutionary artists must be sworn to bring into being. But we cannot do this unless we are part and parcel of the people, no different, except for our consciousness, our role.

Certainly, it should be impossible by now for us to think we can function as revolutionary artists and intellectuals under the hood of the masses Cadillac, making it go. The African people are historic masters of the arts. We are the creators of art, music, poetry. Indeed speech itself. Why should we play Charlie McCarthy, a wooden dummy, to the greedy racists who continue to rule the world.

The imperialists control the arts like they control everything else. They decide what is hailed and what is dismissed. They say what is produced and what will never be. They choose the super stars, give out the grants. They are the creators of the Pulitzer and Nobel Prizes, and indeed they select who we will idolize and follow. They let us know what literature is serious, what is not.

In fact they tell us what is literature. They have a canon in which they have selected white men as the masters of literature (there is one white woman, but not one person of color). They are the genius namers and prostitute makers.

They give out Academy awards for pornography and drive the Great artists and intellectuals into exile, anonymity, madness, poverty. But why do artists and intellectuals collaborate with this? Why do we accept the Devil's sick illusion as the actual? I guess if we are not, generally published or produced, we may criticize but that is the limit. Though some of us, it may be said can wail on these suckers on occasion in our criticism, which is the sharp form of class struggle in the arts, or in the works themselves. But as I said we must do more. First we must organize ourselves. Here in South Africa, and since you are already in the motion of doing this, you must, as you organize help and network with the rest of us around the world.

We must organize nationally, from the cities, to the counties, to the states, to the regions. What we must organize is a Writers' Union. In the tradition not only of Mao but the great Pan African revolutionary writers of our tradition, like Sembene Ousmane, Ngugi wa Thiong'o, Jacques Roumain, Nicolas Guillen, W.E.B. DuBois, Langston Hughes, Margaret Walker. The idea of Black writers or artists was an absurdity to our slave masters, for their avaricious predatory societies enforce a terrible ignorance on them which they in turn enforce upon the world, so that they may exist as parasites and disease upon the people of the world. A class who lives on lies, theft and murder. What about a class that would even steal people, with the help of their various little evil Fausts of the Planet. What about a class who would kidnap people from their homes and bring them to lands which they also stole, put those people in chains. All those they did not kill they made slaves so that they did not have to work themselves. Then call those people who did their work, LAZY! A class that would invade other peoples' lands, destroy their societies, because they loved idleness. In fact they were idol worshippers till some 300 years after they murdered Christ!

Remember it was Africans who created religion and even gave these folks Laws of Civilization and tried to teach Neither Jesus nor Krishna nor Buddha nor Muhammad were ever in Europe! But the question is why do we continue to subjugate ourselves, our consciousness to the slave social orders' of these heathens for whom Gold is the only Deity and slavery the only just form of social relations. And it is the artists, the intellectuals who must provide the catalytic paradigm for our people's continued movement to self determination and democracy and socialism. We should form this organization as a union of writers, not just to talk *to* each other, but to work together to create the collective models of organization that point and work for socialism.

For instance, we should be collectively trying to set up a writers organization that will first organize writers and also help create the process of organizing artists in general in whatever discipline, organizing not just as a union for mutual benefit as far as conditions, fees, access, within that profession, as any trade union might. Such a union, in my view, should also serve to actively influence the political climate of society, playing a leading role in organizing writers and artists and intellectuals as a revolutionary force on the side of the people in the fierce struggle that remains in order to elevate the people to higher levels of democracy and socialism. Such a union would help unify the workers and farmers and progressive and revolutionary allies politically, to oppose the forces of reaction which are still very much alive. Not just in a trade union fashion. This organization should be an expression of the political, economic and cultural process of the society itself. Educating the writers and intellectuals by providing closer links with the people, and at the same time, providing the people themselves with political direction and education. Such an organization should help mobilize the writers to become themselves more truly self consciousness and fight for a truer self consciousness among the people.

Such an organization must itself create publications and newspapers to raise and discuss and expose the questions key to society's development. It must create publications, popular as well as more advanced, not just help writers publish in bourgeois venues. The union must create new venues itself, and by that process raise the quantity and quality of writing itself. Providing more opportunity for writers to publish while expressing the needs and direction and of the people themselves, providing revolutionary leadership. The older forms of slavery left us with low levels of productive forces.

Illiteracy and mass education are still in society. Intellectual workers are critical to building social development, but remember even out of the small number of intellectuals an oppressed people have, an obvious sector of them are completely backward, and work for our enemies, and while the number of revolutionaries is likewise small, we must influence the middle sector, the patriotic center, to take up consciously the struggle for the people's democracy development and socialism. We must become an expression, by our own collective organization, of new venues for publications. We must cease pandering to the purely commercial requirements of writers functioning within the bourgeois society. The union must itself create the weapons for dismantling such a society helping to speed the actual concrete material conditions for broadening of democracy and the coming of socialism. For instance, such a writers organization must create literary vehicles of such quality and impact that these publications become the focus for the writer's desire to be part of the highest quality intellectual, artistic and literary community. The union must create a collective process for publishing, distribution of writers works and see to the republication in mass editions of our classics. Do you think you could go into a bookstore and find Aristotle out of print. Then why should Sembene or Ngugi be out of print? The union must be the seed, a living developing example of the socialist relations we seek for the whole society. Such an organization must itself raise and be our expression of the political, economic and cultural transformation we seek. Unifying writers to struggle, but also helping to create more and more progressive vehicles for struggle.

We must create new vehicles and venues as expressions of the new society we seek and be a catalyst for the creation of others. We can organize collectively supported journals and newspapers and collectively supported publishing houses. We must be creators of the very institutions we must have, which in themselves will be weapons against the opportunism and prostitution with which the bourgeois rewards its pets.

We must create the vehicles, the venues. So that we are providing politically revolutionary, artistically powerful vehicles so that writers can no longer blame their ideological and artistic backwardness on having to prostitute for humanity's enemies.

We must begin perhaps with newspapers, regular, popular yet serious. It will teach us to write more effectively, having to be understood by working people while discussing the most serious topics we know.

If the continuing struggle for democracy, reparations, land reform, literacy, mass education, a revolutionary peoples art and culture, health, are the areas that need the most explanation and discussion, these are what we must pursue variety (in a variety of forms, exposition, fiction, verse, drama, song, opera, radio, TV, film).

So the new newspapers, journals, magazines, publishing houses, little theaters and big ones too, concert venues and clubs must be part of our thrusting mandate. That is, we must create them and help them be created, not simply get writers a better economic relationship to the big capitalists. Producing prostitutes is not our role, opposing such prostitution is. Likewise the organization in its expression, through concrete organization and system, i.e., construction of the new democratic culture, must set its own standards. Give its own awards, recognize great men and women for achievements valued by the people and ourselves as their true intellectual representatives.

I am not dismissing our certainly prestigious awards from the other side. First of all — until recently — no such Awards existed among us. There could be no recognized B lack artists and intellectuals in the old slave world, and the recent international wave of recognition because imperialism denied we were humans; certainly we could not be artists or intellectuals.

But the decline and fall of straight out colonialism and the introduction universally of neo-colonialism meant that they would give lip service and abstract gestures towards our humanity even while struggling mightily to suppress it. But who do WE praise and who do we dismiss. That is the fundamental stance of self determination. Where are our DuBois Prizes, our Jacques Roumain and Amilcar Cabral prizes? When do we honor the Sembenes and Ngugis? Where is the Baldwin or Guillen medal? You mean if the imperialists will not honor Margaret Walker, we will sit silent as other people's furniture and by that act of non-consciousness be regarded in the world like furniture. In fact, we will even let people sit in our faces as we practice the consciousness of chairs.

So such an organization must take upon itself to see to the

establishing of such national and international, awards and likewise such international networks of collectively created self-reliant institutions of publishing, states, and dramatic production. We must stop merely trying to get a story on the bourgeoisie's network. We must help to bring the peoples' radio and television stations into being. Also, the producers and technicians and administrators to accomplish these ends, thereby entering into another aspect of class struggle i.e., the struggle for production.

One thing we must recognize and really understand, that the ultimate resource, the richest resource on the planet, is the people. The people are the most advanced intervention in society, no matter double-talking murderous technology. To build the revolutionary democratic society moving toward socialism, our organization must spearhead the reorganization of social relations, criticizing capitalist and exploitative relations and actually beginning to build the new society.

The democratic struggle for peoples' control of the South African political economic and cultural entities will be long and drawn out, violent and peaceful, open and hidden. But at this moment while democracy and even a socialist mixed economy are still being proclaimed and the people's' memory of your domestic nazis is still fresh, is the time to move.

What is so ironic about the trip for Amina and I is that 25 years ago we faced a somewhat parallel situation in the U.S. What was called the Civil Rights and Black Liberation Movements. Under the broad leadership of a democratic reformist Martin Luther King and the working peoples' leader, Malcolm X, Omowale, a democratic revolutionary.

As a concomitant aspect of the revolutionary upsurge, and explosive united front of working people and the petty bourgeoisie and other classes, a significant sector of people, but particularly the national bourgeoisie and petty bourgeoisie, were thrust up into visible positions of social, political hegemony and authority. And as they rose into these mostly advertising agent propositions, not only cosmetic, however, yet essentially SPOOKS who sat by the door, to give the U.S. some pretense of democracy, as they sat, some from the very beginning of their tenure, it made no difference that it was we, the people, who had worked and fought and went to jail, got killed or beat damn near to death, to get them in those positions. Again, the problem was "the Double Consciousness" accompanied by or exacerbated by straight out bribery and each day of their tenure saw them move further away from the people who had delivered them into their new Heavens.

In Newark, New Jersey, USA, when the 1st Black mayor was elected in a major northeastern U.S. city, I was part of the political leadership of that wonderful and historic campaign. Yet, in a few months after the election, the very qualities that had perhaps identified me as political leadership now "non-plussed" our brothers and sisters who had won electoral office who now drew further and further away, not only from the personal us, but from the people themselves.

In fact, as these mayors and councilmen and appointed officials and congress persons, judges &c...., drew further and further away the people, they began to characterize those of us who openly carried the banner of working people's struggle as irresponsible militants, crazy "white haters," anything but the truth, which was, yes, we were too Black and too Red.

A few of us had started to criticize our new officials as they disappeared into the corporate suites and "godfather" payroll offices. And of course, as our criticism grew sharper, the bigger and badder we became, out of their mouths. You see, as they were becoming more and more openly functioning prostitutes, they were undermining and opposing, secretly or not, more and more of the things they'd sworn to the people they'd do when they got in office. They began to rely on the people for nothing but reference and memory and they, at the same time, relied on the big bourgeoisie, not only for their various "perks" and toys and head pats but for their socialization and consciousness.

In fact, in a couple of years, we militants, the very folks who'd led the attacks on the status quo, and rallied the people to their support, became their well publicized enemies! So we got a portion of the people's army together and put the 1st negro out. But we hadn't learned our lesson. The new Negro, who'd played outspoken opposition, the last repository of integrity in public office, was, if possible, even worse. Because he sprinted away from the people, where as the 1st Negro was too fat to run.

Ironic today, here in a newly post apartheid South Africa, because we thought we were post-apartheid New Ark. We and so many other brothers and sisters and comrades, who'd worked and fought for the end of U.S. Apartheid. (You know, of course, that this is where Apartheid began, The U.S. South!) And just like that part of U.S. history, post-Civil War Reconstruction, it was betrayed. Not just by the so called "Redemption of The South," the betrayal of democracy by the U.S. government and the delivery of the south back into the hands of the dead slave masters' overseers. So that 30 years after chattel slavery was overthrown, U.S. apartheid, separate but evil, became the law of the land. And all the laws and promise of the revolutionary era were betrayed and overthrown. Hitler's racial laws were taken from the Black Codes imposed on the Afro American people as Reconstruction was destroyed.

And today, we have just witnessed the same phenomenon. It is what DuBois called The Sisyphus Syndrome. Where, like the ill fated Sisyphus, we are doomed to forever roll the rock of liberty up the mountain, only to have cruel "Gods" roll it back down on us, as a penalty for our refusing to die! Yes, and just yesterday, 25 years after we brought the Afro American petty bourgeoisie into electoral hegemony in the revolutionary era of the U.S., they have allowed the peoples' enemies to return, having long ago, to paraphrase James Weldon Johnson, "sold their heritage for a mess of pottage."

The point I am making is that we must make certain our leaders our actually working class leaders and not followers of the bourgeoisie (in mufti). That is, they must represent the great majority of workers and farmers. And not be fighting merely to get into the ruler clique. And, alas, that is often true of the middleclass, that they are not struggling to end oppression, so much as merely trying to get the same status as the oppressors. It is the same of writers and intellectuals. If we are not serious representatives of the people, we will wind up on the side of their enemies. And no matter the piles of glittering resources a society might have. Remember the people are its most precious resource.

Our false leaders and turncoat artists don't understand this. They believe being Beggars is the utmost dignity. Just as our Kneeling Negroes In Newark. For instance, isn't it obvious that if we are going to fight illiteracy and push mass education that the arts are one of the best ways to do this? And that there can be no real anti-illiteracy program without mounting a massive arts program. Such a writers' Union as we propose must be in the leadership of this. It should be equally obvious that the old use of society's institutions is inadequate. We must eliminate the Beggar Mode of social life and call for and help implement the self reliant mode. Toward this end even government and other public agencies must be moved to self reliance. Schools, for instance, if understood correctly. are natural economic producers. The combining of the arts with education at these facilities, decentralizing the programmatic functions of arts and mass education, gives more venues and ends the strictly Bureaucrat/Beggar concept of funding public institutions.

Just as the writers' union itself, if understood correctly, must be collective and self reliant. Small capitalism can't compete with imperialism. But self reliant collectives can provide alternative circuits for resources providing aggregation of resources that can be naturally expanded with the development of enterprises. Our focus being on providing more service, more employment, more anti-illiteracy and mass education programs In which the target groups are central to their functioning. If we can implement this collective and self reliant mode of operation and eschew complete submission to begging our enemies and the friends of OUR enemies, we will develop.

If not, we won't. And it must be said for the Pan African people, not just USA/USA. And eventually, it must be said, for all the people. For us in the U.S. our national priority must proceed always with an eye to expansion throughout the whole of Pan America, i.e., the Western Hemisphere. And like Africa, we must also be constantly in touch with like minded comrades throughout the entire Third World. Because they are hardest hit by imperialism. But we must always be open to revolutionary and progressive peoples' internationally.

Where are our Arts Festivals in the great capitals of the world? Our writers' union could do this. Why do we wait for SONY or JVC or IBM? Goree, Almina, Johannesburg, New Orleans, Habana, Beijing, for starters. What a circuit! Why should we wait for "Budweiser." It would be much wiser if the Bud were our own. Where our people are, where sympathetic people are, these are our venues and they must be networked without being dominated by capital. Our union would take the lead in setting up international programs to proliferate collective solutions and self reliance. It is the petty bourgeois beggar mentality of these governments, supposedly sympathetic to the people, that has prevented them from doing these things.

No more complaining that Big capital wont let our writing or other art undermine them sufficiently. That they wont publish our books which tell them to die or produce our plays, exhibit our paintings which show ways big capital can be destroyed. It is we who are fools if we don't understand why. Not them! And Now's The Time! As Charlie Parker said. In the flush of newly won democracy, here in South Africa, we must move. In the Other USA, we are in the backward, downhill mode. Sisyphus' rock has come tumbling down the mountain, once again. We are beset with confederate maniacs. New Hitlers and younger Goebbels, Negro propagandists for white supremacy and Hanging Judges, Tom Ass Clarences abound and Colored Colons to connect the large and small intestine of capital to the "wreck them!" The Civil Rights Movement, like the 19th century reconstruction has been undermined and all but murdered. It will happen here, for the same reasons, if we let it.

In The U.S., e.g., August 17, the government murderers are scheduled to murder another one of us, the writer, Mumia Abu Jamal! It is the most spectacular lying frame-up of recent years. The would be murderers want us to believe that the struggle for democracy and self determination is over and that democracy and self determination themselves have been defeated. And that these Doles and Gingriches, these Helms and Klan militia lynchers have won. And one of the purposes of my visit, aside from the conference is to present a package on Mumia to President Mandela for his intervention. It would be a powerful act, just as millions of us throughout the world swore and acted to see that he would not be executed when Apartheid so mandated.

The ANC, through Cyril Ramaphosa, has already spoken out against this state lynching. Even South Africa has banned the Death Penalty. Only the U.S., of the industrial states, maintains the Death Penalty. Restored to emphasize, in Bl ood, Sisyphus' rock rolled down the mountain again.

But the Death Penalty itself must be banned. You know what it takes to do that. A collective Self Reliant effort. I hope I can get everyone here to sign a petition calling for the end of the legal state murders. And, of course, you must understand that like the old Apartheid government, these legal lynchings are aimed, in the main, at Black people! So let our call for the freeing of Mumia Abu Jamal and the end of the death penalty mark the beginning of a new dispensation. The coming together of the artists and intellectuals internationally to struggle against imperialism and its stifling imposition of the beggar mentality on us. To consistently provide a presence that is unified to struggle at the side of the people to end the old social relations of slavery , colonialism and neo-colonialism and spawn a new era of collective growth based on Self Reliance and Self Determination. We will do it!

Keynote Address: March 21, 1996,

Johannesburg, South Africa

Black Drama
(Introduction)

When the 1st edition of this work came out I was elated because, 1st the historical continuum of Black Art is very much under documented. For instance, of all the great Afro American writers there is none save DuBois (and in a somewhat restricted, by cost, little-known edition) whose works have been reissued in the uniform "classic" editions. The fact that there was a work, of some admirable scholarship, that sought to at least sum up and present some of the notable works of Black dramatists. (Ah, now if we could only get around to putting together a national Afro American Repertory Theater, so that these works could be seen, could tour, could go into the schools...but then that is work we are working on, I hope?) I used the 1st edition in many of my classes through the years, and still instantly recommend it for Black lit and drama courses. This new edition, in two volumes, in paper, promises, on the surface, to be more accessible, so that is cause for more elation. The editors have shown themselves to be genuinely "on the case," again re-presenting a historic selection of what they feel to be some of the outstanding dramatic works produced by Afro American authors. But as much as I celebrate the event and the work and the authors. Ted Shine, in fact, is an "old" schoolmate of mine, years past from "The Capstone" [of Negro Education] they used to call it, Howard University. We witnessed Baldwin's *Amen Corner* make its first appearance down there, and, I guess, we were both touched by it forever. Still I would like to make some critical remarks, call them scholarly responses to the whole, not out of any petty pedanticism, but only out of a genuine desire to enhance the presentation.

Drama is the most interactive (media word) form of Art, simply because it presents persons, human beings in something presuming ongoing life. All literature "is an ideological reflection of real life" (to paraphrase Mao). Black literature, here Black Drama, gives an ideological portrait of Black life. Afro American drama, of the lives and history, the material social life and psychological development of the Afro American people.

Black Americans have gone through three distinctive political upsurges in our history here in the U.S.: the 19th century Anti Slavery movement, which culminated in the Civil War and Reconstruction; the early 20th century, which focused on the Harlem Renaissance, where a distinct Afro American modernism rooted in the "Black Consciousness" that DuBois had spawned and Garvey had popularized and Langston had made great poetry; and then the Black Arts Movement, which accompanied and reflected Malcolm X, The Black Panthers, Dr. King's marches, a literature and art that reflected the real turbulence and political upsurge of the Civil Rights and Black Liberation Movements. A collection of works truly reflecting this historical span and motion should carry the works that try to dig into the essence of those times, dig deeper than the superficial newspaper lies (usually of the rulers) to say whatever was not and whatever is whatever, but we still rule.

These volumes do this, to a great extent. I simply want to mention what is not and why they should be. Though, some of the suggestions I made were taken up, but others I felt should be mentioned.

Zora was missing at first, I wanted *Mule Bone*, which many of the buppie/academic negroes do not like because it talks of uneducated peasants. But what about being an uneducated peasant masquerading as a Professor at Slave Money University teaching that Afro American literature is a marginal form, a kind of Henry James/Derrida scrub team?

Forget that.

I thought that "Yes We Can" as the title of the early twentieth century plays was corny. Though my dialogist said well that's what they (those dramatists) thought. Well,...but I wd say they had no doubt what they could do, they thought the restrainers needed assurance, if the title has any relevance.

In The section titled "Legend and History," I could not understand how Charlie Fuller's, *A Soldier's Play* (which I confess I dislike and have written an essay on to explain) could be placed, anachronistically into a group of plays from the '20s and '30s. If they wanted Fuller, *The Brownsville Raid* is a better play in my view, certainly it is not the "Hail, The Negro Middleclass," drumbeater, that SP is.

Along with that, I wondered where was Ted Ward's *Our Lan'* (although they do have the great *Big White Fog*). Ted Ward is one of the great, dig it, great writers of any nationality and any time. The reason his plays don't get done...well, it's like Robeson said, "Two things these people don't like about me, my views and my nationality." Ward was a Red, like they say, Black & Red. Ain't Black bad enough?

Also, William Branch's important play, *In Splendid Error,* is gone. This play about Fred Douglass and John Brown is pantheonic in impact and certainly its Legend and History qualities should go unchallenged, even as text. Under "Social Justice," I wondered why there were not more of the Federal Theater Project plays. *Fog* was one, but Roosevelt sent Harry Hopkins to squash it in Chicago it was so Black and red.

But this is the root of one aspect of Black national oppression. That we do not have our own venues and networks and theaters and tours. Our art is formidable, but still kept to the margin because we have not achieved self reliance for the Black Arts, as predicate for the Self Determination of Afro America itself. Self Determination must be first, because even to struggle for complete democracy as Americans the oppressed must, themselves, put together the United Fronts and organizations of struggle. That is the 1st degree of Self-Determination. Malcolm called for Self Determination, Self Respect and Self Defense. Respect can only come with creation of self reliant institutions that will carry Revolutionary Art and make Cultural Revolution. This is the only real education an oppressed people can have. The formal public education of the U.S. is at best flawed with the lies and distortions of bourgeois class ideology and racism. So that a few years after the last political upsurge the people make , through the schools or lack of schools, films, television, sick Negroes and regular U.S. nazis they can preach the end of the civil rights movement and the natural hegemony of the petty bourgeois. Just as DuBois said they did after the civil war.

For 60 years, they pushed the humiliation and plantation stereotype slave portrait of the Afro American people(from Sambo to *Birth of a Nation*) to justify the destruction of the reconstruction. Self-Defense is not just military. It begins with organizations and institutions for true self consciousness (again, DuBois) to break down the "double consciousness," seeing yourself through the eyes of people that hate you. The great Afro American dramatists do just that. They cut through the sickening double consciousness (as Langston said in "The Negro Artist and The Racial Mountain") and talk to us about our actual origins and history, draw out our actual Intelligence, touch our 'real feelings. This is why Confucius said, "If the people hear the wrong music the Empire will fall." That's why there's so little real jazz on the stations. Why they cover and hide and melt it down into fusion. The same with all the deep democratic voices of the Black artists. And drama, the most ambitious, because it uses real folks. When revolutionary drama appeals it usually means the other thing is about, or already on. Under "Comedy as Protest" I wanted Ben Caldwell's *The First Militant Preacher*, which was one of the most performed plays of the 1960's Black Arts Movement. I know personally, I directed it, and did performances up and down the West Coast and The East. There can be no registration of this, because we were in cultural centers, schools, playgrounds, people's houses, right where we belonged. And that is what must re-happen.

The arts, the drama, must not wait around for the murderers to discover them so they can make its creators honorary murderers, or real ones. We must do it ourselves. Dig, for instance, the quality of the "black films & drama" on the slavemasters' circuits these days, from *House Party* 100 to *Living Color*, it's mostly minstrelsy. Compare them to *CornBread Earl & Me* or *The Education of Sonny Carson* or *Buck & The Preacher*. Or *Raisin in The Sun, Blues For Mr Charlie, Dutchman* to what passes as Black drama on the stages of dying — killerville. The editors happily also included Caldwell's little masterpiece. (It needs to be played in every church in the country.). In that same category I wondered where was Loften Mitchell? Toni Morrison is one of the most important playwrights around, though I know her plays have not been seen. Like Billie said, you ain't got "your own," you in the wind. But Toni's Emmett Till play cries to be included, not to mention, performed. We saw a performance at the Public Theater. You know the deal, give you a perf, but none really.

Under very big mistakes, I'd say the decision not to include *Blues For Mr Charlie* is the heavy. This is a great play, one that marks, very clearly and indelibly, a transition in the mindset of the Afro American people. The play is ideological struggle between Dr King and Malcolm, in Jimmy's dissociative and sexually oriented perception. A struggle over the youth of the movement. Which way, nonviolence or self defense? After this play Jimmy was demoted to the margins of U.S. literature by the living dead. Under "Black Theater For Black People" where is Marvin, X, Ron Milner, Sonia Sanchez, Rob Penny, Oyamo, Larry Neal, some of the people who actually picked up the Black Arts Movement and carried Black Theater across the country? We could go on with our carping. Where is Wesley, where are Harris, Cleage, J. Franklin? And certainly, of the new folks, Lawrence Holder, that hard working young man should have made the set. But my informant sd, they had a space problem. (Like I told you, Billie sd, you ain't got yr own...&c).

But put all these things I sd in yr notes, and be thankful for the considerable gifts these two energetic archivists have provided. I was deeply thankful to see DuBois' *Ethiopia*. It would be a great project for the churches: and Board of Educations to collaborate on. But like the lady said ... what is important though, is that collections such as these should be made mandatory in all Black Studies programs and in schools across the country, especially those where Black folks are. This is the deep education we need and must have, to stimulate a true self consciousness and begin again to push our Sisyphus like burden up the mountain again. But unlike Sisyphus, one day soon the rock won't be coming back down.
(8/1995)

The Last Poets

On the Cannibal. Remember Sisyphus, but be like Hannibal. This here, is A Book for Booking.

Beauty. Terror. Information. The Buddha Dope Body. To Split Wit. You stand in the middle of reality on one leg. Got to be The Good Foot. The God Spell. The Trance-trans B (2) see! Our Cross is not a murder weapon. The picnic of Not was Ignorant Shadow Distance. Illusion is fake laughter the destiny of the past.

We is the Ptah Baby. Our ancestor sent up out the whale's mouth (ain't that a Pip!), from where we was on the ocean's floor. Mothers and sisters in the middle passage with the whales. And now we is Wailers. Listen to The Big Fish one night. Song for the Fishers of The Human. The Baptizer, The Wailer, Revelator, High John The Conqueror, we is them, the same, when we white we name Brown, if we Black we blow like Trane.

We was Blue when we got here, before that we was inside speed purple, before that we was inside darkness in the womb of night. Why is you qualifying you whisky color was? Who was you is now over revealed as wrong. Look at the racists, how they wrap the Sun in ignorance and keep On off.

Why are you concerned about these things? I is a was a been a, No Shit slave! A nigger, here in, They-merica. Cold slave catcher whip cracker colorless ghost looking actual Oedipus type Mother Fuckers.

For real?

Yeh, the "Fuck up yr life" type real.

And this is what?

This? Scions. Them us was is again & ing. Me. Yr boy, that mad angry unanonymous Negro. Hate everybody.

(No. Not everybody. On the true side—just my enemies. Most people enemies. This ain't personal.)

But the, your, niggers, really, art?

Yes, our Art! Look, you aint John-on-the-one. You John Bull. You the Barbarian, shave, claim religion, call yrself Aryan.

Such dialogue is in the streets, washing up and down. We-Merica to They-Merica & Back. If the truth is refused, the planet remain uninhabitable by Humans, it will be barren and eventually "out to lunch" for a long long time. Evidence will be a Weisehunky Schwarznegger & a McDonald Box- Pictures of Niggers lynching TomAss Clarence.

In the Valley of The Shadow of Death. Behind my Brother, The King, selling me to the Ghost. (On we ark we seed em coming, out of the nigger of slavery, we warned, "Ghosts Ahead, Who are Cannibals!")

"The Valley of The Shadow Of Death." Oh, yes, millions, Jacques Roumain ran it, "At the bottom of the Atlantic Ocean, A railroad of human bones!"

For it is these bones, which still live as the instruments of prophecy, from which to Divine. These dice (speech, like Dicht, Dick, Dutchman calls the poem Dick Tongue) comes out of space as space, into space, as the memory of its history as the measure of expression. Drum sticks.

Art demands its existence to be. The creating is a specific space of making, a beat (Be At!) Black Art is the truth of what is, it was, a ray of YES (we say) ACT YOU ALL.

In West Africa, The Djali was the historic living speech arriving in the ark, the word ship. The Thot of vision (Muse I See), and from us, always, as matter, object and subject. Singing to ourselves, to re/member, re be (Get wid it!) struction. It is science (Knowing, which is the dialectic of No/ing) speed measured in Nots—we see, sea (where you coming from, Wailers). I am Jonah and The Baptist, like I splain you. And Trane and The Revelator woodshedding with the infinite on Patmos, shot out by Devil Vision. Channel 666!).

We cry, "Thou Art with Us," as the I completing I, with the ampersand, dig. The musical connection, the number, with coming—IS STORE—musical sign, the sine is an angle, we made the pyramid to point from ON up at our Soul, Bird, on fire, flying out, giver of life and light. So from the beginning of Human life on this planet, our Art has been with us. Despite the recent centuries of Barbarism and our own personal tragedy. (Which be, at 1st, self-inflicted, by the old Don, Yall Kool, De Kang, made his own mama a slave if you wdnt start no shit wdnt be none...). Yet, Oh historic chain, Oh, Europe, you are the Evil Cannibal Ghost. Yours the Murder of Christ. The Inquisition, The Destruction of the Old World, The Slave Trade, Chattel Slavery. Fascism, Capitalism. Still we remain, like Sisyphus, targeted by Death, yet we is the Jimmie Brown of this ever and we straight armed death like the chump of delusion.

So Oedipus, the Caesars, Alexander, The Crusaders, demanded with one voice with "White America" (a slave ship) that we, each generation, roll a huge rock up a mountain, only to have it roll back down on us. Fred, Harriet, Nat, Dr. DuBois, Garvey. Yet even in the valley of the shadow thou art. It is our breath, our being, our spirit, that is with our coming.

It explodes from out and as a tale, anima, the lying snake, a lion's tail, head of Sister Soul, who is us and chants for life without end, "I Rise In Fire!"

Our Art is as true as the Being that is the living world. And though slaves &c., this last half millennium, our art remains with us. Listen. Oh, Afro Americans! Imagine we is Fred and Highland Garnett and David Walker, The Sorrow Songs, Arhwhoolies, Shouts, Worksongs. They took our drums,
Clarence squealed on Rap, the beat spoke across the world, our being and meaning—Oh Yes. Like JB, when we got on the Good Foot, we knows the God Spell, we "Go Out," "Get Down," Burn! (E.g., these cities, many times, Cry, Phoenix, I Rise In Fire!)

The Djali is the eye, the "I" of change and rise and motion. What life stores in itself to come back from its Western trip. Like us, the Dark, is old and deep and hip. Our Mama is Sky, or Nut or black hole to the Dough Nut. Jazz, they thought, meant fuck, an Anglo Saxon word for violence. Oh? "Fucked up!" means, not Creation and Birth, but tragedy. The frown at the roof of the world—Oh, laughing niggers. That's why you low, the bottom, for laughing so much.

In France, they called the poet Griot. The Town Crier. In the South we said Djali. Like old Negroes on fire with the gospel, in church, and rising, possessed, like Bird, BA, the Charlie Parker wailing his fetish back into the sun. On out. What is created. An Atomic Bomb or The Blues? Duke Ellington or John Wayne? Bette Midler or Sarah Vaughan?

Let it be — but that Art! That Being of us carried as us, seen and been, as and was, to be what we create again. The Real is The Royal (King of Everything) and it is connected — Oh, uncivilized things who ignorantly rule, as savage wizards of cannibal power — connected as what is one and all and every, and that truth is the beauty of what is alive's reason. So, even, half destroyed, humiliated, murdered, enslaved, exploited, slandered, stolen from without intermission, our Art is with us. Be it Billie, or Phillie Joe or Max or Monk or Langston or Zora or Pops or Margaret or Toni, our Art is a great Being towering from Earth to the outer inner of where we was is been and going. The Djali is in charge of the life of memory, hence meaning. What is inside of the living, the constant beat of Is/Is and R/R.

There is no Last poets, really. Perhaps the name, taken as a sign of the cataclysm to come, the revolutions to slay the animals who rule earth and forbid its habitation by Humanity. Science is living wisdom. I & I is the Black Bird, whose speech is a crown. Crow and Raven, Bah Bah, The Black Sheep, who has the wool.

Our history is a laughter, a thunderous laughter, given dimension by tears. We is to Happy moved. We is Orpheus, raising the Sun, so the dark is moved to Fire and Light. We is rhythm, a dividing one ness, that's two for going. That is the beat, the breath, day/night, yes, no, Woman/Man.

Our Art, is the Zen speech that defies illusion, the nigger, whassis name, Boddhidharma, East of the Sun, like we, West of the Moon. Our Art is where we carries the world. When we get into the godspell, speaking in tongues, scat, BeBop, get on the good foot. Good!, I Cry — God only exists in Hell, to replace Good!

Djeli Ya! (Like Mr. B. sung, Djeli Djeli Djeli Ya Get Down to Go Out! Our Art carries the world, as our living, from Ptah Baby, selves. Abiodun and Umar are the most consistent carriers of the name, The Last Poets. For the Knowers, we know the name once meant the great Gylan Kain, now in the Netherlands (as is traditional, for a time, for Orpheus). David Nelson, now a minister in Colorado, and Felipe Luciano, my man, the courageous leader of The Young Lords, a funky warrior, like we usually is — (Check Muhammad Ali waste a doomed chump, e.g, the minstrel, George F.). And Abiodun, on the set, from the beginning.

The Abiodun LPs have established the most known sound and image of the LPs — with Umar and Jalil. These LPs have created a popular oeuvre that speaks and will speak from us, through them, to the world.

The rhythmic animation of word, poem, image, as word-music, is the Djali, and the Djeli Ya! This form came out of the revolutionary '60s Black Arts Movement, from way back beyond sorrow songs and chattel wails. Where we created the word as living music, raising it off the still, Apollonian, alabaster page. Now the words become a score. Like Duke's (we wish) to be lifted off the page, like a composition needing to be musicked, by the Djali, to fully live. "Performance" poetry, the dead people said, to claim a grandness, by inference, for the dead academic, earless, soul sold emptiness of that verse championed by the Beast who is a man! For the Beast loves only death. Only robbery and murder permits this Beast to live. And so all he teaches (Mr. 666) is death. And, replaces Goodness with dead paper and greed. The LPs take life and give it back live to the living. No matter those who will leave only "Gone with The Wind," McDonald's boxes and a reputation as a Beast!

Give Life to the Living, is what the LPs do. They remember themselves through *The Souls of Black Folks*, alive these many centuries, we are slow to anger. Our Art describes our past, the middle passage, Slavery, the struggle of the Afro American Nation! For Democracy, Self- Determinations and the destruction of national oppression and capitalism.

Abiodun and Umar are like a bubbling rhythms spoken out of what the streets themselves can hear. The '60s Black Arts movement, which sought and still seeks, to create a revolutionary, self reliant Art to transform ourselves, as a revolutionary culture, which at full strength and consciousness, will overthrow "White America" (the fascist media abstraction) like the Brown Bomber wasted Schmeling. Oh, yes — it's coming, sure as the world, not even by ourselves, but with all those willing to be human beings, no matter their nationality, it is their Ideology and Acts that define the living from the soon to be dead. "Whose side you're on," as my wife, Amina, says.

"I Rise In Fire"! Yes, it is a prophecy, The Black Bird is prophet against the Devil's profit. The Soul of Blackness sings, chants, even wiggles after a touchdown the ghosts couldn't stop.

The power of the Djali of the '60s, BAM, returns, Oh, Charlie, you hip thang, as Rap, old word, the beat on the wood. The "Log" in which we keep notes (Blue) on reality and history and who am we us i — was is and will be. The LPs are the prototype Rappers, The transmitters of the mass poetry style of the BA '60s, through the whatever of WA and ourselves inside wailing for light, with the hard rhythms of What Is brought into the Now. A Jazz linked Rhythm and Blues feeling the Rappers copped, form a direct connection with content (till the Dangs got in it)! The LPs speak, in the tradition, from Fred to Margaret to Trane, of our real lives. The beat, the feeling, form and content, come from there. From the here we hear and see. Our rising I. It is the Is Story. The seed. The scene. The seen and The On The Un. It is teaching, because it is true not just "propaganda," which could be a lie; Oh, Ali Baba of the Romes.

The LPs' "message" (Self-Wisdom) is Black, is the living history of our consciousness. And who is not "Black," as a historic confirmation of the truth of Civilization's origin, is from outside the Van Allen Belt. A Lien (e.g., the IRS). That humanity will prevail, and civilization begin. That the heinous crime of slavery and which, like the moth wasted by the flame, a teacher said, "You did it to yourself, Krishna!"

The LPs are in the tradition of Revolutionary Art for Cultural Revolution. The RAZOR. And certainly, Hey, Now, a lotta peepas know, "them Negroes carry razors." Or perhaps, for the LPs, their RAZOR is a RAISER, Revolutionary Art for Cultural Revolution. Oh, yes, Freedom is our aesthetic and social and political quest. "FREEDOM!" — we say. We think it is good, We think it is beautiful.

So the LPs sing and chant and speak to us — they say, "Ba, Ba, Black Sheep — You got the wool!" That's the "Mission" they on, and been on, to arm us with true self consciousness. They say, "come together to create life...love...to create create." They say we are..." afraid of revolution, mus' is, mus' aint dont sound right. Even up here in "hip" New York, "a disguised sin."

They say our minds are, "in a state of mental paralysis," "all the while our children are dying...all the while, a fucking ghost is killing us..." Yes, they say, now it is the Will, the fuel of the future. Who loves the world of animal cannibal is both and The LPs are remembering and recreating the science. Yet, like most of us they have to juug themselves and ourselves again and again to re-re-understand that it is a not a color or a religion or a nationality killing us, it is a social economic system, and our collaboration, conscious or un, that allows this humiliation and pain. Understanding, creating, recreating, remembering, the science, yes, the "magic words," actually, formulas, to waste you, Dr. Dracula.

So these are the chants of the creating of the New that comes twisting in struggle with the old. The rational mind of what is coming into existence, at war with what is going out of existence, and hence, irrational. Ah, such beauty, is a rhythm, a song. A formula of what is the science of Beast Killing. For who would slay the Beast must study and learn and understand and then be inspired by the fire of all that will live. For who cannot hate, cannot love...who cannot kill, cannot protect life! (to paraphrase the great Chinese Djali, Lu Shun).

In the tradition of democracy of revolution. In the spirit of Afro America. As creative rise in, who must create a new world, out of fire and like our Ptah Baby selves, rise again, with Art, existence created by consciousness and science. The greatest truth is that which exists always! Art that speaks for the people and to them, functional as lists of things to think and do, things you thought and hate to think about. They wants "Nigguhs" to stop bullshitting and hoping God is America, still disguised as the Devil. They urge us to be self conscious and dig The Beast in The West, and the Easternness and Africanness, the niggers up tight, hard as slavery, still maintains, Ask Rodney!

So they speak as outrage, as the persona of the hip the slick the knowledge speak, the nationalist, the Afro centric, the patriotic and militant traditional Bigger resistance type nigger. Like Sonny's Son (Bubadika's Lumumba) describes, "I'm the kina nigger you don never wanna meet!"

They speak to the necessity of united militant self as defiance, resistance, the magic of "will" as creative elaboration of the living. The Rappers have confirmed that the word is still the power of what it brings. And that our Art is a weapon of our struggle, as anyone's art also relays their minds and feelings, their vision and their direction. And if we understand that art and literary criticism are a form of class (hence, national) struggle, then we should understand that until the revolutionary artist create their own superstructure, their own organizations, networks, institutions, to criticize, encourage, distribute, and teach, we are in a razor fight without one. Say this to point out that the Word Music we make, Poetry-Jazz, Rap, &c., is a sharp weapon needing to be held in our own hands and kept sharp and pointed at the enemy (not our sisters and wives and mothers, &c.) It is time we rallied our troops and began the mobilization of the mouths and the hearts and the brains and the souls. For we must understand, what Fred D. and Mao TT meant when they said, "Find out the exact amount of injustice any people accept, and you will find out the exact amount of injustice they receive" and "Cast Aside Illusion, Prepare to Struggle!"

All these ferocious revolutionary wordships and Djali, we got, must be got together, you know. Let the Revolutionary Festivals and Conferences and Mobilizations of us, begin. Or re-begin. If the word is to be given, let us gather the revolutionaries of the word-music, the LP's, and Kain, Nelson, Luciano, Jayne Cortez her Firespitters, Amina and My Blue Ark, Sekou Sundiata, Gaston Neal, Linton Kwesi Johnson, Mutabaruka, Kalamu ya Salaam, Askia Toure, John Sinclair, Louis Rivera, Sonia, Haki, Little Willie K. from S.A. and Duma, Sterling P, yall know... Pedro Pietri, Sandra Esteves, Miguel and the Nuyoricans, Cheryl Byron, the young folks, Ras & Willie P, Tony M, all those who can run the revolutionary line with hot musicked words. The D.C. oralutionaries, they in LA and Chicago, New Orleans and St. Louis, the everywhere we is, they. I mean all who got the word on fire loaded in the mind and heart, with the soul of the sun, we children of Africa and Pan America, let us get the army together, and begin to create a superstructure, a mass mind of revolution. So, sampling Mao again, "Let A Hundred Flowers Bloom, Let A Hundred Schools of Thought Contend!" Yes, like the Charlie Bird sang, as we-us-i rose straight up, us tale on fire, smoking like blue laser gone, "Now's The Time! Now's The Time!" — we wailed, and the chorus — "I Rise In Fire!"
(3/1996)

Jimmy, The Church & The Spirit

The "Blood of The Lamb" was a sacrifice. Put forward, for us, most popularly in the doctored bible of the mulattoes fleeing from the south and coming up with a text to justify their invasions of other peoples' lands all the way to the north of Africa, under the jurisdiction of a newly reformed African invisible cult master, Jehovah, who, the more tradition bound would refer to only by the initial "G," so that nobody would think they also were substituting God for Good. Because God only shows where Good has been removed to guard against Bolsheviks.

The King James bible itself is a travesty as any scholar of religion and mythology can testify. The old testament, the mouthpiece for a tribe seeking to transform itself from slaves to masters having found out the magic word, civilization, This is important to our discussion, because Jimmy Baldwin discovered quite early, that not only was the bible a reference to the mythology of thieves and murderers, who later would shave and cut off all the hair so they could emerge as "Aryans" where before they had been known as Barbarians. (Barba means beard).

Second, Jimmy had discovered that the deepest and most truthful part of the text had no bearing on the conduct of those who trumpeted it the loudest. That not only had the text been stolen and doctored on (by the scribes, who were the propagandists for the usurers, who were the angels for the new church of the cleaned up barbarians, who were the Romans (that's how they copped, by Roman) Caesars (and that's what they did when they got there, seized every mfing thing in sight!)

Jimmy discovered this because he trusted his feelings about himself and his perception of the world. Even there in Harlem as a child minister, repressed by the will of his terrifying father, whom he loved so much he would not dare to emulate and fail and that was why he could not stand the sight of him.

Because Jimmy knew there was a world, a real world, beyond the text, beyond his father's terror, and beyond the truncated quasi unreality of Harlem and its attendant horrors. Jimmy was bookish, that was clear, but he was sensitive, in a way that made the bookishness an emotional necessity, to reference his feelings with something other than thin air.

Those eyes, my God, I stared into them when I was an undergraduate at Howard. And he there for the premiere of "The Amen Corner" (which a negro prof of mine sd set Black people back a hundred years with its flat speech!). But Negroes aside, Ted Shine and I lived in the same dormitory then, Owen Dodson was Master of the Howard Players, my English professor was named Sterling Brown, and Toni Morrison was the grass roots favorite to become The Kappa Queen.

I paint this detail because I was carrying it all, as it was carrying me. The play touched me as the cry of someone who was trying to tell me something else I yet didn't understand. But it was a cry from within a cramped space. Where the only solace was to lie that you wanted to be there and believe you needed to be there. And you must act and speak as if the lie was real and you were the only doubter present, if doubt from you could be peeped by the peepers. Jimmy didn't really register on me until I had skipped out of this amazing cultural incubator, which I then somehow linked to Jimmy's cry, like I was as cramped, My god, and then doltishly joined the Error Farce, where my frenzied acquaintance with literature was to be bombarded into me by the desperateness of my idiocy which had got me sitting out here under the naked sun trying to read the collected works of everybody.

Coming out of that joint, I saw Jimmy Baldwin for the first time, those eyes, like my own, staring me down, from a bookstore window. *Notes Of A Native Son.* I scoffed it down without a breath, turning back to the cover again and again, at the end of each essay, as if to assure myself that this was my man, this dude, this young black dude, like myself, who had such feelings and such articulation of them. The grace and flawless swoop of language, seamless, more sophisticated than I imagined one could be when telling the truth and with such passion it made my eyes water.

Jimmy's reference and metaphorical touching of religion is constant in his works. It is a touchstone of his, a measure, but one with a double edge. He uses it like we clip relevant articles from a newspaper, throwing the newspaper in the garbage. So that he had always quotes, phrases, understandings he had gleaned from the Bible. Relationships he had perceived and rationalized, which he used to clarify his own understanding of things. But at the same time, because he knew the moral dishonesty, nay absence of civilized measure and morality among the citizens, both in church and out, but particularly those who swore by the church and used the Bible like toilet paper, to clean out their nasty mouths, there was always a drollery that accompanied that usage. A split perception that slid along under the words.

Like David Walker, Jimmy had long understood, that if these people, these people who rule us, believe in God, it's definitely another God. Like Fred said, the worst slaveholders are the religious ones. Or the July 4, speech, where he fastens slavery to the white american church like a chain.

Dig this: (casual) "Though the church I come from and the church to which most white Americans belong are both Christian churches, their relationship, due to those pragmatic decisions concerning Property made by a Christian State sometime ago — cannot be said to involve, or suggest, the fellowship of Christians. We do not, therefore, share the same hope or speak the same language." (Intro, *The Price of the Ticket*.)

Or. this: (like Johnny Hodges on "Blood Count") "The Western world is located somewhere between the Statue of Liberty and the pillar of salt.

At the center of the European horror is their religion, a religion by which it is intended one be coerced, and in which no one believes, the proof being the Black/White conditions, or options, the horror into which the cowardly delusion of White supremacy seems to have transformed Africa, and the utterly intolerable nightmare of the American Dream. I speak with the authority of the grandson of a slave, issue of the bondswoman, Hagar's child. And what the slave — despised and rejected, "buked and scorned" — with the European's paranoid vision of human life was to alchemize it into a force that contained a human use. The Black preacher, since the church was the only Civilized institution that we were permitted — separately — to enter, was our first warrior, terrorist, or guerrilla. He said that freedom was real — that we were real. He told us that trouble don't last always. He told us that our children and our elders were sacred, when the Civilized were spitting on them, and hacking them to pieces, in the name of God, and in order to keep on making money. And, furthermore, we were not so much permitted to enter the church as corralled into it, as a means of rendering us docile and as a means of forcing us to corroborate the inscrutable will of God, who had decreed that we should be slaves forever.

"What a cowardly, not to say, despicable, vision of human life. What a dreadful concept of divinity" (*Evidence*, p. 82–3).

Jimmy tells us he went into the church to become something someone (his father, himself) could love. He wanted to submit to that love and be transformed by it. This submission was a kind of ecstasy of psychological release, for someone so obsessed with self doubt and menaced by others' perception, chiefly his father's and White Americans, that he had a hidden will which he would only reveal as the acceptance of Love. Jimmy did not love anything but what he wanted to love, which he did not yet understand, was himself and the world his self psychologically envisioned, a world where he could be himself, where he could be loved. A world he doubted really existed. His becoming a minister was an emotional dismissal of self doubt. He would love Jesus, and become Jesus' friend, but he would find religion at a church other than the one his father preached in, so that he might compete with his father, show him that he was of some value. And being a child preacher, a mystical miracle, he drew larger crowds than his father. But Jimmy came, very soon, to understand that the church itself, as it was constituted, and as it was used socially, was a game. And he began to think of himself as being one of the gamers. Gaming not only the people, but himself as well.

The most important part of the church, the only real and satisfying part of the church, for Jimmy, was its emotional content and drama. Check this from *The Fire Next Time*.

"The church was very exciting. It took a long time for me to disengage myself from this excitement, and on the blindest, most visceral level I never really have and never will. There is no music like that music, no drama like the drama of the saints rejoicing, the sinners moaning, the tambourines racing, and all those voices corning together and crying Holy unto the Lord. There is still, for me, no pathos quite like the pathos of those multicolored worn, somehow triumphant and transfigured faces, speaking from the depths of a visible, tangible, continuing despair of the goodness of the Lord. I have never seen anything to equal the fire and excitement that sometimes without warning, fill a church, causing the church as Leadbelly and so many others have testified to 'rock.' Nothing that has happened to me since equals the power and the glory that I sometimes felt when, in the middle of a sermon, I knew that I was somehow, by some miracle, really carrying, as they said, The Word — when the church and I were one."

Baldwin's literature and his countless lectures, especially the emotion filled charges to Black and White people, during the Civil Rights movement confirm this church bred word engendered passion. Jimmy's passion is what finally endears him to us, as it rushes out of the grandly constructed sermonic devices of his poetic. That is his impact, that he thrusts the truth at us with such deepness of emotion. He said again and again that he was "a witness" as the believers say. But his belief was in the prophecy of the truth, the meaning of reality.

Jimmy's elegance, his high aestheticism, is a remnant of this religious concern. So is his deeply cutting vision. Because his understanding that White America was neither genuinely religious, nor by any stretch of the imagination, Christian, allowed him to use the very words of the text in all his presentations, to beat the dog doo doo out of White America, and the Negroes and misguided whoever who valued it.

The religious hypocrisy was the same as the social hypocrisy. White America was no more democratic than it was religious. Black people were no more citizens than White Americans were Christians. So that in many critical points of the works, Baldwin would use the biblical text, as the "Amen," the shout of recognition, the "Yes, Lord!" of the witness, that what he had seen and felt was truth.

Baldwin said, "The spirit of the south is the spirit of America." He said this in his last great work, *Evidence of Things Not Seen*, a book he had to sue McGraw Hill to release once they had turned it down! For Jimmy, spirit was the animating reality of our living consciousness and relationship to the world. It was what made us human or not. His constant metaphor for the spirit of White America is menace, danger, murder, atrocity. His own work sought to evoke the spirit and truth of the excitement and drama of the church; From its high evocative word ship. It's altar, from whence the: "Word" would come, that high place, and so the grandness of Baldwin's written prosody was of speech made into text. So that the spirit of the written word conveys the moving life of the speaker.

One of the most important aspects of *Evidence's* style, form, is that in it, Baldwin is able to give us the motion of the peripatetic observer, observing the Atlanta horror, and its complexities, bearing witness to the individual and collective guilt of White America and its petty bourgeois Negro management class, with the precision and deftness of his own Jimmy self at some non cocktail non party where the squares hang on the walls like wallpaper waiting to be pasted.

The spirit of Jimmy's works is of a high moral prophetic vision. The Witness, who has been buked and scorned, like John The Revelator, digging the coming attractions on Patmos. The spirit of that grimly beautiful "Message to the Churches." What was grim, was what Jimmy spoke of when he said, that White America thinks that Black people's religious beliefs are childish. But that's the trick the grim payback. Because, as DuBois laid out in *Black Reconstruction*, suppose you really believed in all that, the old testament, the new testament. Suppose you believed one night you might meet the savior walking down the street. And you were that Blood and here was the Lamb who had promised to deliver you. My eyes have seen the glory of the coming of the Lord, he is trampling down the vintage where the grapes of wrath are stored. He has loosed the fateful lightning of his terrible swift sword. What that eternity of humming meant, even after the drum got took away! At the coming of the Lord, its gon be your ass, all you heathens, its gon be yo natural ass! This was, likewise, Jimmy's religion, and his spirit!
(6/1996)

Larry Neal & The Critical Word: National Black Arts Festival,
June 28-July 7, 1996

Larry Neal and I were fundamentally comrades in struggle. Those of you with even a surface familiarity with the Black Arts Movement know this. And I thought the world of Larry, he was my man, brilliant, militant and hip. In a lotta ways we were alike. We did want to overthrow white supremacy, we did think that our art, the statement of our fully conscious culture, could help do this. Larry was there when we came up with the phrase.

We were gathered in a meeting and someone said, after our all night peregrinations on how to destroy our national oppression, what Larry would call "The White Thing," they said, "What shall we call it?" This new word spun organization of artists and cultural workers we were setting up to organize ourselves for the struggle for self consciousness, self determination, self reliance and self defense, by any means of the Razor, Revolutionary Art for Cultural Revolution. And it swept into my head without a sound, "The Black Arts," I said. And it had meant the simpler construct when it came in, but when I heard it out in the world, all the other inferences began to come in. "The Black Arts." Wow. Not only the mobilization of Afro American artists to do battle with white supremacy, but the ancient magic tip tipped in as well, and I marveled at that, because surely that is what it was, not so much magic, but what Fred said when the master caught him learning to read. "What they hate, I love...and what I love, they hate!" Black arts had to be wizard

187

wrackes spooky ugly, cause hey, aint that what we always been here in White America.

After Malcolm's murder, we moved quickly up to Harlem. That had always been our fundamental plan, from the beginning. That was a central part of it. That we Black artists would move back to the Black Community, so that we could be part of the whole Black struggle for liberation. That we would be an organic and influencing part of it. Our art would move the revolution into being more quickly by raising the consciousness of our people!

But saying is always easier, you know, than the other thing. So, after the blinding fury that passed among us at Malcolm's assassination, by the next month (March 1965) many of our erstwhile brothers heads had cooled sufficiently, so they had changed their minds about moving uptown. One of my closest friends and 'poseta-be comrades even pulled a pistol on me to emphasize the fact he wasn't going any where!

Larry, of course, came up town. But he couldn't cut the mad environs the inside of the Arts quickly became. Especially two of the arch fakers from Umbra, whose sole gig seemed to be to intimidate and alienate the artists and the community and cause seamless disruption inside our fledgling operation. So, although Larry was always up there with us, my constant confidante and counselor, two bizarre nutty Negroes kept him out of the organizational mix. And this was not just idle rumination. One of these Negroes shot Larry in the leg a few days after I, myself, by the end of that furious year, had also split. In terms of Larry as critic, he was one of the finest, I think. Though, and this is the essence of this piece, as we both moved on to engage triple six in our diverse ways, where before we had been critically very close, there developed a space, a distance, a contradiction, never antagonistic, but it got more and more obvious.

To wit: we were Black Nationalists when we banded together as The Black Arts. Some new, some for a minute, some grown to consciousness in that ideological focus. Certainly, I was among the newest of the straight out nationalists, having been hooked up in the Village social scene since the late fifties. It was all the more stunning to a lot of people, then, that I, so obviously well integrated, like they say, would make such a move. For one thing, let me tell you, some people, Black and White have never forgiven me.

What we thought initially, i have stated, that we should and could use our art to attack our oppression and mobilize our people, raise their consciousness to intensify the struggle. We stated (and this is laid out more completely in a pamphlet called "The Black Arts Movement"). What we didn't understand completely is that we had to raise our own consciousness.

Because Black meant anything then to us. And under that rubric a hundred schools of thought did contend. But I had had, before, a left spin on my ideas, even ensconced in pig heaven. The ideas in *Home* will certainly verify this. Though, when The CPUSA, had come to me a couple years before this and asked me to be editor of their literary journal I had declined, not because I had some specific ideological conflicts (I did, of course, I didn't know exactly what they were). I had nixed it because the office was old and dusty, and wizened white dudes crept around, and this gave me the feeling I would be working for undertakers.

I say this, because Larry and I and Askia Toure, met as comrades in political struggle, initially. Not as artists. Askia and I on the skirmish line in front of the U.N. protesting Lumumba's assassination. Larry, along with Max Stanford, who were then both members of RAM, of which whispers spun around the different listening posts telling of their secrecy and militancy and organization. I learned, in a short time that RAM had set Askia, Larry and Max on me to help guide me and direct my energies in the direction RAM wanted them.

Larry's poetry was, for me, along with Askia's then, models of what the new Black poetry had to be. Askia, with his pulpit sermonic sweep and Larry with his dazzling bebop metaphor and rhythm. Both were using the feelings and rhythms inside our speech to open up our consciousness. To what it was, that surrounded us, and who it was that was surrounded.

Larry's early essays were like reinforcements on the front for me. Here was somebody who not only understood what I was doing, but was thinking and doing some things, I had to dig and arm myself with. Read "The Black Arts Movement" essay. Or "Shine Swam On" or the Richard Wright pieces. They take up the question of the meaning of nationalism to the Black Artist and the meaning of Black culture to the artist and the people and how can these be loaded in to the gun of our whole consciousness to blow all enemies away, even those inside our minds.

Of course, there were some things I didn't wholly dig, but they were minor, then. Larry's love of the music was particularly the thing that drew us closest. We were, together with A.B. Spellman, editors of the short-lived (3 issues) *The Cricket*. A little journal, named after Buddy Bolden's old New Orleans whisper sheet, which began to focus on the music with the love and seriousness we demanded. It will come again.

Larry's pieces in *Liberator* were also like mannah to me. Ammunition and reconnaissance in the struggle. Brilliance shining its light on our insides so we could dig it. We had put together *Black Fire*, the signal anthology of '60s Black Arts, Black Power, Afro American writing, as smoothly as we would bounce up and down with our eyes closed listening to Trane.

But as we became aware of our distancing from each other, such as it was, I don't think either one of us ever admitted this. I guess it was rooted first in the Black Arts organization itself. Larry could not dig getting inside there with the madmen and struggling with them to do the things. At first I thought this was some RAM orders. But then RAM leadership was thrown in to a shocking disorientation by some personal betrayals that saw Larry self-eject from the group, as I understand it, and the heads shot off in different directions. But the organization was a contradiction. Larry could not belong, RAM or not, because he did not think the hassles with nut 1 and nut 2 and the crumbs they had with them, were worth the effort. He thought that he could do his work, his writing, his thinking, without going through that. Probably Askia, thought that too. He was also under RAM's command.

But that is, as far as Larry was concerned, where I felt our paths began to diverge. I did think he should have been inside the Arts, fighting these lying neurotic Negroes with me. And they shot him because they figured his council was anti-them anyway, and they were right. Askia was similarly menaced by the same kind of vicious destroyers.

But it is the practice of organizing and the ideas that arise from the task itself that cannot come from the theoretical work alone. Our daily struggle to mount four shows of poetry, painting, music, and drama, and the logistical and administrational incredible snarl of that was a formidable doing that had to effect our thinking.

I knew, as Larry did also, that "Black" in and of itself could not sustain either practical or critical analysis. He knew this because even under the spray of opportunism, metaphysics and idiocy that could come out under the "Black" rubric, that first a viable ideology could not consist simply of "hating our enemy." As he said, in one of his essays, "Hate Whitey" cannot be the only plank of our ideological vessel.

We were both nationalists, but Larry began to see the flaws in nationalism from a socio-aesthetic perspective, and dialectically, that is where he sought to redefine it...My own nationalist trip was jarred from its naive altruism by the Negro destroyers and opportunists and traitors we encountered, from religious nuts to undercover police, all waving the Red, Black & Green. But after the Arts, when I returned to Newark, licking the wounds to my arrogance and my ideological confusion, the fact that we did begin then to concretely and practically organize not only a Black Arts Theater, The Spirit House, that traveled all over the country, spreading the word, but shortly thereafter, got deeply involved with community organizing from the grass roots level and political organizing which led to the formation of the Committee for Unified Newark and the Congress of African People. The election of Kenneth Gibson and the first Back majority city council and then to the Gary Convention and the mobilization of 8000 Afro Americans to begin to put together the permanent political entity that would be the organizational and institutional base for our struggle for democracy and self determination. Though Larry was always supportive, we even worked on the *Cricket* and *Black Fire*, during the earliest period. But it was Larry's refusal to consider organization, again, as the bottom line of political struggle, that drew us further apart.

I'm using myself as a measure, to get closer to the essence of our developing ideological differences. Larry, anybody who knew him. can tell you, was one of the cleanest Brothers I knew. And I likewise, always wanted to be in that number. That was, for us, part of the tradition. That was an aesthetic focus and insistence itself. As Aptheker told us about DuBois' historic sartorial splendor, he considered that part of the struggle itself! As if to say, yall wanta make believe Bloods is unkempt, &c., dig me. I never considered it in this way, to me it was what we had grown up knowing, and loving, the clean mf's we dug everyday, especially the ones playing the music or making the most sense where we were.

But this aesthetic regard was not casual for Larry. It was a part of his persona that ran into the ideological with a heavy impact. Not that I was any different, but there is a point at which emphasis becomes confirmation past knowing. Both Larry and I dismissed the Left, not only because we were Nationalists, but for me, certainly, it was part of the construct of my nationalism, that I had seen and been a part of the sad pageant of revisionist impotence. The CP was backing Roy Wilkins thru then and had even said that "the nationalism of Malcolm X is like the nationalism of the Ku Klux Klan." Which is not even Marxist, much less democratic. People like Harold Cruse actually taught in TBA and his *The Crisis of The Negro Intellectual* was general reading for us. The constant and historic criticism of the CP and the white left in general we had grown up with, not only from Black people but from whites as well, whether Trots, failed Marxists, Wright, Ellison, Baldwin and the bohemian fringe of anarchy that used that tired saw as a legitimization of their own bourgeois penchants.

We dismissed the left as a matter of course, the "white left" we said, to make it plainer. Larry and I associated the white left not only with the CP but with the rigid chauvinistic 19th century quasi-liberal racism and corny social realist aesthetic all the U.S. "Moderns" had railed against. Though what we actually knew, how much or how deeply we had investigated, is questionable. Certainly, in my case!

And it was this "white Left" admittedly, even from a theoretical Marxist Leninist position that was backward, chauvinist and opportunist. They were revisionists. We were correct in one sense, but not for the reasons we thought. But the proclaimed doctrines they claimed they represented and aggressively ran us and a bunch of other young people away from, even today, had more truth than we would deal with And that is a critical point.

Because Marxism does begin its analysis with material social life and emphasizes class and class struggle, even for some while betraying all in practice, many younger Black activists and intellectuals dismissed that aspect of struggle as "outdated," "hypocritical." We knew white people were evil, even the political ones. Lying liberals at best, so we ditched, before we came close enough to understanding, the important truths the authentic teachings carried.

Larry's analysis of Wright's "A Blue Print For Negro

Writing," emphasized Wright's empathy for Black nationalism and his urging of Black writers to come to grips with the nationalistic aspect of Afro American thought, as a legitimate weapon in the struggle. Wright's ejection and rejection of the CP seemed to confirm all this. (*American Hunger*, the publishers made sure not to bring out until 1977, thirty-two years after *Black Boy*, so fewer people would understand the actual conditions and ideological and political context of Wright's well publicized split with the CP. Or understand his assumption then of a kind of professional anti communism, *The God That Failed*), which was actually in tune with a whole petty bourgeois bail out from revolutionary struggle, when it got too hot in the kitchen. Wright's *The Outsider*, should confirm the utter wackiness of both his ideological and social Me Culpa for his entrance into anti communist "existentialism."

Both Baldwin and Ellison seem to confirm this. Both even putting Wright down for his writing of "tracts" and "protest literature" and the function of the CP as a censor to the creative imagination. Ellison from an aesthetic point of view, Baldwin (who was briefly a Trot) from a more socially oriented psychological stance, but still dismissing.

If the whole basis for material social analysis and socially conscious art, was thrown out as the gibberish of white folks, and we had already gotten hip, to some degree, to the utter naiveté of uncritical embrace of "Blackness," then where did that leave us?

For me, it meant that I would plunge, for a time, deeper into cultural nationalism, still trying to find an authenticity in a specific ideological trend of Black nationalism that I could see as more solidly theoretically based, better organized, and about the work of organizing the people, in reality. This led to the Kawaida doctrine of Maulana Karenga, whose doctrine included a treatise on Art, as functional and a weapon in the struggle (some of which, I later found out he had gotten from *Home*.)

The difference was that we were struggling for liberation, we began as militants, as comrades to the Black Panther leadership. And we perceived after a time, that even the emphasis on Africa, which made the Kawaida/Us line more attractive to the youth who now wanted to celebrate, politically and economically support, but wholly identify Africa as the most revolutionary aspect of our concerns.

The political organizing we did in Newark, and nationally

was to overthrow the U.S. system of white supremacy, and as we worked and studied, national oppression and monopoly capitalism/imperialism. We were, by self definition, political at base, not cultural. And certainly not in the patently atavistic way that Kawaida legitimatized.

The basis of our struggle, The Afro American people, was political, the culture itself was shaped by its political and economic base. If we did not focus on the material structure of the society, and seek to transform it, nothing else we did would have real meaning.

Larry could not accept the specific identification of Marxism, yet, like many intellectuals, utilized a line that does not conflict with the class and international nature of Black national oppression. They also cannot come to terms with the question of capitalism directly, not only because of the nationalist bias against "the white left," but because fundamentally they believe that what exists can be reformed, by whatever means, without destroying it totally.

Larry's motion began to consolidate a cultural nationalism based on a reformed relationship to the ruling class. Ellison was reconsidered because Larry thought him correct on withdrawing from the twin political blocks to the creative artistic and intellectual sensibility. Everything was "New," in that sense, since "everything" had been proved inadequate.

Ellison's line that he was more interested in a writers style than his politics, and that no solution to the Afro American question could arise from a "narrow" focus and analysis based on the repressive attention to material social life and the politics of whatever group that considered it. *The Outsider*, like *Invisible Man*, Wright, like Ellison after him, kills both the communist and the fascist, and says he can not tell them apart. Ellison scorches the Brotherhood (the CP) and the nationalists (Ras the Destroyer) and opts for individual freedom and consciousness as a critical requirement for human development and for Black confirmation and strengthening of our ties as Americans struggling to and fit to be a part of the U.S., our inclusion being the major change. But Black people could be integrated, theoretically into The U.S. society, and it would still need overthrowing, since the monopoly capitalist base makes national and international exploitation, and national oppression absolutely necessary for its development.

Ellison substituted mythology and psychology for ideology and politics and the material social conditions of their existence.

This was not unique in 1950's U.S. bourgeois literature. The whole basis of the "New Criticism" and the Southern Agrarian movement was to remove literature (art, intelligence) from any connection with the material social life of the society. "A poem should not mean but be!"

Ellison attacked my *Blues People* as so politically hyped "it would give the blues the blues. "Larry did not agree with this, as his "Zoot Suit" essay states, but he did think that Ellison wanted to write *Blues People* and was drugged that he didn't, I guess, first!

But that is not the question, the issue is that Ellison could not have written *Blues People*, because he did not think the art related to material social life and history. He urged us to seek myth and deal with the psychology of Black people. But that's what I was trying to do, projecting these from the actual life and history of the people. Where do Ideas Come From? Mao asked. From material social life. The psychology and mythology are the result of being alive, not the reverse!

Larry embraced Ellison's alternative to social analysis, as part of his, now much more emphasized, views on spirituality. He chastised the Black Nationalists for criticizing and attacking Christianity and the Church when we didn't have a spiritual alternative.

But spirit is product of real life, not the reverse. Things have an essence, an aura, a life pattern, and this characterizes what they are, materially, in many ways we do not yet even perceive. Again, to remove the real political lives of the people is to have no clue as to what their spiritual condition is. People make music not the reverse. Art is the sensuous manifestation of spirit, as it is mind and ideology.

Larry moved toward a line that exalted the spiritual aspect of Black Art over its practical material raison d'etre. So that art became a "free floating" spirit looking for the correct form to manifest in, collectively and individually. Albert Murray's *Omni America*, which in the overview, has many truths, is at base, aimed not at overthrowing "White America" but claiming a place in it. Further, Murray's emphasis on style exposes his continued bourgeois euro-chauvinistic slant. Where Black people themselves are only a "style" of America, asking to be acknowledged. After all, "we read and dig and appreciate the same things." (This is the undergrowth of Ellison and Murray and their fat blue devil,

Crouch). Ellison and Murray can positively nauseate you with their paeans to the greatness of Euro socio aesthetic and charge to us to be equal to it. Hey, we're hip enough to do it. Duke Ellington is our Picasso, says Crouch! (Does you really believe Picasso is as hip as the Duke of Afro America, Stanley. I'll begin with *Transbluesency*) Murray and Ellison, actually reintroduce the European measure as a reference to style. Larry cannot go all the way over there, consciously, he could not countenance some outright "backsliding," but. he could take the logo of the argument and incorporate it as the practical element of spirituality, i.e. style.

So even as Capt Fuller, the 1st Negro officer in the concentration camp, you would still be your hip Black self. Shit, I dress better than them mfs. They be listening to Dave Brubeck, dig that.

Larry had grown, by this time, absolutely cynical about the political integrity or intellectual and ideological seriousness of "the movement." But style was an element of individualism that still linked him, individually, and as a cultural nationalist. Somewhat like the cultural autonomy sector of the Russian social democratic united front that called for cultural autonomy, but we leave the running of the state to the Czar. Both Murray and Ellison could fit into this, with their emphasis of style over content, and intellectual and social integration into the beast's canon (which, where we lives, becomes a cannon)! Crouch in his "The Half Turn of Larry Neal," celebrates Larry's sliding away from Black Nationalism, dismissing the entire Black Liberation Movement as embarrassing charlatans. That's why he now has gotten a "genius award" and is a consultant at Lincoln Center and a regular on *Sixty Minutes*. Larry did not ever become what Stanley is, a comprador. A seller of the people. Stanley's essay slurps with this poison desire. But what they had, at last, in common was the dismissal of the political for the individual proof of capacity to qualify to be a part of this society. Larry was not going to do that completely on their terms. Stanley is their terms.

So it is the distinction between the Black national bourgeoisie and the comprador. In Stanley's case, he is a tender of the various tables and gates for yo boy. Larry, was in DC as a commissioner of the arts, and in that Black city, still to Black people.

Larry's dismissal of the political aspects of the struggle as inane and vulgar and a refusal to understand the spiritual focus of social development, meant that he could only carry the nationalist

fuse as militance, and an aesthetic declaration which was its practical form. The culture the art could be used to transform society. How? To make people conscious of the spiritual, the highest aspect of humanity. But style and form are linked to the real world, as specific expressions of it. The question of self determination for the Black Arts, which can only be achieved through political mobilization and organization, was let slide by attention to the psychological, the mythological, and the style or form. Which is where them other folks came from in the first place. Form over Content. No, Stanley, Larry was not a comprador, I'm glad you understood. But the $$$ line of the Black Bourgeois always leads to a stone wall. And it is at the base of that wall, that collaboration often begins. Crouch ran into that wall a while ago.
(6/1996)

The Language of Defiance

The language of defiance of the oppressed Afro American Nation today is referenced to our history, experience and the totality of our cultural storehouse, i.e., collective, the whole gestalt of individual variation and summation of where we been, what we seen, heard, was told, used to know, &c. This defiance began as "simple" contradiction, meaning it was not the same. The north and the south of the world, except, as I have laid out, was a million years or so when there could not be that contradiction, since the two was not yet here, and was the one, that always splits into two. Why? Because the dimension of reality is created by being composed of opposites, no up without down, no hot without cold, &c. Is and Ain't was that first contradiction. But the breakup of the world, the opposites, as rendered by the masks of drama, tell the story. The smile at the bottom of the world, the frown at the top. The Africans wanted to "get happy" as part of their word ship, to get possessed with the spirit of everything, the all. This was the good spell, the trans (cross over into) the "promise land" a vision not a colony, like on a spiritual return, not an imperialist invasion, but if you look at the old testament objectively, you'll see things ain't changed much.

The Europeans, all you college causalities can tell us, say, after Aristotle, the thief and plagiarist, that Tragedy is the highest form of human experience. Like the contradiction between the Egyptian Pyramid, "the angle of success" and the Square, which they said was the "angle of failure." The language is full of these kinds of contradictions from its inception. So that we were in contradiction, not antagonistically, from the beginning of our coexistence on the planet. Look at the Encyclopedia Britannica's most recent edition, and you will find that they still do not understand the "purpose" of the smile or laughter. They define it as of unknown usage, and as a set of physical responses.

Our speech continues from the ancient cultures without our conscious intervention. So we speak of Squares, and their walking buddies we called Lames, even before we knew that the 1st Crazy Eddie, was Eddie Pus. The spirit cannot descend without song is the ancient African charge linking worship with music. Since music is the thought made manifest, the self of thought.

I'm speaking of culture, that store house, that where house, tell where you coming from, likely where you going. Blue was our favorite color in West Africa, Equiano tells us, then when we blew, let the kings we still talk crazy about, sell our behind and our a-hind to the ghost, for a mess of pottage, that middle passage changed what Blue meant to us, just as our lives as chattel slaves would change our relationship to everything and everyone and ourselves. So that Blues becomes sadness, a strained mood of loss, like we say, You Blew, my man, that's why you so blue. Our associations follow us even though material social life shifts and twists our previous relationships.

The Greeks deprecated the Africans because they smiled so much. But this is simple enough if we refer to the geo-aesthetic representation the masks of drama make. Our geography and the social life inherent to that made us different from jump. Plus, Africans, we is a very old ass group. Slow to anger. Still believing in Good when these other folks say God, and mean an idol, a lifeless statue or paper statute, like you a citizen dejure but defacto you can get your church burned down smiling and practicing the Golden Rule.

Africans were socialized around the Arts, "We are a nation of poets and musicians," sd Equiano. Like Americans, in these sweat suits, are socialized around sports...(even if they can't play). The wordship was connected to music, to bring the spirit, the living breath of the world, into us, to possess us with the all, so, like Trane and Sun Ra, we could go out! Bird was Bird, because for Black people, the bird has always represented the human headed soul. Hammett's "Black Bird" is The Phoenix, who catch afire every hundred years or so. And rise up with his behind flaming nuclear, screaming, "I Rise In Fire!" (You need to repeat that, so people will remember who we is, and who they is....) "I Rise In Fire!" Like J.B., Baldwin not Brown sd, "The Fire Next Time!

So that the passion that ensued from the wordship, the good spell, where we got on "the good foot," the "frenzy" the young DuBois called it, is not incidental to our rituals, but the point. Integration even got white Rockers imitating old Black ladies Sunday morning swoop into the heaven of pure revelation.

Slavery, of course, made the natural contradiction of our social and aesthetic perception, antagonistic. We was different to begin with. But slavery made us enemies. So Fred's "They hate what we love, we hate what they love." It is antagonistic when the actual material life carried out that is confirmed by this socio-aesthetic contradiction is a relationship based on exploitation and oppression.

Cabral said that finally the people and their culture are the repository of resistance. Because imperialism swallows our lives and our history, our registered experience. Tonto's history is in The Lone Ranger's saddle bag. And will be there until Mr T. cut the masked man throat.

The mistake I made in *Blues People* was talking about African Survivals as if they were the exclusive province of The Afro American people. But the whole of the western hemisphere, the real "Western world" is a composite of African, European and Asian (Native). If you of that people and that culture, you carry all three. The great majority of working people of any color or historic national character don't listen to European music, or deal regularly with European culture. This is a fake out the U.S. rulers use to continue their national mostly brown, more no (like Malcolm was called "moriney") and speak Latino Spanish. They are about as "Hispanic" as the Afro American people are English.

The contradictions of social life, philosophy and aesthetics, we brought here are violently exacerbated by slavery. The Americans from Europe become white we become slaves, Negroes, of which there are still a bunch running around loose babbling about the U.S. being a democracy. The language of the Afro American people carries our history and the information we need to understand this Hell's capital we are enslaved in. For instance, even the word "Dis" which you might disremember as the Rapper's innovation is old and pre biblical. Dis is the capital of Hades. And Hades, dig it, those who are bereft, who have lost. All our language speaks as resistance since, again Cabral, as long as we are where we are, an oppressed nation, super exploited, suffering the added torture of racism (persecution because of physical characteristics) and for B lack working women and women of color, a triple oppression, by means of nationality, class and gender.

The language, like they say about that spaghetti sauce, got it all in there, and the contrast with our enemies is constant and obvious, though they cop whatever we do, since we do not have the focused consciousness to do for our selves and create the organizations and institutions and networks and cooperative entities for self consciousness, self determination, self reliance and self defense. We are the oldest artists in the world. Wherever we are in the world, this is obvious. Yet our disconnected consciousness of individual American slaves leaves us destitute, even though Michael Jackson sells 93 million copies of his album, Mike — don't touch that girl — T is the sultan of knock out, Michael of Jordan the Prince of Air, without the Afro American U.S., Western hemispheric, world culture would be unrecognizable. You say "uptight" the president got it in his mouth by the weekend. You re re re create rap (the 1st ngomas beating on the log, the log the sailors keep to check on where they was &c., did just that, rap, speak. That's why the slave masters took the drum away cause we was rapping to each other after hours). Tell me did the Slave masters remove the drum for political or aesthetic reasons? I remember this crouching Negro whispering something to his boss...oh well...American language like American culture is a composite, emphasized according to class. But because of the still 90 percent segregated condition of the Afro American people, much of our national character persists. Like the music of Americans who ain't allowed in it.

The Europe thing is brainwash for college students. So they learn about European literature, philosophy, culture, as part of the filthy blasphemy of white supremacy. If they so supreme, why is the world so fucked up? Listen to the language, it resists because our denigration (what?) persists. We say "Bad" which means clean, literally. But baths came to Europe later, and were considered an evil practice. Evil we know as the reverse of live. Who does nothing, i.e., who is idle, is rich. They have programs like "Escape with The Rich & The Famous" because they want you to worship the Idol worshippers. We say "Terrible" from it's original meaning, inspiring terror, like awful, inspiring Awe, Corny, on the other hand. How did prophet get to be profit, or soul from sol to sole or sold. Who believes that the man, Adam, whose name itself, means he was added on, came before the woman, Eve. Everybody come out the womb. That's who m b!. Why would paradise (metaphysics or fake speech?) be called Having, oh, you meant haven. Why is God in German Gott? Or Good Gut? Why are the Vandals called that? Why are the Anglos Saxons (Sackers). Why did the original symbol of christianity, the fish get changed to the weapon of execution the empire used to eliminate slaves? Why is the day of Christ's murder called "good Friday"? Who made his betrayer, Peter, the Father of the Church? Who put out the lie that Paul was an Apostle? What does Judeo-Christian mean if the money lending collaborators with Rome betrayed Christ and The Romans (the so called new Christians) killed him?

Why do you believe "Confession" was not a state program to suppress rebellion? Why does their so called trinity have no women? Why is "God" an adulterer? Why are the holy women of the church called Nuns? Why are the committed soldiers of Christ called Monks?

Our speech, carries our whole existence. We say Jazz, for Jism, because our music was creative, spontaneous, improvised. If we know who Ja is, digging Marley and know the double z is the symbol for Shango, then how come we don't understand that Jazz is saying like Jesse, which means the same thing, Je suis, I Am, and that's what the music is called. I AM. that I AM. If we know that Eve means before, and night is Black, and that the clitoris becomes the navel chord, and music, the soul's music, like the sun's rays.

We get down, like in the Congo, touching our alma mater, the earth, the terra, to rise, go out. Our city of ON was directly under the measured track of the Sun, so we would dig by understanding. My sister and I used to love our grandmother so much when she spoke, because that was some other speech. Like DuBois sd about his Zulu grandmother singing, "Do Bana Coba, Beneme Beneme" i.e., to the tune of "You can shake it to the East, and shake it to the West, but you know which one is the best." It reached beyond us into the was, so we could be wholly here. (*Nothing Missing*)

Scat and BeBop language always impressed me as Black people trying to reunderstand their ancient tongues. Speaking in tongues, what tongue? What the past laid on you, interpreted in the now. Cool is still contemporary and it had the same meaning in the

Congo. Just like "getting down." Our struggle for liberation is found in our songs and dances, our stories, our labor and our spirit. These, the Gifts of Black Folk, Rap is as old as the African speaking with rhythm, beating on a log. We were Shine from way back, in fact, The Djali (not the Griot, a French word) was called The Gleeman. That's why we shine. Like Louis said, Just because my hair is curly, just because my teeth are pearly, just because I wear a smile on my face all the time, that's why they call me Shine. The Gleeman. To go up, the smile, not get dragged, which is why we say, "that's a drag," the casual meaning of tragedy.

We are different peoples shaped by different material reality. We have never been citizens. The U.S. has never been a democracy. They be calling us monkeys, apes, &c., but Lucy was human #1, and I ain't seen no great humanity coming out of Europe or the Imperialist white supremacy of the U.S. But dig, it was the Monkey, who broke his front feet leaping up in a tree to get away from the lower animals. And with this broke foot he made a hand, and when he dug he was safe he started talking much shit. In fact, he would throw it on em if they got too out.

It was at this point that the animal sounds were differentiated, at the same point the hand developed with the opposing thumb, which allowed for the making of tools. That's when we became the Signifying Monkey. The key to man. Hey, man! we say. Why, cause that's what we dug we was, Mtu, the Ptah baby, Black as Ptah.

Our language rests on image, sound, meaning and metaphor. Just as we could speak through the drum because of the significance of tones. A cymbal was a hard leaf. We was communists when we got here, then them apes got more stuff than everybody bit they mama in the neck and made the sisters slaves.

But the language of the world has its roots in Africa, the differentiation time place and condition. When the Rappers say "Word," it is old. That was the beginning of the human world, word, as opposed to cries. We is Djali not town criers (griots), we create Djeli ya, like Mr. B, Djeli, Djeli, Djeli....drove my mother crazy made my old man blind. Djeli Roll Morton told me he created jazz in one afternoon. We say Jam, from Jamaa, the family. We say cook, smoke, dig, (under stand) get down, investigate. We are underneath what you see, and come back into sight purple and indigo and blue.

Like Max sd the Hermosa All Stars were talking about Pop,

they meant Paul Whiteman not Louis Armstrong. Our Duke is Ellington not John Wayne. Our Divine One is Sarah Vaughan not Bette Midler. Most of the meanings of Black in American are negative, you know, blackmail, blackmagic, black Tuesday, blackguard, black heart, kinky, niggardly, Clearly political and social. They had a term they claimed scientific in the 19th century, called, Draptomania, where we would drop the tools and split, We didn't want freedom we were just feverish with illness. (I'm sure a crouching house nigra told the boss that for an extra pig foot!) So much of American speech, and what passes as American rationality and logic is irrational and crazy. Like The Bell Curve. Like disconnecting economic conditions from crime. Like calling the U.S. a democracy, when there ain't never been none. Like talking about the good old days, when was that? Langston sd, America never been America to me.

And in Fred's July 4th speech is contained, the prosody, the rhythm, the tonal variation and emphasis, the metaphor, the grand sermonic sweep, that incorporated all the language Americans knew and some they didn't because of the different actual experience and the method by which that had to be and was historically told. Only Melville approaches the dramatic poetic of Douglass in the 19th century, but some of his bite is symbolic and articulates the inherent censorship of the society. Douglass is straight out preaching and quotes from his work are more alive today, in the context of this society, than mighty Shakespeare.

Our language is of resistance because we are. If we did not we would perish. What we produce as art, for instance, must constantly be renovated and reformed, for the same reason the escaping slaves had to move from place to place, very quickly. So Rap will soon go through changes because triple six corporations have coopted much of it to make it attack dogs on Black life. The very meaning of your life is saddled like a mule for work, to make the idle profit. Whatever you say is copped. Whatever you do is seized or coopted. We outta here was coming out of Clinton's mouth by the weekend. Like "We Shall Overcome" came out of Lyndon Johnson's and "Power to the People" came out of Nixon's.

You create New Orleans collective improvisation, triple six comes up with "Dixieland," which he immediately uses to "cover" us. That's what Dis/Cover means, to cover you with Dis. Joe Turner opens his mouth and it comes out in Elvis Presley's bank account.

He is the King.....(poem).* Like Whitman was the King of Jazz. Goodman the King of Swing. Like Fred Astaire is the King of the African dance known as tap. You come up with it, they will cop in a few days because of the powerful productive forces, so you have to switch up for it to maintain any meaning. *(In the Funk world if Elvis Presley is king, who is James Brown/God?)

When they found out they had to appropriate our poetic, they called it Language Poetry, then Performance Poetry, as if dead style was classic. They found out about poetry and jazz so it is new, when that is what Djeli ya has always been. Drama and poetry were always constructed of music and dance, it is only the northern cradle that lost this.

Finally, our speech is defiant because it is direct. It must be. The Americans like the Victorian colonialists, must use a language that is everyday less direct, less instructive and more abstract, because everyday they have so much to hide. That's why the Victorian literature is so unreadable, hung and dried with an ornament meant to disguise. Like Disinformation. They tell us Downsizing when we know they mean layoffs. They talk about the national debt when we know they are stealing. They call white players intelligent, ourselves, natural, we know they are beating their chest Tarzan style.

Today, more and more American books purporting scholarship, science, research or seriousness are asinine and dishonest. But then look at the movie industry, the television industry, the publishing industry, the art galleries, and tell me what is serious or even relevant there. American speech is like American newspapers, all the news fit to print. You mean all the news that will not expose your historic criminality.

If we seek merely to tell our story it is "too political," if we even show photographs of our neighborhoods, it is social protest. The recounting of our history, like the Godfather said in the flick, has to "blame some of the people in the room," and they do not dig it. How can the native people be "Indian givers" and these imperialists took their whole land. They blame scalping on the Indians when it was the Americans who started it and became famous for it.

Our language seeks truth, because only truth will set us free. The obvious contradiction with the sorry, slave, colonial, so called Euro-White Canon, which is really a cannon to destroy the truth of the world, is simply a prescription of what we need to think so imperialism can survive. Today, many of the buppies, and neocon Negroes can get over, because they speak with the word of the rulers, and as such are their mercenaries of class and national oppression. This is how you see the sharpness of class struggle rising even among the Afro American nation. Bunches of dishonest whores and colored gun bearers can get over preaching that art has no relationship to reality and the world — that thought is only just, if it blames us for the devil's evil.

We said, tell it like it is. And that is a serious weapon. But we cannot hope to launch it from triple six's war room. We must create our own cooperative networks of institutions and organizations. We must speak as an oppressed nation, allied with the exploited classes of this society and the world. We must speak as outraged slaves, determined to be free, determined to liberate ourselves. Don't worry, it will swing, it will still be hip, you can still dance to it. Like Martha and them said, you be dancing in the streets!

NBAF '96

Rhythm

Rhythm is the natural motion of matter. What exists is presented to us by our sense organs. Though, the very understanding of just what sense organs exist, is still only primitively partial. Physically, for instance, cannot be defined simply as a known paradigm, if we understand dialectical materialism. The contrasting motions of matter, the continuous development as change, understood, perceived, by us, (any thing — Consciously) cannot limit what actually exists. Our knowledge limits us, not what exists.

Our approach to truth is always partial, advancing in stages (some regard as "Gaps"). Motion is and isn't what is moving. Yet the oneness of matter exists because of its twoness, which is motion. A thing is it and not it at the same time, (i.e., it is what it is and what it is becoming) as a property of motion. The present is a connector of the past and future. Yet it is more transient than either, but always remains what exists. What exists as "truth" is also matter in motion and also a reflection of that Being (process) where ever it is expressed, as what it means.

African Religion sought to discover the human relationship to what exists always by "tuning" in to it, and becoming, at whatever level, at one, cognoscente, conscious, "with knowing," be possessed, by it, as the direct expression of the whole, and as a direct experience. This is the "Holiness" (Whole/ness, at/one) the revelation.

The Joy that animates The African, "the laughter at the

bottom of the world," because Ecstasy is the motion, the livingness of the motion. Jazz is literally I AM! (JAIS!). The IS NESS of AM. 1, I, Aye, Eye, Si, IS - ING (I SING). Conscious Come! Creating The Semen of Consciousness, JISM'S mind. The G, sensuous life. With the circle, existence as motion, energy. GO. To be it must be dialectical as well, which is its expression as Dimension. GO-OD. Like BE-AT, it is expressed as rhythm—matter in motion. What is "dead," non-existent, the lie, delusion, is irrational. Reality cannot "die"—What R(AM) I.

Consciousness is degree, stage, motion, speed, intensity. So Rhythm, From the meaning of the alphabet signs themselves, Exist-Develop(Build/Bild—Ger. = picture, image)—Split (Quest, mitosis or Elegba, the cross roads-Rests at-Builds-Moves.

The composite rhythm of everything is everywhere. The whole life, (Time Place & Condition) shapes the rhythm, the where you be at (Bloods say). And it is a physical/mental construct. Finally it is deeper, because it goes deeper. Will grow deeper, i.e., the perception of the finest(?) particular (of a) rhythm accesses properties in the perceiver (or confirms them). Rhythm's infinite "circles" of transformation, in modes and forms and directions we do not even know exist.

The whole of what we, as matter in motion, are, in whatever degree of particularity, are connected as part of "Nature's" rhythm. It is entirely possible to "trace" all the whatevers of whatever as specific (compound complex) network of sense, at whatever level, able to be understood by it's rhythm (or its sound, smell, &c.)What the physical, social, &c., reality of the world is, we are part of, as matter, as rhythm. Our closeness, our distance, our awareness—the heart speeds up, in relation to what? Color is the same reference. Number, Letter, Sign, Symbol or Cymbal. The actuality of our total objective relationship to whatever forms of motion and mode matter we are and in and part of is us.

Africans used rhythm to speak and sing, to dance, to communicate over long distances with each other and to the forces of the universe. This ancient grasp of rhythm's relationship to everything is a feature of the "Primitive Communist" (Engels) social organization of that epoch. The Call & Response, Preacher to Congregation forms call spirit through rhythm, enforced as dance and song, as music, the drum, the voices, the flutes and whistles, rattles, balaphones, choruses, athletes, poets, actors, calls the spirit and from the place of our regular selves we are moved, until we rise to "frenzy" DuBois called it (*Souls of Black Folk*).

We rise like the Black Bird (BA, The Phoenix, The Soul). We reach for intuitive meaning and understanding of Existence, of what exists forever! Which is the ultimate Goodness. Like a temperature rising, the possession by and as the spirit (that hot breath...lives "before" with "after" us as us in us in whatever form "continues." (Who thinks this is 1996 is The Johnny-Come-Lately of Civilization). The "Going Out," the Trance, Trans, Cross into another consciousness. Go inside the Known outside the seen. This is the spiritual form. To know the Beyond!

"Divine" means to know the future, not "GOD." The degeneration of the ancient religion into Deism, reaches its extreme with Egypt and the Pharaohs becoming "God," though not apparently Good. The creation of God must coincide with the ending of the communal societies and the emergence of slavery.

Awareness, i.e., the degree of Consciousness, is a sensitivity to what exists. The rhythms of Africa are so deep a human characteristic, as history and presence and one aspect of the Black aesthetic anywhere. Five hundred years of African slavery yet their rhythms dominate most of the world, even while its creators are in chains. One reason, because the ancient drum so basically replicates our hearts and the changes everything it goes through. Day Night-Good Bad-Wet Dry-Past Present Future, the endless beat of breath and life.

Using rhythm and vocal verbal tonal expressions, as MUSIC (you could DANCE!), but as a technology of communication! So the political opposition to the drum in the U.S. and Western slave kingdoms. It was Seized! Censored! So is the European minimalization of the drum political or aesthetic? The communication of the drum was political and musical. By its conception. So the aesthetic functionalism as emotional expression of consciousness. Djali (Griot). History its Poetry-Music. The rhythms of the African are alive, living as part of the world. Not removed as "ART" in the bourgeois Western sense, though Art it certainly is. But not alienated from the pulse of the greater mass world. Not exclusive, now abstract, not as design or utilitarian, but as recondite predicated on willful obscurity. Reducing "understanding" to the bio-subjective arbitrariness of "The Pose" of distance, from real life!

What is expressed from the old communist reflection of the

connected world of essence and effect. The masks of the theater outline as geography and aesthetic, the South & the North, the Woman & the Man, Hot Cold, Valley Mountain, Smile Frown. One noted Greek philosopher spoke of his disgust with the constantly "smiling Africans." They laugh too much. So in slavery, this feature is turned into an expression of ignorance. So too, the dancing and singing that have registered the history of the human world.

The geo-climatic character of Africa, its natural richness, was especially suited to support the "natural economy" of the early Communist cultures. The communal nature of the southern culture, as a result of the relative ease with which the natural economy supplied most needs, could be maintained for a long period. This is in sharp contrast to the frozen inhospitable unproductive north, which likewise put an indelible stamp on the cultures that came out of there.

The Afro American use of African rhythm is obvious, but finally more "integrated" with European musical conventions than most of the other African based musics of the world. (Except the creation of Rock & Roll, the "slavemaster" of Black White social Slave/Master relations!) The Afro American drum is a machine, "The Set." It is an industrial product, as reflection of U.S. industrial capitalist culture. "The Set" is descended, says Max Roach, from the "One Man Bands" that arose after the Civil War. The singer performer covered with a snarl of instruments, some of his own invention — bells, cymbals, whistles, horns, drums, wood blocks, might have a harmonica in a hookup on a bass drum, sumpin might have wheels on it.

The reintroduction of the word into the very body of the music will come again. It is the very levels of the advanced corporate imperialist social economic technology that are and will be absorbed into the speech and rhythm of the Afro American use and response to the rhythm of time, place and condition.

Rhythm is in the essence of what exists and we are expressions of rhythm as are described by our lives (t,p,c). The Afro American flows from Africa to cross where and become themselves or that experience dissociated from the African past. Yet that passage is an historic documented rhythm. The speech of real life expressed like the heart does, from the life the heart keeps alive.

All life is rhythm in that sense and expressed, registered as such. Afro American rhythm is African West as slave and victim, as pre and post U.S.; American and to that extent individualistic, yet Eastern and Collective, Communistic. Existential as Improvised and Spontaneous. Experimental and deeply Traditional.

It is the speech of those who yet have not become what their words know is absolutely real. The Drum is real, like the heart of a living being. The soul is the heat and birth and ejaculation—to express the Material Life Force ("God's" i.e. "The Creator's" obvious residence).

I AM is what "God," the creature created by a slave culture (when nothing can say that, always but what will always exist) says. JA, the Hebrew G., Shango's twin lightning bolts. JAZZ? AM (The motion of the "I" =Eye, Sun, Son &c). But it is everything real which is the real exclaimer, and we respond, like the music, screaming YEH! YEH! JA! (RA) ZZ!

The communal improvised Blues (bending light) history, memory, feelings, vision &c., are old and visible as the seasons. Which rhythm we are part of as much as sea and moon. Or the schedule of the radio station— History's self portrait as human feeling and communication. Where from within We make the self-entering arc of reflection as it is as live report we register with our senses (on up to Use).

Where we are as to the newspapers description of "where we're at," is a song and a story, a dance, part of the whole music of the Here. Even as Style and who digs it! Rhythm, on the other hand, does have the truth of science. Even to explain why we are where we are (physically or mentally). Monk or The Osmonds? TV Commercials. The Catholic Church offices are connected to us as part of what we are receiving and broadcasting as the world.

Death is a rhythm and terror, Fascism, just as Beauty or Ugly as objective descriptions of who is describing. The social life of the rhythm's "other" visibility, remarks culture, class even nationality, perhaps gender, philosophy, &c. What Black Rhythm (ridm, ritm) worldwide and historically is, is "The Call Of The Living" and as such it describes and fuels a real world other than itself to exist. Communication includes Desire. Even Hope—Expectation. Confirmation, Identification, History.

The Rhythm connects nature to itself as material self-consciousness and expression. We create the feeling we can feel and what we think therefore matters. Reality's Self Confirmation. And it draws to it what it expresses and sends out what it is.
(1996)

Rap & Primitive Capitalism

Rap murders should make it clear that we are witnessing a kind of "primitive accumulation," the flow of money into a small portion of the Afro American population. It means that capitalism itself is rising within the community, and the penetration of money into the very center of the ghetto, is the prerequisite for the rise of capitalism, when the accumulators of money transform that money into capital, i.e., wealth used to exploit.

Slavery and its subsequent national oppression meant that large sums of money could not penetrate the heart of the Afro American community. There is a Black bourgeoisie and petty bourgeoisie, they are a bourgeois class always at the margins of capital. But the huge sums of money snaking through the various ghettoes, in the combination of entertainment and narcotics, and the more mainstream whoredoms of Americana means that there is now a basic "primitive accumulation" necessary for a more advanced stage of commodity production to emerge within the Black community.

Leontiev, in "Political Economy" says, "primitive accumulation creates the necessary prerequisites for the rise of capitalism. It creates the necessary conditions without which capitalism cannot exist....these conditions are....on the one hand, accumulation of wealth in the hands of a small portion of society and, the transformation of a vast mass of workers into proletarians having no means of production and therefore compelled to sell their labor power. Primitive accumulation thus effects the separation of the producer from his means of production. This separation is brought about by the cruelest methods of robbery and plunder, murder and violence."

First, the "Gangsta Rap" was a trend that developed under the money "guidance" of the big corporations. Early Rap, Grand Master Flash, Africa Bambatta, Curtis Blow, &c., even early Public Enemy rapped about the political struggle Black people must wage against their historic national oppression. The violence in these early raps is a political violence aimed at Black Liberation. Under the bought and paid for insistence of the corporations this political Essence was changed to thugism and anti social, particularly, anti-Black woman sentiment.

The values of the later rap became the values of gangsters not revolutionaries or even radicals resisting an oppressive system. These thug values, if we think about it, are the same values as Rockefeller, DuPont, the imperialists themselves, that's how they got rich, murdering and stealing, from peoples all over the world.

Some of these rappers are even calling themselves Gambino and Gotti, paralleling their own intentions to that of the straight out mob. In a mixture of ugly romanticism and catalyzed by the economic and social force of big money flowing into the ghetto which accumulated becomes capital, while most of the community is being pushed in the very opposite direction, laid off, cut back, downsized, &c.

So the small group in the community accumulating such wealth is going through similar social convulsions that the Jews and Irish and Italian mobsters did around prohibition in the '20s. They also favored flashy consumption and a violence that shocked the world, killing each other for control of their "territory."

Tupac, Biggy Smalls, went out the way large and petty gangsters did, for about the same reasons. Tupac, the son of Panther Revolutionary Afeni Shakur, should make us understand the horrible waste that this primitive capitalism is bringing to the Black community. Not only for those whose dead bodies have names familiar in the newspapers, but everyday, young people are killing each other, deluded that such acts make them more important, more independent, and except for the cases of self defense, more able to bend other people to their will. Ask Al Capone or Lucky Luciano.

The rise of capitalism in the oppressed Afro American community is an expression of the elimination of legal apartheid by the Afro American liberation movement. And though we might understand the basic illusion that is being mashed on the people, that somehow the struggle is over, and we are all equal, still even in that pimple worth of social development, the democratic crumbs obtained, mostly by the petty bourgeoisie, allow for the development of capitalism in the Black community, and while such cruel aspects of that development, as the Gangsta Rap transformation of Rap, are vicious and negative, we must understand that not only is this capitalist development normal with any expression of democracy (without the guidance of a party of the proletariat to push forward past capitalist development to socialism) it is the higher existence of capitalism that will allow more and more people to enter into the democratic struggle, and more to come finally to fully revolutionary positions, based on the higher level of the productive forces, ie, the expanded education and more advanced tools that are the result.

One of the reasons why propaganda should be the main form of struggle to build a revolutionary party, at this point, is to explain exactly what transformations are going on in the communities, and their causes, and how, ultimately, the people can win.

(3/1997)

Margaret Walker
July 7, 1915 - November 30, 1997

You cannot even spell here without Her. First, Margaret Walker, Margaret Walker Alexander. She is one of the greatest writers of the language. She is now the grandest expression of the American poetic voice and the ultimate paradigm of the Afro-American classic literary tradition. Margaret Walker Alexander is the living continuum of the great revolutionary democratic arts culture that has sustained and inspired the Afro-American people since the middle passage.

Here is an American art, but an art deeply rooted in the actual life and history and feelings of the African chattel slaves, transformed by the obscene experience of slavery, from humans to "real estate," as DuBois shocks us into understanding in *Black Reconstruction* Many — were suffering throughout the world, the good Doctor said, but "none of them was real estate."

It is from this basement of the human repository of recall and emotional registration that our lives in the western torture chamber began, and it is out of this ugliness and oppression that we have still made our judgments and created our aesthetic. So it is, like Douglass, Harper, DuBois, Hughes, the high-up near heaven thunder mouth preachers, laboring in the darkness of our willed salvation, that Margaret Walker Alexander reaches us. Carrying our will and our history, our pain and our precise description of what it is, what it was and who the great beast rose smoking from the Western sea, snatched us way from home and brought us here to be et, what ghost and pirate. What did this.

Margaret comes from the way back. She has clearly been touched by Douglass (look at the July 4, speech...that modernism post-Shakespeare and contemporary with Melville and Whitman,) you will find that same chronicling of pain and place that Margaret immortalizes in "For My People." It is no accident that that poem has touched so many. Because it comes from so far back, so way before ourselves that when we open our eyes our minds, she is telling us what we had up in us and never not understood but could not find the words again to say, so perfect were it said.

Margaret is the human speech itself, raised like DuBois or Langston to reach past itself. To be itself, simple and open and daring to be paraphrased. She needs no hocus pocus, no abstractions, save language, full open, itself. For Margaret, like those others in the tradition, the language itself is the monster. The sounds we make everyday, stirred up, rolled around, these are the whatnots and what it ises of what we slur as literature.

Margaret takes the highest of the oral tradition. The oracular divinity of high religious speech. The Preacher. But not just the preacher, like Jimmy B, for instance, she reaches past the preacher to where the preacher spose to be getting his stuff from, the all-the-way-out, past the Waygonesphere. At that point, just before your eyes roll up in yr head and you screaming hallelujah, or death to slavery, there is that place, it's moving — of high up sequential reasoning. Where Perception have took us to meet Rationale and we have persisted past that to Use and that use has rose us up from ON to reach Dig, before we see Serious. As the Dogon would say.

Margaret takes the Douglass mode, the grand sermonic speech form, as Bible and as Prophetic hymn, which both Blake and Kit Smart and Melville & Whitman copped on that other side, and rises up through the intense self-consciousness of the Harlem Renaissance re-expressions of assaulted humanity, wailing its beauty from under the beast's foot, no matter, "Beast, Beast, I'm from the East"...what DuBois' Zulu grandmother chanted in the kitchen. That music from way back, as the preacher carries, as oral, as old bible and the cap of revelations. The symbol and metaphor — but straight on out, not dry as a bone meditations over the paper word, while your boy up the street murdering peepas for they oil or whatever they got (check that white skull branded on your Black "Flag of skin"). But Margaret carries the flesh and blood of the oral as the written, making the page rage, the type sing, the form animate.

The reason Margaret Walker Alexander is not as rich and famous as she is beautiful, is because if you tells the real life of the living peepas you is gonna, minimally, get hid, covered, as the slicksters in Warner Brothers said, as they draped the hid — cloth over Big Joe Turner, making dollars heave out Elvis — The Pod of Jackie Wilson-Presley's mouth. Because after the great Langston Hughes and Sterling Brown, the twin headlines of literary divinity were Richard Wright and Margaret Walker Alexander. Both come from Mississippi, like William Faulkner (the Hunchback of Notre Dame). But Wright, always upheld the mass history and experience, the mass emotional recall from the solid viewpoint of singular clarity.

From the time she says in her first published work (published by DuBois in *The Crisis*), "I Want to Write," at 19 years old, "I want to write / I want to write the songs of my people. / I want to hear them singing melodies in the dark. / I want to catch the last floating strains from their sob torn throats. I want to frame their dreams into words; their souls into notes," through the great "For My People." The panoramic drama of the novel, *Jubilee*, until her most revolutionary, "I Hear A Rumbling," Margaret has stayed on the case. She has always stood up. From her earliest WPA days, even though, like many of us who are whipped and 'buked and scorned for telling the truth, still, Margaret has always stood up. She has always spoken with the open recognizable voice of the people. A tradition she carries as strongly as Langston Hughes or Sterling Brown.

Margaret's work has always been an expression of creation from a deep knowledge of Afro-American, especially Southern Afro-American culture, as deep as Zora's. But Margaret has never despaired or been turned, in her words or her vision, around. She has remained clear and beautiful, moving and prophetic. Margaret Walker is part of our deepest and most glorious voice, dimensioned by history and musicked by vision. What she tells us in her books, with that voice of sun and sky, moon and stars, of lightning and thunder, that oldest voice of that first ancestor, who will always be with us. That is what we people have, inside, to reach where Orpheus goes each night end to raise day again. That voice to keep us live and sane and strong and ready to fight and even ready to love. Like our mothers' mothers' mothers' mothers' mothers' mother and our wives and sisters and our daughters and our comrades and our mothers' mothers' mothers' mothers' mother. Margaret Alexander Walker.

Artist In Residence Program Celebrating MARGARET WALKER with Amina Baraka, Sonia Sanchez, Ruby Dee, Vinnie Burrows, Joyce Joyce, Janus Adams, Furaha & Nandi Broadus, Rashidah Ismaili, Sarah Wright, Sandra Esteves, Louise Merriweather, Clyde Taylor, Sigismund Alexander.
(4/1998)

The Lone Stranger
or
White Supremacy Strikes Again!

Actually Bloom's book, *The Closing of the American Mind*, reveals how much the American mind has closed. His, the most obviously referenced! What is most predictable yet saddest to observe, is that there is nothing very new in Bloom's book, It could be called, "Finally the Immigrants are Sycophants of their own Exploitation." It could also be called, "The Bull Europa's Droppings are often called Judeo-Christian in Polite Society." The thud of the other shoe hitting the marble floors above our (imprisoned) heads in which the jailers stare in static luxury, is ironically summed up— Robert Paul Wolf in Academe winks at us that University of Chicago literary tombstone Saul Bellow is really the author of this Fleurs du Mal.

Wolf cites Bellow's "bent" for "daring satire....to write an entire coruscatingly funny novel in the form of a pettish, bookish, grumpy, reactionary complaint against the last two decades....As part of the fun." Wolf continues, "the book is published under the name Allan Bloom—is even copyrighted on Bloom's name."

"Evocative," Wolf calls this pseudonym. In meta-actuality, Bellow rights the ghost's foreword. My own salute of Wolf's Bellow bashing comes because I once thought Saul Bellow, the Saul Bellow of *Augie March* was the mensch that Walt Whitman would be as a Chicago Jew in some heroic post holocaust struggle to find real meaning in the world, and create himself as the human expression of that meaning.

Bellow's recent ghosts have shown that he made a right turn about the time the University of Chicago paid the Black Stone Rangers and Jeff Fort money to drive out the Black residents of Hyde Park so the University could expand. (Yes, it was the same doctor of Robert Louis Stevenson's fable. And the same recurring monster identity that finally gets him iced as an exceptionally schizophrenic murderer.)

Bellow said nothing in our own confrontation over Augie's disappearance. But now it's clear he thought he looked like Spencer Tracy. But, it was Jeckyl who eating too much that was dead became a Jackal and why the working class visionary was gone, a ghost, why he hide. And what we saw hideous and alien.

The immigrants' torture is that they had to hide and they could only cease being aliens as they amassed green cards. Apparently millions of them with pictures of American slave holders and war mongers. Who they now could salute, as a pledge of allegiance to death.

The pantheon of so called Western culture, Bloom cites as the absolute from which other angels can only be refracted, hence mostly colored. In fact these colored Rays, Sun Ra's, worship coming, not going. The Spirit not the Ghost! The ankh with its fat full nuts bursting with seeds (and vision) plunged erect into the open space, the whole of creativity where the only eternal life we know is re-layed with the electric Jism that binds the S-U-N, the Earth, Nature; i.e., the Father, the Mother in their sweet baby-making musical frenzy!

Just as The Father, The Son & The Holy Ghost is a formula for a new economic system's line of inheritance, which is the result of the overthrow of the matriarchy of the Ancient Southern World. The Enslaving of Women. The Enslaving of Africa. The destruction or ridicule of the ancient arts and science. The death propaganda of the separation of thought from feeling. The separation of form and content.

But, I'm leaping a little ahead. Bloom, "Chicago's Grumpy Guru" Atlas shrugged, is another alarming sign of how far to the right even the once democratically-inspired sons and daughters of the immigrants have become lower post pillars of world reaction.

Whether highly visible pitifully tardy colonialists as in Israel or South Africa (the last pitiful defenders of the vanishing empire of Imperialism) or pseudo slick yokels hustling crosses as fascist nostalgia! The "Great Books" chauvinism which the guardians of White Supremacy and Imperialism seek to show or re-show us was a standard '50s argument. It is the rubric of the colonizer. It is the continuing lie of European world domination, since the social philosophy of capitalism is White Supremacy.

The entire situation is side splitting. If we are not cooled out by the deep tragedy it reveals. Is this also Joyce's Bloom? The un-Christian outsider after circling Dublin on his day finally repeating aloud the Molly Grabbing (Mali, Zulu for riches). Yes, yes, yes, I will — give it up. Sidney W. Finkelstein's books, *Jazz: A People's Music* and *How Music Expresses Ideas*, point out how the new lovers of riches (Americans) had to give up their otherness, their "lack of polish" as the New York Times informs us, to get in on the banquet of human flesh. The admission to white cross land was your soul! Its spelling was changed from s-o-u-l to s-o-l-e then sold. The elitism of cave creatures trapped by the Ice Age above the Mediterranean.

The prophets became p-r-o-f-i-t-s! The Ankh had its inseparable balls and head broke off and became a cross and nothing is worse than being put in a cross. But disconnecting the balls from the brain is tombstone symbolism. So one worships what is dead or in the past hence cannot change (BS) is therefore absolute. The joke or lie (interchangeable) of Bloom as gesture (jester; i.e, minstrel) of his tribe's executioners is that he becomes like the colored cop who wants to prove he belongs (with the other dogs, man's best friend — the opposite of God — part of D'evil. Not live hence evil!

Bloom's saying, "Black slavery was an aberration that had to be extinguished not a permanent feature of our national life" is Jekyll Hydeing! He says like Jerry who will Fall Well that slavery, aristocracy, monarchy, theocracy were laid to rest by the declaration and the constitution is Hyde. Yet, if Jesse Jackson is "un-electable" then the U.S. is not a democracy! Bloom's own writing, even Cliff Wharton says, is proof racism lives. Bloom's democracy like his imperialist orthodoxy is "Greek." It hides an elite that lived off slaves.

The nut is that the Greeks were not only white supremacists since the great books of their great philosophers were patriarchal proto glosses of African ancient teachings gleaned by his boys at the Egyptian Mystery School as told in *The Book of the Dead.* (or by

Churchward, James' *Stolen Legacy*; Higgins' *Anacalypsis*; Heller's *History of Philosophy*; Clyemer's *Fire Philosophy*; Max Muller's *Egyptian Philosophy*.)

The neo-German worship of Greek plagiarism (only because it is theft not mere influence) is so classic a recruitment into the land of the willfully dead, one shudders. Bloom is assaulted by relativism because his Readers Digest sycophancy of Western culture though still riveting his soul to the Icy (only I see) elitism of northern isolation, has come apart before his eyes. But since he did say, "Yes," they gave him a play. He, himself, says he's a "schlemiel," a self hating would-be stealer of the flame of intelligence – he wanted out from the provinciality of his social working Indianapolis parents. Chicago was Dublin (his mentor is a Dublin Bloom).

But the stink and chaos of the death philosophy he cannot understand. He wants his second class citizen dream of Chicago as Athens to yield an ecstasy of wholeness as acceptance. "Look at me," he says, "I'm not a gentleman. I'm not T.S. Eliot." Bloom's relativism is his code word for the real. His ideal is the unassailable ahistorical (but finally social and assimilationist dogma of the philosopher king, a benevolent despot.) So kind he (it) would even accept a secret barbarian like He! (Only, of course, if wearing Saville Row.) (Like Cary Grant or a rock star!)

The fact that such heel clickers as Reagan's anti-education ubersturmfuhrer Bennett is in Bloom's corner and together they oppose the Stanford University (largely Black and Chicano and Progressive) student attack on the so-called "Western Culture" course ties the knot very neatly in the oxbow.

First, only the savage purity of Nazi cultural nationalism will march to the drumbeat of the pristinity and greatness of European culture. Culture is a continuum of rise and falls, as variegated as the sun's rays – and as measurable. Progressive students and the oppressed nationalities reject absolutism because it is simply a rubric for colonialism. Bloom's horror at the student rebellions of the '60s and his labeling the rebels "fascists" is the modern storm trooper talk (echoing William Buckley) and knowing that fascist is a bad word. To call the rebelling slaves the slave masters when you are the assimilated overseer, now an "honorary whiteman" saying the terror that spooked you into submission. If one survives fascism one can either swear that it will never be allowed to re-occur or join it greedily as Fanon says, now being

222

allowed to oppress someone yourself.

Such as Bloom are in utter ignorance and semi-literacy of such rants that Africa and its children are the first to stand on two legs and even passed out the Ten Commandments Negative Confessions to civilize the late comers. What the Stanford students want to do is add the other side of the pyramid to restore wholeness, put form back to feeling, north to south, east to west, man to woman.

DuBois said that imperialism in its greed would even destroy its children's education than teach the truth of history. He also said by what measure do you uphold the greatness of European or Western thought and look at the unending massacre and torture and slavery and mindless pain that rule has represented (and as for the Stanford students, they know that the Blacks, women, and third world, since the slave trade, are too — but the slaves of the west are fighting for equality!) The Bloom book is another blast of backwardness and justification of the status quo of a dying uncivilization! "Who is the Tolstoy of the Zulus," says Bellow, Bloom's Dog Father, "I'd love to meet him." The Bellow of a slave master's house servant ignorant of the world outside the castle of Hyde.

He was called W. E. B. DuBois! And that's expressly why all students need Black studies, third world and women's studies. The universities of imperialism training turn out white supremacists not intellectuals!
(5/1998)

Urban Culture and The New Politics of Cooperative Development

Over the past thirty years I have proffered, in the context of being a spokesperson for the democratic and collective rebuilding of this city, a great many proposals to various city officials. One of them: conversion of WBGO from a marginally used public school outlet into a citywide arts station. This was rendered as it is in the present.

I have, as well, proposed* an International Writers Conference, *Renovation of the Train Station on Broad Street to a Black film center and mall (this long before Spike Lee and the Black film initiative from Hollywood) this with letters of support from important Afro-American cultural workers and stars. The present mayor,* though he told me he would support this, promptly gave the property to a Mr. Grant, where it now stands yawning like the other Broad St. bureaucrats.

When the present mayor entered office, I was, at my own urging, part of an Arts Task Force (that I had suggested, but was almost excluded from) that included Clement Price, Miguel Algarin, Philip Thomas and others, who proposed a broad arts and cultural program aimed at rebuilding the city and converting its still somewhat negative image. The mayor, at that time, was poised to give Symphony Hall away to corporations for one dollar a year. Prior to this, under Mr. Gibson, we had proposed the acquisition of Cable Television for public school and adult education and an arts channel. This was turned down by the Mayor and his Model Cities

224

staff. New Jersey cable was then put under several years moratorium, until it was given to a group of small Negro entrepreneurs who, after some years of limited productivity, sold it back to a large corporation, allegedly linked to Prudential.

We have, since then, made proposals to* convert Symphony Hall into the site of a city wide and area wide repertory theater, consisting of the main self producing arts groups from Newark, Essex, New Jersey, NYC and environs. The formula, exchange of the companies' services as artists, for the provision, by the city (and other agencies) of regular publicity and operating expenses for the hall, the net proceeds to be divided between the hall and the companies. In this way a continuous spectrum of groups like African Globe, Kimako's, Sumei, Cross Roads, New Federal Theater, NuYorican Theater, Newark Ensemble, Theater of Universal Images, and the myriad musical groups, vocal groups, drama groups, comedians, young performers, talent shows, would form the permanent, ever changing repertory for a completely renovated Symphony Hall, which would easily become a unique arts center, created from the cooperation of municipal oversight and indigenous arts groups, institutions, foundations, and the private sector. This proposal has been sidestepped, agreed upon, obscured, but never carried out. (It is ironic to note that just recently the new director of New York's City Center revealed in an interview that this is how the new programs at the Center are being supported and planned!)

I also proposed several years ago, *an Anti-Graffiti proposal, aimed at mobilizing area graphic artists to teach mural arts, as in Los Angeles and San Diego, to young would be artists, thereby redirecting the graffiti trend to a constructive renovation of the city's environment. This was also rejected. Some of the Newark Council members did not understand what a "mural" was. The *Krueger Mansion, as well, was a proposal of mine, to convert this historical landmark into a Central Ward and All-City Afro-American Cultural Center, such as the Schomburg in N.Y.C. (which is part of the NYC Library System) or similar institutions in Chicago (DuSable), Boston, Philadelphia, Washington, D.C., Detroit, &c.

Mayor James brought in, as usual, a would be administrator from New York, who, not knowing much about the city or its capacities and personalities, could do very little. Now *The Star Ledger* claims $7,000,000 is missing in this project. As well as the millions of dollars wasted or unaccounted for, as a result of the continuing incompetence and cronyism at Symphony Hall, again, WHY? Again and again, the powers that be in this city, have either co-opted proposals and messed them up or hid them and did nothing, again, as usual. Why? One reason is that too often our political leadership lacks the foresight to see that any real positive development under their watch will be credited, rightly or wrongly, to them. But the reduction of a great theater to a pork barrel for patronage tars the Mayor and entire municipal government, with the same absurd costume as the recent director of Symphony Hall, who *The Star Ledger* reported as having had to be escorted physically from the premises. How bizarre that the previous director of SH was also summarily removed, receiving a note, he explains, when he came back from lunch telling him to turn in his key!

Too often Newark politicians and, I would suppose, their advisors, feel that they must have absolute proprietary and veto rights over everything, opting for less and less democracy and public cooperation, even though they were elected on those premises. One proposal that I offered before the city council and had accepted and voted on positively by the city council in 1987 and 1992, is the "Coast" Proposal which seeks to transform the old "Coast" Black entertainment and "red light" district of this city into a contemporary multi national multicultural arts district that would reach northward from Lincoln Park toward the center of the city, thereby lighting up the entire downtown area, bringing in new businesses, new institutions, social and economic productivity, and a new and more positive image for the city. (See NAC newsletter, for an essay by this writer outlining The "Coast" proposal in more depth).

The "Coast" proposal would also be the catalyst for new low and middle-income housing, including artist housing. It would seek to concentrate the multinational cultures in the city, through the arts, i.e., music, dance, drama, create a dazzling complex of national cuisine, Afro American, Italian, Puerto Rican, Portuguese, Haitian, Jamaican, African, &c., so that Newark would become a "destination city" not a fearsome media specter. The obvious boon to businesses of all kinds and attraction for new businesses should be obvious.

But another aspect of such a development would be the general new context of education and social progress such renovation on the south end of Broad St and across Washington and

Martin Luther King Blvd. would provide. The arts provide new business, housing, employment, education and a share enhancement of tourist attraction. This proposal, we are still working to implement, now under the organized efforts of the Newark Music Project, an independent research and development entity sponsored by Kimako's Blues People.

Kimako's is a multi media arts center operated by my wife, Amina Baraka, and I for the last fifteen years, from the basement turned theater, of our homes. The last Saturday in each month. All are welcome. During this period, we have brought in internationally known artists as well as the unknown and local.

What are the major obstructions to these projects, I feel is simple misunderstanding, albeit the often solipsistic power urge of the parochial politician's personality. In addition, we understand that there is an institutional and corporate view that the self-proclaimed omniscience of power and big dollars is all one needs to create. Alas, too often what is created from such a premise is sterile and superficial, or at least does not reorganize and renovate the fundamental productive forces of the presumed target area. In this case Newark, and environs.

The NJPAC is a welcome addition to our landscape. Mr. Goldman* and I met some seven or eight years ago, long before the building became a reality. The purpose of that meeting, for me, was to express support for the NJPAC idea, but to register the continuing need the indigenous community had to convert sites like Symphony Hall into productive centers for local and area groups and performers, so that the development of NJPAC and its audience would proceed side by side with the development of Symphony Hall and the rest of the city's arts and cultural potential. So far this has not been the case. *(Lawrence Goldman, CEO-President of New Jersey Performing Arts Center, in Newark, after sitting in meetings of the Lincoln Park/Coast Cultural Project for one year took our ideas, e.g., making a "Downtown Cultural District," then distanced himself from us, especially after being questioned about what happened to monies for the "Lost Jazz Shrines" project.)

The problem is that NJPAC tends to be a rental agency for road groups and performers. Much needed and energizing, yet there is no attempt to create the stable repertory of indigenous groups and performers who in the long run could enhance NJPAC, and certainly form the basis for a new Newark image and raise the level of the entire productive forces, i.e. the education and social conditions of the majority and their access to the instruments of cultural and self development. Particularly in light of the well advertised plans to build an arts district around NJPAC,* Ironbound, and in the north-central part of the city.

The parallel development of the South end of Broad St., the Lincoln Park and Coast area would be a critical addition to this desirable renovation, but only if community, indigenous artists and organizations are included in such a plan. Otherwise, it will, in a very short period, go the way of SOHO, which began as a new arts' district, but has been slowly transformed into a downtown extension of the posh Upper East Side of New York. Why? Because the planning was done, in the main, by the private and institutional sectors with minimal inclusion of local artists and the community. What must be done is 1st Cooperation must be emphasized over domination and exclusion. Cooperation between indigenous artists, arts groups and institutions, and public institutions the municipal government and private corporations.

The arts and cultural development of the city must proceed from this reference, the focus on cooperative development, partnership, a mixed economic thrust, where public and cooperative resources are joined with private and institutional resources in profit making or non profit operations designed to create a stable resource structure for arts and culture and education in the city.

All privatization, for instance, must be analyzed to see how these thrusts can be modified to include public and cooperative popular entities and enterprises. The city should be analyzed according to its present political division and Cooperative units made up of artists, cultural workers, cultural institutions, educational and religious institutions, businesses, and city governmental aspects should be designated by a city-wide "Arts Authority." These forces should be combined in open coalition and assigned those various parts of the city to develop. The Oversight, Focus and Legitimization of such an operation would be a critical and innovative thrust from such a collective and inclusive "Arts Authority."

For instance, if we pulled together such a cooperative economic and social alliance for X ward, then arts groups, artists, institutions, businesses, city government collectively could put musicians in many of the restaurants, bars, supermarkets, churches, hospitals, union halls, various commercial sites and other desired institutions. This would be organized so that the fundamental needs of these businesses, &c., institutions were met in a collective contractual arrangement. Principally by utilization of city governmental resources and business productiveness, we might see each area of the city transformed.

What about a city gradually famous for having music, whether a single piano player in a tiny restaurant, paintings in tailor shops and laundromats, poetry readings in the churches and day care centers, or singers in the branch libraries or in business centers and other population centers? There are a great many grants already available for such work, but it must be focused on and a master plan produced. A small group of professional grant proposal writers (with provisions to intern younger people) available to the collective sectors of such an "Arts Authority" could bring in millions of dollars in a relatively short period, with one goal, trying to establish a higher degree of self-reliance for Newark arts!

Each school in each district is a potential arts and culture center that can bring enough resources to support employment of several people now unemployed. This is also a popular form of adult education, through the arts. It should not have to be emphasized how important it would be to distract the youth from negative paths, and involve them in the creation of renovated educationally enhanced communities.

Such a development would not detract from present large arts and culture organizations, actually it would build new and larger constituencies. Create more relevance for ongoing programs. Send a new generation of arts and culture workers up out of these communities with progressive skills and provide new vital links between private corporate interests, public interests, municipal and governmental aims and the presumably collective need to recreate these urban centers as new and revitalized centers of urban contemporary popular culture.

Such conferences as the one recently sponsored by Rutgers and a diverse speckle of the corporations, with high priced admission and addresses largely from pre-packaged "advisors," might serve as confidence builders for the corporate and institutional and municipal and other governmental circles, but frankly, they add only suspicion and alienation among indigenous and popular community forces who are disingenuously excluded, when, in the main, the "grass roots" seek only to enhance their lives and get their two cents in (remember slavery made many of us only 3/5ths human...hence our burning desire to get that other two cents in).

The recent abortion that city appointed forces made of the Newark Jazz Festival and First Night Newark should be loud and obnoxious cases in point. George Wein was hired by city consultants to do something that any number of indigenous artists, scholars, jazz lovers, scholars, in committee, could have done, and for much less money and with continuing and lasting impact. For instance, to drop Sarah Vaughan's name from the Jazz Festival is an abomination, only possible because of the publicly ignorant mismanagement that the festival enjoyed. People close to the administrators of the festival say the Sarah Vaughan's name was dropped because her family wanted too much money for the rights. At the same time, we find out that hundreds of thousands of dollars are unaccounted for. And who are the administrators of the festival, or who WERE they, since the festival is all but eliminated? What are their qualifications? Certainly, administrators of any city funded program should be scrutinized by the public just as if they were a new surgeon general, not just be examples of political patronage.

The Sarah Vaughan Jazz Festival in Newark should be one of the great arts and entertainment and economically and socially enhancing operations emanating from the city. Yet, for the sake of petty political short-sightedness and the blushingly ignorant exclusion of most popular forces, for the sake of a circle of political yes-persons, with neither the information, skills, track record or serious concern for the music, an important Jazz Festival, with unlimited potential for tourism, scholarship, education and economic uplift, is trashed. If there is to be an authentic "Renaissance" in Newark, this kind of "patronage politics" in opposition to genuine municipal development, cannot go on!

In order to proceed with a truly cooperative agenda, it is necessary to call a working and planning summit of the forces mentioned, not merely toss out window dressing such as today, to divert the average from understanding that most of the real agenda of the powers that pulled the Rutgers/Private Sector arts conference together, has already been decided! With the almost total exclusion of Newark residents!

A unified task force of all the forces I mentioned, and a focus on unifying, under one cooperative umbrella, what I have called "an Arts and Cultural Authority" that can re-organize, make joint proposals that would provide a basic flow of resources for indigenous artists, institutions, organizations, build methods for total accessibility, issue regular publicity, provide workshops and features for public and private institutions, institute new programs, build new audiences, attract new business, create housing and employment.

For instance, a Mural, such as has had great success in the West and South West, can newly animate communities; refuse piled vacant lots can be transformed into mini parks with regular performers or exhibitions small and large; businesses can be invigorated with afternoon or morning performers, or graphic artists drawing portraits of customers (whether churches, schools, welfare and unemployment offices, union facilities.) All can benefit, and the city can benefit, by recreating the environment with indigenous multi-media arts contributions.

Newark has been a major contributor to U.S. popular culture: the list of famous performers born or raised in Newark should be better known. The development of self-consciousness in the city about the city, creates minimally a new sense of pride in "place," but has economic potential. The creation of small business today is very difficult because of the so-called "globalization" of the market economy. In such a situation, it must be understood by corporate America, both international and strictly domestic, that only by revitalizing local markets and expanding existing consumer bases, can the economy continue to expand. Otherwise, the globalization of the economy will be a simple act of cannibalism, as it is now configured, expanding production access to all corners of the earth, essentially by decimating the productive and consumer potential of what remains the most important market for U.S. business, American citizens.

The development of U.S. productive forces can only be accomplished by allowing the multi national multi cultural diversity of the nation to express itself and reproduce itself as a productive enhancement to the whole of the U.S. social and political economic fabric. This requires a broadening of the educational and socially uplifting elements of popular culture. So that the arts and culture do not remain, more and more, mainly commercial products of international corporations. But the emerging reproduction of the real lives of the American people.

One of the reasons for the U.S. continuing trade imbalance is that the U.S. imports untold millions of products from across the world that are the result of small, commercial and culturally oriented enterprises. We can go to any fashionable shop or mall or various festivals and we find small items from all over the world, artifacts, art works, handicrafts, village products. U.S. citizens, from their multicultural backgrounds can produce such a formidable array of artifacts and cultural products, for a world market. The prerequisite is cooperation across economic sectors and the allowance of a locally Self-Determined focus, of a community.

The urban centers of the U.S. can blossom and revitalize the place and people of this nation. Just as the Italians say, "Culture is Our Oil," any fascinated tourist to that country, as my wife and I have been many times, understands just what is meant. The indigenous traditional grandness of ancient Rome is a day to day social and economic boon to the Italian people. Just as the indigenous culture of this city, for instance the fact that between 1942-45 the significant history of the Jazz style called BeBop as well as Rhythm and Blues, Gospel and Blues was recorded here in Newark, at Savoy Records. Savoy is owned by a Japanese company now, but the Lincoln Park/Coast Cultural District is already looking into what kind of Newark enhancing arrangement can be made with this company.

Newark the birthplace of people as diverse as Willie "The Lion" Smith, Jerry Lewis, Joe Pesci, former Mayor Koch, Allen Ginsberg, Sarah Vaughan, Eva Marie Saint, Shaquille O'Neil, Wayne Shorter, and so many others. At the Lincoln Park/Coast Cultural District, we know what to do with this information. It is our hope that a citywide Newark Arts & Culture Authority can begin to meet earnestly and regularly, so that such information can be transformed into social, economic progress for the entire city.

Note: * In a recent conversation I had with Mayor Sharpe James** and some members of NJPAC staff, Mayor James agreed to call a meeting between himself, Ray Chambers, Larry Goldman and I, to begin discussing some of these ideas. I hope that he has already begun the process.

**Sharpe James, as mayor, decided that 5 million dollars be allocated to the Lincoln Park/Coast Development and 15 million to the restoration of Symphony Hall just before he suddenly refused to seek re-election. Subsequently the new Mayor Booker, led a spurious drive to seize their money (along with money allocated to the Newark Library and Newark Museum, 80 million total) saying later he had this money to pay down the city budget.*

(10/1998)

Allen Ginsberg: Bless His Soul

"HOWL" reached Puerto Rico, late 1955, whenever the early *Village Voice* did. I was there disguised as a colored Airman second-class, lower left gunner and weatherman on a B36. Reading at nights and 12 hrs every day under the Latino sun, while guarding somebody else's airplanes, and scoffing every stationary word in English Literature, all the Best sellers in the *NY Times* and with seven or so comrades in an underground airman professional killer salon learning the history of western music and literature as night librarian at Ramey Air Force Base, Strategic Air Command, Aquadilla, Puerto Rico. At least two of those guys, both photographers, lurk somewhere even now in NYC, to tell the tale. James Mitchell and Phil Perkis!

We read and kicked Hardy, Proust, Kafka. Hey, What's a Kafka, we yelled? I donno...Hey Roi, order it. And the night librarian did, plus a fifth of Rum. Motets, Gregorian Chants, Bach, *Ulysses*, Tess Durburville, I mean some under the earth dull as shit, but *Ulysses*, Rimbaud, Baudelaire, Satie. We were getting our under over graduate readiness preparation to return to Civilization, we thought, after roaming the sky scaring the world with nuclear frustration, American ignorance and young arrogance, wondering what the big world wd be.

For me, the *Voice*, was just more confirmation that like my High School hero Allen Polite, who I first was turned on to The Writer, him a still great unpublished Poet. He said, we thought, The VILLAGE, YEH, that's where everything was at! Oh yeh! That's

234

where the world class intellectuals and knowers wd reside. Oh yeh!

And finally, 1957, they booted me out as undesirable, you bet, I had already got booted out of College as likewise, but now as a fucking commie Buddhist colored guy, busted for books and an alarming hostility to dumbness. You ever dig Curtis Lemay on his stomach on a "Go-Cart" speeding across the flight line Saturday mornings. Wd instruct the hell out of you. With both stripes now ripped off along with secret clearance, Gone Gone, and so we shot off in ecstasy to the City the Apple, New York, Bohemia, The Village, to try out our vicious learning on those we were sure wd dig how heavy we had got.

And it was "HOWL" again, plus Allan Polite and his cohorts, Cunningham, Cage, Charlip, Czernovitch, R H Blythe, Suzuki, Zen, gals in black stockings, Yeats, Poetry Poetry Poetry, that brought us panting into the Village. 1st crib 104 E.3d Street, $28.00 a month, 3 rooms, no heat, my mother wept. But hey wasn't this the joint?

But Alas! and Alas and Alack. It was not that what that was in my head. Not the GV of PR. The west village was full of poseurs and empty bags of old pretense, where was Poetry? Where was heavy intellectual outness after all? But "HOWL" was emerging full then. Being talked about. Given Ink emerging full and clear. What struck me...an Audaciousness I needed....in that McCarthy Eisenhower seven Types of Ambiguity '50s. That oatmeal lying world. In Puerto Rico, I'd sent my stuff to Kenyon, Sewanee, Hudson, Partisan, and all the cemeteries, and it came back almost before being mailed. The New Yorker's poetry actually made me weep, at the deep nothingness they touted as feeling, yeh, but only of deep disgust.

So "HOWL"—the language. The stance. The sense of someone being in the same world, the defiance. Yeh—to the Dead and somebody else's version of a Bohemian Intelligentsia there was here this HOWL So I wrote Allen on a piece of toilet paper to Git Le Couer asking was he "for real." He answered on French toilet paper, which is better for writing, that he was tired of being Allen Ginsberg. And sent a broad registration of poetry from a newly rising objective united front of young and younger poets, for the new magazine YUGEN. And that began some forty years of hookup.

Allen was finally what I thought was everywhere in the

Village, a genuine book stuffed intellectual, and as well, a publicist, perhaps the best we knew of poetry itself. There were so many bullshitters and tasters and energetic dilettantes otherwise. Jammed in the coffee shops imitating Marlon Brando. Except Jack Micheline wasn't imitating, in those jazz poetry sessions he was who Marlon Brando was imitating.

And we remained friends Allen and I for forty years. His takes on Williams, and the variable foot, American speech, the breath phrase, the existence of an American language and literature, which the colleges still deny, was what was most important to me. The anti Moloch heavy anti imperialist line that wove through HOWL. AMERICA GO FUCK YR SELF WITH YR ATOM BOMB! Now that was poetry! Plus talking to Allen about Western poetry was always part of a course. On Blake, Smart, Rimbaud, the troubadours, we visited Pound and he apologized for being anti Semitic, at least Allen heard that, that crazy motherfucker. Wms' funeral, we trooped over for, once read together at Weequahic high school, in Newark, where we was both born. Howard U, that historic trek, reading on the campus, refused from all buildings.

Allen was a font of ideas and publicity for the new word, a new generation, on prosody, America and intros to the whole united front against dead people "they don't like the way we live" was the way AG summed it up. And for this, that we cd bring the SFPs, the Beats, the Black Mt., O'Hara and the NYers together to do battle against the zombies of Euro-formalism, neo colonial death verse, academic glacier-jingle lobotomy, was where our deepest comradeship was formed.

Allen and I argued relentlessly, from sotto voce subtle earlier to staccato hand waving shriek, as soon he and me, in our ultimately contradictory rationales of the world, went our separate ideological practical day to day paths. But we could always talk.

Malcolm's murder shot me out of the village for good, and our greetings and meeting became measured and less frequent. The gap between Black Nationalism and Tibetan Buddhism, I wanted to make War, Allen to make peace. For all our endless contention, often loud and accompanied by contrasting histrionics, we remained, in many ways, comrades in and of the word, partisans of consciousness!

The day before he split, Allen called and sd he had to see me. Very important he sd. Can you come? Yeh, what's up? Well...he paused, then as usual, matter of fact—I'm gonna die... OH bullshit, Allen Why're you saying that? No—it's true. I just got out the hospital. Maybe a couple months...not long. Hey don't say dumb shit like that. No, No its true...Anyway, you need any money'? Money? Naw Naw I don't need no money...and you ain't gonna die. Well, you still gonna come Monday, it's important. Yeh, I'll be there....but nix on that death shit. Ok, see you...we exchanged our outs...the phone hit.

Then the next day, the newspapers carried their stuff. A big drag...Man, a big big drag, you know. Because that fundamental struggle for an American poetry. For our speech and consciousness as part of the energy and power of the United Front against the dead and their Ghosts. All that I first was drawn to, though we might argue where it all went. Still, right now, The anti imperialist revolutionary democratic struggle itself is about to be running again at Rage Pt. And I guess Allen figured the exit would be his final argument. Like, I told you I was leaving...

But then a last word for Allen, gone now, turned completely into spirit on us. What we uphold of him, for all the, to me, completely objectionable, out to lunch postures he can be identified with, is the defiance and resistance to Moloch, in the collective tongue of the multinational multi cultural American speech, rhythm and voice. What it was I first dug he was saying in "HOWL". And the great line from America. America go fuck yr self with yr Atom Bomb. Now that's Poetry!! That still rings and will ring true. And for this sentiment, and stance, and revolutionary democratic practice, part of an often revolutionary art for cultural revolution, we say Hail and Farewell my man, Hail and Farewell! (I know, you told me....) (6/1998)

Zora Notes

Herself, the phenomenon....
Eyes tells the background,... *Dustracks*.... Plus Langston & others
Herself as Black and Equal....(the question of Self Determination
and the absence of a formal restraint....Eatonville
(absence of Whites)
Mule Bone tells the primitive, naive, yet more civilized...all Black
town.....(the argument between Two Churches over whether or
not to have a Jail!)
So Zora felt EQUAL, not being earlier subsumed with the weight
of separate (in contrast to the other,) and inferior!—i.e. segregation
vs. autonomy!—not Black &White Signs, &c., not the overt
repression of general southern and U.S. racism as aspect of
national oppression. (A feature of post civil war south, was that
many all-Black towns sprung up as....) and much migration out of
into West, Southwest, and North, when equality did not follow
civil war, and Klan, &c., showed.
Dust Tracks, Eyes, and *Mule Bone* tell a lot about Zora early and her
attitudes. Eatonvilled Autonomy created a contrast a contradiction
between Zora and other progressive Harlem Renaissance peers...
Zora felt, from jump, that she could only be judged by herself, that
she was an autonomous entity.....character of her own making...
The weakness of this is the political context of Black life, as
defined as having less democracy...racism for Zora was an
ignorance (of her and the wonders of Blackness.....) just as earlier
DuBois thought racism i.e. national oppression, was a form of

ignorance and that education would eliminate
it...and that the talented tenth wd lead the way...

Both think of themselves as individuals..... Neither understood
their Blackness....DuBois in *Souls* where it is revealed at a kid's
party and his resolve to outdo all of them....the veil....the double
consciousness... "how does it feel to be a problem" ...the journey
south to Blackness.
Zora, an individual, without the contrast to oppressive
whiteness....Who returns south after studying anthropology with
Boas....and also makes profound anthropological aesthetic &c.,
research as DuBois southern pamphlets and his entire study of the
south. It is Zora who matches with her aesthetic and
anthropological studies, DuBois social econ historic studies....
Sorrow Songs, Religion, Africa, made the creation of US
sociology...likewise
Zora has created a Afro Am Anthropological study of which is
unparalleled (& with the African Continuum)

Language, Religion (Biblical work Moses as Black), Custom,
Aesthetics,
...her other works reflect this...
DuBois Langston, Zora....
Quote Jump At The Sun
I am A Negro.....Oyster Knife
Quotes of Negrotarians
So *Eyes* tells us about Afro American Class contradictions and
relationship of men and women.... Until last part with Picker
(romance, from Haitian sojourn??) but again class struggle, blk
men and women....
Consummate telling of oppression of male from each class strata.
Dirt farmer and low as opposed to her 1st context and "quote
about love, and women, and life...and what she
wanted...consciously and unconsciously
1st hook up...old feudal...given to man....as MULE...

Second encounter with Male is Romance, as Leaving feudal, dirt
for....slickness of new Black petty bourgeoisie...bourgeoisie and
AYE GOD (!!) and the critical distancing....and destruction of man
by his own chauvinism and removal of the SUPERIORITY of

MALE ROLE (context much like *Mule Bone*)

3rd new romance,...wander lust with WORKER.....promises of
equality in everything but again chauvinism wandering eye of
male...jealously with both
.....woman after man..... light skinned dude after woman
Tragedy and Madness Mad Dog Chauvinism as Disease....
He is bitten
Court Room Scene and contrast between white and Black...Blacks
still in feudal mode....whites more liberated....capitalism brings
more advanced social Relations...

Janie's last statement re returning...(Amina's poem).....
her wandering
for all its negative...is still a positive in memory and emancipated
thinking...she is more sophisticated and passes it on
NYC Harlem (Remembering We Selves)
Zora's attitude toward Niggerati
(Quotes)
Her independence autonomy seemingly quizzical relationship to
whites including patron....Dodge.
She and Langston reveal deep instability of HR ultimate lack of
self-determination
which Zora thinks can be manipulated because
she knows, she thinks.
Margaret on Zora and on the lack of visibility of Black women in
Renaissance...Quote Her independence as a brilliant artist caused
her marriage to fail, Black writers were jealous of her because she
was a.. woman...she was as brilliant as any of them Zora's
scholarship is REAL and VERY IMPORTANT
Her gathering, for all its contradictory urging and funding by
Dodge are still important to her and to US
Her anthropological, folk, aesthetic studies are in need of wide
review and dissemination! The Black Aesthetic....African
continuum and Afro American re invention

Slang Story
Zora with Language and Style are liberating in
approach and finding!
Afro Am language glossary

Style Definitions
Sanctified Church
Zora descriptions and use of language and place contexts in her
fiction....voices, sights, customs...psychology, mores.
Fundamental theme....women's oppression, choice, tragedy and
frustration....and the happiness provided by CHOICE.... And
freedom
Mule Bone....Break up of Langston Zora friendship....fading of HR
Langston's description where...everyone went...and Zora's fate
Oppression as Black and woman, once the HR exotic Hullaboo is
over Zora's later attitude, was that the negrotarians were
false...she found it demeaning to beg for admission to U.S.
Conservative in that she did not see democracy as Integration, but
sought autonomy and self determination...one side of the coin...
Problem is that DuBois "Double Consciousness" is real, but we
must use both sides...struggle for democracy and question of self
determination...
Zora did not want to leave the fundamental Afro American
Cultural specificity and brilliance (Ditto DuBois, Langston, &c.,
maintaining the culture...which is at its most brilliant in the
U.S south,
but at the same time
W.E.B. fought for democratic entrance of Blacks into U.S. either
Black people will
enter the US as a democracy or U.S. will cease to exist..
But both approach the question of Self Determination as Cultural
History with no wish to "assimilate," Similar to Cultural
Autonomy Lenin Speaks of where they wanted Cultural
autonomy but still to be politically
dominated by Czar, and bourgeoisie In some ways, WEB reflects
this by refusing to see Political Self Determination of Afro
American Nation, (though in Black Reconstruction saying that
only thing that would have brought equality in the South post
Civil War was Dictatorship of the Proletariat 1935)
WEB politically sees this as the struggle for democracy...though
he moves to Communism and picks up before Garvey's insistence
(which he abandoned) on "Nation within a Nation."
Which in some ways replicates some of Z's attitudes...use
segregation.....need
cultural educational, education cooperatives, and unity of Black

political struggle.

Tragic Sexual scandal cemented her obscurity

DuBois, Langston, McKay, Garvey, Cullen, Thurman and Zora and contrasting views within the Spectrum of HR....

WEB, Zora, and Cullen clash with Langston over *Nigger Heaven*

WEB & Langston clash over McKay *Home To Harlem*

Role of Art & Politics WEB "No art that is not propaganda"

LH "Negro Artist & Racial Mtn" (vs. Cullen) — Mckay's primitivism in *Home* and *Banjo*...yet Shakespearean sonnets...

Langston and Zora's precise reflection and inspiring use of working class and peasants' (Zora) customs...and language

Why *Mule Bone* is beautiful and understood very little and embarrasses petty bourgeoisie,

just as LH embarrassed petty bourgeois Negroes re Blackworkers in urban setting...vicious quotes, "Poet Low Rate."

Mule Bone is high art as language, mores, song,

LH later refusing to put Robeson in his music anty, and DuBois faulting him for it...LH at McCarthy hearing denouncing his own poetry...Zora, anti

FEPC...."Blackness"....was not for her anything but a self determining,

autonomous presence, whose democratic place was its own self's existence as valuable

not a permissioned entity by white folks(see earlier)

Later between the poles

Langston's move from Black consciousness (later the Negritude) Which is also Zora....and her research and style),

McKay to primitivism rubs against ML, Russian opportunism trip.....To Catholicism

So later repositioning of HR figures is at first obscured, as in '60s Black Arts Movement, by Blackness....(even so, Cullen,

Locke are Right wing of HR, LH

center moving left but petty b waffling at McCarthy, McKay finally (like Social democrats Bunch, Randolph) Garvey from Black Self Determination and Africa

for Africans to Purity and Meetings with Klan) LH backing away from militancy of his reflection of '30s ML influence, and Zora, differs only in that she returns to the one sided insistence on an autonomy based on her own presence,

as independent as she finds Black Culture and aesthetics.

....(remember she did not know she was Black...physically different...and with that, a politically defined subordinate...till the flick with the children...this is the reprojection of that...I'm here, and me, and that's what that is....

The HR breakup is like the '60s Black Arts Movement, indeed the entire Black political upsurge of '60s where as the next phase of struggle is reached the strands of the whole UF unwind, with the sharpening of class struggle...and the emergence of a revisionist petty bourgeoisie replacing the more militant leadership of the earlier period.

(1/1999)

Ed Bullins

I met Ed Bullins in San Francisco early 1967 where Amina and I came because I had accepted a job as visiting Professor at San Francisco State. The purpose of that visit was to set up a Communications Project, whereby we could send Black Drama throughout the city and the area, and film it. This was part of our conception of how the Black Arts Movement was to be pushed and people organized around the idea that Black Art had a political and mobilizing aspect to it that Black Artists could utilize as part of the Black Liberation Movement.

The earlier Black Arts Rep Theater in Harlem had already made somewhat of a national impact, though it only lasted a year. In Detroit, Woodie King and Ron Milner had opened Black Arts Midwest. Bullins and Marvin X and some others had initiated Black Arts West in San Francisco. There was a Black Arts Group that had opened in New Orleans under Val Ferdinand (Kalamu ya Salaam), in Chicago OBAC, and by this time Amina and I in Newark had been operating Spirit House.

So the upsurge of the Arts Organizations was paralleling the swell of the movement itself, which Robert Williams in N.C. and Malcolm X had moved from Civil Rights to Self Determination, Self Respect and Self Defense. Our conception of Black Drama was that it had also to take up these calls to the Black Masses.

Bullins and Marvin X, Duncan Barber, Carl Boissiere, and Rosita Broadus formed a kind of activist center for Black Arts development in the Bay Area. There was even a Black House, where the most militant groups met. And we read poetry there, it's where our drama groups with the communication project rehearsed and performed with the Black Panthers as security.

The play, *We Own The Night*, which Jimmy Garrett wrote with my poem of that name as inspiration was performed at a Black Panther Party Benefit. Now it is the slogan for a Death Squad of fascist New York police. Talk about influence. Though they twisted it, since WOTN showed an attack by white racist police on Black People in all the major cities of the country.

Bullins was an activist in seeing Black Art, Black Theater, forwarded through the Bay Area. With *How Do You Do*, he presented another absurdist tinge, highly effective, one-act, *The Electronic Nigger*. Strange, absurd then, we have only but to look at the George Wolfe's example, particularly behind the attack on Black Theater, Lorraine Hansberry in *The Colored Museum*, which were to forge credentials for entrance into the Big Top.

In fact, *The Electronic Nigger* is the paradigm for the Tom Ass Clarences, Armstrong Williams, Crouches, Benjamins, Ward Connerlys, manufactured Negroes whose affluence flows from dismissing and attacking Black self-determination. Charlie Fuller's Negro captain, in *A Soldier's Story*, is a perfect electronic nigger.

But Ed would move more directly into a kind of quasi naturalist theater, with a surreal undertone that came from the emptiness of direction and alternative of some of the characters, as if walled in by ignorance and misunderstanding. *Clara's Old Man*, with the hulking lesbian as villain running the young suitor off; *Going To Buffalo*, In *The Wine Time*, where the lives of working class and aspirants to the lower middle class take up their time and space bounding off each other assailing each other trying to love each other, unsuccessfully, or dreaming about another time, another place, another love...

The naturalist aspect of Bullins theater has probably been the most replicated in looking at Black theater generally. August Wilson, modifies his naturalism with a poetic and sometimes mystical mooding. Marvin X's theater is closer to Bullins' flat out attempt to reproduce the empty squalor of some Black lives.

The Bullins' play, *The Gentleman Caller* in *Black Quartet*, with Milners' *The Warning*, Caldwells' *Militant Preacher* and my *Great Goodness of Life*, was a presentation of the earlier more absurdist, more surrealist Bullins, where the Maid wastes the caller because of his attentions to the haughty alabaster disaster he was calling on.

What is important in Bullins' work, and I think in most of those identified with the Black Arts Movement, is the projection of Self Determination. At the BARTS, we had called for Black Art to (1) Be identifiably Afro American, to come out of our own traditions. (2) To be mass oriented, to come out of the schools and libraries, so during the 1965 Black Arts Harlem campaign, we brought poetry, painting, drama, music, across Harlem, in the streets, bars, playgrounds, parks.

Third, we wanted our arts to be as revolutionary as Malcolm X and SNCC, to march with King and take up arms like the Black Panther Party. But I think the most serious affront to the Negro backward and to reactionary whites was that we insisted that there was a Black Art. We insisted also, that in order for this Black Art to emerge as it should, strong and transforming Black peoples' lives by showing them their lives, and in that, reaching for development and new vision. It was certainly that self-determination, the autonomy, the independence that most irritated the guarders of Black National Oppression as Art.

And this remains the key contradiction between the revolutionary wing of Black artists and the retrograde trend. The retros, the buppies, neo cons, displayers of extreme negrossity cannot, will not, understand that we are not attachments to imperialism's fingers. That we can create independent of the master. The most insidious aspect of chattel slavery, and it remains even now as a kind of chattelphilia, the love of slavery, is that too many of us believe that we have no lives, certainly no lives as artists, unless we are connected to the lobby of the great torture chamber of bourgeois culture.

Bullins was a leader of the movement to create an authentic art that reflected Black lives and history. A movement which sought and still seeks to create the independent venues and networks and theaters and halls necessary for a wholly self determining expression of our lives and direction. This is the most lasting influence and impact. Bullins' plays, like my own, are not done because they would interrupt the sham flow of success and Negro making it in the big top, by laying out the continuing death whistle underneath the billionaires cheers for rising Negroes and their useful Negrossity.

(3/1999)

Doc-I-Meant (for Gaston Neal)

Word Music Dun Dun mean Drum Speaks. Talking Drum. Music must speak from the word. Whole word—Sound, syllable, rhythm, content, forming tempo, meter, cadence.

To express at another level the entity of which it becomes an aspect of Music must speak out of the word for the content as part of both. Sad songs need no lyrics. Wordmusic has lyrics-ideological-emotional statements even as only sound/music. As another word (sound) self, as word must be another music self.

Djeli Ya, like Yell wiggle move—Jelly Jelly Jelly cause Jam—(Family)—don't shake like that. It is the glistened consciousness—shake you up—now glistening. Shake! That Shines (Louis, i.e., "Just because my hair is curly/Just because my teeth are pearly/Because I wear a smile on my face all the time, They call me SHINE."

One of the complaints certain of the Greek and Roman Philosophers and Statesmen had with the Ethiopians (Africans, Blacks, &c.) is that "they are always smiling." The Djali is also called The Glee Man (where we get Glee Club). So you can understand the dual masks of "Theater"...which are a geo-aesthetic (not only) portrait of the world. The smile is the bottom of the world * the frown is the top.* The Africans were always so disposed, as from as superficial a characteristic as their weather and the ease of self-reproduction ie food clothing shelter. Whereas in the North, hey, New Jersey is bad enough. (See the poem "Allah Mean Everything") To wrest one's life out of the snows, &c. But then too much of the south had fat decadent Kings selling our behinds to the northerners.

Word is Who-Where- (Wear-Ware-Wore) Past, dynamic past is what is passed-Music is the your motion of rising & changing as thought given form & feeling as an object. The living reflection of material life the Thoughts I see I hear Son ideographic graphs grams Sound-Sign (Sine — off to the side as a composite of Drama — the smallest reflection of what it is &c., in word as music as the connected body of the more combined the closer to the Dun Dun — and if we work — the music by itself will talk laugh cry speak and (Re: Tony Wms, film by Bill Ferris, new NEH Head, where they bring TW to African Coast, install the set,* TW plays, in few minutes from across the bush, he is answered. They say, "We hear you (PL) but do not understand what you are saying." They think it is Plural, because of the polyphonic polyrhythmic TW can put out on the set, which is a western industrial instrument...created by the Black one man-bands after the civil war (sez Max Roach). Researching the UN NEW This writer has been studying and experimenting to introduce an un-new scale (pentatonic in inference) relating specifically to WordMusic. Where in the words relate directly to the music as NOTES. So that to write a poem is to write a piece of music. We request that this institution join us NMP and Ks BP & yrs truly in writing a grant to study this phenomenon as it comes into being and also Part Two to recreate the Talking Drum the actual word music for Afro American speech and The Set. (History WISE 1 "...ban yr boom boom ba boom...you in deep deep trouble..."
I RISE IN FIRE!
WORD — WERE — WHIRRED
MUSIC
Who & Where exists. All History & The Gone that is infinity.
Word is sound of thought précised w/ specific image — the word is a Sound-Picture
+++The Was The Wered The Who
Word is itself History, literally &metaphorically. The Alpha Bet is itself
Hieroglyphic Ideogramic, Ideographic. When Commerce became heaviest in Egypt, the old hieroglyph was transformed to the Hieratic, abstract, the symbols were maintained.
(Whales were among the early "
speakers;" their
"singing" is tonal communication
The breaking the "big toe" by the Monkeys raising eyes off

the ground is not only the hand making evolution, but as the fingers are differentiated from Paws, the Wails/tonal Pre face was articulated into separated speech sounds, as Vowels — also the basic form for the Pentatonic Scale (Black Keys). See Paul Robeson. *(Check CT's Boesendorfer, which still carries the Black Keys as part of the white key configuration)

Speech is Educated Space. Song is emotional dimensioning of Speech.

Where rhythm is synchronized and the meanings of "words" given emotional pattern to introduce the "story."

Story is a carrier (store — of meaning. Connects self to infinity as each beat is sound & not sound (BEAT), Time Place...The Heart, The Breath — Night

Day. The Tides. Everything is TIED.

Language (Land Long Measure Laughing and Crying (The Masks of Drama) are actually a *Geopsychosocioaesthetic* World Picture

Crying * N

=

Laughing * S

Talking Drum *Dun Dun, Ngoma*

Notes to "Letters i.e., Words...essentially Tonal

Speech to Song

Letters to Notes (b) TASKS!

Bill Ferris Tony Williams Film

Drum & Africa (Dig, Pygmies had neither DRUM nor GOD! Very Old Folk)

Drum & Europe (Why the European essential marginalization of Drum....Aesthetic or Political?)

Ebonics & Standard English...Both not accurate...Language a living composite

of All who contribute to it. Albeit Class dimensions.

Witness that as soon

as a word, phrase, usage come out "our" mouths

(See Zora Neale on Afro Am

dramatic shaping of ANY THING particularly

see Language, *Sanctified*

Church. See Jimmy Baldwin "If Black English Ain't A Language, What Is It?" *The Price of The Ticket*)

Music as Dimensioned Thought

Language is History

All Language Begins from A SINGLE BASE! (See Robeson on
Pentatonic found, e.g., as disparately as Russia
(e.g., Volga Boatmen & Deep
River), Mexico, Africa, U.S. South, including Appalachia, &)
EXCLAMATIONS are the Oldest continuous speech forms.
They are all essentially
African!! (See G. Massey,) e.g., Oh, Boo [war cry],Wow, Gee, (Must
make Rhythm & Blues
of Music ie MusickedWordWordMusic)
The DJALI function is to LIGHT UP the mind, like the RAISING of
THE SUN to make DAY! *(For instance the ancient Zen Texts ask
"Why did Boddhidarmha—called bringer of Zen or The Great
Vehicle—Come from the West? He definitely must have laid over in
South Eastern Asia witness Khmer)
dig, CAM KAM CHEM) people and the huge Mountains of Louie
Armstrong folk throughout Cambodia, &c.)
Word must tell Deep and dimension reality as an emotional
intellectual
sound-image of material concrete life as the ideational connection to
is (understanding &) USE
—The Word is the FIRST DRUM
—The Drum then Follows
The Sound & Rhythm of the Voice the Instruments molded with the
words are
ANOTHER dimension of feeling, physicality. —The Instrument
would then be part of a more ( ) Natural Rhythm & harmony. The
entire dimension of the instruments are then more fundamentally
Human. With those short stops,
incisions of momentary multidirectional pre-opting....(Trane's
greatest and least imitateable blowing is of a multidirectional, it
seems, omnipolyphonic tonality that is not just virtuosity of
instrument but omni- embrace of the mind's everywhereness, then!

It is a collective improvisation, as to how they fit and make the
abstract aspect of music as playing the instrument as an
independent dynamic and adjoining but not whole.
The quirky, more specific complex of the Word is Music which the
instruments are merely machines which can express human

feelings...so the Human speech song word syllable sound What dazzling Monk Beethoven Jr. Walker of the flesh wd create the story. The instruments tuned
to the voice as it moves, and pauses and Says
EMOTION & IMAGE DRAMA
DAbDEb
FGb—
EbBbC=
"word
music"
The Music would Jook & Pop, stretch out scream laugh and cry, with the whole
dimension of the Word as Sound Music'd into "meaning" more direct yet more complex "unsure" —Exchange Collective Improv Musical Dramas Realer by combining as the beginning of Everything (I read) In the
beginning...i.e., The WORD.

The Word is the Bottom & The Because, it is how Music was Created. (as an aspect of the Productive Forces and, at same time, Super-structural)...contrary to Stalin's line on language... ie language is neither, but ONLY Collective...but certainly Classes have USAGE.

The principal of "Opera" is united expression, but in an (ie, the status quo, for us, here,) unrealistic formality... as the coopted "creation" of a specific class.

What is improvised is the connection of voice and music into each other! A Theater of Human Feeling! We are Speaking & Singing in a balance of The Word being the Source from where what comes after comes from. A Human Being of its specific beat & prosody. The Instruments should be (like Louis, Cootie, Tricky Joe, Charlie Parker) the vocal tradition continued
as e.g., The Blues.
By speaking we are instruments together, but Created by....In The Beginning.
The What When
The Why
The Music should be the exact expression of The Word (Story word)

TELLING

PROPOSAL FOR COLLECTIVE COOPERATIVE RESEARCH AND DEVELOPMENT OF TASKS MENTIONED AS AN 'OUTSTITUTE OF (IDEOSONIGRAPHIGRAMISTRY? VERSONIGRAPHIC STUDIES? &C) GRANTS &C.

TO BENEFIT FIRST LOCAL ARTS AND EDUCATION, E.G. (KIMAKO'S BLUES

PEOPLE, NEWARK MUSIC PROJECT, LINCOLN PARK COAST CULTURAL DISTRICT) AND

NATL ARTS ORGS, PROJECTS, &C,

The voice can go Anywhere except where it don't know to go.

The longevity of the Djeli Ya is an expression of the longevity of the DJALI!

SHINE! The Gleeman ! What we want is a confirmation of who and why and where in the smallest and most intense form of Drama to get word drum rhythm meaning re ordered re organized, so as to speak music and play words regain, it is a Necessity. We don't generally understand the gravity of our drum's removal from (our) words!

Now it is abstract, in the main! Like Hieroglyphics under the weight of commerce becomes Hieratic. DrumWord, under the weight of middle passage and *Homolocus Subsidere* betraying the method to Slave Master obscures its

ultimate Science and becomes abstract expressionism! The Drum Speech the

ideosonigraphicgram,... idea sound image word versonigrams —

Is more accessible, as concept, because of computers. But everything can make a sound be rhythmic, as everything can be a weapon!

And then how wonderful a concept from the laughter at the bottom of the world. To create something aesthetically pleasing and absolutely use-functional.

Of Politics. People Engine. (tick tick tick) how it run.... Lenin sd, Politics is the most concentrated statement of Economics (*State and Revolution*). Karenga sd it was the "Gaining Maintaining and Use of Power." (The difference is that there is No State Class designation, ie what class, &c. Lenin by speaking of the

connection between politics and economics gives, at once, the question of For Whom!

Mao sez, We should create Works that are Artistically Powerful and Politically Revolutionary! (Yenan Forum)

252

That is the essence of WordMusic, that our speech as a lever of Consciousness, aesthetically moving and politically powerful. That is the Two Edged Sword DuBois raised in his polemics with McKay (re: *Home to Harlem*) and Cullen with this dismissal of politics, saying he didn't want to be a Black
poet. Langston jumped him hard in "The Negro Artist And The Racial Mtn." "One
of the most promising of the young Negro poets said to me once. 'I want to be a poet—not a Negro poet,' meaning, I believe, 'I want to write like a white
poet,' meaning subconsciously, 'I would like to be a white poet,' meaning behind that, 'I would like to be white.' And I was sorry the young man said that for no great poet has ever been afraid of being himself."
To McKay's arrogant Negrossity that "DuBois worked only in Propaganda so he did not recognize Art," the Good Dr. said simply, "I don't give a damn for any Art that is not propaganda!" OK?
Add Mao that "All Art is Propaganda, But not All
Propaganda is Art."
DuBois said it like this; "The Disciple of Art must of necessity become the Disciple of Truth!"
We strive for Truth, since propaganda is not necessarily true.
Propaganda is a word coined by Pope and the Jesuits.
Truth and Beauty, said the Doctor, why does it sound to some folks more profound if we drop it as a quote of John Keats?
We see "through a glass darkly," and from a class perspective. Hence Cabral's admonition to the would be revolutionaries of the petty bourgeois, that they must "commit class suicide" / Again. Mao, "For whom do we Write?"

"What do we praise and what do we attack?"
It is as disingenuous to say Art is apolitical, as it is to say, "It's only a movie." The arts, the entire spectrum of the superstructure, is utilized to lie to us, to distort reality and convince us that the artist's role is to sell thems soul (or ass as they case might be.) From Soul to Sold. For a profit, we abandon our deepest function as Prophets, to tell the world where it is and where it was and where it going. Divine means to Prophesy.
So from the deepest container of Self, the very construct of Dun Dun, the talking drum, the WordMusic, the ideosonigraphigram, The

Djali's Djeli ya
is to create that stunning revelational socio-aesthetic alloy of truth
and beauty.

   That is the concept from its creation, the DrumVoice whizzing
above the trees, to tell the truth, this is the work of the Gleeman. Us
is JoJo (Swahili) the Story Teller, Shine, the Raiser (never leave home
without one), Orpheus' parent Thot, Hermes Trismegistus- past
present future...man woman child, Isis Horus Thot That, definitely
not the fake trinity of adultery, anti-woman viz made into Nones,
the "boy-love" of Grease, money, before the son of the Wind

God, Sisyphus of Corinth, got popped for refusing to cooperate with
death and
made to roll the rock back up the mountain for eternity,
after the most powerful
"Greeks" hurled it, they think, eternally, back down from Fred,
Harriet, Nat or Garvey, DuBois or Malcolm, Dr King heights.
So the work (who where when (time place condition) are
you......(Que?) K-the Wordship) Djali (Griot is cry !Not Laugh! A
French word
evokes the frown of Oedipus, the Blind Lame obsessed with
tragedy... doing a paper for class...a drag, Papa Slayer Mama Layer,
the frown at the top of the world. A Square.
Does Ye dig how yet the word, exists within us from its
contexting as Culture,
the Socialization of our specific Class History and Practice. E.g., even
as we Afro-Americans (our nationality) a Western People, use the
Words, albeit beyond our analysis, to come to similar descriptions.
The Egyptians sd the
"Angle of Success is The Pyramid. The Angle of Failure is The
Square." All us
has called some whatever Mother Fuckers (Oedipus, ie Club-
Foot....i.e., A Lame!)
"Lame Mammy Tappers!" What constancy that sobriquet.
If we were Colleged, we was bent with the definition that the
highest
form of art is Tragedy...(literally, "A Drag" the corners of the mouth
turned down, &c.) So the gravity
(if it ain't took up it gets so grave as to put you in
one.) Dis, the youth say, from way back, The Capital (sic) of Hade!

In love with his bowels, stomach and genitals,
whose grandest creation
is expensive feces. Who worshipped Idols and now Idleness — the
rich (the devil's workshop) or Idealism-the misguided or slick.
"When the Word is Given," we have heard that all our lives, let us
do our utmost to give that word beautiful and true.
(10/1999)

Black Poetry & the Oral Tradition

1st — The Oral Tradition, so called, is too often, the sleekest form of socio-aesthetic "Dis" going around. That is, to harp on the Black Oral Tradition sometimes is a *screen* for distorting the fact that African cultures were also the earliest to commit their oralture to artifact. (There are hundreds of books attesting to this fact.) But a history of Facts challenges a history of militarily and dollar enforced Lies — so the obvious is obscured and the wholly fictitious trumpeted as a license to rule the world.

About language, any near-scholar with some scientific intentions should come to the conclusion that language arises from a single source, the earlier cultures in the world. (See Churchward, *Signs & Symbols of the Ancient World;* Cheik Diop's *Unity of African Culture, &c.*) The obvious testimony of the *recentness* of the mongrel-fraud "Judeo-Christian" Europe is the fact that anyone thinking it really is 1999 is too much of a neophyte to be embarrassed by such an ingenuous admission of how recently they grasped civilization.

Both Diop & Churchward's books or David MacRitchie's *Britons, Ancient & Modern*, Vol. 1 & 2 (1884) relentlessly attest to Africa as the origin of writing and the word itself seems clearly related to *Rite* as in *Ritual*. So that writing can be understood as the method of committing the ancient rites to a medium that wd outlast the priests. (Whose very title suggests that previous to writing they were the final *before — diggers!*)

The general accessibility of people to the term hieroglyphics has never stopped the profits of enforced ignorance. For years we have been told that the framework, aesthetic-scientific moral of what we call civilization has either not come from Africa or that it came from Africa, but was brought there by either (1) Europeans (2) Asians or (3) Space People. Even today, Phoenicians, Chaldeans, Sumerians, Assyrians, White Egyptians are still being credited as the originators of written language. Why? B ecause White Supremacy is not just an idle chauvinist papal bull. Historic distortions such as this are part of the weaponry of white supremacy. Because the general and deeply held assumption by societies of their supremacy provides carte blanche(!) for them to do anything — from oppressing the majority of the world's people, as colonial possessions to (mistakenly??) bombing the Chinese embassy.

Yet the reality of Black predilection (& perhaps other non-eurowhite) for the spoken, the at-the-time-of, the importance of improvisation, "accident," as even the Chinese refinement — throwing the bones — called the Tao (today in the U.S. it is Dow-Jones) emphasizes the at-the-time-of-the living, the spontaneous, the still to be understood. But certainly not to the exclusion of the written or formal.

For all the Jazz players' emphasis on improvisation, the greatest figure in the music is Duke Ellington, who registered 2000 compositions (w/another 20,000 pp of mss at the Smithsonian)!

For all its bogusness, Black folks quote the *Bible* as the Supreme reference &/or the Qur'an at least as much as "The old folks." For that matter, earlier European cultures put value on improvisation, not to mention the avant-garde of the last 90 years. Herr Beethoven and Herr Mozart were formidable improvisers.

The carnard that Black culture is Oral & Spontaneous hence not literate or historic (as one L*a*n*g*u*a*g*e poet recently asserted) is just racist bullshit. A funky lie intended, even unintentionally, to justify not only white supremacy, but ultimately Imperialism. They say, "We rule the world because we are historically & always & forever Superior — That's why its alright for us to steal, kill, destroy..."

In the arts, such bullshit allows musicians who play bourgeois concert music to dress in tails have stable careers in music, to make hundreds of thousands of dollars a year more than jazz musicians. The conductor of the NY Philharmonic makes 2.5 million dollars per year.

In the U.S., even though the market share for jazz CDs and so called "classical" CDs is the same, 7 percent. The latter are given all kinds of props & dollar superiority to confirm their superiority in the colonial-imperial lie.

As for the arts, the world has not died. What was & is written does not stop the flow of revelation, of seeing & feeling & transforming.

Monk sd, "There's two kinds of mistakes — the regular ones — and the ones that sound bad!" Most of life is oral not written. The unplanned, though possibly remembered, dominates real life, not the prescribed or the formal.

Formalism is valued by the backward because it obscures the principal function of content. Certainly for me, content is principal over form — that is, What you say is more important than How you say. But at the same time, if the form, the How, does not enhance the What, then the What will suffer.

The Bourgeoisie prefer formalism for this very reason — if we are entranced by How then we might not seek to know What. The various non-representational graphic arts are certainly like that. As Brecht sd, "How much safer is non-representational Red than the Red of blood bursting out of the slain worker's chest."

The cultural worship of the written over the oral, the improvised, is another of such formalism. The silent manqué of the written word over the spoken word is haughtily held by the Tyrant Rexes of bourgeois arts & culture. Anything written, they hold, is superior to the merely spoken and to word-music, the talking drum.

But in Africa, the *dun-dun*, talking drum, provided a means of expression that was formal & informal as speech itself. And it is not Morse code, but adapted to & expressive of the tonal variations & rhythms of language.

The spoken word/word music/Oral Tradition is valuable because the written is *fixed* (unless being read or changed at the time of). And while valuable, it can never replace the moment-to-moment revelation that life itself is. Being, coming into and changing its existence every moment w/every breath & heartbeat.

Like improvisation in The Music, *life itself is alive!* What we know translated by what we feel — what we feel modified by what we see — what we see dimensioned by what we hear — &c.

Like the improvising musician the poet must tune in to the

totality of T-P-C (Time, Place, Condition). The relationships of everything Sense & Intellect can conjure & describe.

Black people, world wide, are, since the 15th century, at the bottom of international social life. Internecine wars, internal slavery then external slavery, colonialism, neo-colonialism have seen to this. Part of this is to be obstructed from education. The fact that most people in the world *cannot read* any language, is a testimony, in addition to the Black situation, to the place the written has in most peoples' lives. Albeit, somewhere anyhow, some other writing does affect them.

But it is the "natural evidence" of the world that is its truest testimony & liveliest reflection. Language itself is the longest measurer of presumptive humanity on the planet, but the written is barely evidence of this. So much more, so boundless is the obvious historiography of speech. To make a thing of space, an entity carrying oneself & its reflection w/it.

The poet wants life because the poet is alive. Not paper or plastic. The poet is an organ of registered flesh. The poet registers much of that flesh and its multi-various extensions and endlessly reifying reflections, which is a reflection of matter. Ideas come from social life — art is an ideological reflection of life (from Lenin & Mao).

To disconnect one's self from oneself, as a non-world from a world causes the Beast to trumpet the tiny fragments of World distortion, As the World.

There is in any circumstance a dialectical dimensioning that must be understood e.g., the prevention of the Black slaves, or poor people the world over, from getting formal education, truncated their lives but at the same time, provided a grim sanitation process preventing some of the dumbest ideas on the planet from being as deeply assimilated among the oppressed as among the smaller group of oppressors and those living on the spoils as middle management and running dogs.

The absolute openness of All Things, that anything can be approached "Oye Como Va" (Puente) is the best aesthetic and social legacy of slavery, colonialism &c, though it has obvious drawbacks.

The blues voice is "natural evidence," and a reference, not the sleek artifacts produced by music lessons. The "trad" is whatever exists and what doesn't exist as a teacher.

The last poem about slavery being educational is the sense of this. In overview, in brutal detail, in grim reflection — what it is

& was can never be fully written or formally registered — like the Holocaust, it is a combustion of the universe that smokes & flames & sizzles some invisible gas, maybe a little sliver on an old woman's hat. Not isolated, but to look at this one lady here & that reflective combustible hands on the flower that lights just above her eye near the nose Sunday's come late morning in church it rolls into her sense being & she raises straight up ten feet, even tho 134 years old and starts hollerin hollering "Oh God Oh Lord Oh Savior Ohhhhhhhhhhhhhhhh!" The pictures in her mind make no sense — nonsense a Negro preacher from Rutgers murmurs this ain't sophisticated. "Jesus ain't in Georgia." But the old woman is whoopin & whoopin & hollering & crying & she falls into the arms of two specially assigned nurses & Aretha & James Brown in the Congregation copping — & they know it!

The Oral means that the word lives where it is living aloud. An Ellington score is a marvelous thing. We're doing a Happy Birthday to Duke & to look at that score, one of 2000, is to be genuinely fascinated. And if you can read music, even better, you can dig and silently light yrself up with lilting.

Ah, but to give it to an orchestra and let them breathe human life into those signs & symbols is to experience resurrection.

Words on a page are a *score* — but no more. For the words to live they must be played. By that instrument in contact with flesh, then likewise, Ourselves.

The Black experience in the fields — where the music was called Hollers, Yells, Arwhoolies, &c, meant it was loud & open, the song. It was against the law to read or write. It still is. Ethnic Cleansing is going on in the US with Anti-Affirmative Action in Colleges!

So the opposition to Black matriculation in the oppressor society, except as slaves, meant much that was valuable had to be oral, verbal, remembered.

Luckily, we have the slave narratives & writings, like Fred Douglass's "Narrative." But what if we had the free & open replication of what it was to be there, in that, then, open & clear.

All of us know we have heard the living jism of what is being, through us flashes of what is greater than us, as all, from time to time. That sudden shocking Revelation.

The access to Books. The Oral was the All (Fred — On learning to read, How his head almost split open w/ the revelation of that ugliness—"Soul Thieves"—"What I hate They love, What I love they hate" And then that itself was committed to paper by him, before the end of slavery.

The oral gives more life to be heard by itself, ourself, to then know, the hear the here what's sound, so you are connected to dimension—The word-music raises both poetry & music back to their sets' echo, its mouth searching its ear for what its eye heard.

As in Theater—talking heads is recent—the staged word—the ritual, the rites were all of the disciplines—acting—dance—song—music—poetry. No page can contain that.

Like those who think the sign is the scion is the son—The Sun the soul encompasses all Where the U get in is you.

The world values life since it is squashed by death. (*Allah Means Everything*). That's what's going on. The Living ruled by the Dead—that's corpsocracy. The Corpse state Corporate world.

Body is ignored yet they say its all there is. Soul is Black entertainment that, like the rest of it, has changed the spelling to SOLD—What is Oral is accessible in ways the page cant be. And even accessible, the living orifice makes a relevance no bloodless artifact can. Besides we are the Blood. "Gimme some Skin, Mr. Bones."

> Dice—Say
> Dicht—Thing (Dig?
> Dichtung (The Poem!
> Dichter (The Poet…the spoken)
> Dictate (Written)

The Bourgeoisie profits by pushing the Dead as superior to the living. The museums, galleries, libraries crammed full of all the paradigms and models. (Ouote *Heathens* "Heathens think anything alive is their enemy"

The Petty Bourgeoisie, the loyal or soi disant disloyal fox hounds are trained to be entranced, enthralled by the Dead. Middle class folks can sit & watch & listen to dead shit (even play live dead shit—with absolute attention, giving great boasting critiques of what is most boring.)

To dare life is the focus of not just Black culture, but real life and any who actually live (Low Coup…Has the room ever been so quiet.)

The bourgeoisie eschew & hate real life. The path of life must lead to revolution. The path of revolution is the restoration of life to the tentatively alive, the poor, the oppressed, the multinational, international working class.

Socialism is the name for the beginning of real life—itself struggle at a higher level. Ultimately life, as it rises, will destroy Monopoly Capitalism and Imperialism. Life almost fully realized is what we children call Communism.

The Oral, the Live, breaks the dead mold, the wax statue of the cannibal chomping on us lambs—Ba Baa, Black Sheep—in Silence!

BA BA, Black Sheep, you got a bunch o wool. "Our souls our souls are in our wool" Our will...—Rap makes it clear that the Black Arts thrust of bringing poetry to the street—out of the class rooms & libraries & elitist enclaves is still present (but distorted by commerce). We sd we wanted poetry that (1) was AfroAmerican, as Billie or Duke (2) was Mass oriented (3) Revolutionary as Malcolm X.

For all the establishment poison that nobody likes poetry & that great poetry is dead on the library shelves, Rap proves a lie. Now our children walk down the street reciting poetry at the top of their voices.

The genre called "Free Style" especially interests me. Open improvised by sound, rhythm, cadence & rime. My sons Ras & Amiri Jr excel in this. Ras' CD "Shorty for Mayor" is a superb example (w/Lauryn Hill; Write RasBaraka@Aol.com).

But, as usual, under monopoly the international commercial culture, which as all but co-opted actual popular culture has diverted much of the early *freshness* of the genre into the garbage dump of cash for trash, crap for rap. So the genre must like escaped slaves, get up and move in order to survive!

Those who denigrate Rap (Rap—On the Log...naval record
    The Sailor (Say Lore)
    Djali—Gleeman
    Djeli Ya (must be Jelly...
    Shine—Louis Armstrong
Rap+Dun Dun—Talking Drum
Wise 1...If you ever...
    Those who denigrate Rap do not understand poetry—
    "past present" (end of)

The Oral values Aliveness & that makes it primitive
because it cannot be possessed as & possession is where the
stupid world is at, The Devil Insists
(As usual He Lies!)

(8/26/99 Saalfest, Austria)

The Millennium

Letter

Today, more and more American books purporting scholarship, science, research or seriousness are asinine and dishonest. But then look at the movie industry, the television industry, the publishing industry, the art galleries, and tell me what is serious or even relevant there. American speech is like American newspapers, all the news fit to print. You mean all the news that will not expose your historic criminality.

If we seek merely to tell our story it is "too political," if we even show photographs of our neighborhoods, it is social protest. The recounting of our history, like the Godfather said in the flick, has to "blame some of the people in the room," and they do not dig it. How can the native people be indian givers and these imperialists took their whole land. They blame scalping on the indians when it was the Americans who started it and became famous for it. Our language seeks truth, because only truth will set us free. The obvious contradiction with the sorry, slave, colonial, so called EuroWhite Canon, which is really a cannon to destroy the truth of the world, is simply a prescription of what we need to think so imperialism can survive. Today, many of the buppies, and neocon Negroes can get over, because they speak with the word of the rulers, and as such are their mercenaries of class and national oppression. This is how you see the sharpness of class struggle rising even among the Afro American nation. Bunches of dishonest whores and colored gun bearers can get over preaching that art has no relationship to reality and the world, that thought is only just if it blames us for the devil's evil.

We said, tell it like it is. And that is a serious weapon. But we cannot hope to launch it from triple six's war room. We must create our own cooperative networks of institutions and organizations. We must speak as an oppressed nation, allied with the exploited classes of this society and the world. We must speak as outraged slaves, determined to be free, determined to liberate ourselves. Don't worry, it will swing, it will still be hip, you can still dance to it. Like Martha and them said, you be dancing in the streets!
(6/2003)

A Series of Poetry Readings
at
The Newark Public Library
January through July 2003

Presented by
Amiri Baraka
New Jersey Poet Laureate

An I-Logy for Boobie Heard

Quite a few people know Nathan "Boobie" Heard was the author of the Newark Hood '50s novel, *Howard Street*, the slashing heart print of the Brick City's old Third, now, Central Ward. The center of an older Black Newark. But by the '60s this third oldest city in the U.S. had a population 65 percent Black, spread out across everywhere.

That *Howard Street* was the most authentic blood filled reflection of those days and folks in this town's Blackest, poorest, angriest, add hippest, community, should not be doubted. But the "fiction" of the book is in the creativity of its sizzling motion and precisely nuanced narrative. The book could have been both a master work as well as a very popular film just as Claude Brown's *Manchild in the Promise Land*.

Boobie spoke often about various half steps by filmmakers to do the film, but of course, Boobie's problem was that he was Black in a white racist society. There were other books that followed *Howard Street*, *To Reach A Dream* (72), *Cold Fire Burning*, *When Shadows Fall*, *The House of Slammers* (83).

But I always thought that the scam offers, frustration and subsequent creative constipation served, as it does with most artists of an oppressed people, to keep them dribbling the ball back and forth under the hoop of "American Success" knowing they have no shot!

I met Boobie in Trenton State Prison in 1967, a "minute" after I was locked up there, delivered by Newark Police after blazing, getaway-car style, down the turn pike at 90 mph, with the siren

269

blasting, from Newark Court House to Trenton. I had been sentenced to three years, no parole for possession of 2 guns and a poem, during the Newark Rebellion in 1967!

Boobie came to my cell told me that the guards would show up soon demanding that I shave. If I refused, Boobie hipped me, they would put me in Solitary because they wanted to get a potential trouble maker "out of the population" Of course, following the jail house sage, I didn't refuse, so I stayed in the tiny iron box. But later, going to the mess hall, I saw this Blood, at the end of the Hall, with a full beard. "Hey man," I said to somebody, "Look at that dude, he got a beard."

"Oh, that Nigger crazy!" We laughed, you dig?

Boobie was in the joint, with the 9-year sentence, for "Armed Robbery," one of his many trips to prison as a young man. It was *Howard Street* (68), he thought, caught the attention of some folk in the parole system that got him sprung.

The book was published just after his release from Prison. Ironically, *A Cold Fire Burning* was finished in 1963, but he couldn't get it published until 1974. I was at Trenton State only a couple of weeks before an appeal and new trial let me out. But while I was inside, Boobie and I talked as much as we could about the world, philosophy, Black People, Literature and the future, and got even closer after we got out. We were always meeting Boobie, usually Amina & I, at some club where there was music, and a lot of folks we knew rapping at the top of their voice.

Boobie came to our house a lot, for the parties Amina & I would give, or just to stop and talk. Amina had known Boobie before the book, she lived on the actual Howard Street as a young girl, and she often talked about how sharply the book rang true.

Like I said, Boobie was an on-his-feet philosopher, plus he hated the corny Negroes we would bump into from time to time, who didn't know what time it was or where they were or how they got there. That meant some times when we were trailing in and out of the Clubs, Boobie would get into a heated polemic with some turkey that often threatened to explode into boxing.

But Boobie was a positive influence on many young Black folk during that period, that time, place & condition. When many of us quoted Mao Tse Tsung that "Revolution Is The Main Trend In The World Today!" *That* revolutionary optimism kept Boobie from cynicism which opposed the fundamental truth of Nathan Heard's take on life in this world. That it is ugly but it can and must be dealt with. That we are what we make of ourselves once we find out where the poison and inhumanity lurk. That we owe it to ourselves, our people, anyone we love, to be strong as we can, by knowing everything we can and taking on everything we must.

His voice, Not only in the books, his teaching gigs at Rutgers, Fresno State, Newark College of Engineering, as well as his legendary persona as the guardian of New-Ark night life/But Boobie "talked much stuff' every night, everywhere he went. It was his way of teaching even up and down Newark streets leaning on the bar at The Music Room, or Len & Len's, or Sparky J's or Troxler's or The Bridge Club or The Key Club or any of the other spots and spas that he and we hung out in.

Born in Newark in 1936, raised mostly by his mother, whom he remained very close to, Gladys Heard was a well known Blues singer and Boobie himself, a drummer, sat in regularly with the various bands coming through.

So many of us miss Boobie, larger than life, all city night club host, first to toast, ultimate defender of common and not so common sense, because it's like part of our self has gone with him. Those times, that aggressive deeply sweet charm, that laugh that could overturn the dreary corners of Newark's grayness, that big hand he offered, that experienced history in the real life tales he spun and by which he measured the world, your words and whoever he met, and the people he met. All that is gone, perhaps we can glean some of Boobie from the living flesh and breathing consciousness of his books, from the stories many of us will tell about him, our individual and collective memory of Nathan The Large, Newark's Main Man, We called him Boobie!
(3/2004)

Vincent, the Hip! Chronicler of Color: My Main Man

Any body been to our house probably been in the Vincent Room. That's what Amina & I have called it for Thirty Years. The Vincent Room. Why? There are 14 Vincent's in this room, drawings, water colors, oil, crayon, mixed media, Harlem, Mississippi, Brooklyn, Newark, Funky City Bloods, Black Peasants in the Southern '50s confronted by the Flesh of the living confederacy "Her with her baby in her arms." Civil Rights, Black Liberation, the Glorious Music, Negroes behind bars. Trane's Funeral, Africa, the Black Power Conferences, Militants, Magic masks all glowing there.

In the next room 3 Vincent's, Blue deep Jimmy, eerie twisted wailers, & up the stairs, Ralph Feathersone's car blowing up, Rap at the height of his rapping, "Black Lovers" eternalized in Red, Black & Green, and down in the kitchen, one time held blues singing lady. All those on display and perhaps a couple dozen hid off.

Our house insides are Vincent created spirit of the great wave & overview of ourselves. Laid down with the eye, mind, brush of the young master, Vincent Smith.. I met Vincent way back, way way back, back before that. He called himself, like another of our fallen Cultural Workers, Tom Feelings, And may he always rest in the glory of our minds, hearts and eyes…They called themselves *The Paul Robeson Generation*. To give resonance to the measure and method of their developed consciousness. Telling us it was Paul the great Warrior Artist who pulled their coats and minds to what Art must be to serve the people who birthed us, nurtured us, taught us, defended us, and indeed to fight For the lives of the majority of people on the planet.

What a horrifying loss this is, you must see that, to lose both Tom and Vincent this same insane year. For our family to our daughter Shani's ghastly murder, from which we will never recover, we must add Nina Simone, Benny Carter, and great masters like Vincent & Tom of the arts, my man Modibo Baker and Sonny Carson Black Revolutionaries. But today I want to give my heart to Vincent. We have a great many Vincent Smith works, a bounty bestowed on us, not by mystery, but by our own good taste! Or, say, our sense of always wanting to be close to the Magic. (Says Kain) Because we have always loved the brother's paintings, Vincent, because he was truly like they say, My Man. One of my main men, like we say. And god, how many such intimate friends can you stand to lose and not lose your mind and heart as well.

In the day to day practical side, you can't even reference or get historical on people. Your witnesses to great events, fantastic emergences, historical un-precedents disappear every day. So how can I explain to folks what the so called Village looked like the first day I hit the streets and was introduced to Vincent by the also vanished Allen Polite over on Bedford Street, where another painter, Virginia Smith still lives.

Vincent was in his stomp down Bohemian days then. And all these new and wanna be Bohemians don't know what a sho nuff old time, classical Bohemian is, until they come acquainted with Vincent living in an abandoned building where NYU now glowers and towers, with no light but the sky, and painting and chugalugging, and rapping the days and nights away, but still bright as sunshine, knowing somehow, from the messages from our souls that, yes, the future wd come, and we wd somehow rise up on it, in it, despite it, to say or paint or play what we had to, no matter who and what and why, because, dig, we knew we were Somebody long before Jesse J quoted us! Vincent's work still digs into me and makes me grin as now, and imagine him imagining it and naming it. Because whatever we were or wd become one thing was definite, we was hipsters, in the old sense, before the mainstream got it. We were BeBoppers before we even got there. You know. Everything we did, even if we was on the ground broke, turned down, talked bad about and daunted by the ignorance and ugliness of our environment, we tried to be hip.

Everything about us had to be hip to be on or with or about us. We had to walk hip, and talk hip, and look hip. And have hip ideas. The only other thing serious to us was our lives and hearts & souls and love and truth and the people. Everything else was, and still is, jive and that's the way we talked the way we greeted each other. Sliding in like the music, & laughing we were always happy to see each other & open our minds again! & stare at stuff and look at each other communicating with our eyes what it was or what it wasn't and what we thought. Whenever Vincent & I met, it was an event. Because so much about one another would flash through our minds, that laughter would invariably accompany those meetings. "Hey, Man, What's Happenin? What you doing? I heard you be in the bank all the time, counting yr gold."

"Yeh, I'm in there lookin for you ..."

We laugh, each knowing the bizarre audaciousness of that conversation. For one thing, as great a painter as Vincent was, as long as racism exists, as long as the defining of what is true and what is beautiful is the exclusive property of a small class of lying predators, then great artists like Vincent Smith ,or for that matter Nina Simone, Tom Feelings, Benny Carter will never get their Just acclaim. Like I said in a poem, "In The Funk World," "If Elvis Presley is King,! Who is James Brown! God!" But that is our work, those of us who understand what the total social and political cause of our creativity must be.

Look at Vincent's "Mississippi Series," done in the '60s with those wild looking sheriffs whipping on people, or the multicolored masks of Vincent's musicians their own selves awed by the music, or his work iconographing the militants the Raps, and Featherstone's, and Malcolm's, with that fantastic color sense, giving people, objects, nature, shapes and dimensions created by Vincent Smith alone.

Vincent's trips in reality and in his mind, to Africa ancient and Africa now and yet to come: created a world of color and magical perspective. Vincent, was the first to admit, that Jake Lawrence had a heavy influence on him. Just as I would admit that Langston do get in my jingles from time to time.

But Vincent had an adventurous sense of place and presence, and where Jake had the magic of a cubist symmetry going for him, Vincent had the elongated, truncated, reconfigured Eye, Head, and Mind world of himself to twist what we saw another way. He was a chronicler of Black Life, of Colored Life in Color in the Pan-Colorederistic chromatography of the Harlem's, Brooklyn's, Newark's, Mississippi's of the World.

It is difficult to say what it will mean for me that Vincent has turned completely spiritual on us! What that going will mean. Except, would you miss laughing. Would you miss a food belly warming story from a venerated old friend? Would you miss the deep conversation of a great artist? Would you miss how evening looks? Or the colors bama lamming off the sisters hat under the street light rapping to a red negro with his hand held in the air and the light glaring upstairs in the tenement. Oh Yeh. HEY man, take it easy, greasy...,you got a long way....Later Man, see ya in a minute.

WHOA!! or put it this way, would you miss Day light or the Blues, would you miss thought, would you miss the unlimited Zen Negro laughter at the actual meanings of things? Yes, that deep feeling and intelligence, casual as nature, heavier than everything you think is hip, I do, will miss it. And missing it will be part of me gone, and if you knew Vincent or go look at his work, you can feel what is missing.

We will always see Vincent's work in our lives, and at the same time hear that insinuating urban hipster drawl, "What's Happening, Baraka, You Cool?" No, that cool is forever passed. But as the great artists always do, Vincent has left us his life and his word, his mind, his feelings, his politics his ironic bebopper humor. It must be enough for us to go on, and we will go on. We can still do things that would make Vincent laugh and flash those knowing eyes. As if memory was a deed, of what we seed. Confirmation of what we need! Plus, we all, who has dug, dig, we be going to meet Vincent, in a New York minute!

I remember when I was inducted, like they say, into the American Academy. After tip toeing up on Albert Murray, and in the lounge after dining with the immortals, was My Man, like a rush of the hip, and we hung with August Wilson and then with us two and talked much what not, there in the American Fun House, And leaving; as he always exited, Vincent's "Take it Easy, Baby." And me, "Hey my man, Vincent, you take it easy." And some—times, though I didn't have to, "Don't Take No Wooden Negroes!" Cause Vincent was much too hip to do that! Hey, Later!
(2004)

Statement For Haki Madhubuti

Haki Madhubuti and I knew a couple of brothers named Don L. Lee & LeRoi Jones a long time ago, I know the Brother Haki is going to say something about Brother Lee, in fact I understand he's written a book that covers the life of Brother Lee. Good thing too because Lee split a while ago. And he would know about the whereabouts of Brother Jones as well.

I'm sorry I'm not there to question him closely about the whereabouts of those two brothers. Nevertheless, Haki and I have knowed (that's an Afro-American term "KNOWED") each other for more than a minute. I checked him and right after Lee's book *Don't' Cry, Scream!*, I guess that's when Brother Lee gave him permission to take over his writings.

And though Haki has added some new perceptions and rationales to his use of Lee's song book, we must admit that Brother Lee gave him a powerful tank of Black Arts solid fuel to zoom his unique upwardness path into the waygonesphere of the Black soul's future.

Haki was never just a writer, the fire and focus were a Lee legacy, but from that launching pad Haki went on to pick up very specific political determination. His undefined "Scream" was quickly self-defined as a Black Nationalist wail. And like quite a few of the artists of our generation, touched by the flame thrower of the Black Arts Movement, Haki boldly numbered himself among activist artists. Not just a speaker, but a Doer!

As Mao said, "the highest form of knowledge is Use!" Most

but the absolutely wooden headed Negro perceives that "something is wrong" with the historical and contemporary relationship of the Afro American Nation and people with slavemaster north America. But perception is the lowest form of knowledge. The next level is rationale, that is, what you make of what you perceive. In *Scream*, Lee's vivid perception was already in transition to Haki's *Direction Score* (71) which included his earlier *Think Black* (65–67) and *Black Pride* (67–68) and the hugely influential, *We Walk The Way of The New World* (69–70).

There is much growth in and through these works. And that was the period of the explosive productivity of the Black Arts Movement, in which many of us Negroes became Black, at least by word, but some indeed by deed! The highest form of knowledge is *Use*! I can talk a whole lot of stuff about the piano, confess mucho knowledge about it, but if I can't play it, I really don't know it at the highest level.

So it is and was about the Black Liberation Movement, many can grunt and grumble, some can even raise that to a higher level, write poems and books about the struggle.

But during the height of the Black Arts-Black Power years Haki wrote poems that served as guidon to the struggle, but even more important he was an activist in that struggle. By the time *Direction Score,* he had even gotten to the point of making keen analysis of that struggle and it should be clear that that is where the fire and clarity of his poetic works came from, the struggle itself. Haki and I were both members of the Congress of Afrikan People, the African Liberation Support Committee, and we have argued, marched and fought with both friends and enemies and we have remained, with legendary bumps and shudders, comrades in struggle, despite the fact that we have not agreed on an encyclopedia of things in the world.

I am a Communist, Haki, I think, if not unreconstructed, is still a Black Nationalist. Yet I have never hesitated to recognize the great good that this brother had done for Black People, and by that paradigm and struggle, for the world. The fact that Haki has taken our commonly held goal of Self Determination and made it the narrative of his own work, with the Institute of Positive Education and Third World Press should proclaim very clearly that Haki is not just a talker he has taken the forms of knowledge about our struggle to the highest point. USE. In fact, Third World must be among the leading Black publishers in the world.

Don L. Lee was screaming and he needed to, there were too many criers and liars clogging up our movement back then. But unfortunately many of these are back, even though they disguised as Black. The intense irony of our struggle is that its success has created phalanxes of Negroes who benefited from that struggle but who are now part of the forces that obstruct it.

This is so much the case that, like the Sisyphus Syndrome to which DuBois paralleled the Black Liberation Movement, we roll the rock up the mountain and have it rolled back down on our heads. Not quite as far down, but as a glance at the Swine Bush and his wooden Negro heels should put us all painfully in the picture.

One celebrates Haki Madhubuti (Don L. Lee as well) and recognizes that his work is still the paradigm for a form of Black Self Determination in our struggle for Equal Rights and Self Determination, a Peoples Democracy. We know Haki recognizes the need for another Black Arts Movement even more so A Cultural Revolution promoted by Revolutionary Art.

One that will help build the United Front of Political Action against Imperialism and National Oppression, White Supremacy. But an Art that will answer the criteria of John Keats as well as WEB DuBois a commitment to Truth & Beauty! Hail Haki. Right On Brother!

(12/2005)

Part Two
Fearful Symmetry:
The Art of Thornton Dial

Bessemer, Alabama. Through a broad sway of windows. Or just outside on an expansive deck, which wood is gotten dark and pressed with the green of mold. For me it is still the middle of winter, Mar 92. But here in Bessemer, the weather this morning is mild, though there is a crisp blowing to the day and a dampness from yesterday's all day all night storm, including a tornado watch. But this is the house of one Thornton Dial, a painter and sculptor. Yesterday afternoon is the 1st time I've met Dial. Though I'd seen his work a few months before. The house is impressive, an uneven gabled wooden structure. Big and full of uncharitable rooms. He'd moved to this house two years ago, as part of the "new dispensation" his art has begun to produce in the last few years.

All day the rain had blanketed Atlanta and the highway, Interstate 20, on which we had come out to Bessemer to see Thornton Dial. It was wet that evening, and through the night the rain poured down. It was sloppy when we went with Dial to visit Dials's brother and 2nd cousin, who calls him "Buck" in a small house in Bessemer. These relatives, as well as Dial's sons, daughters, cousins, nephews, and even grand children all make art of one kind or another. The variety and diversity, yet fundamental profundity, of it all is astonishing. As when we rode then walked through the mud of the Bessemer ghetto Arnett pointed out a not small brick house, the 1st one in this part of town, which Dial built himself when he was still an iron worker! One of Dial's sons now lives in it with his wife and daughter. The son is also a sculptor and painter.

At Dial's brother's house there were also sculptures in the yard, with wild religious motifs, e.g., "Jesus and The Two Thieves." The thieves and everybody else is Black. Only Jesus is white—seems logical somehow. The cousin. Reginald Lockett, 28, does multimedia constructs of a staggering kind of grim, yet eerily "graceful," tragedy. He has a theme, repeated again and again, of animals, usually deer, trapped behind actual fences. His allusions to the parallel of young Black life in the U.S. is piercing. Dial's oldest son, Thornton, Jr. worked at the Pullman Standard box car factory the same as his father. It is from this work that both developed their sense and feel for the rough carpet rope and metal that they use in their works. The younger Dial's work is clearly inspired by his father, though he still works a great deal in sheet metal, except instead of the Tiger as the ubiquitous totemic symbol, for Thornton Jr. it is the Lion, "the king of the jungle."

Richard Dial, a younger son, heads up a small family company that makes lawn furniture, but he also converts some of his lawn chairs into a more ironic kind of art and religious signification, e.g., a metal chair with rope, wood and wire, he calls "The Comfort of Moses and the Ten Commandments." The chair itself is Moses, one of the holy scrolls of the Ten Commandments in each arm.

In all, there are some twelve artists in the Dial extended family, encompassing three generations. Obviously, the elder Dial is the font and the catalyst for this broad outpouring of aesthetic power and statement. No art schools or guided tours through museums have provided this. Dial, on first glance is, as we say in the movement, "the basic Blood." That is, the mass man of the Afro American nation. A worker, and from advanced production, a pullman car making iron plant, where he worked for thirty years!

Shaking his hand, you are aware immediately of the iron hardness of it. Like all those industrial slaves spread throughout the world. Hands of iron, their whole bodies compact and exercised to athletic slenderness against their wills, without jogging or aerobics. They carry a kind of reticence, in a sense. Looking at things as closely as they can, almost squinting their eyes, to make you out, or whatever. Refusing to be cavalier in their rationalizations, seeming somewhat conservative, because of this. Except, as you listen, you realize this is not the case. It is just that they have been taught by a long and painful history of exploitation and oppression not to be glib and not to be careless.

But also you realize, almost from the beginning, that Dial is listening closely and evaluating what you say and what he is going to answer. The voice neither loud nor soft, his eyes pointing directly at you, talking pleasantly, about Bessemer, his job, how he got into "Art" and what he is saying in the works. You realize, thinking about the works, and listening to the man's engaging unfolding of his life to you, that this is the kind of razor sharp intelligence and evocative imagination that millions of these advanced workers bring with them.

During most of the years Dial worked in the pullman car factory he was "making things," "making ideas." Not for any market, or for any abstract conceit. He was merely extending his day to day contact with the world, his all absorbing perception, into ideas that he could translate into real things. Dial's art is how he makes his statements about the world he is in, the world he has encountered going back and forth to work, on the job, in the hell's cauldron of the American south as a Black working man. It is, in one sense, the best "use" he could make of the world. Where the world could be rendered directly from his feelings, replacing the enforced alienation of industrial labor, with the emotional statements of having lived and registered and reflected and remembered.

One important idea that should come out of Dial's show and the ones he will have, and the recognition he eventually must get, is that he represents a broad spectrum of Black creativity, particularly in the Black south. This is so important because the south is not only "the scene of the crime" (slavery), but if you read DuBois' *Souls of Black Folk* or for that matter the most recent U.S. Dept of Commerce maps and statistics on the Afro American people you'll find out that even in 1992, 6 out of 10 Black people still live in the south, and 8 out of 10 were born there (no matter what they might say now.)

So that it is truly the landbase of the Afro American nation in this country. It is the heaviest source of Afro American culture and history in the U.S. And even after the mass migrations out of the south at the end of the 19th century, by the '60s, not only had that out migration reversed so that there were larger numbers of Afro

Americans returning to the south than were leaving it. But even after fifty years of "getting their hats" and splitting the south, to go north because they thought, like Richard Wright in *Black Boy*, that that was where their lives "could be lived with dignity," by the end of the '60s there were still more Black people in the south than anywhere else.

So that Dial is not "the one and only" he is representative, if you will, of a mass Afro American culture that is the mainstream, but still unknown to most Americans, the one exception being the music. To a large extent there is some mass American perception of Afro American music, because it is the most persistent shaper of the whole of American music. Even though, as the real southern Afro American musical culture reached a general mass American confrontation, from the '20s on, it was "covered" as the people in the music business call it, by white artists. That is, they would get white artists to record the same songs as the Black artists. Whether it was called "Dixieland" or "Swing" (the noun, usually, not the verb its originators intended), or "Rock & Roll" or "Cool" or "Fusion."

This is because in a society where economic advantage is sharpened because of racial exclusion it is important that the powers that be keep the music lovers segregated. Otherwise, they might just take on the ideas (as sound and form as well as content and lyrics) of working class Blacks, and then where would we be!

In the graphic arts, like most of the other arts (the exception being athletics, which the bourgeois taste makers deny is "art") it is much more difficult to breakthrough for the Afro American or other oppressed nationality artists. Music has its "abstractness" going for it. Particularly recorded or such where the artists cannot be actually peeped. And now traditional American minstrelsy (demeaning stereotypes of Afro American people and culture used by racists for "entertainment" and to debase the Afro American people) has become an acceptable commercial "white" style, complete with big time sales, since Elvis. In my own research I have found that after every Black political upsurge, like the civil war, the Harlem Renaissance/DuBois-Garvey '20s, the '50s and '60s Civil Rights and Black Liberation Movement, there is an upsurge of minstrelsy, along with the so called "white backlash" of reaction that seeks to put the niggers back "in their place."

The word that there is a large surge of so called "Self-Taught" Black graphic artists emerging from the Black Belt should

282

not be shocking. That's where they would be. The schooled artist, is the minority, in any case. But particularly in an oppressed nation, there are very few Black people who can go past high school. (Only 50 percent of Afro American youth finish high school). Something like 5 or 6 percent even get to get next to a college or higher education of any kind. And very few have the "luxury" required to become formal "artists." That is why, even among white folks, art in a capitalist society is reserved mostly for the petty bourgeois, the middle class, which explains much of formal art's irrelevance and dullness.

So the norm among Black artists must be the self taught artist, in whatever discipline. The apparent readiness, happily boosted by Bill Arnett, for a whole swell of Black self taught artists from the south is something to be awaited with great expectations. 1st, because, like Thornton Dial, there is a revelation in these works, of what the actual life of the Afro American people is. Both the day to day life and the spiritual and intellectual life.

If one can listen to the stomp down country blues, or Bessie Smith or Louis Armstrong, or Duke Ellington, or Billie Holiday, or Lester Young, Charlie Parker, Ella Fitzgerald, Miles Davis, Sarah Vaughan, John Coltrane, and still not understand the deepness, the profundity, the shattering penetration and understanding of the totality of American life in their music, the transcendent expression of its essence, its actual being, using the lever of Black life in America, then it will be hard to "understand" or appreciate the Black self taught artists, or even those who have been lucky enough to have had some schooling and still not be catatonic Negroes "whiteboying" for a living. Like the slave narratives, the Black telling of America is its completion.

Much of U.S. 19th century "official" literature is too embarrassing to discuss even for the academics, e.g., "Cannibals All" or like the 1868 best seller by J.H. Van Evrie, M.D. (published by Van Evrie, Horton & Co. 162 Nassau St, New York City) entitled *White Supremacy and Negro Subordination*; or *Negroes A Subordinate Race*, and (so called) *Slavery Its Normal Condition*. With An Appendix "Showing The Past And Present Condition of the Countries South Of Us." Though, goodness knows, those same sentiments still animate U.S. society, up to and including its governmental organs, But the narratives show not only the slavemasters' America, but the other side of the "Land of the Free, Home of the Brave" tip, the reality of slave life, and as well, America the hypocritical, America the lie, America the slave state.

Any Black artist possessed of the will and expression to tell the truth about Black peoples' lives and history in the U.S. will tell a similar story, The Black self taught artist, coming from even further outside of "the loop" of American respectability, can penetrate even more deeply into the funky reality of the American soul. And in ways that are even more "shocking," because the images depart from the standard academic rendering in both form and content. Dial's work is exactly that. There is such power and feeling, such depth of recognition, even in the most "abstract" or bizarre seeming juxtaposition of forms. So that Dial's forceful smash through of conventional "painterly" imagery, reduces much American art relating to Black life almost to the flour boxes, salt shakers, water pitchers that carried humiliating racial stereotypes, that are now collector's items.

Works

One thing about Dial's works is that they might be anything, They might look like anything, they might be made of anything. They are at once, seemingly a mixture of narrative and signifying. The images are not so much "symbolic" in the sense that they are supposed to represent something else, as they are merely a Blood signifying in form and color. Signifying in the sense that the images are what they are but say more or go deeper. I mean, sometimes after I look at the image, the jagged maelstrom of color, fabric, rope, rug, wood (it could be anything) I hear the word "Shiiii..." go through my mind. Like Dial had said what be was going to say and at the end of it, just as it bounced off your eyeball there is the punctuating Afro American scatological benediction, like Magic might, stuffing one night in the face of the whatevers, the release of breath and tension at the dismissal by example of the proposition that you cannot do (or maybe, even conceive) whatever, there is upon the completion, that "shiiiii...Dial's works celebrate perception, that he has felt and they celebrate rationalization, that he has not only perceived but knows something to say about it? And his works definitely celebrate the how to, the use, he makes with art, of the world.

You see and hear! like a juxtaposition of the eye and the ear, along with the parade of other sensuous connections the work makes, certainly, the tactile, the mounds of color, paint that can actually be touched. Like you can feel the tigers! I say, hear, as well, because the titles themselves, especially from my literary view, are, like we say, "out to lunch," and then some. He might not be back till breakfast. Like here is a working man, you say. He did not know anything about "art" someone tells us, and Dial probably told him that. But I know he heard of "art" in the church. For instance in the Lord's Prayer. "Though I walk through the valley of the shadow of death I shall fear no evil for thou art with me!" Most church folks heard of that and know what it mean. I'm saying that Dial's sense of himself, in the world, from back there in the church, from the raising, the socialization of himself in the Black working class world, would have given him a sense of art, as a sense of the I—Thou or (I & I) relationship. The God sense, the goodness of myself objectified in the world, in what is created, to pass me through the darkness. Again, the Art vs. the Art-Not.

That is the pursuing over-image of these works. "I shall have no fear for thou art with me." That is the prayer like quality of the works, not as the quiet murmur of the priest in the confession, but of the Black preacher praying against all odds, signifying even if "Uncle Bubba" sittin in the church. I heard a Black preacher once, in Atlanta, Jesse Jackson had introduced as "his preacher," get next to "my peepas enemies" with them right jam up in the place, smiling like Swiss cheese the whole time. And Rev. Buck lightin em up like candles, I mean in detail. The Negroes in there like to fainted they was huffin and puffin so hard tryin to keep from fallin on the floor howlin. But there is a great deal of fallin on the floor howlin humor in Dial as there is horror and terror and tragedy and frustration and tears and anger and love. Whatever can be ascribed to feelings, waves of emotion, couched in the language of the hands and eyes and ears.

Titles?—what about "Black History Coming Out of Darkness Into the Light" The words alone carry such a transfiguring depth if we pursue them. Any why's asked would make U.S. that much wiser. A black tiger, in fact a black palette, but traces of a red white and blues flag. Black bird, black nest toward the center, metal trees. brown face, brown hair, a mask. Black ghost figures, black images. Brown and black forms. Inside the picture all the images are bound together speaking. As all paintings are literary, the more abstract ones depend totally on literature. For instance who would know what Jackson Pollack was saying without the titles. Who would know even with them. Except the energy and dynamic of form.

But Dial's murky moving forms pushed out or broken out of that dark palette are knowing. Their aptness is already spoken (painted) except when Dial tells you (titles), the telling makes the painting tell more of itself. Though it was always there staring, just like him, straight ahead, eyes slightly squinting. "Buffalo Man: People Have Learned from the Indian" — there, even without the image Dial has spoken. Just as the image, even without the words has spoken. It is all in there, like that tomato sauce they advertise on television. It's all in there. The pain and history.

Did he say Buffalo Man or Buffalo Soldier? Either way. The Buffalo is extinct. The Buffalo soldier helped try to make the Indian extinct. Buffalo Man? Again a palette of blacks, browns, white. Indians profile holding birds. Hidden tiger scratches. Scratches as if made by tiger's claws. With plywood cutouts. You're looking into an expressionist face. The Buffalo Man (you see the Buffalo head off to the Left) better turn into the tiger, lurk and survive. Scratch the surface, leave tracks, but not be caught up by the frozen Custers. Not all Dial's works feature the tiger motif, although this show is built around that constantly reoccurring signification. I am the Tiger. We is the Tiger. You is the Tiger. My sons and daughters, My brothers, My sisters, My parents, My people, Your people. The ones that fight. The ones that struggle, The ones that struggle and lurk and survive. We is all, who feels this, the tiger.

That image of unimpeachable strength, the terrifying power, always at the ready, for use, whenever the prowling beast desires. And while, like Dial's oldest son co-signs, the lion might be, traditionally, the King of the Jungle. There is a grandness to that, of course, the regality of acknowledged domination.

But the tiger is not the king, he is just that, "burning in the forests of the night." That is what Dial captures, with his tiger sightings. That crouched tense dangerous energy, however displayed. Not just leaping at some unwitting trespasser, or bystander, or unwitting yokel, but even standing and watching, as Dial frequently has his tigers do. Watch the monkeys. (Another recurring image, the monkey, as the… "gofer," half victim half naïf, perhaps a yeasayer of that which does not need to be yeasayed. The terrified, the uninformed, the duped, the needlessly slick.)

Watch the citizens, the events, the sameness of beginning, development, benediction. This tiger is also always learning. This is a smart tiger. A big tiger. A strong tiger. A tiger who don't give a damn that anybody dig he's a tiger. A tiger who might want to be seen, who might not. A tiger who figure he can kick any body's behind (or they A-hind for that matter) if he "have to" But, still generally, don't too many people fuck with me, you could sense he felt that, you got next to him.

There is that sense of independence in all Dial's works There is a bursting loose, a bursting through. A revelation (Like how "for thou art with me" can be carried even beyond the valley of the shadow, yet shape the works true to the shadow of the valley. Not just memory, but the living sights and sounds of life going now going on. The memory, the reflection, makes reality understandable. Guides how we act, Like our grandmothers told us, "...you better act like you got some sense..." or "you don't even know how..." to act. The tiger is summing that up. Much the observer. the eye of the artist, the I, the ego, the mind and experience of the artist, but also the being, of humanity, those who watch. Those with eyes. The millions of recording I's. The tiger is a being who knows how to act. He is different places, doing different things, because he finding out how everything acts, and acting, himself, as he does.

This is a playful tiger as well, the tiger will signify much jive, Act the fool sometime, and laugh at himself, but just to let you know that all the fool we done acted he is just recording it for everybody's use & delectation. What is sweeter than foolishness recalled as education? There is a hardness. Even harshness to the works. They bite. They maul. The steal up on you. But they growl. They make noise. They are like the tiger. Not vicious, but a tiger. Nobody ever hipped you to tigers? It is so true. That quietness. That watching. Dial too, I swear, is like that, in my brief meeting. So quiet, even polite, in his way, well spoken like they say. But that's what's offered, no matter how sweet his intentions might be, that's all that's offered.

There's a sweetness to that jungle, that comes from you not knowing everything that's happening. A pacified surface you can live with. But there is something burning in Dial. That tiger is stalking and walking and talking. And burning, That life, as a tiger, burning, burning, burning. And many of his images have that explosive, fiery presence. Like they have combusted into view and then been torn and ripped into hot wholeness. It is the hand and the eye, (as in "What immortal hand or eye...") the physicality and materiality, and. the mind, the consciousness.

Like "Blood and Meat" is worthy of Oliver Stone, in his relentless *JFK*. The impact of that film is considerable because story can lay out the computer roll of villains and events that make his thesis. Dial piles these whole momentary flicks, dialogues and statistics on top of each other. Some crazy blazing impasto, a frenzy. Like the Zapruder film, blood and meat. "Back and to the right," Kevin Costner kept repeating, like in a seminar on assassinations. "Back and to the right...Back and to the right," as we keep seeing Kennedy's head in its final explosion, and Jackie K climbing insanely over the back of the seat Kennedy's head blown loose, like democracy, by an invisible government a secret clique of slavers, laying Caesar low. How can we tie all that craziness together, alive, as it is? It's reality continues to be reality, however moved and transformed, A moiling twisting screaming whirlwind of exploded flesh and ideal. This piece can actually "spook" you.

It speaks to the King assassination as well, and a crucifixion image is included, as well as star pierced image, from a "3-dimensional palette" that is yellow, white, orange, red, with rope, carpet, tin cut outs (the faces of MLK and JFK) a taut explosion of painted rope, steel bands, copper wire. The work itself monstrous, vicious, full of conspiracies and convections. (And the tiger lurks there as well, in fact the whole piece could be formed out of his hide! Yet he is "hidden.") The recent academy of abstract expressionism speaks constantly of "painterly" uses of the image, the surface, the entire canvas. Both Dial's built up paint surfaces and impasto are akin to the "hardness" of the real, offered for the proof of the hand as well as the eye. Even the soaking of paint, pigment, oil, into the surfaces, as aesthetic processes.

Dial is painterly in the sense he uses all the dimensions of the space. He does not cut off his ideas. They are there in motion. The tiger keeps stepping. He is different places, when he pauses, it is only to see. To understand and then to move on. (Next "canvas"!) Even the biological image of the tiger, signifies. Stripes, for instance. One out of four Black men wear such stripes in America. And Dial constantly represents those stripes as the emotional color of the work. They might be Black and white (we know that common

American social contradiction. You might even know some cats like that) or yellow and black? or red and blue or red, white and blues. (Check out "The United States Tiger Cat" [89], like the tiger flying his skin as a flag!)

Whatever the tiger carries is a "statement," what he looks like, how he is seen. Half hidden in the "forest" among the proximity of other "images," humans, monkeys, the encircling familiar anonymity of the form the unknown provides, the shape of our lives, the known, restricted by what and who we are not. By what we do not know. We are where we are, in all ways, described, defined, outlined, by all that is not us. The us-not. The forests of the night. Meat and Flesh imagines the creation of what exists, an artifact of how reality is both destruction and the remains, the body of memory and ideas. As if emptiness had a violent birth which explained it as an illusion.

This frenzy is repeated many times. Like a monstrous organ, hysterical, constant, like a beat, a component of the world's rhythm. An insane heart, full of exploding blood. A recurrent whirlwind of searing comprehension.

That's why the tiger is always on watch. It is a forest, a jungle. It is always night, whatever it look like to you. The "day time" like poured colors from everywhere, an illusion as well, when the tiger enters the dream of the endless continuum of his life. His "showtime!" But track the tiger, record his whereabouts and the context of his appearances. His "experiences," his winding in and out of everything, his looking at and being looked at by everything, his amazing convolutions and the way he is excreted from the color, or deceives you into not seeing him at first. And who are these various wild women's that he be creeping between or standing over, they peeking out between, his big paws. He is a cat, definitely, and cat like. But like we always say, I rather be a cat, anytime, than a dog.

The Track of The Cat

The cat might be inside an "Alabama Coal Mine," where everyone is "struggling for life." The yellow, white and black palette, with all the figures colored the same. Dial says, "Everybody is the same color when they come out of there." The slashes of expressionist imagery. Huge faces spaced around held in those colors, with that daunting textural presence, thrusting up off the surface, mixed and tossed by adversity.

Or, Dial could take ideas from television, like "Lady Caught Up Between Two Fishes: Tiger Looking in," "two males throwing female between them, cheerleader." By twisting oranges, reds, with the tiger or observer, what is this stuff all about? You can see him thinking smaller than the spectacle, yet measuring and judging it.

Then Dial can see that even the tigers can be transformed. Even a cat can be "caught," trapped and used—white smooth going cats going to the top, reds, maroons, whites, blues, these are successful cats. "And success makes a man attractive, even at 60 years old."

A light tiger and a dark tiger, going up. A "yellow woman" and a "red woman," "gray woman" head on looking at these successful tiger buppies. Is this what they wanted? What do people want? What they don't have? Or what they think they need? What they dream?

"I Had A Dream, A Dream About Heavy Burdens." Again the Martin Luther King resonance. From a dull green palette, the swelter of images emerge. Stencil, traced drawings of faces. Like an overgrowth, the forest, with the faces and shapes, like the jungle with eyes popping out. Hidden faces and other colors hidden by the green overgrowth. What was King's dream, actually?

The image of twisting hammering confusion is one constant in Dial's works. Usually with only the tiger's presence as some "stable" reference of consciousness. "Heckyl and Jeckyl: Pleasure for the People." Who are these barely observed characters camouflaged in the shifting forms and color. The red, orange, black palette, with electric wire, screens, rope, plywood cutouts, steel bands. Here there are turning, roped in, tied up figures apparently caught under the confusion of ties (like the monstrous "Meat and Blood"), and somehow objects of "pleasure" They seem caught, in order to give pleasure. And the cat's tail, suggests that it is his tale that we are drawn into.

And the tiger got tales. "Tigers Making Business," for instance, is an allegory about "The idea of wood—begins with trees." This is plywood cutouts mounted canvas. In bright yellows and oranges, with green (leaves or backs) strung around as partial frames for the two tigers looking somewhat timid or like they've been "framed." And they are watched by barely seen "ladies and gents" expressionless and floating toward the edges of the surface, to further frame the tigers by what they are not.

The tigers stare out at us, in this allegory, also, of life and history. In conflict, in combination, they are "doing business." This is, perhaps, the prerequisite for doing business, to be fixed in one spot, posing for the world. But like that battery, left to himself, the tiger keeps going. Like Dial says, "Life keeps going on." And it is everywhere. "Pieces of The U.S." suggests this scattered, fragmented wholeness. It is an expressionist iconography, with an emphasis on simultaneity, overlaid heavily with multicolors. Faces, heads, profiles, twisting to stare straight ahead, sideways, upside down. It is a white cat this time, with black and red stripes, floating up and to one side. Blending in with the whole, but himself one of the U.S. "pieces."

The August 1990 piece, "Men on Alert: All Eyes on Iraq" made just before the war, The heads and faces of men stare trying to fathom the future, the meaning and morality of the world. Even the tiger is turned upside down, by the prospect of war. Again, there is a commonality to the figures, not just because they spring from the same palette and colors, but they are linked in form and expression. The tiger(s) too is part of it, though his tigerness, the whole catness of him. seems to have him float in relief against the turmoil of this square world.

There is a figure that looks somewhat like Saddam, almost as if there are scrambling tigers swarming around him, tying the coming war and the displaced people also from the layoffs in the U.S. A dual anxiety, to which all eyes are turned. The significance of all of it ghostly as the steadily rising screaming sirens of a coming war. "In Struggling Tiger Proud Stepping," which is a two-piece work on Clarence Thomas, Dial once more steps to the topical. But all of his works, if you ask me, have some topicality to them. Some spirit of our current bubbling, babbling, world, its day to day expressions. In "Part One" a net is spread over the whole work to suggest that both Thomas and Hill (and indeed all these blacks or all Black people here) are caught. There is much foliage, in bright green, the color of the mazoola, the rope for instance is also green, and in all that green there are suggestions of an audience.

The Tom cat seems to be dancing, or trying to maintain his balance on the net which is above Anita Hill. Like she is caught under it, he above it. The tiger is black and white and red. The principals in the real and the metaphor and the blood spilled to maintain what ultimately cannot be maintained. Hill's arms are outstretched as if she is terrified yet expectant, below the cat. She is the trapped figure as she seem to scream up at him, the tiger's legs akimbo trying desperately to keep his balance. So it seems that Dial sees both Thomas and Hill as victims to the audience stuffed inside the green foliage.

But what of the "primitiveness" of these concerns? When we walk into the Museum of Modern Art and see boxes and squares and circles or sweeps of "profound" color, or maybe see a French woman shoot an air pistol into balloons full of paints, all that, somehow is "high art." But like Brecht said, how much better to make the red on your canvas a purely non-representational red, how much safer, than a red that is "blood pouring out of some slain worker's chest."

Yet the formalists and academics claim the high ground of intellectualism in American art. But you could go into these exhibitions, or view hundreds of them and never even know what species inhabits this planet. And how much more pleasant for the banks and the academies where the big abstractions hang. After getting a slow start the biggies now realize that the safest art in the world is the most abstract. Unlike the mural commissioned by Rockefeller from Diego Riviera in which Lenin's head popped up, so that it could not be exhibited.

The ideas and concerns in Dial's work are the day to day concerns of the world. The comings and goings, the pain and tragedy and comedy of our everybody visible and invisible world. Yet Dial is a "primitive," they say. The world is off limits for art, they tell us, not wanting their big playhouse shook up. To be really profound it is necessary to talk about nothing, as if it was something. Like the new New Critics called deconstructionists who say that literature is about literature, that is, important literature is about literature, only vulgar literature is about the world.

In "Strategy of the United States: Black Storm Coming On " Just the title itself must be considered vulgar by the masters of the art-not. Two tigers ridden by two white men on each side of the canvas, and in the center, the ancient black bird, Ba (the soul), the primordial symbol, the phoenix (The half lion/half woman changed to a bird—the evolution to spirituality—the sphinx become the phoenix) rising. "I Rise in Fire," cries the phoenix... "I rise in Fire."

Bursting out and up between the common slavery of American class, national and gender relationships. Blowing up in flame from the midst of that madness, man riding man, humans riding "cats" (and "chicks" too), so the species, the society itself is half human half animal. The reduction of the human to the animal makes the society half human half animal.

And so the bird, Ba (Ancient Egyptian) the Soul, must reassert itself. As that is what is being destroyed in the lowness of our world. Because the humanity is denied, the human headed soul must assert its presence (like after the Rodney. King verdict, "I Rise in Fire," screamed the Phoenix, rising out the ravaging flames that sought to destroy Dis (the capital of Hades)!

This place, America, Black people always speak of as Dis. Like the rappers make it contemporary, "Don't dis me, sucker....Or I will Rise in fire!" And Dial carries it in him as a feeling, an idea, a project his hands make from the outline, pouring cat of his heart. The "Black Storm" is the Phoenix rising. (How "on it" is the fact that Arizona where they at first would not honor King's birthday (M.L, not Rodney), that their capital is Phoenix! But how chart a society where the oppressor nation's king is Elvis, and the oppressed nation's King is Martin Luther? How understand a culture where the oppressor nation's Duke is a patriotic cowboy, named Wayne, and the oppressed nation's Duke is the greatest composer America has produced, last name Ellington?

When you say Bird, are you talking about Charlie Parker or Larry Celtic? Is it Bette Midler who is Divine or Sarah Vaughan? There is a fragment of the antagonistic psychological development. Common psychological development is what produces a common culture. But in America we have the culture of the oppressed and the culture of the oppressors, like all nations. And that contradiction is based on different material social lives. The view from the bottom vs. the view from the top. Dial speaks from the bottom, from the culture of the oppressed, whatever you think about that, it's true. And it has a significance that "rings" as Abbey Lincoln sings. Like that Bird, where it came from to get into his psyche. It was rung in by his whole and our whole, and the whole line of us, whole lives and history. It is his history that Dial is telling, looking at it one way and another.

Looking at it as it is being acted out, yet feeling it inside and through his fingers as he picks up his materials and proceeds into the valley of the shadow, thou art with him... thou feeling, thou mind, thou memory, thou registration of everything that ever happened that you could possibly register, to be you, to be Dial, or that cat stalking around the forests of the night, somewhere in that Blackness, burning.

"Everybody Can See The Tiger Got A Monkey On His Back" says a great deal just from the words. However you take that. Since that tiger is in a sense the singular and the plural as is that monkey. But magnified by households and offices into the huge metaphorical ones. This painting is one of a pair (#2 is called "The Monkey Will Even Screw the Handicapped," again a cold American truism). But both canvases make their icicle hard point. The 1st has the monkey made of red and orange checked rope carpet unwonen and rewoven and pasted on the surface. (And Dial frequently uses fiber board or wood to paint and fix his cut outs on. "Back" has a ridiculous red orange monkey riding on the Tiger's back, while this cat seems to be sniffing flowers, the tiger almost seems a trifle high, as if he is being seduced or momentarily zapped by the scent or cent of illusion a pretty surface, a pretty smell.

Yet a very Dial-like looking man looks on at the tiger, at a tiger, getting took off. This human figure seems? also, and this is sharp? a black bird stuffed inside him. That is that human headed soul, retained inside, as the tiger lets the monkey ride him while getting ripped on the smell of flowers, the illusion of power. While the monkey rides. The monkey of grim idiocy, himself a signifier, both victim and victimizer.

Remember, in the African tales the monkey is the signifier, the trickster, identified with the Orisha, Elegba, who holds the power of the crossroads, the slickster, the gambler sometimes identified with a huge phallus, the animal that went up in the tree to get away from the other animals, and by inference became man. Twisted Euro American appropriation of this figure sometimes equate Elegba with the devil.

In the U.S., the Afro American story tradition transforms the Signifying Monkey into an indigenous creature, the rabbit. Brer Rabbit to you, translated into American popular culture as Bugs Bunny. The one "who is never at a loss." But in Dial's iconography, the monkey, while resonating a questionable identity as victim or helpmate of the victimizer carries a negative connotation. Here as user as well as in the "Screw" image. (That image of the tiger as white and faded blue, unwoven and woven carpet, with the tiger neither color, but equally striped. The monkey in white and red and black fixed to the tiger, screwing him, the tiger or the tiger standing above another figure with red hair and black face, screwing it? While other faces, both "human" and "monkey" stare and undulate from all sides.

As a Black man, and the principal tiger signification we can understand the directness of this message. As Black people are "handicapped" in a white supremacist still slave society. But, the monkey that screws them, are they the backward Negroes who go along even with programs designed to screw them, are they the various caucuses of Negroes who ride the great collective back of the Black masses? As witness the myriad anxiety ridden faces poking out of every which where.

The tiger knows, as the tiger in us knows, we got a monkey riding our backs, or the monkey in each of us, the exploiter in us, will "do it" (rip off) to anybody. Does the tiger know he is being ridden? In piece one The tiger is seduced into being ridden. Or has a grim symbiotic relationship developed between the rider and the ridden, between beast and burden? But it is Dial's tigerness, his tiger-tude (to paraphrase yet lecture Soyinka) that gives contrast between the tiger and the monkey rider. That is why the tiger constantly recalls and even celebrates his "tiger-tude" as the advanced Pan-Africanists historically evoke their Negritude to confirm the long trail of the oppressed and when the oppressor got on to ride. That is precisely what "the man" say. That's what the man train the dog to do. That's why dog is man "the man's" best friend. (He ain't got many human friends on account of his fucked up behavior in slavery, colonialism, neocolonialism, et al.)

They called such dogs, "nigger dogs," in the old days (when was that? next week?) now they might call 'em anything, Mayor, Congressman, Supreme Negro, Chief Joint, call em, literally anything, and they be anything too. It is an excellent composition, combining an abstract expressionist like surface and an Afro American expressionist convergence of painterly effects. The Tiger is hidden you see his head woven among the reed like strokes. The eyes anxious and seemingly vacuous or terrified. Like the nigger dog would make your face turn chasing you through the forest.

On the back of a carpet, a yellow, pink, blue palette of house paint, the colors seemingly applied with palette knife or whatever.

The dog's head also just tippling through the surface snarling with twisted mouth, a grimace a jagged smile, probably that he is so hot on the trail. Dial's works, no matter of what unlikely materials, are always well constructed. They are mainly sculptor like, not only from the build up of paint, the heavy impasto, but a direct" hands on" the surface. You always see evidence of Dial taking the matter into his own hands. Those hard as iron, iron worker for thirty years hands. As Arnett says, "The guy's a builder." And that's the way he approaches the works, like works of construction. Layer after layer, of either paint, carpet, wood, metal, directly applied and under the direct feel of the hands.

Since his earlier works, or the 1st works to be shown to people outside his home, there has been a powerful maturation process. The very fact of the works being shown has contributed to that process. Dial's reclusiveness was not some middle class conceit, he was an iron worker and the ideas he wanted to break down to reality, to create or recreate, were meant for him. Not at the exclusion of anyone, but because it didn't dawn on him the extent of the outside interest his ideas could generate, but obviously in the situation he was in, many of the feelings and ideas he expressed, even way back, he could hardly feel the powerful arbiters of his environs would be sympathetic toward.

But as the Arnetts got into the picture and people from everywhere began to come to see him, and he has traveled now himself. (See the hilarious masterpiece "The Tiger That Flew Over New York City.") There is a growing self consciousness to the works, a truer self consciousness to the eye of the painting's ego. A growing willingness to speak more directly and be the identified self, the I of the staring cat.

It is something like Heisenberg's theories of uncertainty, that things change when they are observed. Certainly this is obvious with humans to the extent we understand that people react to our reaction to them. Though Heisenberg might also be implying that there is no objective phenomena and therefore extending idealism.

What there is that is constant is change. In each element of our perception or of our being perceived, who we are is changed, that is the continuum. We are not who we were this morning, nor will be same tomorrow.

(2005)

Culture, Language, Media, Meaning

Culture, we should understand by now, determines what and how we think, to a large extent. Culture meaning "how we live," both the base, which is economic, and the super structure, which are the institutions, organizations, shapes of governance and education created to forward and maintain the philosophy that animates the base.

The economic base of the U.S., for instance, is created by Monopoly Capitalism, Imperialism, National Oppression and Racism. Hence its superstructure, it's educational institutions, its social organization, it's aesthetic rationalizations, it's political culture are created to enhance, maintain and forward that loathsome economic base.

So that the most ubiquitous ideas and philosophical concepts within it are shaped by that base to such an extent that what is true and what is false are determined by the content of its structural desire, not by objectivity. Without being contexted by U.S. imperialism, and that as a historical development of slavery, capitalism, white supremacy, national oppression, racism, monopoly capitalism, imperialism (now euphemistically referred to as "Globalization") many of the basic presumptions, rationalizations and ways of understanding things within the society would simply not seem plausible. Not only would basic rationalizations and use of the world be very different, But even the shape of our psycho linguistic gestalt would be altered. The ubiquitous use of "Black" as a negative could not have developed.

Black mail, Black sheep, Black Tuesday, Black day, Black comedy &c. Language contains and is a philosophy.

The terms used to define and legitimatize the U.S. Policy in the Middle East such as "Bringing Democracy" to the region when it is the blatant feeding behavior of Imperialism, are outright bizarre. The explanation to Americans that Terrorists exist because "they are jealous of our Democracy" is as crazy sounding as a President of the United States landing on an aircraft carrier disguised as Tom Cruise. Yet it is the ideological culture of imperialism, white supremacy, that can use the tacit code words and psychological distortions of its history to convince innocents of various degrees that it is good and true and kind and always doing the right thing.

In this operation language is the most facile operative impacting upon the society. The content and structure of the base and superstructure are the source and reservoir, but language is conduit, the connection. When something is no longer a war but "a police action," when it is no longer a lie, but "disinformation." When unfortunates are no longer kidnapped and sent outside the country to be tortured, they are "rendered," it is rendition. When the Devil is no longer Satan but Dubya.

The word: "Terrorism" itself is such a Rube Goldberg construct of the dead entrails of oppressive U.S. & European culture. It can only be believed because of the mind set of the people themselves. The slave owner and colonial nations, who themselves have brought and still today continue to bring terror on the world's majority, can be made to believe (what ever percentage of them continue to believe these things) that some mostly Colored errant miscreants, for no reason, have decided to bring terror upon the light skinned residents of the planet. There is never a need to explain in detail why this would be so — it just is because those Colored people are up to no good.

If we think that now the mindset of these societies has advanced to the point where no longer is outright chattel slavery or loudly proclaimed colonialism their work, and the basic economic engines of these societies. We have but to look anywhere in the third world, the Colored and formerly colonized nations, including Ireland and we would see that though the terms of oppression and exploitation have been modernized, Afghanistan, Palestine, Iraq, Darfur, Somalia, the threatening of Iran, North Korea, Venezuela, Cuba, Bolivia the implicit terror of naming countries an "axis of evil" continues the intent of the former "lower stages" of oppression. And by what right and presumed morality dares predators like the U.S. and Great Britain to call any people an axis of evil, when they have long been themselves Assholes of Evil.

Can anyone speak of Terror without acknowledging the terror of the Slave Trade or Colonial rule? This is what my poem, "Somebody Blew Up America" was about. Yet after the initial terror of the attacks (by whom is the question I still ask), nothing was as abusive and infuriating as to hear Bush and the rest of the A.O.E. speak of terrorism. Yet it is the language playing on the historic mindset that denies to the U.S. (& British) people that they are the world's primary terrorists, and except for the German Nazi, Italian Fascist, Japanese Nationalists brief attempt to best them, have been the world class terrorists for hundreds of years.

The language masks intent rather than illuminates it. One of the striking aspects of the decline of the British Empire, even during the supremacy of the Victorian Empire, was how ornately euphemistic that English language became. Because when the sun never set on the British Empire, there was so much hideousness within that Empire to hide and cover, the language itself became a barrier to direct communication. So now U.S. factories are "downsized" rather than closing, jobs and technology are "outsourced" rather than removed to countries where the overhead is lower, no taxes, no unions, which means U.S. workers lose jobs.

Just yesterday, the Attorney General of New Jersey was sued by the Federal government for subpoenaing local telephone companies to find out whether they had been violating citizen's privacy by sending phone records to the National Security Agency. To find the truth is, as the Bush feds say, to violate and...compromise national security.

So that the very distinction between Fact and Fiction is made ambiguous with the use of language within a certain culture. A culture which has produced a perception challenged mode of receiving data as well as a thoroughly incorrect system of rationalizing that data. The use of such data is war, crime, greed, exploitation, oppression, racism, homophobia, &c.

Information and knowledge itself are thereby challenged and ignorance is the prescription for such a corrupted order to remain intact. Ignorance and of course coercion, but enforced ignorance is also a form of coercion. I want here to quote from a poem of mine "Allah Mean Everything" (99) which shows how language is a reflection of the culture it originates in but also helps shape that culture and others in whatever associative relationship they might have, e.g. U.S., German, English.

Close reading can show us the similarity between the same words with wholly opposite not just different meanings. Prophet and Profit are the most spectacular, but as Karl Marx tells us in his work on The National Jewish Question, when the Christians used their always flawed version of Christianity as their moral grounding they might adhere, at least in language, to the biblical prophets but when that Christian ethic was wholly replaced by the morality of capitalism, monopoly capitalism and imperialism the Prophet in question was no longer Jeremiah or Moses but the bottom line.

MEDIA is itself a distorted usage. And certainly we should be aware by now that the so called used to be Third Estate is no more. The original French categorization of divisions in society — the nobility, the clergy and the people, which supposedly included the press — when the people became the National Assembly in France the revolution began (1789). But now the process has long been in retrograde. The U.S. press is almost wholly controlled and is a shameful extension of corporate power. Just as is the government itself.

Language changes mean changes in society, changes in the order of things. For one thing, Terror is from Terra, a Latin word for the earth itself. How then does that get to be Terror? Intense/ear (C.T. Onions). To scare, to make one tremble (W.W. Skeats). And then to relate that to the U.S. use of Terrific meaning quite the opposite.

Media meant medium, the middle of two extremes, implying objectivity. But also, one supposes like the Medium that speaks messages from the other world, the dead, as a means. But the Media is not a medium except in the sense of a conduit, but a conduit for corporate and right wing ideas. Even the "alternative" weeklies are mostly instruments of corporate expression. The electronic media almost wholly owned by big money. ABC, CBS, NBC, FOX, MICKEY MOUSE are the big five in 5 the U.S. and they are Right of Center, Right, Righter, Rightest. Even the so called left of the U.S. media is right wing. In fact, though there are many certified Right of Center pundits on Television and Radio, the single Left of center program I can think of Bill Maher's "Politically

Incorrect" which is humorously and probingly Left of Center was eliminated from the regular television menu and allowed only on the less accessible Cable television channels. Fox is simply a right wing propagandist. Where once Afro American programs might at least cast an alienated look at mainstream U.S. society, the two biggest shows on television are Oprah Winfrey and Tavis Smiley, who are to the right of Maher. Most of the '60s Black shows have been long eliminated and the corporate government connection learned from the '60s that it was detrimental to allow people like Malcolm X and Martin Luther King, Stokely Carmichael, Rap Brown, &c., to have any consistent access to the airways. Most of the Black faces one sees now are fools, entertainers and athletes.

The media is one of the main shapers of society today, psychologically and as paradigm, using outright lies, disinformation, empty entertainment, right wing talk shows, as disseminators and popularizers of the amalgam of imperialist commercial culture. Fewer and fewer of the old classic movies, the pre fifties social commentaries even reach the small screen. Remember there was social commentary even in the Film Noir detective stories, classic westerns, and tales of class struggle, ancient and modern.

So the media is not medium, it is decidedly right wing. And though it can use words coined in popular use, it can quickly subvert those words. How did kinky, an adjective describing Afro American hair, get to mean weird sexual appetites? How did the term Politically Correct which was the sought after correction of phenomena that were Politically Incorrect (such as in the Arts and the Academy and Government) get to be a satirical term for what is the least desirable aspect of a thing? Something drained of all life and meaning was what the media transformed Politically Correct into in a short period. Many of the people using the term no longer know what it means.

When the people's oppressors co-opt and take from popular language and make it their own, as for instance when Lyndon Johnson used the term "We Shall Overcome" stolen from the very movement he was repressing or Richard Nixon shouted "Power to The People" ripping off the Black Panther party's slogan at the same time he was killing Black Panthers, it is one continuing technique to confuse and counterattack against the people's initiatives. Any kind of language made popular among the people will be copped by the media and the monsters its serves immediately. Bill Clinton saying, "I'm outta here" or "Illing" (he was).

There are also not quite subliminal manipulations of language to render progressive categories passé or confusingly redefined. For instance, get a definition of what "Post Modern" means. Except as I define it as a linguistic method of derailing historic experimental and progressive art. But what is post modern a "Road Warrior" society or simply as evidenced in the dialogue of some of the most backward L*a*n*g*u*a*g*e poets an excuse to sit in the tenured office and denounce literary political activism as an "impossible ideology." But ask the next user of this gobbledygook what it means.

The term Black Exploitation films which at best means films with mainly Black actors and themes focusing on Black people, released during the period of upsurge of the Black Liberation Movement which sought to oppose the exploitation and oppression of the Afro American people is transformed into a dismissal of these films as movies exploiting Black people — it's the exact opposite. Yet those films were in many instances (*Superfly, Buck & The Preacher*) infinitely superior to the garbage offered with Black faces today. The industry discovered (as did government &c) that they did not need to help create Black films which might be radically critical of U.S. life, history, and society itself when all they had to do was to put a Black face in the most disgusting mess and Black people would go see it. *Training Day* and *Monster's Ball* attest to this. To give Denzel Washington and Halle Berry Academy Awards for these is the coup de grace (actually the bribe to join the volunteer army in invading Iraq!)

In the arts as well as social history the events and personalities of the '60s are being consistently covered (music industry word) and hidden. The great poets, writers. painters, musicians, dancers, thinkers of that turbulent period are being covered up. Martin Luther King is "sampled" superficially to support exactly what he opposed. When King said we did not want to integrate into a burning building. The elevation of Black Secretaries of State and Supreme Court Justices are done exactly to affect that suicidal entrance. The former to threaten and lie to the largely Colored world. The latter to second the initiation of criminally reactionary legal and political action. For instance the sanctioning of the Bush presidential coup in 2000, or the elimination of the Knock & Announce requirement for Police entering a home. Again in 2004 there was a Negro, Ohio Attorney General Blackwell, who sanctioned the second criminal possession of the white house, that fraudulent election. There are microcosmic examples of criminal Negrossity throughout the country.

Even among the oppressed the change of language reflects a change of mind of time place and condition. Black is no longer motivational. Actually the address of the term to politics is called "Old School." When I asked Danny Glover, the actor in San Francisco in 1967, to come and join our Black Communications Project attached to San Francisco State and the grass roots Black Arts West, "...to do something for the people," he did. I doubt if that plea would work today among many Black youth of the same age.

Paul Robeson said, the artist must take a stand, either for fascism or democracy. The greatest writers have always stood on the side of freedom and human development. Whether, like Shakespeare, they characterize the idiocy of a society that wants to behead scholars who wanted to bring a formal grammar into the language. Writers like the great Chinese author, Lu Hsun, still barely known, in his masterwork, *Diary of a Madman*, was able to characterize the repressive Chiang Kai Chek regime by using the metaphor of a mad man to disguise his attacks. He speaks of some people eating children and of course he is mad. Kafka's *Metamorphosis* or *The Penal Colony* or *The Hunger Artist* clearly presages the coming of fascism in Europe. Langston Hughes' *The Ways of White Folk*, are sharp, terrifying sometimes tongue in cheek descriptions of the racial fascism that has existed in The U.S. since the Slave trade. Ousman Sembene is able to characterize the neo colonial manipulation of the African people in a story like *Mandabi* and his many other works.

This is critical because the artist can make critical analysis of a society a more accessible quality of people's thinking. To make revolution understandable and desirable, to paraphrase Toni Cade Bambara. The artist can show the world not through a glass darkly but with the clarity of aesthetically and ideologically enhanced vision. No matter what style or technique. Realism is not necessarily realistic, abstraction, surrealism, fantasy, not necessarily obscure. I uphold Mao's "Let a hundred flowers bloom, Let a hundred schools of thought contend."

What is ironic in the present ugliness of the U.S., is that Bush and company have reversed Dimitrov's definition of fascism but to the same end. Dimitrov sd Fascism was the rule by terror by the most chauvinist, imperialist, jingoistic sector of finance capital. Bush and company use the fear of terror as the rationale for terror.

So there has been in the U.S. especially a terrorization, an attempt to eliminate really creative and daring socially responsible and progressive intellectual pursuits. The re-emergence of the dullest kind of poetry and writing, fusion or confusion in music, reaction and shallow commerce in film and on stage all of it resembling the McCarthyism, Seven Kinds of Ambiguity '50s, The U.S. pre Civil Rights, Black Liberation movements pre Beat Generation & Theater of the Absurd, pre Black Arts Movement, pre anti war anti imperialist and student movements. Pre King, Pre Malcolm, Pre Panthers. But worse. All that is being subsumed into the rhetoric and material life of a nation whose memory of Left Unity and often victorious struggle is being wiped away by the hollow ugly footsteps of a people being led into Fascism.

It is one absolutely critical task of artists and intellectuals to oppose this dangerous political and artistic retrogression with either art that is artistically powerful and politically revolutionary, scholarship that can engage in the "struggle of ideas" as Fidel Castro puts it and political activism. Our lives depend on it.
(6/2006)

Black Fire: A New Introduction

Black Fire was intended as a statement, a declaration and a "roster" to inspire "recruitment." A statement, in so far as the book itself, that such a body of work existed. Not only Black & committed to the struggle, but also to demonstrate, as Mao sd, that we could be politically revolutionary and artistically powerful. That was, likewise, its declaration, that the assembled were artists and militants, directly involved with the struggle to liberate the Afro-American people. It was meant also as some kind of "list" of the troops, a role call of the willing!

Remember, Malcolm X had been murdered & most of us in the book were Malcolm's sons and daughters. And this was a period when "Revolution is The Main Trend In The World Today!" In fact, it was Malcolm's murder that sent many of these artists out of the Greenwich Village & other similar integrated liberal arty "cool-out" zones up to Harlem & other Black communities to take up what we felt now were our "responsibility" in the Black Liberation Movement. In New York that was the setting up of the Black Arts Repertory Theater School on West 130th Street and Lenox Avenue in Harlem. Most of the writers are young. This was the generation that came up after Jimmy Baldwin. Some of us were accused of actually hectoring Jimmy to return from Europe & join the struggle, which he did in a gallant way (See *No Name In The Street*).

The BARTS had fallen apart after a year of fierce & finally even gun violent internal struggle. But as far as some of the work we pledged to do, it was an auspicious start. Six days a week we sent four trucks out across Harlem. One with Poets, one with a graphic arts exhibit. Another with actors to do some of the plays featured in this collection and others. A number of the writers in Black Fire rode those trucks and mounted the homemade stages painter, Joe Overstreet conceived from banquet tables, riding under The Black Arts flag designed by painter William White.

Another truck carried musicians like Sun Ra (whose poetry is in the anthology as well) Pharoah Sanders, Don Pullen, Milford Graves, Albert Ayler, Grachan Moncur, organized by Andrew Hill to vacant lots, playgrounds, parks, to bring the most advanced Black Arts to the people of Harlem. It was a wonderful summer's work.

The Black Arts Repertory Theater School self- (and FBI) destructed because "Black" is not an ideology and so the unity gained under that finally nationalist but reductionist label, though it was an attempt to locate & raise the National Consciousness, could not hold. In that emotional spontaneity there was not an advanced enough unity to maintain the eclectic entity that "Black" had brought together, Nationalists, Muslims, Yoruba devotees, Marxists, under the cover integrationists, Christians, all the above-ists. And I repeat the FBI was hard at work, Harold Cruse had two agents (we took photographs) in his political science class at the Arts.

But though that institution failed, on the immediate practical side, it was the flare sent up that marked the explosion of Black Arts institutions across the country. And this book was but one fragment of that burgeoning movement. What we said we wanted to do at BARTS was create an art that was (1) Black by form & content, as Black as Billie Holiday or Duke Ellington (2) An art that was Mass oriented, that could move easily in and be claimed by the Black Community as part of a Cultural Revolution. (3) We wanted an art that was Revolutionary. As revolutionary as Malcolm X or the new African revolutionaries.

From the anthology itself, it is possible to see our intentions & our contradictions and eclecticism. Still, it is a powerful document of that time & of the BLM in overview historically and yet it focuses on aspects of the struggle still very much in evidence today. Larry Neal and I were, indeed, comrades in struggle, although ultimately our paths diverged somewhat. Still, he was to me, a kindred spirit. He was one of the most influential publicists of the Black Arts Movement, and one of its most powerful artists, as his poems here attest.

By the time the book was put together, I had returned to Newark as BARTS imploded. The original book jacket photo of Larry & I sitting on the steps of the Spirit House, in Newark, which my wife, Amina & I had organized to continue the cultural revolution of the BARTS always has a special significance. Razor sharp, Larry Neal & the recently Dashiki wearing "Roi" Jones. It is an image, in some ways, of the united front inside the book against white supremacy & submissive "integration into a burning building" (as Malcolm and Dr. King both told us).

A Real Note: What is so frustrating, though scientifically understandable, is the muting of the most militant of these voices as well as any similarly "Black Militant" or revolutionary voices by the accumulated "covers" (record industry word), co-optations & betrayals attributable to what DuBois called "The Sisyphus Syndrome," where each time we roll the huge boulder of soi-disant U.S. democracy up the towering mountain of U.S. hypocrisy & resistance, the "Gods" roll it back down on our heads.

The present incredibly tepid face of American (including Afro-American) literature confirms DIS! *Black Fire* was meant to dismiss such passionless employment applications (in the racist bourgeois establishment) passing as poetry, drama, &c. But the present state of U.S. literary affairs, which of course, mirrors the present state of US social-political affairs confirms that fact of how much another Cultural Revolution is needed here in the U.S. & all over the world.
(8/2006)

Why Most Poetry Is Boring Again?

You look at these various chapbooks and magazines, with wild titles — titles that announce that the titlers think they're "way out," with the "work" inside. These same folks and their "critical" extensions think it is "the cat's pajamas." But if, like me, you receive maybe a hundred of such works per year, what you notice is that after a few minutes of perusal, or a few more, if there's some sign of life, you can close the opus without much reflection.

The crux is that we're caught between two trends which are actually forces. Because the dialectic of the world permits not only of the objective, the actual, the real, world, but also of subjective, distorted reflections of that objective reality. Of course, reality itself, though diverse, as the exact context of time place and condition can still be objectively determined. Mao sd that art is an ideological reflection of the world in the mind of the artist. The key phrase here is "Ideological reflection." What you think is what you see. But then the measure of sanity must be how close one's perception & rationalization of the world corresponds to objective reality.

The bourgeois intellectual (or to place it at the level of bar room dialogue) viz. most of these dull ass writers, eschew the actual for some tamponed version, which pleasures their ideological & socio-psychological persona. Another, more or less spontaneous, aspect of this dullness includes the desire to be "included" in the social diarrheic of the society's value and meaning. Not only those "Academic Cowards of Reaction" (the title of a poem of mine) about e.g., the conjurers of the phrase "post modern" which cd only mean a society in retrograde, where the believers in such are passive road warriors of tenured security. Answers to the Bushmen's need for "intellectual" justification for the march to fascism.

This would include certain babbling crypto-Babbits – of the so called L* A *N*G*U* A *G*E poets whose theoretical quasi "Left" masquerade seeks to obscure a limp conservatism that opposes (e.g., Ginsberg's) political activism by artists as "an impossible ideology." And with that construe their dullness to be profoundly arty. There is certainly the blunt consideration of "being safe," not rocking career, academic, employment, boats by "saying something." As the poet Michael Pingarron sd, in a poem defending me (*Big Hammer*, 4/05) "we're free to speak/provided we keep our mouths shut."

In the case(s) I speak of, it is the tail waggling flashily out of Bush's behind, like Gerald 2Xs '60s devil cartoons. One wonders is it still called "high art." Now too high to deal with the angst and pain and ignorance of the real world. Though certainly it is an obtuse registry of it. Content with the masturbatory inoffensiveness of an actual loyal opposition, inferred loudly as "deep" intellectualism. Childish feints at surrealism, useless abstraction, jokey pop art, inside jokes for the un cognoscenti, all pass as, wow, poetry!

Actually, for all the self hype that such posturing is "far out," in reality it is all the way in. As Brecht sd, how much safer is abstract red, because it does not have to "take sides," like blood pumping out of the slain worker's chest. Duchamps commode is in the most revered of bourgeois showplaces, and after a brief shuffle of recognition, the banks much prefer abstraction, pop art, the weirder the better, so that there are no living images of this hell we inhabit.

Part of the impetus of the Black Arts Movement, created after Malcolm X's murder by the same forces that control the white house today, was that we wanted an art that actually reflected the culture & feeling of the Afro-American people, and by extension what existed in America itself. An art that wd come out of the classrooms & elitist dens of obscurity & help move the masses of people to revolutionary positions.

Today, that movement & its paradigm are either covered or reviled, usually by establishment call persons. One who sd, he didn't know anything about the Black Arts Movement but he was sure Black people didn't dig it! But these kinds of attacks are not just aimed at the BAM, the most moving arts of that generation of whatever nationality (e.g., The Beats, SF School, Black Mountain, New York School) The whole generation that formed an active United Front against boring academia are dissed directly as they have done recently in the *New York Times* to Frank O'Hara and Ginsberg. The entire generation of artists who actually worked to register some understanding of "the great outdoors" i.e., the real world (outside the classroom) & all its bloody turbulence and contradiction, have been systematically kicked to the curb. The literary establishment has always tried to do this, but there has always been a parallel movement by those artists concerned with transforming the world by trying to create an alternative superstructure. The generation of the '60s were exploding in reaction to the pit of abstruse irrelevance the academic conservative, often anglophilic literature that dominated in the '50s which co existed with and was a microcosm of the vicious backwardness of McCarthyism.

In part such a literary trend, in itself, was a repudiation of the socially engaged and experimental writing of the '20s and '30s, just as McCarthyism was a "correction" to the red '30s and the U.S. war against Nazi fascism which hoisted expectations of a post war progressive democracy. But the retrograde superstructure and political fortress of monopoly capitalism opposed such idealism. BeBop, one anti progressive sd at the time in the '40s, was another form of Stalinism.

But just as Langston Hughes and William Carlos Williams (or Henry Dumas & Ed Dorn or Larry Neal & Charles Olson) were in the real world and DuBois is excluded from the latest Britannica list of "100 greatest writers" because he stooped to talk about the world, the institutions, publications, media of the bourgeois superstructure influence and dictate to artists and intellectuals that art should not be used to directly transform society, but is more profound when it is a solipsistic individual gratification, a mantra of the grand isolated elitism of aesthetic billionaires.

The "Thermidor" to the revolutionary period is not only being insufficiently resisted by all of us, particularly the artists, since ironically the civil rights and anti imperialist movements of the period have, at worst, enabled a class of neo-con slackers to step into positions of prominence and power, claiming to be "new" but actually carrying the very ancient baggage of minority rule. *(9/2006)*

Creeley Tribute

The United Front against academic poetry was best sounded by Charles Olson's "Projective Verse," "The Open Field," "instanter upon instanter" Allen Ginsberg gave me William Carlos Williams' "American Speech," the "breath phrase" (*Le Fou*, p. 32 for *Charles*). But that teaching from WCW (*Lion & Dog* p. 28) a more dissembled metaphor of Thought Knowledge Action (See intro to *Selected Poems*, p xxi) A Poet of "Love" & "Words" to say that précised "What must be sd."

The convergence of Creeley & Olson is gigantic ideation of the world. Going in both directions past through here. The Pre Sent (from there, the past, the present passes) Creeley names Pound, Zukofsky, Williams as mentors, included bigly Olson & the wealth of the assembled Levertov, Duncan Dorn, Wieners, McClure, Ginsberg, peers. Words Love, (*The Sentence*, p 26; *The Immoral Proposition*, p. 36; *I Know A Man*, p. 40; *The Whip*, p. 45: *The Hill*, p. 71) *Language* Complex & Simple.

But what we shd be keenly aware of is that the THEY we know to be animatedly evil, has now, to confirm DuBois' Sisyphus Syndrome, which he ascribed to the Black Liberation Movement is, in fact, the response imperialism, national oppression, makes to any form of rebellion or assertion of an alternate way of living or thinking.

So that of the great & glorious phalanx of ourselves in the post-McCarthy '60s, for at least until the late '70s, all that rush of poetry & music, that would be the beast's response. Even though there was always the tit for tat answer to our struggle to advance human life & Mind. Through all our advance, Kennedy, Malcolm, King, Kennedy were gunned down, apparently by those forces that sit in the Caucasian Crib at this very moment!

So they have tried to cover & obscure all we have done. Who but the few of us knows Creeley's work? Even fewer know the great Charles Olson. Allen Ginsberg is given notice, but in this age, given a debunker's analysis. Check out the *NY Times* review of "Howl: The Poem That Changed America."

They have even told us recently that Richard the 3rd. was good guy & now Judas is rendered hip. All a reflection of the time we live in. The post 911 world of 911 lies, false wars, now completely privatized except for the dying. (*Plague*, p. 33; *Ever Since Hitler*, p. 344)

Two stolen elections testify to the post democratic obviousness of this, our country, which, in truth, says DuBois, "has never been a Democracy." When Malcolm was murdered, I thought there should be (there was) War. And so I moved away from what AG called "the era of Good Feeling" which was Greenwich Village & the Lower East Side, ending with the flight to Harlem. And so ignited, with others, The Black Arts Movement. Because in M X's murder which followed JFK's it seemed to me (we) that the Racial Fascism that we had always known & thought as I got older and met intellectual & artist friends that that horror cd be transcended. But alas, it has merely grown into Globalization, Tsunamis, Katrina's, Iraq, Guantanamo's.

But during that passing time there was between a few of us AG, Dorn, Creeley Joe Early, &c and what passed for a "New Left" some useful connection. Read CO on his reflections on AB at the time of the Cuban revolution. Read Creeley's review of AB's *Transbluesency*, there is in all that dimensions of a changed and changing world. Now they have endeavored to obliterate &/or lie about everything valuable from that time of a mass willfulness not only to break out of the money jungle of obscene America Monopoly capitalism and imperialism politically, but of a generations attempt to poet its way out of the colonial prison of American Academic Anglo stoogism. In this nation's rightward plunge that single phrase "the '60s" is used more an more by the enemies of humanity to represent things obscure, ugly or irrelevant. Best we resist this as we would resist our own murders.

(2006)

On *Blood Luxury*
by Ewuare Osayande

What a title! It washes over and through you, combining and overrunning with relatedness. Blood as Blood, itself, a toxic swagger let out mostly everywhere, not anymore as much some life circulating fluid.

Or Blood as stole in. To Be, then, "The Blood" as we is called amongst we…(and even A *Gang*—past tense of going, i.e., gone) We are most familiar these days with the Blood of vampire Killer appetite Bush Fiends. Definitions summarize power, place, energy.

To run that into "Luxury" is to make an image of exquisite "insanity." Like the "Caucasian Crib" where Wheaties cereal killers, live. What kind of hideous "light" seeps out: Luxor was "the light of the world"; Elegba left the "y" to question.

Ewuare is young, strong-minded, full sensed and aware and yet aware he must get to wear the world like an inside the head & heart stocking cap. The outrage is the opening of the senses to reality—The dismissal of "The Given."

So begin with "A Defiant Grace" another wonderful title (to Gwen Brooks), then to "Buck" (Dolor is pain and literally Bread FR< > SP, depends on the accent.)

What makes for the strength of the young poet's seeing is the constant "dignity" that the slave has. Yes, Buck the system, but know that it must be finally destroyed. As any such "liberation" within it is just a dance step, necessary, difficult, sometimes exhilarating but if not understood as "a stage" becomes a twist.

If we are past being outright Chattel, how come the whole two cents never got here. If 89.9 percent Bloods "voted" (we know that's a lie), they thought, against Bush, then 1.01 has been copped, and we still have not received all our sense, and remains at 3.9. But at least, you say, we ain't wooden Negroes who is only 3 cents whom E refers to, the "Hoes" found in all sexes.

What makes the book alive is that at each turn the poet reaches to grab the ugly and wrestle with it, and as contrast/contradiction to DuBois-Keats' "Truth & Beauty," for instance, sensitive to "the woman question" and how well paid "Hoes" have contracts to demean Black women. He says the women "the sistah" (the Black Man) harassed/is Black/too." So saying, the old cultural nationalist saw of African Traditionalism covering Male Chauvinism is pierced.

We won't go on, just to say that Ewuare is like the image Mao posed about Revolution, a ship yet some distance away, but whose tall and inspiring sails are already visible. Or as my ultimate artist-philosopher-teacher, T Sphere Monk said, upon visiting one of my painter friends, "Man you in a tough bi'nezz." So, say that for the poet, or the one who carry the RAZOR (Revolutionary Art for Cultural Revolution). Take this book as this brother's imposing sail, already aware of how to use the turbulence of the crooked to give fuel to his focus.

One more word, check the poem "It Must Be The Shoes." Re: not only Error Jordan, but of the heaping compost of nouveau coon petty and comprador Zapalote who ironically, but quite scientifically predictable,* have grown big butt stomachs on their "next!s" as a result of the peoples struggles, and whose gig is now to suppress, silence, sit on and lie to us. This work, already passed around by mouth, based on the poet's hot *Djeli Ya*…is, in its solid composition; its raging metaphor; its relentless ideological (class) analysis, is one coming attraction of how tough this lad gonna be. The Goodest Knews is that Ewuare is one of a dozen or so really significant younger *Djali* who seem to know where they wants to go, in fact, they is already going…and got a RAZOR in each hand!

(*See Lenin, Vol 15, 18, *Collected Works*, "How Liberalism Separated from Democracy")
(2006)

Notes on Culture, Art and More

Spirituality & Religion:
The Views of Three Giants

Recently a book was published by my bad friend, Marvin X. I know most people speak of their good friends, but they don't be talking about Marvin. The book was called *Beyond Religion: Toward Spirituality*. Marvin says that quite a few ministers & faithful have condemned the book, sight unseen, for his, to them, unseemly title.

But it is a good title, although I certainly don't agree with several of the ideas in the book. Still, the idea that we must make a distinction between Religion & Spirituality is very valid. The formal corporate "church" is an abomination before any God, but theirs, which is Money. But it is a fact that so-called organized religion does not promise much of anything but Sunday morning release, after a week of work.

The stunning fakery that churches lead us into, whether Catholics vs. Protestants in Ireland (which any thoughtful person knows is not about Religion but about British imperialism's 700 year domination of Ireland) or the fakery of the trumped up Islam vs. Christianity or Islam vs. Judaism are likewise fraudulent political scams meant to take people emotionally, but hiding the reality, that each is about U.S. & Western (including Israeli) Imperialism. The so called "Faith based Charity" is little more than a bribe for churches & ministers big & small, to follow George Bush into fascism! But the church, as an institution, has always suffered the uncertain morality of its shepherds, face it, that is one of the abiding strains of humor in Black American religious lore.

Like most of us, I was raised in a Baptist church, where my grandfather was president of the Sunday School, my grandmother a mover in the Ladies Aid Society & my mother one of the stylish educated young ladies who saw to much of the church's social functions. My uncle was a trustee & later, after my mother died, my father, who never went to church before that, became a Deacon. (Deacon Jones — the one who Louie Jordan accused of "throwing the whiskey in the well.")

But I confess, though I was given a great deal of helpful instruction, some of it rude and very physical, my grandmother could pinch my thigh when I was "acting the fool" enough to make a tear pop up. I got beat half to death when I went into the church basement & turned off the electricity — they thought the organist had had a stroke — but for all the wealth of religiosity, when I got baptized at twelve & popped up out of that water underneath the pulpit and felt nothing had happened, the formality of religion was laid to rest for me. And, alas, today still trodding that same road, I am a Godless Communist. But then, spirituality for me is quite another presence. Certainly religion is to co-opt & take advantage of human spirituality. Spirit (from Spiritu) means literally Breath. It is the Breath of Life. What comes through us, in and out of us constantly. If Breath is the cymbal, the heart is the drum. From the Sun, the Soul, the essence of our lives.

So that, for me, spirituality is that character of ourselves that lives through our body. It is the essence of our being. So that there is a spiritual quality about living things, even animals. But human spirituality is supposed to confirm that they are of a higher order; living in America these 300 odd years has sometime made us doubt it.

It is the life force of something: how totally alive it is. Because just as I believe we have yet to develop all the senses, still restricted to the easy 5, I believe, I sense, that there is much more to life than we know or comprehend. It is our spirituality that puts us in touch with beauty or can make us sensitive to truth. Though that is one of the horrors of living in this still undemocratic neo slave society....Beauty & Truth are always the first things to be attacked or smothered by the ugliness and greed of our oppressors.

That's one of the tragedies of an imperialist hyper mercenary society for the expediency of monopoly capitalism and its hand maidens Afro American National oppression & racism, and the general suppression of democratic rights. A popular peoples' culture has been replaced by vulgar commercialism. Whether it is the straight out filth & pornography of films and television or the radio and music CDs. Whether it's the creep, Imus, who the people finally brought down, or the 50 Cent & Snoop Dog, who want to make the same attack on Black people & Black women in particular. But we shd understand that both Imus & the more reactionary Rappers exist because of corporate dollars.

When Proctor & Gamble, NBC, Staples and General Motors saw a broad spectrum of Unity & Struggle against the idiot Imus they pulled out & that was his b hind! So when we look at the filth, the anti spiritual, the coarse racism and anti woman stream of filth and not only that but the no where, ugly, uninspiring, dead end themes of this stuff, finally they exist because of the corporate ownership of the U.S. The corporations oppose what is overtly spiritual, what is out front trying to raise human consciousness, in music, literature, media, politics. People are easier to rule when they're ignorant & believe they are in the best of all possible worlds.

Compare the literature, music—jazz & Motown, painting, poetry, drama of the '60s, '70s early '80s, during a period of Cultural Revolution & you'll see. From the Impressions "Keep On Pushin,"' "People Get Ready," Sam Cooke "A Change Is Gonna Come;" Marvin Gaye, "What's Going On" even James Brown, "I'm Black & I'm Proud" or the Max Roach-Abbey Lincoln works, Nina Simone "Mississippi Goddam," Charlie Mingus "Fables of Faubus" Sonny Rollins, John Coltrane and the great Duke Ellington. Listen to "For My People" or "Black, Brown & Beige" among many others. I mention just these things so you do a mental comparison of the inspiring yet even intellectually daunting art of that period of open declaration of Cultural Revolution & today's Eddie Murphy, Tyler Perry, The Wayans family (they even want to play "white chicks" not only that but as FBI agents!) The powers gave all those Academy Awards to Negroes (notice) a few years ago because they wanted you go to Iraq with them. But they didn't give an award to Denzel for *Malcolm X* or *Hurricane* but for playing a corrupt Negro cop who corrupts this pure white rookie cop. And the flick with Halle Berry was simply garbage, the moral of it being "you can fall in love with the racist who murdered your husband and end up eating ice cream on your back with him looking up at the stars."

Awards for Sidney Poitier with Whoopee Goldberg

emceeing "Now that you all are Americans, you can go to Iraq, (since you don't have a job & can't go to college) & get killed" What are the highest & noblest feelings and impulses & ideas—what do we aspire to? What do we see as beautiful? What do we denigrate? These are measures of our spirituality. What in life animates us? The first chapter of DuBois' great classic The *Souls of Black Folk* begins with that, "On Our Spiritual Striving." He is saying that the act of trying to be human in a world that has chains and whips to keep you from it is "A Spiritual Striving."

It was DuBois who said, "Many people have suffered as much as we..." but none of them was Real Estate!!" That is his genius to understand the specific damage done to us. God knows we been "buked & scorned," lynched, burned, robbed, historically segregated, discriminated against, but none of this was as evil as to be made into "Real Estate!" That is the attempt to remove us from humanity, to de-humanize us, to eliminate our spirituality is what it was. And in many ways, when you see too many of a whole new generation willfully playing "Sambo" it makes you angry.

My wife, Amina stopped our boys from running around calling each other "Dog" (which Spike Lee made popular in his flicks by having Black women in reaction to male chauvinism, calling Black men that) by telling them that if they were dogs that made her the B-word and that was sure gonna get them knocked in the head! To raise the human consciousness, to drive it yet to higher levels of contemplation, like my grandmother used to say, we were gonna meet again "on higher ground" (Thank you, Nana). This should be the general thrust of *Our* Spiritual Striving.

It should be obvious that this society, led as it is by corporate savagery & greed, whose mouthpiece is the foolish son of oil billionaires, can only lead the country, all of us, to Hell, to Fascism. To fiery doom. Bush and his other figure heads of corporate capitalist rule might claim to go to church, but it is a church run by Satan's earthly surrogate. Bush's mother's remarks in New Orleans at the Superdome when Black children wallowed in excrement that "these people were doing better than they usually do," had all the spirituality of a shriveled old vampire. Now that they have allowed Katrina's destruction of the levee to eliminate a large part of the Black Community, in New Orleans which I'm convinced was as accidental as a firing squad, they will now recreate the place exactly like Bush's mother, dead white and absent of much spirituality. But what intrigues me in DuBois' Credo which says he believes in a "...God who made of one blood all men, "the vision of what that God would have to be when that consciousness is opposed on Earth? Is it a spiritual paradigm or a personal God? Certainly the God most Americans believed in was not that God.

In the second paragraph, DuBois' focus on Spirituality, the spirituality of Black folks, "Especially do I believe in the Negro Race in the beauty of its genius, the sweetness of its soul & its strength in that meekness..." "Finally, I believe in Patience...patience with God" It is interesting that of the three writers I want to mention today that DuBois is the most God speaking, but he became a Communist! Perhaps he had run out of patience with God or was practicing what the Christian communists of Latin America called Liberation Theology.

Another quote of DuBois that we should remember was that Black people had given American three gifts: The Gift of Labor, The Gift of Song & Story, The Gift of Spirit (in the struggle for Democracy). Our spiritual striving. And in the great chapter from *Black Reconstruction*, "The Coming of The Lord" he characterizes 19th century Afro American Religion and Spiritual Culture And I paraphrase, suppose one night you might meet the Lord walking toward you in the street with his head ringed with stars and you'd say, Lord why am I a slave? And he told you, you had sinned and fallen and now you must redeem yrself. So that when Chattel Slavery fell, Black people thought, It was The Coming of The Lord!

Langston Hughes said the book that most influenced him, he said he read it three times, was DuBois' *The Souls of Black Folks*. One reason I tend to think of DuBois as the Father of the Harlem Renaissance. Langston talked about God, Jesus & Christ in his poetry. And the church itself was touched on & frequently & warmly as the butt of humor in his writings. But for Hughes, the Black church lent a cultural specificity to his view of the Black community. DuBois did a classic study of the Black church in the chapter "Faith of The Fathers" in *Souls*, analyzing the history & cultural impact: it's triumphs & it's foibles and foiblers, his writings, like the music of Duke Ellington have a classic spirituality about them.

But Langston, from jump, is secular & very much the Djali, which is what the French word Griot means to describe except Griot means "Cry" like the northern expression on the Mask of Drama. Djali is just what it sounds like, the African word for the poet, story teller, musician, historian who moves through a community to raise its consciousness like the poet's most ancient job is to raise the sun each morning like Orpheus — to maximize human spirituality! Yet Langston's work, the poetry most of all, but also the drama, short stories, the novel, the two-part autobiography *The Big Sea* & *I Wonder As I Wander* are clearly the Djali's Djeli Ya, the inspirational aid to our spiritual striving.

While DuBois holds his reference to God as a presence of highest Power & Meaning, Langston sees God or The Lord or Jesus in all kinds of otherwise mundane situations. "Caribbean Sunset," "God having a hemorrhage, Blood coughed across the sky Staining the dark sea red, That is sunset in the Caribbean" (Hughes).

See, there he just created the sunset with, of all things, a hemorrhage. It is actually a kind of downsizing of the Deity & giving it an unlikely human ailment — to explain nature. What about "Ma Lord" where Langston says directly "My Lord ain't no stuck up man / Ma Lord, he ain't proud / When he goes walkin' / He gives me his hand. / You ma friend," he 'lowed" (*Collected Poems*). It is the religion DuBois' cites in his "Coming of the Lord," the faith of the Black slaves, then of the Black poor, farmer & working class.

Hughes' love poems (118-9) bring the God & Jesus reference face to face with Black life. A savior but one that must understand the hardships & slip ups of being Black in America. Yet in the "Angels" poems e.g., "Angel's Wings" (from *Collected Poems*) you can see that he is mocking, perhaps, the big house Negroes in their Big House churches. Wings "white as snow" can't fit the Black working class, farmers and poor, who've been dragged through the muck of slavery and oppression in America.

When the more politically intense '30s comes along, Langston's use of God & Jesus images becomes more pointed & political, either the sassy directions of "God Slumbers" (136 op cit), which is now not just wanting to beg & whine to God & Jesus but is urging that God "stand up and fight like a man." Perhaps believing, as he has characterized in some of his factual pieces, individuals who use religion to avoid dealing with the brutal racist world! Langston even sees Christ (and this occurs in several poems) victimized by the racist society In "Christ In Alabama" "Christ is a nigger / Beaten & Black / Oh, bare your back!"...The poem ends, "Most holy bastard / of the bleeding mouth / Nigger Christ / On the cross / Of the south" (*CP* p. 143) It seems that if DuBois's God

"Who made of us out of one blood" wd come to earth, the Alabama poem wd be his fate!

By the middle of the '30s Langston had become heavily influenced by Marxism and his trip to the Soviet Union. The poem, "Good Bye Christ" gives us yet another one of Langston's changing characterizations of Divinity. Here as dupe of the rulers to divert working people's mind from making revolution! Ironically, Langston's "Red" period which you can check out if you find the book *Good Morning, Revolution!* Was where he had to pay a price for his '30s views (including the poem "Put Another S In the USA)" so like the Union of Soviet Socialist Republics it would be the Union of Soviet States of America!

He was attacked in the '50s by HUAC & made to testify where he "copped a plea" saying he no longer had those views. His readings by then were picketed by right wing groups including the religious zealot Aimee McPherson. Because of this, he seemed happy in the '60s when we young Black nationalists come uptown and began to talk bad about white folks. In honor of that (or so it seemed to me) he issued the book *Black Panther* dedicated to Stokely Carmichael, the leader of SNCC, who was organizing then in the South. To bring in a third great writer, I choose James Baldwin, who confirms the great wealth in the treasure chest of Afro American culture and the duty it is for all of us who claim to be conscious to go to that treasure chest & spread the word & teaching about it to produce the works, plays, readings, study circles to reignite the Cultural Revolution, like the Black Arts in the '60s to counter the low level of cultural awareness this down cycle of the Sisyphus Syndrome has brought us to!

For Langston, it was the culture itself that was spiritual, the way he describes it in "The Negro Writer & The Racial Mountain." What makes Jimmy Baldwin such a paradigm of sharp analytical comparison between spirituality is religion. "The Spirit of The South is The Spirit of America" (*Evidence of Things Not Seen*) He says about the white Christian church "...we were not so much permitted to enter the church as corralled into it, as a means of rendering us docile and as a means of forcing us to corroborate the inscrutable will of God, who had decreed that we should be slaves forever. What a cowardly, not to say, despicable, vision of human life. What a dreadful concept of divinity." (*Op Cit* p 82-3)

Baldwin's understanding that "White America was neither

genuinely religious nor by any stretch of the imagination, Christian...The religious hypocrisy was the same as the social hypocrisy. White America was no more democratic than it was religious. Black people were no more citizens that White Americans were Christians" ("The Blood of The Lamb").

The contradiction between Religion & Spirituality is between that existent quality of actual life, as it is lived, & as it is envisioned, that is reflected in the persona, history & practice of a living being or a group of beings. Religion is the all too often flawed institution proposed to reflect & project the Spirituality of a people. Fred Douglass, in his July 4th speech, criticized the American church to such an extent he had to write disclaimers at the end, confirming the fact that he was a Christian and that he was, after all, simply urging people calling themselves Christians to stop the hypocrisy of professing religion while continuing to be slaveholders.

The Black church, through our years here, 1st held in the forest in secret, because we were even forbidden to seek God and then as the breakaway institution of a soon to be emancipated people, has led us, whether Douglass or Nat Turner or Malcolm X or Martin Luther King, but their religious stature was a reflection of the high level of spirituality which their lives expressed — not the church, per se.

These Three Giants of Afro American culture, I have barely touched on this evening, each express their relationship to the church & religion & to their own spirituality in ways which identify what their actual lives were! It is our Spiritual Striving, our struggle through Unity & Struggle to raises the level & quality of our lives that in turn raise the level & degree of our spirituality, the expression of our soul lives, the nature of our actual selves through the character of our actual deeds, our livingness.

Remember it is the Afro American people who have produced the Douglasses, Tubmans, The Sojourner Truths & DuBoises, the Langston Hughes & Zora Neale Hurstons, The Duke Ellingtons & Paul Robesons, the Margaret Walkers & Billie Holidays. It is our spirituality that leaves its historic finger prints on this world, whatever our individual churches might do.

Cultural Revolution and
The Literary Canon

The reactionary trend of the 1950s which produced McCarthyism and the Hollywood and academic purges, the Korean War, and Eisenhower was reflected in American literature by its domination by a punishingly dry, highly mannered magazine verse equipped with hot and cold running Latin and Greek phrases, footnotes and the emotional significance of a *New York Times* crossword puzzle.

This kind of literature was trumpeted and proselytized by the so-called New Criticism, which sought to remove all social relationship from poetry, from literature generally, making it a completely solipsistic and an elitist artifact that jingled stiffly about its not not self.

As it turned out, the New Critics were hardly that. Their leaders like Allen Tate, John Crowe Ransom, Cleanth Brooks, and Robert Penn Warren were identified with the Southern Agrarian Movement. (Allen Tate's book *Reactionary Essays* says most of it!) The Southern Agrarians preached a national chauvinist and metaphysical sentimentalization of the Chattel Slave Empire, claiming that industrialization was destroying the South, and a culture that ranked with the Greek Attic.

But the raised level of U.S. productive forces after WWII and the Korean War expanded advanced industrial labor and educational access to a much broader segment of the U.S. population, particularly to the second-generation immigrants and new generations of Blacks. There were ideas set in motion that disrupted the basic disposition of class forces in post-Korean War U.S., that challenged the basic social relations of the society, particularly to class privilege in the U.S. and white supremacy, the fundamental social organization of imperialist U.S. society.

On one hand, there was the group of largely petty bourgeois white youth who were called the Beat Generation, who claimed to rebel against the complacent mediocre hypocrisy of American fife. This middle-class rebellion appeared in literature heralded by Allen Ginsberg's poem "Howl." The so called Beats, along with other young American poets (e.g. the New York school of Frank O'Hara. Koch and Ashbery. The Black Mountain poets identified with Charles Olson and Robert Creeley) challenged the polished ready-made academic poetry as lifeless and socially irrelevant. They also challenged the American petty bourgeois lifestyle with their varied versions of mid-twentieth-century American bohemia.

But on even larger and even more sharply anti-imperialist development in the 1950s was the rise of the Civil Rights Movement and the most recent major upsurge in the continuing African American National Democratic Movement—the 1960s Black Liberation Movement—from the 1954 Supreme Court decision to desegregate public schools "with all deliberate speed" which apparently is extremely slow. (But that's just 35 years ago!), the movement took on momentum with the MLK-led Montgomery bus boycott of 1957; the formation of SCLC and SNCC and the student movement. the sit-ins; freedom rides, and countless demonstrations as the MLK-led "non violent" Civil rights phase peaked by 1963. Then the March on Washington and Malcolm X emerged as the new maximum leader of the movement, ushering in a more militant period with Stokeley Carmichael, Rap Brown, Huey Newton, The Black Panthers, U.S., RNA. and CAP rising to make revolutionary challenges to imperialism and white supremacy.

The largely white anti-war movement that rose at the same time took shape as part of the general resistance to Vietnam era U.S. imperialism but influenced in great part by the African-American movement.

Any period of sharp social upsurge produces a corresponding arts and cultural movement reflecting the social motion in the arts and culture. In the nineteenth century. the antislavery movement gave rise to the slave narratives, a whole genre of powerful American writing revealing the material, ideological, and psychological basis for continuing U.S. racism.

At the same time a more original (i.e., less imitative of Europe) native U.S. literature arose from other sectors of the Society as well. The work of Melville, Whitman, Dickinson, and Twain revealed this development, but such work was attacked or ignored by the still Tory dominated academic and official culture which was, and still is, English and European. The works' very "Americanness" made them untraditional in form and content. Part of the backwardness of official U.S. culture is its continued domination by Europe, and America never has been Europe.

In the early twentieth century. as whole cities of African-American people moved from the south to north and were transformed from rural dwellers to urban, from farmers to industrial workers, an anti-colonial,. anti-imperialist movement came into sharp relief throughout the world — particularly throughout the Black world. The frenzied industrialization of and preparation for World War I itself raised the level of productive forces so that the newly developed world girdling form of capitalism — imperialism — also gave rise to ideas in its superstructure advanced enough to counter it.

DuBois founded the Niagra Movement (1907) and the Pan Africanist Movement (1901). One was the first major integrated domestic organization of the twentieth century to fight for democracy and equality for the African-American people. The other was the beginning of the effort to unite African peoples world wide to resist their common enemy, imperialism, in the form of colonialism and white supremacy.

The African-American people had been betrayed by the U.S. government and the destruction of Reconstruction after the Civil War. Instead of reaping the fruits of Emancipation (1863) called for by the Thirteenth, Fourteenth, Fifteenth Amendments and forty acres and a mule, Black people had been reattacked by the newly formed Ku Klux Klan and gradually forced back into a neo-slavery. They were disenfranchised and legally segregated by the end of the nineteenth century. The so-called Black Codes imposed on the Black population in the South instead of full U.S. citizenship proved to be the model for Hitler's racial laws. This is understandable since fascism is fundamentally about slave labor. But under fascism even white people can be slaves!

The Black arts and cultural movement in this early part of the twentieth century was called the Harlem Renaissance, but of course it was not limited to Harlem. Harlem had become the largest Black city in the world. And that was where the unifying force of the newly rejuvenated Black thrust for democracy, in its domestic and international forms, was focused.

This literary arts and cultural movement produced great writers like James Weldon Johnson, Langston Hughes, Zora Neale Hurston, Jean Toomer, and Claude McKay. Not to mention Duke Ellington, Louis Armstrong, Bessie Smith, Aaron Douglass, among so many others. It was an art that reflected the social movement of the Pan African peoples as it expressed itself through every aspect of their lives.

Hughes's "The Negro Artist and the Racial Mountain" was even a formal challenge to the social and aesthetic values of the segregated white supremacist U.S. and called for an attention by Black artists to the mores and culture of the Black masses as the inspirational muse that would create a great African-American Art.

The more genuine American theater that O'Neill helped create during the same period saw Black characters on the stage in something approaching realism for the first time, as well as, an American working class. In fact, the so-called age of Modernism, one general reaction to the breakdown of the nineteenth-century formalism. metaphysics. and idealism to the Western world, its passage from competitive capitalism to monopoly. cannot be fully explained by telling us about the O'Neils, Steins, Pounds, Eliots, WCWs. Stravinskys, Picassos unless we also hear about the Harlem Renaissance. This is with that the Negritude, Negrissmo, Indigisme movements in Europe, West Indies, Africa, and Latin America which it catalyzed.

The outbreak of the 1960s, the third major political upsurge by the African-American people in a history of continued struggle for equality and self-determination, also gave rise to an art and cultural movement. The Black Arts Movement and, with that, The Black Theater Movement, wanted to create a poetry, a literature, which directly reflected the Civil Rights and Black Liberation movements. We wanted on art that was recognizably African American like Duke Ellington or Billie Holiday or Charlie Parker that was mass oriented. We wanted a poetry, for instance, that could come out of the libraries into the streets where the people were. Not a poetry whose very profundity was measured by who it didn't reach, or by who was not relevant to. We wanted a poetry that was direct, understandable, moving, and political. And lastly an art that was revolutionary, poetry that would help transform society, not merely lament or mystify the status quo.

People like Larry Neal, Askia Toure, Henry Dumas, Amus Mor, Carolyn Rogers, Mari Evans, Sonia Sanchez, and Leroi Jones emerged along with thousands of others to raise a Black art that was a continuation of the social uprising that fought to change society itself, as well as writers like James Baldwin and Lorraine Hansberry whose great writings began just before this period, and in some ways even set the tone for it.

The challenge to society brought with it a challenge to the philosophical. aesthetic. and institutional superstructure of the society as well, since it is not just the material base of the society that is imperialist but the ideas reflected in its superstructure as well.

The idea of Black Art was to challenge the "whiteness" of art as posited by a white supremacist society, as it somehow the society could be a slave society but the art does not reflect that slave-owning and slave-being mentality.

The literary canon, for instance, that accreted self-aggrandizement and solipsistic conquerors' mentality that is referenced as the greatness and profundity of so-called Western Art. Western Philosophy, is simply that, a body of materials whose content supposedly is the aspired revelation and evolution of humankind, but is in reality nothing but a justification (not very convincing) for imperialism. When Bloom and the other mothers accuse anti-imperialist thinkers of relativism in opposition to his colonial absolutism he is correct but unenlightened.

The attempt to re-establish the power of the actually nineteenth ¬century imperialist retake on so-called classic Western values and their fragile but sweaty kitbag of "masterpieces" is part of the normative reaction to any progressive or revolutionary social period. That is, like the Sisyphus myth, the rock is pushed up the hill, but then it is rolled partially back down again.

After the 1960s attack on the social and aesthetic values of U.S. imperialism, the late 1970s saw reaction rising by the time of Jimmy Carter, with both Malcolm X and Martin Luther King shot to death, and both Kennedys shot to death, equally mysteriously. The 1960s had raised the questions of the multicultural and multinational character of society and had challenged the white supremacist origins of the so-called literary and artistic canon.

In education Black Studies was set up in many schools, though it has yet to reach the high school and elementary school level and is still shaky even on the university level. To show you how deeply and profoundly cultural revolution is necessary to continue any political advantage the insurgents make, understand the falsity of an English Department when this has never been England, and the strength of the English Departments in contrast to American Studies or Black Studies. After the U.S. Revolutionary War, the Tories continued their hold on the superstructure until this day. We still have a colonial relationship with England in our arts and culture. Broadway, for instance, is still the home of old British play wagons.

The social thrust of democracy and anti-imperialism carried with it ideas that attacked the Eurocentric bourgeois nature of American education and official arts and pushed for a multinational and multicultural American culture and art expression that reflected reality. Just as the society was attacked as on oppressive exploitative one, so the literature, the art, was attacked as merely reflecting that exploitation, and being equally exploitative.

Mao Zedong's prescription for Cultural Revolution was as a continuing political struggle in the sphere of arts and culture to maintain the dominance of the working class and revolutionary ideas in the superstructure. Mao said further that if the Chinese Communist Party could not mount and maintain such a cultural revolution then the party would "change colors" and become a bourgeois party, even a fascist party. We can see from events at Tiananmen Square the tragic accuracy of Mao's teaching.

In the U.S. since the revolutionary trends of the 1960s there has been a distinct counterrevolutionary and reactionary trend. On one hand assassinations, jailings, and exiles disrupted a great part of the movement, both black and white, according to the Cointelpro documents and papers received through the Freedom of Information Act. This meant that not only were the basic gains of the progressive period called into question as surely as the Baake decision called into question affirmative action. but as the Carter years gave way to the Reagan years many of the things we had struggled for in the 1960s were openly agitated against. Witness, for instance, how the term "Liberal" by the late 1980s had become almost akin to how "Communist" was used in the 1950s. Opposition to Affirmative Action was made vague by opposing "quotas" instead, but the effect was the same.

By the same measure calls for a restoration of the Eurocentric and white supremacist so-called Greco-Roman, Judaeo-Christian standard of philosophical and aesthetic measure are really calls for a restoration of the social norms of the pre-rebellion 1950s. For instance the way subjects ore understood and classified and taught in the university confirms the segregation and white supremacy of the foulest aspect of the material base.

Historical periods of American literature are routinely taught in a divided notionally segregated fashion. Twentieth-century American literature is taught that does not connect Euro-American Modernism with the Harlem Renaissance, or the Beat Generation with the Black Arts Movement. The nineteenth-century literature removes Fred Douglass, Moses Roper, William Wells Brown, Nat Turner, Linda Brent, etc., from the literature and any aspect of the slaves' life is made sociological. But to quote Bruce Franklin, "African-American culture is not peripheral to American culture but at its heart." So that by ascribing some metaphysical racial greatness to the role of works corresponding to the bourgeois American canon not only is the history of the world distorted for oppression's, sake but the very psychological development of the American people. certainly its soi-disant intellectuals on these campuses.

For one thing the African people had a different aesthetic basis before our transportation to the New World. It was based on the animist philosophy which sees everything in existence as "living" but to different degrees, in aesthetic whose ancient religion was characterized by priest and congregation in a call and response relationship, in which the spirit that was to be sought could only be brought into proximity by music, and whose highest aspiration was to become possessed by that allest spirit.

These multi-registrations of being were reflected by the polyrhythms of the music (speech and thought) and by the polychromatic registration of bright color. Art was always preeminently social for all from all, a port of the very development of the total society.

The separateness of art from mass concern, the emphasis on Apollonian attributes of form and restraint, the enslavement of women by the rising philosophy and society of the northern cradle of Greece and co., the ultimate separation of thought from emotion as Nietzsche testified to in his *Birth of Tragedy* (Hamlet's disease of liberalism) are all social, philosophical, and aesthetic verifications of the culture manifest above the Mediterranean, after the ancient African-derived cultures were put in check politically and ultimately dominated. Women still carrying on the Dionysian ecstatic culture of the southern culture cradle were lynched by the Apollonian demagogues up into our own society at Salem witch burnings.

In addition to the traditional and historically developed differences of the African aesthetic, certainly the role of slave in relationship to slavemaster creates even larger distances of social and class perspective that must inform any black aesthetic. To impose the Apollonian, the formal, the academic above the creative, the womb man ness of art, is part of imperialism's continuing work which seeks not content but only form, not ecstasy but memoranda, and chauvinism and narrowness instead of the cosmopolitan, and the spontaneous or improvised, is imperialist superstructure work.

This is why the cultural revolution is so important today. We are in the midst of a deep reactionary period when revolution is once again held up as fantastic and only cynicism and betrayal and upholding the status quo qualifying as realism. In the 1960s indeed. "Revolution Is the Main Trend in the World Today," that's what we used to say. "Countries want Independence, Nations want Liberation, People want Revolution." But that is when the principal contradiction in the world was Imperialism vs. the People and Nations. But soon after, the contradiction of Imperialism vs. Imperialism which is the trend that leads to imperialist war, became principal, and me revolutionary movements were turned around by rising fascism.

We are at a crossroads in that struggle today. The attempt to restore the so-called literary canon to make political prisoners of world art and culture in the name of some self-aggrandizing super culture with neither origins nor relationship to the rest of the world is simply white supremacy returned. You cannot speak of Greek culture without relating it to the whole of the ancient world from which it sprang and which it continues to reflect.

In the Channel 13 bit of Goebbelsmania called The Art of the Western World, a statement was made that "Creativity began in

Greece." Naturally I wrote letters to them and a number of other folks challenging this mindless protofascism. A white rock critic for the Star Ledger told me "Creativity did begin in Greece ... for the Europeans." Any way you take this it's gas chamber logic, but then this was Boy speaking not Tarzan.

There is no life or culture, no art or philosophy separated from the whole expression of human life and being on the planet. It is the separation that is the first strand of barbed wire for the fences at Auschwitz, the more modern versions of southern plantations.

For those of us in the arts or the universities, those of us involved with the institutions and ideas of the U.S. superstructure, we must see that the only positive direction we can go, that is the direction of life supported over death, is cultural revolution. We must oppose the reinstitution of the racist canon, like we resist Part 25 of *Friday the 13th* or *Rambo XI*.

For instance, we must join forces to socialize the university and all institutions that affect our lives. By socialize I mean to make the university deal with real life and the actual society in which It stands. If the university is the repository for higher learning, advanced philosophy, and innovative technology, why are the cities in which they stand so bereft of these resources? There is no other way to measure ideas' usefulness except in the crucible of real life.

The university professor is never made to measure his ideas in relationship to the real world, in relation to how much change (i.e. human advance) or how close to reality the world measures those ideas to be, but is valorized only by the abstract and frankly elitist inter-academic dialogue. We publish for each other or to get tenure, we create and do research for the same reasons. While the great challenge, real life, real society, stands ailing and ill because our resources have been removed.

Why poor education, unemployment, no housing, drug panics in these cities and communities of our world if the universities are full of so many self-proclaimed geniuses and mountains of ominously profound conclusions? The university must be made to relate to these cities, to establish partnerships in developing real life to higher and higher levels of understanding and sophistication, not stand aside and praise itself for being so clean and so heavy and so outside everything, as is mostly now the case.

The cultural revolution at the university must see Black

Studies, Latino Studies, Women and Labor Studies, as the missing links of progressive education and preparation for a new and more humanized world society. Ignorance and lack of education must be made extinct. It is dangerous to the whole world for uneducated masses to exist. The extent to which we raise the world educational level is the extent to which we raise our own consciousness and the level of human life on the planet.

Such studies must also be extended to the high schools and elementary schools, and used in psychological tests for public employees to make sure none of them suffers from the vicious illness of racism and male chauvinism or some other fascist malady which we will lament once we see another black youth stretched out on the ground with a bullet in his head, not for playing his radio too loud but for being black or Latino, or raped not for playing her radio too loud but for being a woman.

Another critical aspect of Cultural Revolution is that we must support the presence of art and artists in the educational process from elementary through university. Art is the main force against Aren't. It is the creative aspect of being through which It is maintained. The development and destiny of humanity is contained more directly in essence in its art than any other dimension. The very devaluing of art is evident throughout society. There is no university without art. Art is the social life of humanity, its philosophical expression the ideological reflection of human life. To devalue it is to devalue creativity. Talk about creativity to the big money guys, and it's, ha ha, a joke, you know. Yet their big money comes from the control of people and society the control of their art, from the most basic art, the creation of society itself, to the articles of its expression. Whether clothes, furniture, music, food, houses, it is all art. Let us be clear it is not academic life that is principal but creative life, the question of human development and evolution. The critical, the academic, are secondary aspects, absolutely necessary, but not to be confused with the making of what is, the continuing of life in opposition to death.

• • • • • • • • • • •

BARAKA: I guess I'm supposed to take some questions now. If there're questions, I'd be glad to answer them.

BOBBIE LOUISE HAWKINS: I don't have a question so much as

something you brought up earlier in the panel. It went by really fast and I'd like to see it brought back. When you said "representative democracy" — I think there are probably people in here who don't understand the functioning of representative democracy as opposed to a party system.

BARAKA: Let me say this: this is a republic, actually, this is not a democracy, which is the great jammed toilet of the age...this is a republic, which means indirect representation, see. When they say "democracy" they actually mean the old Greek model in the first place, they mean two hundred guys living off the backs of a hundred-thousand slaves, is what they mean. And that is why you can see in the Southern culture a continuance of the old Greek Attic philosophy. What I meant when I said "direct democracy," I meant that there should be no electors in our way. For instance, I mean you don't vote for the president, the whole thing is a joke, a canard from the beginning. And that democracy should be in the schools, in the factories, it should be direct, and in the place of it should not just be, "Uh, you vote for Jojo & then Jojo goes right on ya," you know what I mean? I mean, it should be definitely direct democracy. The whole Constitution needs to be grappled with by those of us who think we've gone beyond the Constitution. Because we haven't even gone beyond it, we haven't even got up to it. That is, bourgeois democracy has not been sufficiently flushed out of its corner. In other words, we can't take people to socialism because we can't get them past the limits of bourgeois democracy, because we haven't taken bourgeois democracy to the hoop. We have to take bourgeois democracy to the hoop and dunk it. And then we can be talking about socialism. That's what I was saying.

HAWKINS: I was thinking of the Danish system, which is a representative system. For instance, in a representative system you would not have such a thing as an appointed vice president. In a representative system, if you had these offices going begging, a presidential office, a vice presidential office, what would happen is every one in the country would vote, and the one who got the most votes would be president, and the one who got the second most votes would be vice president.

BARAKA: Absolutely. See, you're saying "Denmark" but that's the

U.S. Constitution. Party politics have obscured the Constitution. If you read the U.S. Constitution, you'll find out that that's the way it's supposed to be. It's still whoever gets the most votes is president, but in the U.S. Constitution, it's whoever gets the second most votes is vice president. But they're two separate elections. You know, I tried to mash that on Jesse Jackson in 1988 in Atlanta, to tell him that this was the time to do that. They were stalled on the floor. I told him, "Now if you were to move for vice president, the sentiment is such that you could get it. You could go back to the Constitution to justify it. and you could push It over." But his addiction to the Democratic Party is what stifled that. You see, if you go back through the Constitution, you'll find out that there's more democracy in it than we know. But what they do is wave their hands at the Constitution, knowing that the radicals will never even look at it. "It's a corny document, I don't even want to see it." The radicals go past it, then wonder why they can't get people to go beyond it. It's because they haven't got up to it yet. That's really the question. You know, direct democracy, we have to begin to talk about that. All of these so-called intelligent people ... it amazes me that we're always putting down these policies. We're talking bad about "Reagan is an actor," "Bush is this," and so on — but if they're running our lives, then what does that make us? If all these people are chumps, then what does that make us? That's my question, you know. A chump's chump's chump's chump.

HAWKINS: I just want to say two things and then I'll sit down. One is, get rape off TV!

BARAKA: Yeah. Get rape off TV! Get TV off TV!

HAWKINS: And one is tax the robots.

BARAKA: Say what?

HAWKINS: Tax the robots. The reason they're running out of money is because they're financing factories to robotize, and all those people are out of jobs, and there isn't that tax income, so we have to tax the robots.

BARAKA: Now let me pose this to you all. In 1945, when we "won" the Second World War, our enemies were Germany and Japan. Remember that? Since then, we have trashed our allies, who were Russia and China—those were our allies in the fight against fascism. The two fascists have become the masters of the world economy—check it out—and you should check that the transfer of capital from the United States to Germany and Japan, since 1945 to now, is where your jobs are. All the manufacturing jobs—look in the back of your clothes—you want to know where all the jobs are? Look in the back of your clothes.

Before the Second World War, the corporate powers effected an alliance between Standard Oil, Krupp, the people who made the cyclone-B gas that they used to gas the Jews—what's the name of that company?

ANSELM HOLLO: Farben.

BARAKA: Farben, right, Krupp, Farben, Standard Oil, Matsushida, and Mitsubishi. And they said this: no matter who wins the war, that all these corporations will not pass into the public coffers. You remember that the spoils go to the victors? Well those corporations never passed into the public coffers. They were held in blind trust so that whoever won the war, private enterprise would come out with the same pieces. That's why there's no money here. All that money has been invested in Germany and Japan, who now control the world economically. But the United States, since it has to trash its own economy to do that, can only rule through military might. So now it becomes the international Samurai of the Germans, who're going to rule through what they call the "European common market" which is going to be a German control power block. The French and the English are dragging their feet. I think the Danish refused to sign the accords. And of course the Japanese are going to use Southeast Asia and the Far East as their block. The United States has no economic base at all, just a sword to run around and threaten people. No jobs internally, except they can threaten people. And they can only threaten people here since it can't keep up. So there is the question of the transfer of funds. This country is run by imperialists. These people are not even capitalists anymore, you know what I mean? I mean, they don't even wanna make a profit here anymore. They want to take the money and invest it other places, make jobs other places. That's the problem. There ain't no jobs here. That's essential.

The only way we can get that away from them is another party, is a third party. And I understand what the brother said there, "Its never gonna happen, it's never been done." Well, in the United States there's been a history of third parties that have come and gone, come and gone, come and gone. The question is, How can the independent, intellectual and radical. revolutionary sector of the United States of American society create an institution for once that will not be destroyed by opportunism? You understand what I mean? That will not be destroyed by sell-outs and co-optation? And that organization, that institution has to be more than just "take people to vote." It has to publish books. It has to create television programs. It has to open art galleries, it has to open hot dog stands and bars. It has to create an alternative life to these people, while fighting them.

You understand what I'm saying? You learn more in a bar or sitting there looking at stuff on a wall or listening to music than you do from some lecture. I teach music for instance simply by putting a record player in the hallway in my department with the music playing. And it plays all the time. And people come by there, you know, they're going someplace else, they're not going there, And they say "Professor, what is that?" I say, "That's Duke Ellington." "Oh yeah, who's that?" What I'm saying is that even the most minute aspect of our lives has to be an area in which we struggle to create an alternative to this. But what we usually do — and I myself have been as guilty as many people, although at the same time I can say maybe less guilty than others — we denounce imperialism twenty-four hours a day, yet wait to be discovered by it. We wait to be made successful by it. We're lamenting the fact that so-and-so won't publish our books, when our books are saying death to so-and-so. Why should so-and-so publish a book that says death to them? Why should they produce plays that lay out that they need to be iced? There's no reason at all — if you want that done, you have to create that yourself. And I'm saying all these cities that you're going back to, in those communities where there is nothing — you can tell there's nothing — just go look at it — there's nothing! You can't get in where there's something, cause that space is already taken. Where there's nothing, where there's vacant lots, where there's empty playgrounds, where there's abandoned buildings — where there's nothing, that's where you have to take up that space. And fight that space for influence, you know.

PETER LAMBORN WILSON: Well, I wish you'd been around all month. There's a lot of other issues that have come up around here I would've appreciated your comments on. There's one I could briefly describe, and I'd love to hear what you have to say about it. And that is this question of the Language Project, the language poets, and the revolutionary potential of Language Poetry, as expressed in certain theoretical writings by members of that school. Are you willing to put your foot in this one?

BARAKA: Sure. Absolutely. Why not? It's always about content to me. Content is always principal. So if you're talking about another way that you want to fiddle with the language, it's perfectly all right. But at the same time the content has to be dealt with. And if you're talking about language qua language, what's different about that from the New Critics? What's the difference between that and the Deconstructionist folk? It's the same thing. Finally, to remove expression from its social context—I don't know. If you're not talking about the question of content, what are you saying? Now, obviously as writers, particularly as poets, we're in love with language, we want to use language, you know, to express life, to express the need for change. But finally, what is it that you're saying? And that to me always remains important. And if you arrive at a new-fangled theory of boring people, if you can find out a new way, you know—I mean avant-garde boredom—well, I guess every era has to have its own boredom, so that it knows it's alive, you know what I mean? But the question always is how do you raise the level? And what makes me happy about what's going on generally, you know some of us older folk—I see Allen here, and Victor Cruz I don't know if he'd call himself old or not, maybe middle-old— what is important to me is that when I heard the rappers some years ago I knew what we had been doing was not in vain, that no matter what these bullshit academics had told us—no matter how they waved their hands at us—I knew that the living word—that the word was alive—that after they got through putting us down—like I said in a poem, "Oh, you thought it was over, huh? You thought it was over" —that then the young people come around—and just like they wanna attack Souljah, just like they want to attack Ice Cube— it's the same way we were attacked, I mean, do you remember how we were attacked? "HOWL" is the worst thing in the world! Who ever heard that language? Get him outta here!!" The same thing that we suffered. "Whoa, he's anti-this, he's anti-that, get him outta here!" Why? Because we dared to make language live. We dared to make poetry that people could actually remember and go down the street saying—bebupebupbebupbedadup. That's right.

When I went to jail in 1967, the judge actually read my poem in the court. And he kept saying, when he came to the words, he would say, "blank" and I would supply the word. "That's motherfucker, judge." The newness of the language has to do with how you take the content that is most relevant to the time that you're in. How you take that content and shape it, so that it actually becomes a conscious part of the psyche of the people, you know. And that's why, finally, poetry's so dangerous. And these people are trying to tell us, "Well, your children don't know anything about the finer things in life." Our children walk up and down reciting poetry twenty-four hours a day. In my house, that's all I hear twenty-four hours a day is poetry. I'm talking about POETRY badapadapda, yeah. But that's the way it is. You're surrounded by eight, nine poets. little teeny poets that are getting to be big poets. And that shows you the kind of violence that they see in your work. Because you're trying to do violence to the status quo. You know, like I said, Set. The Egyptians called it Set. If you try to fix anything—you can't fix anything—that's death. You can't fix anything—the thing's in motion—everything's in motion. So you Set it—that's a death grip. So they're trying to Set this thing, this status quo.

But it's up to us, as poets of truth, if that's what we wanted to be. Obviously that's why we have class struggle because some of us are not—we have to face that, we have to be willing to struggle. I've never been afraid to struggle. But some people say, "Well, you struggle too hard." I think as long as you're principled, as long as you're not trying to wipe anybody out, kill anybody—I'm talking about the world of literature and art—that you have to struggle above board and forthrightly to try to get a higher level of unity. That's what I've always wanted. And I think if we can't pass out of this world without leaving something of value, some kind of institution like a political party—cause when I say political party, all people think you mean is voting—but if a political party has to do anything it has to lead demonstrations, open museums, fight economically—it has to do anything it has to do, you know. Where are our revolutionary filmmakers, for instance? We've already seen that the camcorder is a revolutionary object. Every time we look up, we see another camcorder film — "The Rodney King Story" — we see another camcorder epic. But where are our camcorder films? We can't make eighty-million dollar films about Batman, nor do we want to, but where are the two-hundred-dollar films? Where are the thousand-dollar films that we circulate ourselves? You know what I'm saying? Where are little art galleries that only fit ten people at a time where they sell the painting for a dollar and a half or ten dollars? Where is that? Where is that little mimeograph stuff that we sell for two dollars or a dollar? Where is that?

We're not fighting these people. All we're trying to do is get in it. You have to fight these people, you have to fight'em even when you're locked up, you know, bite'em. DO SOMETHING. Don't just stand there lamenting, you know what I'm saying? I get so tired of lamenting. Just fight them. I believe there's enough resources right here, in this tent, to set up at least one theater somewhere, one film studio somewhere, a network of nightclubs, a network of poetry readings. I mean something, but don't just wait to be accepted by the NEA, I mean, we have to fight Jesse Helms. Don't wait for them. That's what I'm saying. Are there other questions?

Q: This is kind of a broad topic, but it's from the previous lecture, I was wondering what your take was on the genesis of the crack/cocaine epidemic? I know that all my dope head friends and I when it first come out in the eighties and they were publishing the formula for it in the Miami Herald — nobody had ever heard of it before — it was like, what are they talking about, free base? Where did this stuff come from?

BARAKA: Well, the same place most bad stuff comes from: the state. I think the Iran Contragate thing and then the whole Noriega scam revealed very clearly the connection between international dope pushing and the state. That's why I kept saying you need the legalization, the decriminalization of drugs. Same way that you had with prohibition. All of the murders and violence and craziness during prohibition — that's why they got rid of it. And this whole so-called moralistic — I mean more people die from cigarettes — it's an old cliché — I never heard about anyone dying from lung cancer smoking bush. Maybe because we haven't smoked Bush, and he's still in Washington, maybe that's the problem. All of those things definitely are the state. We got Freedom of Information Act papers — I've still got about a thousand of 'em to get, but they cost a dime a piece, and I'm reluctant to pay that money to them. When you look at them, it's clear they spare nothing — they sit in audiences like this with tape recorders, when they could just buy the book. See, the poems in the book, they could just go buy the book.

STEFAN IELPI: I just want to add to your feelings about Rap music in general. Some people wonder why I'm even here. I'm kind of a punk rock singer. And there's some teachers here who believe that this is a valid form of music as well as a valid form of expression. I'm here nosing around academia, kind of checking out what's worth seeing and stuff, and I think, I guess I'm trying to use your impetus and strength and stuff to say that the non-academic poet, the nonacademic music and word is still a valid, live, in-your-face form, and that I want you to read all the books you can possibly read, but if you can, take your poetry and just calmly put it in front of someone's face and say "check this out." Cause when I started, the only poetry reading I ever got was by standing up in the middle of Washington Park and acting like — I put a garbage pail over my head, threw out the contents, and started screaming at the top of my lungs.

I think the best poetry readings are downtown like at Life of Brian, Monty Python's. Just go out there and scream and yell, and don't worry if you can't quote somebody in your work, some dead person four billion years ago. I think that's what we're going to hear — I hope that's what we're going to hear when we hear you perform. I've seen you perform many times, and it's always like, I can walk away singing this man's words! Emma Goldman said you've got to dance to the revolution, well, you've got to be able to sing to the music! I think a lot of people have to loosen up a little bit, maybe put the book down for a moment and jump on a table and get in people's faces. People walk away remembering that. If they're not scared they get some kind of reaction instead of confusion. That's what I mean, the Language Poetry — there were some great language poets here. I mean Harriet Mullen — she had this content inside her work — about advertising, manipulation, politicians, and then the word play went out from that point. It wasn't a bunch of straight arrows shooting at one elusive target. I'm encouraging craziness right here. And never mind male-female, it's all just crazy children under the Muse now.

BARAKA: Well. I certainly agree about rap—I mean, that's the oldest form of poetry that I know of—rap. That's the way it always was. It comes from the whole African rap, to beat on the wood. That's the way you communicated. You beat on the wood, on the drum, you know. That's what it always meant—rap—to communicate, to speak. What they disagree with is the content. The form's the same. I mean whether you listen to John Henry or "The Signifyin' Monkey" or back to the ancient chants beating on the wood, you know, (drums on table) "Meet...me...tomorrow night...7 o'clock...down by the water...bring your knife...don't be late." It's the some thing. That's what rap means, essentially. Beating on the wood, the rapping. And Rap Brown from the sixties, who was a revolutionary leader at SNCC—we called him Rap Brown because he could speak, because he spoke, he could talk, he could verbalize. You know, every nation has two cultures—the culture of the oppressed, and the culture of the oppressors. And ours does too. And it depends on what you identify with, the culture of the oppressed, or the culture of the oppressors. Rap is about speaking, talking. But they trying to co-opt that, as you well know. There're serious rappers, but at the same time we're getting a whole kind of bourgeoisified rap that wants to sound like soap operas. You know, Jazzy Jeff, and the dude that was on television—what's his name?— Fresh Prince and all that kind of stuff. I mean, there's a lot of garbage, Vanilla Ice, MC Hammer, "We should pray"—probably he means p-r-e-y. All these kind of people who come up who really are representing less than nothing in terms of intellectual and political confrontation. But it's like everything else—they always co-opt you. They always buy and sell.

(Unintelligible comment from the audience)

BARAKA: Right. That always works. That's why you have to keep the music segregated. That's why in America you always have what they call "covers" because you have to keep the music lovers segregated. Because if the music lovers ever come together and hear what's in the music together, and what they need to do together, then they will change this together. So you have to keep them segregated. Like what Columbus did — he discovered America. He dis-covered it. Discovered is to be dissed and covered, if you understand what I mean. You get covered which means that the content which is the truest content gets covered up with b.s., you understand? And the dis of course is to be disrespected, dis-whatever. Which is interesting, because the capitol of hell of Hades, was Dis. But what they can always put on you is to make you disappear. Which is always the final dis.

(1994)

Black Studies & Public Education

What was called "Black Studies" emerged in the late 1960s (1967 San Francisco State University) as part of the overall mass social movement for democracy and self determination during that period. Although that overall movement was, like the society itself, multinational and multicultural, the spearhead of that thrust was the African American people because they alone in the U.S. have been chattel slaves, and along with the Native Americans whose native land this country is, remain tethered to the bottom of U.S. society still suffering denial of democratic rights as well as super exploitation and national oppression.

Black Studies represented the attempt to democratize the American Education system, just as the famous suit *Brown v. Board of Education* (1954) which called for the Desegregation of American Education "with all deliberate speed." So the struggle to democratize Education i.e., to transform it from being, as it mostly remains, elitist, white supremacist, Eurocentric and narrow in content, and formalistic and rote oriented in form, was one of the critical elements of the Civil Rights movement and the continuing struggle for equality and democracy in the society.

The U.S. is a *multinational* and *multicultural* society; it has *never been* Europe and it fought a war to declare independence from England! But the recognition of this fundamental character of U.S. society would seriously undermine white supremacy and the racist social organization of the U.S. which, historically have provided super profits from the more intense exploitation of the African

American people in continual slave relations.

The raison d'etre for Black Studies then, is not nationalism, but the quest for democracy! At S.U.N.Y. I proposed, as Director of the Africana Studies Program, that at least one semester of Black Studies be *required* for *all* students, as a method of using education to dilute the ignorance which remains the best condition for the spread of racism.

It should be equally apparent that the inclusion of Latino, Women's and Labor Studies, plus the other oppressed nationalities within this society is also important to make U.S. education more democratic and must also be pressed for. Here is a brief overview of the elementary approach to Black Studies or Pan African Studies (to include not only Africa but the peoples of "African descent" internationally).

****

Methodology: Formalism is the fundamental flaw in American education. That is disciplines, ideas, subjects are approached from the dead and abstract, the mechanical and theoretical point of view and seldom from the living, social (i.e., connected to "real life") constantly changing and developing point of view. So that education now very seldom is measured or has as its valorization real life, certainly not the real life of our largely African American and Latino student body.

A renascent approach to education must be the analysis and refining of human experience for the development of society. Socialization of topics and subjects should be a tool for building participants. All topics and subjects, through departmental focus and overall administrative structure, must be connected to their counterparts in living society — whether history or math or physical education or literature and languages. Students through city, state, county, federal govt or private and philanthropic sectors must be aligned to practical expressions of otherwise abstract disciplines.

The universities and public education system itself must be connected to the day to day life and needs of the cities. Now we have institutions that have the personnel, skill, and resources, yet the cities where they need these and don't have them, and are places where the people remain without needed access and the students and faculty in these institutions are relegated to abstraction instead of a socially transformative practice of their disciplines, which is the only way they can actually know their subjects, alive.

Every department of city government, every office of the private sector has operations that would speed the real and practical , socialized education ie, ideas as they are used to develop and maintain real life.

Arts, fundamental to a renascent approach to education, must be the understanding that the arts are primary to education not secondary. The emphasis on the critical and the formal over the creative is a reflection of the society itself, where the actual creators of wealth are always deemphasized in favor of the middlemen. So in education, creativity is deemphasized in favor of the quantitative or the interpretative.

But without the art there would be nothing to study. Human society is itself the fundamental art and science of our life, not the formal texts codifying it. Whether we mean language or clothing, food or automobiles, it is all art.

We must maximize the students access to all of the arts because in the creative is contained the motive and history of developing life and society. So that graphic arts must transform not only the look of the school, but its real life. Music, literary arts, dance, &c., must be a basic educational approach and means of providing the students with true self-consciousness.

Art and Culture, including sports, must provide the Basic methodological approach to education not formalism or rote memorization. Our study must be of actual human creation not merely the formalization and secondary interpretation of this fundamental human activity.

Reading can not be correctly taught or Languages without reading. One cannot teach reading, as many of these instructors attempt, by saddling the students with parsing diagrams and not giving them access to its living use, as literature, &c. Reading is how language and grammar must be taught, not mechanical rote.

Curriculum: The basic approach to Black Studies should be teaching of Social History and its Cultural Development (primarily as Arts) as reflective of the general development and changes of society itself.

Africa
    Glory of Africa
    Reasons for Decline   See DuBois *The Negro*
    The Slave Trade   Equiano's Narrative
    DuBois's *Supression of the*
    African Slave Trade
    L. Bennett *Before The Mayflower*
    Western Slavery & The Development of the African
    American Nationality in the U.S. & Carribbean & c

    Slave narrative: Fred
    Douglass's *The Narrative; My Life As A Slave;*
    The Speeches
    Woodson's *The Negro In American History;*
    Foster, W's. *Negro History*
    DuBois's, *Black Reconstruction*

Nineteenth century chattel slavery and societal change is best understood by reading the slave narratives of Douglass, Linda Brent, Roper, Wells Brown, H. Box Brown, &c as well as the text of the Negro Convention Movement led by the free blacks of the north. The speeches of Douglass, H. H. Garnett, C. L. Remond, C. H. Langston plus works like *The Appeal*, David Walker; Nat Turner's *Confessions*; the poetry of Francis W. Harper would give a much clearer picture of slave U.S. society and the anti slavery struggle. Civil War — *Reconstruction of Society*, DuBois's *Black Reconstruction* and *The Souls of Black Folk* are the two most important works giving access to this period.

Arts & Culture

A study of Black music and the Black church are the principal focus that will cover pre-19th century and reconstruction eras.
West African Music
DuBois "On The Sorrow Songs"
"Faith of Our Fathers" (in SOBF)
    The transition from African music to African American focusing on work songs, spirituals, hollers and shouts, and the eventual emergence of blues and gospel are most important to show the social development and aesthetic reflection of society of the

African American people.
Unesco African Music series
Folkways series on Early African American Music;
Alan Lomax
     series &c.
    Blues, rural and urban
        Blues People   Leroi Jones
    20th century

Post Reconstruction era of disenfranchisement, Klan repression, and emergence of "separate but equal" and the new "leadership" of Booker T. Washington in conflict with the young DuBois is the basis for transition from 19th to 20th century *Souls of Black Folk* is principal text *Up From Slavery* Booker T. Washington sets context.

Harlem Renaissance is the major period of focus beginning with DuBois founding of Pan African Conference 1901; Niagra Movement 1907:

Garvey Movement; Rob Hill; *Crisis Magazine,* DuBois Editor

Literature by DuBois, Langston Hughes, Zora Neale Hurston, Claude McKay, Jean Toomer, Countee Cullen, James Weldon Johnson, Georgia Douglass Johnson and others should be studied as cultural reflection of social movement of the period.

Music of Bessie Smith, Ma Rainey, Louis Armstrong, Duke Ellington should be studied in relationship to this period for further dimensionalizing of it and provides the whole picture of the period, ideologically and culturally.

Graphic Artists like Aaron Douglass, Edmonia Lewis, others should be studied.

Middle of 20th—The Civil Rights Movement and Black Liberation Movements of the '50s through '70s provides the basic social history of the period. Martin Luther King, Malcolm X, The Student Movement, Black Panthers, &c. People like Stokely Carmichael, Rap Brown, Huey Newton, Angela Davis, Fannie Lou Hammer, SCLC, Rosa Parks should be studied.

Why We Cant Wait, Martin Luther King; *The Fire Next Time,* James Baldwin; *Blues For Mr. Charlie; The Autobiography of Malcolm X; The Making of Black Revolutionaries,* Foreman.
(1980s)

The Fights

"Tyson looked outta shape," I put it on the management. The grocery stores and barber shops rang with it. Kids in the street, teenagers shot it back & forth. How Tyson got wasted. Nobody knew much about Buster Douglas, who did it. Midway through the fight my oldest son called, "This man's beatin' Tyson..." He seemed about to conclude. He could hide his surprise and put it on me! "What? You lyin...He beatin' 'im...He jabbin him all over his head!"

Buster Douglas, who was that? Another "opponent" was what I assumed. Tyson would stalk him and bust him loose from his consciousness. It would be painful, even humiliating! He knocked him down! He knocked Tyson down! "You lyin," I still had not gotten to the TV and when I came into the bedroom where my wife had it on, there was Tyson, transformed completely, in trouble, sluggish, overweight so that his once wraith like waist has relaxed so that his body is square less dynamic and athletic. He is a heavy stocky completely out of shape foil.

The narrator told me about the death of Douglas' mother, and how this and some other personal tragedy had dedicated him and endowed him, it seemed, with a skill and aggressiveness that was, by the time I entered, overwhelming Tyson.

I did not recognize Tyson except in the printed and televised fantasies of his torturers — those who make money and propaganda with his life. As a script, it will sell wildly; I hope someone asks me to write it. The delinquent brutal youth adopted by Christian fight manager — who becomes champ, wild slightly crazed, animal-like —

350

who becomes champ with the brutal finality of force. And it is worth millions.

The ghetto brute Romeo and the television Negro gold digger Juliet. Made into a Coney Island media artifact to sell the drama of social disorientation in this jungle of legal exploitation. To further it, incite and create the situation where corporate groups used trainers, or the media, to stop Tyson from disconnecting himself from the favored ownership and go to Black Don King.

The missionary goodness plus the "superior" training and conditions techniques are used to justify and vilify Tyson and King as Black secret racist no-goodniks. Tyson has been shown as ape like, Simple minded, Victim of a Buppie career person and her mother what sued a baseball player for giving her a disease. I think she won! I remember reading about the celebration. And her career, did soar, not at the same pace, but pinched by the drama, the confessions, the fights, the mad interview she made on television, a loaded bitter drama. And we took sides.

The car crashes, Jose, the ex-Light Heavyweight Champion, Ex boxing commissioner and current writer with the *Village Voice* proves Tyson is F—up!

We wonder is it as simple as Tyson being disinterested, the focus of his life, its very pressures, might have caused him to be more interested in ease and personal self fulfillment or revelation or delusion so that training is more mental, one begins to think and practice a noble abstraction! It might be some subjective self delusion or celebrity dissipation, or all together lack of motivation.

I saw Douglas chasing and blasting Tyson with both hands. Tyson gave no lateral movement none of his characteristic bobbling ducking moving his shoulders as he set up the hooks and overhand rights. He stood more than moved, wheeled sluggish at times. He it seemed dazed, unclear, not fully coordinated. His desperation, a thick stiffness launching inaccurate punches after the fact.

Douglas wheeled and lunged, roundhoused and upper-cutted the heaving missing slow...Suddenly Tyson was falling under Douglas' fierce overhands and uppercuts—he was down, like knocked and crumpled near the ropes. Is this the wages of sin? Are white well meaning people right again? Mike Tyson knows and probably Don King. Aside from the gospel of the media which will be sensational with white supremacy and commercialism. Fights. Magazines. Advertising. Self congratulatory hypocrisy. Cynicism.

Money. Perhaps Tyson's personal life contradicts his training and conditioning. Perhaps he will reorganize his life — the defeat makes his real life Black Rocky knock out return match media gold. It puts life back. Now Tyson has been whipped sloppy, a host of challengers and deals can be *re-cut* Holyfield. Even Foreman. Others.

Douglas is still an unknown flash — a mediocre record, presumably psyched by his emotional state and enabled by Tyson's lack. All this will be found out. He has a belligerent "chilly home boy" persona. Still uncollected and running on perception and strength. Tyson did not seem to have fighting uppermost in his feelings. Therein is the Drama. What he will do and who Buster Douglas really is will be compelling. Like who is the group that owns Douglas? How are they connected? Where are the big dollars going?

It is the tale written in lives we want to understand. Past the glitter of employment — the real life Mike Tyson is living is real. Who knows if he could win it if he wanted to? Perhaps Buster D is as he says. finally self realized. He seemed relaxed, confident and effective. The challenge to Tyson's crown was not taken seriously. Even by Tyson. He is a creature of immense pride and perhaps this will be a catalyst for his successful return if this is to be.

But I want to know who is making the big money? And the identities of the various interests struggling to control and exploit Tyson and Douglas. The general skirmish between "Black" and "White" owner trainer, groups is constant with predictable media sympathy for the latter. Calling Tyson "ungrateful" apparently for demanding self determination.

Tyson is a whole era away from the positive revolutionary expressiveness of an Ali. But his appearance on the Arsenio Hall show with Ali and Ray Leonard showed him both sensitive and respectful.

We hope he will be as clearly and objectively self-conscious as he needs to be, and do what he determines he wants to. (Don King, of course, must also accept significant responsibility. How is speculative?)
(1990)

Symposium on Institution Building
A Reanalysis of the Role and Nature
of Arts Organizations

The mainstream institutions in U.S. society are part of the *superstructure*. That is, at the base of any society is its economic foundation, its material base. The institutions raised upon that base, reflect it.

So that since the U.S. is an imperialist country, with a monopoly capitalist economic base, the institutions raised upon that base, as well as the philosophies expressed within them, are in the main expressions of imperialism. The role of the superstructure, actually, is to put forward the ideas that ensure the continued existence of the economic base.

But most people in U.S. society are exploited by this economic base, particularly the Afro American people, Latinos, Asians, native Americans, the peoples of the Third World, women, particularly working class and oppressed nationality women, who are triply oppressed by class, nationality and gender. All suffer forms of national oppression in addition to economic exploitation.

For these reasons, it should be obvious that those of us so exploited by this economic base especially those of us who understand how the superstructure of institutions and philosophies continue our exploitation and oppression, must seek to create alternatives to those institutions normally created as the superstructure of U.S. imperialism.

Certainly, in the years since the Vietnam War there has been a marked tendency in U.S. society as it pushes ever further toward the right, to more and more undermine and weaken any institutions in the public sector, particularly those aimed at supporting and developing the great masses of the people.The twelve years of Reagan-Bush reaction even openly took resources and power from all public institutions and blatantly sought to give all power to the giant corporations of the military-industrial complex.

The intense reactionary thrust of recent U.S. government has left even fewer institutions in the society, in all fields, directly accessible to the people. In the arts and cultural development, a U.S. which has come to focus on business and corporate power as the ultimate arbiters of meaning has steadily converted art to simple commodity.

In addition, the very ideas that the imperialist superstructure pushes, individualism, the sanctity of private enterprise, the "impossibility" of collective or mass concerns, mean that paradoxically many people believe that by being an impotent individual employed in the mock achievement of corporate solipsism they are really doing the greatest work for themselves and all that can be rationally done for quote the Community unquote, when that term comes up at all. Usually the word community only comes up in regards to consumer campaigns.

It has gone so far that even though we have daily proof that western Europe and Japan experience the degree of prosperity they do based on the strengthening of public institutions and the expansion of a social democratic approach to the public sector, particularly in education, the arts, health care &c. the U.S. has grown, particularly under Reagan-Bush aegis, even more withdrawn from the concepts of an expanded and indeed semi-independent public sector.

Year after year, the concept of the Corporate State, the Hitlerian ideal, looms as more and more possible in the U.S. Even the so-called Founding Fathers never envisioned that the private sector was to dominate and govern the public sector, yet it seems more and more like reality. Public television and radio are under outright attack from the partisans of big private enterprise. And corporate radio and T.V. reach ever lower levels of disgust. And with the greater private control of media, the once proud U.S. film industry is a planetary embarrassment.

In the various ghettoes of the U.S., not only Afro American

but other oppressed nationalities and poor whites, these same corporate forces are always aided and abetted by the "half-hip" petty bourgeois, who are usually the finders, the spotters, the ones who tell the "big guys" how hip our stuff is, and how much it needs to be on the "Great White Way," &c.

So that with their help, but essentially because it is a more profitable concept for the bigs, and even more enriching culturally, they bring the various ghetto arts out of the ghetto and bring it all "downtown."

Gone are the days of the limo trips, like the old wagon trains, up to the various Harlems, not only to witness but to contribute resources to their Harlem renaissance. Now they send for it and bring it "downtown" so that both the money and the art stay in their neighborhoods. (But then both Greenwich Village and the old Hell's Kitchen black entertainment district "Black Bohemia" were once black communities and big spots of Afro American art and culture. Now the Village is the world famous and Lincoln Center sits where the old black "Jungle" and San Juan Hill used to be!)

After the H.R., the next renaissance (around the '40s and the creation of BeBop was *transported* out of the ghetto and *downtown*. This development was sharpened by the gradual quitting of the cities by middleclass whites. So that even the old "going slumming" hijinks and curiosity of the white petty bourgeois going into the ghettoes in search of excitement was largely ended. Especially since from the suburbs, anywhere in the city would represent excitement.

So now the ghettoes, where others used to come and slum and be entertained have had their highest forms of artistic culture removed. And where once the most spectacular artistic innovation was taking place in the ghetto, now there are mostly clichéd organ trios, if anything, in the bars. But not only are the arts' institutions, such as they were, stripped from the ghetto, but the leaving of white folks, and the petty bourgeois in general, from the cities, saw a withdrawal of resources from all aspects of the urban culture, including education and employment. So that the "new" institutions that we must build are described for us by what does not exist. That is, the institutions we build must be to supply the various things missing from our communities.

We must build to address the whole spectrum of what we call culture—no matter what field, it must be connected to what we call social development. Because ultimately, no matter the form or details of its expression, or no matter how broadly defined, what we need most must have some relationship to education in essence and the production of a new society over all. The mainstream provides enough titillation and superficial gratification. However, we take its unseriousness, seriously.

It is not just that we seek ways to connect our developing institutions to other already existing institutions. Many times it will only be by utilizing now underused (for our purposes) schools, churches, labor unions that we can find the venues we need in which to operate.

It is better, for instance, that we use these churches, schools, unions, as sites of performance, rather than stand around waiting for the bigs to discover us. And no matter how large the institutions we are building, these community institutions must be at the core of their development. Because from these institutions will come much of the "new" audience we must animate.

But the idea is not just to "bring Broadway into our communities," but to create alternatives to "Broadway," including an alternative audience, which is actually the people newly animated by self description and self determination at whatever enhanced levels.

The institutions we want must be examples of awakened motion toward self determination through self expression to elicit what DuBois called "true self consciousness."

This means not only do we want to see ourselves, but by that act to make ourselves more fully conscious of who we are, as history and needed development, they are the requirements of our revolution.

This is why such empowering institutions are forms of class and ideological struggle. That's why building new "people" institutions that speak the truth about reality must speak with such power that they are part of the force we need to change reality.

Our need to network with other such developing institutions and across the whole spectrum of nationalities and focused on the bedeviled U.S. majority, the exploited and oppressed Americans, is also a form of expanded institutional development.

We can not exist outside of our immediate localities unless we can put together broad networks and national circuits of our own design. The present circuits and networks of arts and cultural development are flawed at best, in one aspect, because they can not accommodate the true consciousness of the multinational U.S. majority of working people and oppressed nationalities. Even though the imperialists have developed a native agent betrayer in most nationalities, accents, both genders and most sexual orientations. That is they can lie and fake with any mask they need. But the totality of U.S. establishment culture is as closely related to the peoples' real needs as the U.S. film industry is related to truth and healthy social development. The Broadway-Hollywood-TV-Radio media-land projections of reality are as much lies as they are inappropriate standards for mass human development. Just as we must develop the missing links of our own needed self consciousness and social development, part of this development will only come from the enhanced production of revolutionary social values. We must begin to valorize ourselves, to paraphrase Sekou Toure, not only by what we say, but also by what we do.

The imperialists give awards simply to spread their poisonous values of submission, individualism, self hatred, exploitation, chauvinism, racism, internationally and connect us to their production as well as being their objects. The creation of awards in the arts, valorizing the people themselves, and the values of collective unity and collective struggle, collective education and collective development is one thing we must begin to do more aggressively. The creation of such awards as alternatives to the Pulitzers, Nobels, Oscars, will contribute to creating a mass appreciation of revolutionary values. By rewarding what expresses such values, instead of standing around complaining about what our oppressors do or boohooing the awards they give.

But this entails the creation of whole new forms of socially oriented expression. Instead of being awed by the 60 million dollar hymns to animalism and human devolution, we must create institutions that develop and teach practical, low budget, revolutionary progressive innovative techniques as well as content. Where are our camcorder Sembenes, our $5000 video masterpieces, our network of distribution that catalyzes the 100 dollar videoteks and instant theater spaces?

It is better that we be able to get twenty people in a room and perform the great works of history, the present and the future than be murdered mentally, metaphorically and literally by yet another Anglo-Broadway garbage can or funky Schwarzenegger or Weissen Hunky epic.

The concerts, forums, exhibits we need must begin perhaps in our own developing institutions but also initiate activity, performance, development in newer and smaller venues. The audience we know that exists, but must be pulled together, is a small part of the audience we don't know and have no idea how to pull together.

We must abandon the traditional concept of the audience, and we can do this if we are clear on "for whom" we create and "to whom" we would like to communicate.

These new institutions must be forms of concretizing true self consciousness. They must be forms of class struggle, but expand as forms of new organization, expressions of innovative techniques and instruments of social change.

They will also be literally something to replace the nothing that exists. And even where something like we are talking about does exist, the essential difference will be who it serves. The class stand and point of view it takes, the activist nature of its concerns.

But obviously, from the communities we come from, there are few theater, movies, videoteks, bookstores, publishing companies, popular education institutes. Few youth organizations other than reformatories or gangs. Our institution building must answer existing needs and catalyze new solutions.

The imperialists actually use very little of the accreted human values, though they distort and exploit them all. For instance, the mountains of neglected masterpieces, true classics of all peoples and nationalities, the willfully obscured democratic and revolutionary culture of all peoples.

Part of our mandate must be to uncover and undis these materials, and by constructing broad networks and new associations re-educate ourselves and the people. As well as creating new classics, new masterpieces and relating the most ancient of human rituals to those not yet created.

To do these things, it is necessary as well to find new sources of energy, resources and revenue. If not new, at least newly related to the needs we identify.

But witness the churches, for instance, the most superficial of institutions, as far as their metaphysical teaching, yet the most essentially human of institutions as far as the real need they answer. The emotional and psychological values they provide.

No matter how impoverished and degraded the community,

there are always churches, by the dozens and double dozens. How do they exist, by the will and to the pleasure of the people, no matter how false, exploitative and superficial that finally turns out to be.

The churches exist because the community wants them. They are funded by no body but the people, not even by God (no matter what the preacher says!)

Our new and developing institutions must seek as organic a relationship with the people, although a more scientific and revolutionary one. Because it will be the people Themselves, who produce the innovations and the innovator, the youth, those denied access. We must be able to provide that access, not because we are smarter than the people or better educated but because we are their sons and daughters!

(1980s)

Don Imus and the Sham of American Democracy

It should be clear that poisonously ill shock jock Don Imus should be cut loose by MSNBC, CBS & WFAN. And from the feeble little slap on the pinky the corpses have given Imus as "punishment," we should be able to peep the scam ahead.

Not only Imus should be fired but the little stew of ball-less imbeciles. "Producer," Bernard McGuirk with his "hard core hos" comment; Sid Rosenberg, who sd the Rutgers girls looked like the Toronto Raptors (a men's professional basketball team.) Rosenberg also made the same kind of statement a couple years ago about Black tennis sisters, Serena and Venus Williams.

In measuring the trend of the times, We should include not only the Sean Bell assassination, with one cop shooting 31 times, all shot 50 times total. That's 9 more than the 41 shots at Amadou Diallo under the mad dog Giuliani regime. But the equally mad dog comments of the Michael Richards, the "Kramer" of the Seinfeld show actually praised the days of straight out lynching as something he would welcome again. No matter what "we" might do, he said, in the end he would still be a rich white man.

There have been indictments in the Bell travesty. But indictment is not conviction. As far as the other evil confrontations what will happen? It depends in part on what we do. One wonders why only the two female councilpersons speak out on this issue. Where is Mayor Booker's voice thundering for justice? Too many of us still do not know what Fidel Castro told us the last time he was in NYC, reading from a United Nations document. Viz THAT IN THE HISTORY OF THE UNITED STATES, THERE NEVER HAS BEEN A WHITE MAN CONVICTED OF RAPING A BLACK WOMAN!!

Certainly there are so many other likewise evil targets, the radio/TV tandem; "Mike and The Mad Dog" show no love for Black Athletes. *New Jersey's Star Ledger's* right wing garbage makes it a dreadful read. Including their columnist Robert Braun (Eva's grandson?) who thinks the problem with the evil Imus is we should just not listen to it. Like Germany's doomed democratic Weimar Republic, just let the Nazi's pile up until they take over the entire state mechanism.

We should see how the Nazis are pilling up across the board in the U.S. Certainly from 911 onward. That 911, which was like "a new Pearl Harbor" which has allowed the invasion of Afghanistan, the support for Israeli Ethnic Cleansing in Palestine, the invasion of Iraq, support of the Israeli invasion of Lebanon, and the resulting U.S. created civil wars across the middle East.

NOW WE GO TO THE EXTREME COURT

When my poem SOMEBODY BLEW UP AMERICA was written a month after 911, I was trying to sum up all the people throughout the world who had suffered some form of terrorism or another. The poem was sent around the world with positive feedback. It was not until my reading at the Dodge Poetry Festival that Gov. McGreevey's office called me to apologize & resign. But unlike Imus and the other's what I said in the poem needed no apology, and as it turned out it was Gov. McGreevey who had to apologize and resign.

I mention this because the poem caused such a torrent of gibberish and hysteria on the media and the statehouse that finally when the little hypocrites could not fire me as New Jersey Poet Laureate, they got rid of the Poet Laureate position in New Jersey. That's why I sign my letters "The Last Poet Laureate of New Jersey," Just to piss these buggers off.

So now because I asked "Who told 4000 Israelis to stay home that day?" "Why did Sharon stay away?" I was called an anti Semite. But the point obscured by so much bureaucratic and otherwise insincere BS is *that the Israelis and several other governments have admitted that not only did they know about the coming of 911 BUT THAT THEY HAD WARNED THE US!*

What the Israelis were doing is the same thing any nation does (except in this case with the U.S.) if there is danger they warn their nationals, sometimes like the U.S. to citizens in Iran and Lebanon. So that Israel warned Israeli Nationals in the World Trade Center, just like any nation would do. The Question is why didn't the U.S. warn its citizens.

Two weeks ago my attorneys William Manns and Robert Pickett and I received notice that our SECOND attempt to sue McGreevey, et. al., was rejected by the 3rd circuit court. SO NOW WE ARE PREPARING TO GO TO THE SUPREME COURT. The 3rd circuit seems to believe that I have no simple first amendment rights. Because I asked a question about Israel, another nation. The double standard in this country is still bold enough to say without fear of Realistic contradiction, what DuBois said, "America Has Never Been A Democracy!"
(2007)

Sam Abrams
Around the Block a Coupl'a Times...

Sam Abrams is a poet of incisive explanation, so compact and modest, that his rationales seem revelatory in the way that the Zen monks sought. He is out of a tradition we can locate in W.C. Williams, Zukofsky, Robert Creeley, Joel Oppenheimer, Max Feinstein, and perhaps the polite agitator stinging almost unseen from the less visible ring of the crowd's core. Still, Sam, with his subtle weapon of longevity and willed stability has made a poetic that is casual and intense at the same florescent moment.

Not that he is florescent. It is just that what he leaves, after his quiet intriguing asides, stays and fluoresces in our memoried quotes of random beauty and intelligence we have picked up somewhere in this (Be Moderate!) less than perfect world.

I've known Sam almost from the beginning. His discreetly distributed seif-wires of perception have been rendered indelible by a deeply ironic summation of what it was and who we is, trying to dig the world, with or without our selves. Sometimes, because of his tacit commitment to logic and precision, over the easy brassiness of florid metaphor, we might miss the cut, the vital incision, into our knowing. But when we return, the words sit as they were placed, and the somber vision, the ironic twist of light on speech details our feeling. As if, at each ending, there is an explicit breath we must take, better to dig it with.

The "unrecognized" aspect of Sam Abrams' work is part of the wardrobe of his persona. His quiet persistence at "description" is a natural evidence of our lives. It is not the special occasion where the band comes out and hurrahs us into awe, but it is the awe that will come, for the serious reader, for those of us who realize that words carry and signify and quarrel with our previous perceptions, scattering our comfortable rationalizations of what we do not understand.

Sam Abrams is an old (sic) very skilled craftsperson of word made flesh. And as unlike the soaring halalas of the prophets his work might seem light on approach, however, Abrams work is for the "get down," as we say, inside the monster cities. He creates artifacts of breath and feeling, of which commerce has little use, (except to sell perfume or deodorant). Abrams' is a poetry of confrontation with the demands of unobvious exactness. It takes some concentration and some storehouse of life to know his work, how graceful and well honed it is.

Plus, Sam, like very few of his peers, has stayed around to get the final score. There is a heaviness, a consolidated "presence" in that. The work reflects like the easy light of a new day or the disappearing glimmer of what we have almost lost. If the name and the work seem somewhat obscure, remember that hereabouts, truth and beauty have been given the same treatment.
(2007)

A Graveyard with Trees *Ginsberg*
Review of a Biography by Barry Miles

Barry Miles' *Ginsberg* is a litter of collected event, like the coffee table photo album of a slightly academic groupie. Dry, yet mildly in awe of anything dignified in animation, energy, revelation (also as uncovering) &c. The style of Miles' book is laboriously academic in tone yet riotously chaotic in summation and developing analysis. We do not find out anything directly from the book but a pot full of "chronologically" serialized events, which say only those as that.

There is no thesis no specific development. We are left with a maze of things, images, rationales whose use is ambiguous. We do not know what Miles is saying about Ginsberg. Unlike Quincy Troupe's *Miles* which is tape recorder verite' and an important contribution to the oral history of the music, hence a concrete accomplishment of American musical history. Barry Miles does interject himself into the narrative, but his voice is dry, unfocused, unconnected wires carrying "uninformed" information, a kind of academic perception.

For instance: "On March 19, Allen and Peter docked in Casablanca, where they spent three exciting days. Disregarding Burroughs' grim warning never to enter a Muhammadan establishment, they headed straight for the Medina, with its narrow streets and archways. They wandered down a dark alley and found an Arab cafe, where they were given the national drink of sweet mint tea. Someone produced a long stemmed kif pipe and passed it to Allen."

However, the book is useful and interesting for the same reason an old trunk in some wealthy relative's attic might be. Each chapter supposedly lays out a place, a time, an era, (e.g., "ONE CHILDHOOD: PATERSON; TWO A COLUMBIA EDUCATION: THE ORIGINS OF THE BEAT GENERATION") &c., but we are not made to understand Ginsberg, his work or the era as correlatives even with the dimension of contrasts.

For this reason the book is "gossipy," not visibly grounded in any specific idea or expressed understanding. Except the telling itself, of course, expresses Miles' ego, how it sees, its interests, &c. For instance, the book is definitely not literary, yet those are its only merits, that it is written, more "lasting" in a sense than conversation. There is no developed or developing understanding of literature, certainly no theory.

The author does seem interested in Ginsberg's sexual, religious, drug, bohemian observances. But he is no advocate, rather a collector—maybe underwear, socks, locks of hair, &c. So Barry Miles' work is like a scrapbook of such concerns, sensations, pinned on each page like stiff butterflies, a collection of Dis.
(1997)

New Jack City

I "heard about" the flick from the many diverse sources and perhaps, naturally, was at first, appalled. Van Peebles, the younger and VP the elder, are both, to my mind, straight o.t.l. (out to lunch). That is, I thought *Sweet SweetBack* was "venal garbage and was drugged." Huey Newton and the Panthers supposedly thought it "revolutionary."

And from the 1st time I saw the younger Van Peebles, in this same flick, as a naked infant being sexualized by that prostitute of his father's grim imagination, he has not meant anything good to me. I thought the new flick would be a rip off, something tres corny, like all his old man's films (e.g., *Watermelon Man*) and plays (e.g., *Ain't Supposed to Die A Natural Death*, &c.) or corny like the hopeless TV set rags of impersonation the young VP was complicated in.

Yes. Rap, for instance, had come to that point in its development when it was ripe for the Am rip. Where what was Black is replaced with white or those ideas and what has deep meaning is replaced with $. The use of Ice T, a name rapper, seemed to confirm this, and even he said, in a tv interview, that he was dubious about the movie and his role as an undercover cop, because he didn't like cops. (As in NWA's landmark piece "Fuck The Police!")

But since there was much discussion about the movie, and the Rap element, itself, was of interest to me, who with many young Rap aged children, perceived that I had better at least know from whence I spoke, &c. Okay, the form of the film is genre cop cliché.

367

As such it is merely what is the state of the commerce as far as contemporary U.S. cop films. What needs more analysis is the passage of American popular art from earlier, more democratic imagery and story, to the present, where both film and video are flat out dominated by the cop story.

There was a time when the cowboy image, just after the pioneer, just after the socially aware '30s and early '40s of America's class struggle, dominated American film (and radio) image, but since the McCarthy-'50s (See *Naming Names* by Victor Navasky) this has changed completely. But th ere is a livelier interior to this undercover anti-drug cop cliché, expressing finally ideas a little more advanced than the main stream standard bearers of the genre.

What comes across as a more "authentic" mise en scene, the total physical and psychological expression of the drama comes from the actors, the setting, the music, the situations, but also what the film says as a summation of its story. And story and summation do not jibe all the way down the line, but they have some relationship. Yes, the worst actor in the flick is VanPeebles, but his directing is not bad. It has promise, like they say, definitely. What it does is move the material, provide tension, suspense, humor, as mined from the script with some effectiveness, but importantly, it identifies conflicting "types" in the story as acting not labels.

Wesley Snipes as the black heavy "Nino Brown," dig that, Brown Boy, with the Latino moniker to implicate our neighbors as well; Allen Payne as "G Money," his funny but finally tragic right hand; Bill Nunn as "Duh Duh Duh Man" (Spike's Radio Rahim); Chris Rock as "Pookie" the "chilly home boy" turned crack addict, are very effective.

Ice T is uneven (as proof this is not his regular gig) but he is generally effective, Judd Nelson as the low profile emotion "white boy," and the general crowd of faces, and characters are all close to on it. The story, the cliché is rags to riches to violent demise of an American crime figure (Snipes) has been beat to death. But the topicality, the still living day to day of these kinds of lives as headlines, like a blow by blow account of contemporary slavery. This is the film's strength; its evocation of real life is its most powerful drama. While the plot is generic Hollywood contemporary, because the characters breathe through our everyday social practice they seem electrified. Even superficial as these portraits are, they are attached to the unresolved misery of contemporary America: its lies, its bloody class antagonisms and failure.

Snipes is the American Success Story of Mr. Hyde successfully destroyed (exorcised!) by Jekyl's hyped up neo-immigrant/buppy helpers. The excesses like Pacino's in *Scarface* are designed to justify Hyde's annihilation, like any "monstrous Negro." The trio of *Mod Squad* Jekyl agents are near caricatures, their Van Peebles supervisor, a disgusting "Negro" bureaucrat, jr grade.

Like the right wing of the genre, the film's "solution" to the war on drugs is vigilantism (revolution from the right). Here committed by a crazed old blood outraged by the slaughter of neighborhood youth by the New Jacks' crack. He has also witnessed Nick Ashford as a preacher accepting the Jacks tainted drug money. Especially since Snipes, at the end, testifying in court, exposes the bank and corporate and government complicity in the drug trade and will walk in a few months. Imperialism must destroy (any exposure by) competitive capitalism. That is how it got to be what it is. Its legality is its Bigness, the small locally vicious, the people should destroy!

Unaddressed and unanswered, Decriminalization and the forces in opposition; "Prohibition" and the second wave of Robber Barons rising out of the new capitalists; the parallel projection to the social identity and future of today's drug bootleggers.
(1991)

The Selling of CBS Records & Columbia Pictures Is A Crime Against The American People!

The recent sales of both Columbia Pictures and CBS Records to a "foreign corporation" is a monumental crime against the American people! If the U.S. corporate monsters can no longer hold their own against other such beasts, as international finance capital now moves against even the national sovereignty of imperialist countries themselves, then those "holdings" of theirs that directly carry the history, the art, the national culture of the people, not to mention their "holding" of their exploited labor, must be sold to a National Trust, and controlled by the federal law.

By selling Columbia Pictures and CBS, Rocky and His Mothers have sold the life blood of the people, not to mention giving away thousands of jobs, in what are the most internationally critical areas, communications and culture.

Think about it: Columbia, Records, just off the top, means that great works of American culture like, Duke Ellington, Miles Davis, Billie Holiday, Louis Armstrong, Benny Goodman, Max Roach, Glenn Miller, have been summarily and almost clandestinely sold away with no consultation with the American people. It is simply Grand Larceny. And it must be stopped. We are doing the research now, but just quickly some films and stars in the Columbia Films archives: *It Happened One Night* (Gable/Arthur); *Miss Sadie Thompson* (Hayworth); *On The Waterfront* (Brando); *Mr. Deeds Goes*

To Town; Mr. Smith Goes To Washington (Capra, Stewart, &c.); *Taxi Driver* (DeNiro, Scorsese); *Dr. Strangelove; Raisin In The Sun* (Hansberry, Gossett, &c.); *Bell, Book & Candle; To Sir With Love; The Way We Were; Cant Take It With You; Razor's Edge; Secaucus Seven; River Kwai; Lawrence of Arabia; Kramer Vs. Kramer; Gilda; Easy Rider, A Man For All Seasons; Big Chill;* and many, many others, including stars like Elizabeth Taylor, Richard B urton, Fred Astaire, Joan Crawford, Holden, Widmark, Cooper, Streisand, &c., it is truly obscene.

The Rockefeller Center debacle just demonstrates the complete moral and intellectual bankruptcy of the U.S. not-quite-so-big-anymore-shots. Not to mention somebody got a cash flow problem? Eh David? At any rate, if corporate capital can not do the job, then we must have some legislation, suits, &c., opposing this. Opposition to such outrage is part of the Cultural Revolution. ORGANIZE!

(1991)

Shorty Is Alive & Well & Making Movies For Warner Bros.

Over a year ago when asked by Spike Lee to write words of praise for his film *Mo' Better Blues*, which is one of the most embarrassing and corny films purporting to be about "the music" I know, I wrote instead about all of his films, and the essence of this was that in general Spike Lee's approach to Black people in the flicks was very superficial that he tends to view Black life as a cartoon, and instead of seeking depth and balance in his portraits of Afro America, he usually opted for caricature.

Spike has been quoted saying how outraged he was by my analysis. I went on to say, when asked by a group of young people what I thought about Spike's making the *Malcolm X* film, that I hope that he could not do to Malcolm what he has done to Black people generally, i.e., approach Malcolm's life superficially or as cartoon. I hoped, for instance, that he would not make the film mostly about that part of Malcolm's life when he was known as Detroit Red, the pimp, dope dealer, hustler and thief. But I predicted that he probably would do just that.

I said I hoped Spike would not distort Malcom's life, or make it seem that in the end Malcolm X and Martin Luther King's views were indistinguishable. So that ultimately, Spike's Malcolm, would be a typical bourgeois attempt to deMalcolmize Malcolm, and allow petty bourgeois Negroes who always hated or were disturbed by Malcolm the militance of the actual Malcolm, to breathe easier knowing X had finally been laid to rest.

There has been, since then, a lot of back and forth. For one thing, Spike Lee has never been able to answer my question and charges and prediction with any open defense of his ideological stance for making his movies the way he has made them. His trashing of Black women in *She's Gotta Have It*. His trashing of Black schools in *School Daze*. His belittling of the Black Liberation Movement, apology for the police murders of Black youth (Radio Rahim is killed for playing his radio too loud) and early attack on Islam and his open embrace of middle class nigger prostitution by kneeling in the dust to scoop up the cash, in *Do The Right Thing* (which he said was to be about Howard Beach !) His trashing of Black music and Black artists and Black family in *Mo' Better*. His upholding of apartheid and sexual racial stereotyping (why was the sister making so much noise when she made love in the flick?) and the need for the Black community to kill Black youth hooked on drugs in *Jungle Fever*.

He could never exchange ideological polemics about these because he is a Philistine, i.e., someone who pretends to welcome struggle, but instead is, to quote Lenin, "a hollow gut of fear," instead he would simply talk bad about me and even lie. As he has in his latest, you've seen the flick now read the book about X.

But for all Spike's attempts to divert attention from the ideological and political essence of my analysis of his earlier films, what I said and what I feared he would do to Malcolm's life have been proven very clearly in his distorted version of Malcolm's life. If anything Spike has done even more damage than I expected.

For one thing, he has completely destroyed the actual chronology of Malcolm's life. Just as he had done in a "4th draft" script I received anonymously, shortly after our public exchange began. Spike claimed at the Abyssinia Church at a Malcolm X memorial that he had changed that script. But the essential foulness of that script remains. For instance, Spike has completely distorted the actual chronology of Malcolm's life. He has almost completely removed Malcolm's childhood and youth. The film begins focusing on Malcolm as Detroit Red. And the first person we see in the film is Spike Lee as Detroit Red's "sidekick" and partner in crime, getting ready to "conk" Malcolm's hair.

The entire early part of Malcolm's life is nixed, and appears at most as flashbacks in the pimp's mind. The life and influence upon Malcolm of his Garveyite father and Grenadan nationalist mother, are almost totally absent, except for superficial and abstract fragments "imaged" from time to time through Detroit Red's mind.

The Klan attacks, his father's brutal murder, his mother being driven crazy by the state and his brothers and sisters dispersed just as in chattel slavery. All this material is dispersed as well, shredded, disconnected, used, at best, to give some very minor tragic dimension to the general hahaha "carefree" life of RED and SHORTY IN COON TOWN, which Lee (&, of course, Warner Bros.) seems to relish.

In fact, there is a severe let down in intensity after the long long focus on the pimp dope white prostitute life of crime of Shorty and Red, whom Spike has outfitted in Zoot Suits that seem to have come straight from Barnum and Bailey. Spike has not sought to recreate the actuality of the Zoot Suit; he thinks it's simply clownish attire. By removing the chronological development of Malcolm's life and using it only as random flash backs the psychological and philosophical raison d'etre for young Malcolm Little becoming partially lumpenized (destroyed by capital) and being transformed from the son of two righteous Black nationalists, one murdered one driven crazy, is destroyed.

We never really know, emotionally, why Malcolm is doing what we see him doing. And Spike thinks its all fun. Spike, by the way, appears in the film as Shorty for a longer period than Al Freeman's Elijah Muhammad! The Detroit Red business runs at least an hour. It is almost a film in itself! There is a marked let down of passion throughout the rest of the film, even though the time, place and condition of the rest of Malcolm's life, his continued political development, and the historical context and impact of his changes are among the most objectively passionate nexus of personalities and events in recent history. And even though the film is over three hours long, Spike chooses to leave out some of the most important aspects of Malcolm's life! It is as if the film had been shaped by the "powers that be" to remove what is most harmful to their interests and to leave in that which helps them out the most.

The two most damning aspects of the film, and the acts that identify Spike Lee clearly as a dangerous opportunist and mouthpiece for the most backward sector of the Black petty bourgeois is his willingness to blame the Nation of Islam for murdering Malcolm X, thereby absolving the government (the CIA and FBI). In fact, Spike uses the only dialogue he gives the FBI to trash Martin Luther King on the way out.

He gives, Malcolm a throwaway line about how perhaps the FBI or CIA is helping the Nation of Islam stalk him. But this is all. Spike never looks with any depth on the work of U.S. government agencies to undermine Malcolm, Elijah Muhammad, the Nation of Islam. For Spike, like all liberals, Black peoples' worst problem is, ourselves, and Malcolm's betrayal and assassination merely one more Black on Black crime.

Whatever we believe, Malcolm X is dead, and The Nation of Islam and Louis Farrakhan are still alive. For the most reactionary sector of U.S. society the idea of making Malcolm a confused and naive martyr betrayed and murdered by the Nation of Islam is perfect. This is the reason why the film was made, to use Malcolm against the Nation of Islam. And how slick to get a Negro to do it.

Equally as deadly is the completely superficial versions of Malcolm's trips to Africa. Malcolm's visit to Egypt, in this flick, is as a tourist, to see the Pyramids and the Sphinx and nothing else. There is no mention of his visit with the revolutionary Egyptian leader Gamal Nasser.

The rest of Malcolm's African tour is not mentioned at all. Nor his private audiences with the leading African revolutionaries of the time. Not only did he meet and talk to Nasser, but Nyerere of Tanzania, Toure of Guinea, Azikiwe of Nigeria, Kwame Nkrumah of Ghana, as well as Obote of Uganda and Kenyatta in Kenya. On this trip to Africa Malcolm spent 18 weeks. And he talked to many other African, Asian and Arab leaders, and some white ones as well. Malcolm openly speaks of the influence of these meetings on his thinking. Malcolm says of those meetings, that they were so important because, "it gave me a chance to sample their thinking. I was impressed by their analysis of the problem, and many of the suggestions they gave went a long way toward broadening my own outlook."

Spike wants this "broadening" of outlook to be simply Malcolm's no longer saying that the whiteman is the devil. This is the reason for the colorful, though hardly enlightening, pageantry Spike gives Malcolm's Hajj to Mecca. Malcolm is betrayed by Elijah Muhammad and so he embraces the true Islam and no longer hates white people. He is then murdered with a smile on his face, knowing his martyr time has come. Like the doomed idiot in *Of Mice & Men*.

It was important that the further transformation of Malcolm X, who had become El Hajj Malik Shabazz after the Mecca trip, never be revealed, or what he found out as Omowale, the son come home, which is the name he was given in Africa. Why, because even though Malcolm said his trip to Mecca did help him understand that it takes all the varieties of people in the world to make up the world, the final expansion of his thinking was the consolidation of a sharper anti-imperialist edge to its focus.

True, Malcolm was no longer satisfied with being a Black nationalist, but having seen that African revolutionaries were also anti capitalist as well as anti racist, he is quoted on returning from Africa. "You show me a capitalist, I'll show you a blood sucker." On Dec 20, 1964, he said, "It is impossible for capitalism to survive, primarily because the system of capitalism needs some blood to suck. Capitalism used to be like an eagle, but now its more like a vulture. It used to be strong enough to go and suck anybody's blood whether they were strong or not. But now it has become more cowardly, like the vulture, and it can only suck the blood of the helpless. As the nations of the world free themselves, then capitalism has less victims, less to suck, and it becomes weaker and weaker. It's only a matter of time in my opinion before it will collapse completely." This last quote was made one month before his assassination.

In the old Muslim coffee shop, in Spike's movie, when Malcolm asks Shorty to come with him into the Nation of Islam, Shorty says, naw, he loves pork and white women too much. And Shorty insists to the end that it is all a con anyway. We know now, that when Elijah Muhammad is shown in the film, principally as a lecherous womanizer and Malcolm's best friends in the Nation betray him that Shorty was correct after all. It was all a con. All serious struggle against the status quo is. And just to make sure we believe this—Shorty has made this film for us. We saw him on television at the premiere—he calls himself Spike Lee now.

(In my opinion the best thing Spike and Co. could do if they have any relationship to the masses of the American people would be to permit open discussions after each showing of the film, in theaters all over the world. Then, even though the brothers Warner are going to make at least a quarter of a billion dollars on the film, there would be some value in it for the people as well.)
(1993)

Henry Dumas:
Afro-Surreal Expressionist

Dumas's power lay in his skill at creating an entirely different world organically connected to this one. The stories are fables; a mythological presence pervades. They are morality tales, magical, resonating dream emotions and images; shifting ambiguous terror, mystery, implied revelation. But they are also stories of real life, now or whenever, constructed in weirdness and poetry in which the contemporaneity of essential themes is clear. "Fon" is strange, exuding a fantastic aura of ancient mystery and a quality almost Biblical, yet the story moves around a kind of Black liberation motif which sees would-be lynchers killed. "Will the Circle Be Unbroken?" Connects Black art with anti-white Black nationalism. A mysterious Black musician will play the afro-horn. Whites are warned to leave, staying at their own risk. The solo is described in a brilliant poetic intensity; when it is finished, a white man slumps dead. The resistance motif in *Poetry for My People* exists in the dynamism of Dumas' imagery—plus an electric persona of Black folklore, history, language, custom.

The strangeness of Dumas's world resembles Toni Morrison's wild, emotional "places." Both utilize high poetic description—language of exquisite metaphorical elegance, even as narrative precision. But language tells as well as decorates. Both signify as powerfully as they directly communicate. The symbols sing, are cymbals of deeper experience, not word games for academics. The world of *Ark of Bones*, for instance, shares a Black mythological lyricism, strange yet ethnically familiar! Africa, the southern U.S., Black life and custom are motif, mood and light, rhythm, and implied history. Zora Neale Hurston, Jean Toomer, Toni Morrison, and Henry Dumas are the giants of this genre of African American literary Afro-Surreal Expressionism. Jacob Lawrence, Vincent Smith, and Romare Bearden are similar in painting; Duke, Monk, Trane, Sun Ra in music. Dumas, despite his mythological elegance and deep signification, was part of the wave of African American writers at the forefront of the '60s Black Arts Movement.

The Black Arts Movement was a reflection and important element in the '50s–'70s social upsurge of the Civil Rights and Black Liberation Movements. In each of the major upsurges of the African American freedom movement — the anti-slavery movement, the Harlem Renaissance, and the '60s Black Liberation Movement — an accompanying artistic outreach shaped by and endowed with the energy of Black rebellion would also emerge! (The whole nation is inspired.) The most important and significant art uses the revelation of truth (fact, reality, etc.) as a function of its beauty! Pythagoras' number as essential symbol of reality means that correct is legitimate and provable, as is incorrect. If there is real and unreal, there is also wrong and right, scientific and unscientific. The liberation of African American people and the ultimate destruction of Imperialism are *inherent* in nature itself, scientifically predictable. So the great African American artists are these people and their development. The artist carries real life's *number*. Art is science because it is a form of knowing.

The historical existence of Africa and her scattered children, the tragedy and transformation — these form the material, hence spiritual, essence of ourselves. The whole of our story retold and foretold. Modern tales and old! Art is the life of people, society, and nature. The theme is always our real lives in actual society, as unbelievably complex and dialectical as they are. Creativity is the basis of evolution.

The Afro-Surreal Expressionism of Dumas and the others mentioned unfolds the Black Aesthetic — form and content — in its actual contemporary and lived life. MUSIC (drum — polyrhythm, percussive-song as laughter or tears), preacher and congregation, call and response, the frenzy! The color is the polyrhythm, refracted light! But this beauty and revelation have always existed in an historically material world. The African masks are shattered and cubed. Things float and fly. Darkness defines more than light. Even in the flow of plot, there are excursions and multi-layered ambiguities. As with Bearden, Dumas's is a world in which the broken glide by in search of the healing element, or are tragically oblivious to it.

The very broken quality, almost to abstraction, is a function of change and transition. It is as though the whole world we inhabit rests on the bottom of the ocean, harnessed by memory, language, image to that "railroad of human bones" at the bottom of the Atlantic Ocean. But in this genre the most violently antagonistic of contradictions, colors, shapes animates the personalities, settings, language of the work. History and culture are expressed through detail and emotion. Real and unreal, it would seem, defining the disintegration and the "crossed Jordan" of wholeness or liberation, are contending themes and modes. At the same time, they are naturally twined, as fall and rise, tragedy and transcendence, slavery and freedom—parameters of the Black Aesthetic: Africa and African American, Death and Birth and Rebirth. And because so much of our collective feeling is invested, the "meanness" of the genre is literal!

(1986)

Ark #2 Dakar

Forget the fact you're broke or just recovering from hospital time with newly detected diabetes, you're invited to Senegal, to Dakar, the "Bijou Francaise" of West Africa. A place so hip its last president was a poet and a Black poet. Hey, La Poet deNegritude, Leopold Sedar Senghor. (Now, six months a year in Paris, six months in the Dakar suburbs.)

What is new is yourself going here, back to Africa, yes, and why not?, after so long. Last trip 1975, Mogadishu, Somalia. Also new, my second son, Ras, fresh from being a leading part of the takeover of the administration building at Howard University, and hopefully speeding the slide of HU's main Greasy, a cheeky Negro to be sure, as in the old saw. "Take it easy, Greasy, thou hast a long way to slideth." Hopefully, he slideth soon!

But Dakar, Ras and I see as an endless night airport on arrival, and then a squall of American tourists, conference going literary types, and the inevitable poor people, these naturally Black, Africans, & in their own (no kidding?) country. I gotta friend always talkin about going back to Africa and he live in S. Orange a few miles north of me. Bein that close to Seton Hall drives you to think like that.

But these poor are Blacker and even more aggressive. So the cops ("flics" they are called in Paris, in the U.S., our flicks are full of flics — so its a matter of sophistication) are poorer and Blacker and even more aggressive, but they are not also pathological white supremacists. Legless beggars birddog anything smelling strange.

Clean is a verb here you see, not animals with Luggage. There is also the African time set required to set in. The waiting and disorder or re ordering to a slower earthy gait.

As we pass through the gate into DAKAR. A city which meant for me, from pre McCarthy American films, adventure, intrigue, merciless sophistication in the hip East! One immediate spectacle, like in the movies, repeated endlessly, is the attack on tourists by vendors, soi-disant guides (really dudes trying to get over by walking around with various outsiders showing them "safely" through vendor and poverty infested waters).

The vendors surround an obvious tourist and assail them until the would be buyers relent. How gross the tourists say, dashing away in groups, but television beats on groups, but television beats us with a more insidious finality and a more hideous result. We are sold horse manure as Rap (Brown) said, just by its endless repetition as environment.

But like Rushdie being condemned to death by Khomeini. Khomeini is more gross, but Western imperialism more final in its death sentences, even on artists, albeit the subtlety money brings. Wealthier criminals are always smoother.

****

We had set out to see the anti-Rushdie demonstration we heard was planned at The Great Mosque. Our hosts could not change our few pennies and so we had to go stand for an hour in the Citi-Bank Dakar branch and watch wealthy Dakarians walk out with arms full, bags full, briefcase full, of Senegalese Francs.

When I came out the bank Ras was in conversation with a slender brown brother with a USS Destroyer Commander's battle cap on. He spoke, a clear non English American. We began, he hesitantly, we less than at full, but moving straight ahead. Thirty minutes or so we cross into the yard of the Grand Mosque. Huge and imposing, but now empty. But still we stare at King Hassan of Morocco's gift. And ponder the strength and unifying power of Islam! Libya and Morocco, for instance are in Africa, and the people look like most African Americans! We never hear that from the nickel bag smoking up the white house.

By this time, the merchant seaman (we find out) is our walking buddy. Full of description and analysis of anything we ask about or see. When we asked our new guide where was the unpainted pottery, at the end of our long twisting incredibly scenic route we come directly to the stacks of unpainted pottery. Just what Amina ordered.

Later we'd track down a beautiful chair carved from a log, the original way back "folding" kind. It came apart easily on demand for decamping. Looked light but scienced out perfect distributing weight pyramid fashion across the flat surface.

Twice we went to Goree Island, the slave point of departure — from Africa or from this world, depending on the toss of the dice. The weight of Africa's diverse imagery is warm no matter the rude neo-colonial poverty. It's home still. The amazing colors, of the people, their clothes, nature, all reorganize the eye the nose the whole of the sense organs, and there is on top a constant slap of being "stunned" by the look or smell or sound or speed or height or fineness, &c.

It is the bottom line of your real emotional life. So Goree, the small island like a beautiful vacation spot, that floats a few miles away from Dakar. It is a ferryboat ride away, like the Staten Island ride from Manhattan. Its scenery big Russian boats unloading, loading; Black sailors loading or sleeping jet Black under glowing skies, still cooled by the dry season's breeze skimming the eternally rolling Atlantic.

Goree looks like a little resort when you arrive, coming in past small fishermen and the low flying birds. A row of small stores and cafés sit just behind the sand, with tables where we can take the morning or afternoon or evening, as sophisticatedly as you can stand. But then when you walk down the sandy dusty road to the Maison des Esclaves (House of Slaves), there is a different life to the place, a different you, it will seem. For Goree (the name itself is the origination of the concept) is something else again.

Go in to the half palace of murder and look. No matter what the brother speaking on the place, its murdered Black slaves, its tons of weeping and pain, its historic tragedy as site of a holocaust still going on. You are not prepared for the dark of the cells. The dankness and persisting odor of death. You are not prepared for the visions, the images, the death cries you conjure up in your mind. The mean look you give all around you toward what is not Black. The final pitiful hurt of knowing all of what can never be repaid and all of what must!

The narrow places one can look out and see the sea. How often could you see it if there were hundreds packed in with you! The hole in the back of the wall where the weak slaves, the sick, the underweight would be kicked out onto the rocks below, and the hyped up blood crazy sharks waiting as they circle in the red foam. Many of the slaves were from the interior and could not swim anyway. And the sharks circled, from habit of a good thing, waiting. That darkness, that smell, the still swallow ready hole, and now European and American tourists press in, you ain't too sociable admittedly. My son wants to know why they come here. "It's complicated. Criminals always come back to the scene of the crime," is the best I can do.

But Black people, from wherever, seem transfixed, hyped down, if you will. One woman cried as my son and I raised our arms in the chains and bracelets left from that time the speaker held aloft. "I can't take that shot," the woman said. But she did and tears worked her face. I guess, out of a latent terror that it's not completely gone, our Black holocaust. The echoes and vibrations and actual death poverty still is with us strong as escaped murderers.

This summer we're planning an international gathering of Pan-African poets and musicians "to mobilize for the final elimination of slavery on the planet!" Goree will be the site naturally, and the attendant theme is *Death to Apartheid*!

These are some ideas I have as we motor away from the castle of doom and Black death. Our thoughts militate against tragedy against death. We are full of life now though, as we feel Mother Africa breathing through our consciousness. Dakar just ahead!

(1989)

Souls Grown Deep

The South is still somewhere else. Still a mysterious something or another attached to the sputtering fathership of the U.S. nation state. It is not the fabled mystery wrapped in an enigma. Actually there are about 20,000,000 enigmas in which the place is wrapped and a bunch more of "white" people. The enigmas, of course, are Black. Afro Americans to be precise. And the South is wrapped around them as they are wrapped around it, but the South is more like a lie wrapped in a million more lies. And the Afro Americans are not mysterious, they are just routinely obscured, covered, lied about, slandered and called out of their names.

Why? Well for the more intrepid, I suggest you read W.E.B. DuBois' magnum opus, *Black Reconstruction*, the great searchlight on American, Afro American, and Southern history But there is another problem. "White American" history is what exists "officially," thoroughly off the wall and criminal in what it excludes and sick in what it includes. There are no Black people in "White America" history. There are only a few Black people in "White America." And they are not all honorary, some actually belong. (Do we have time to discuss the Negro who wanted to belong to the Klan because he was against segregation? No? Good!)

"White America" is the slave ship, the plantation, the Klan rallies, Emmett Till's smashed body held under the Tallahatchie River by a car engine, Chaney, Goodman and Schwerner, Bull Connor, The little Birmingham children blown to kingdom come for wanting to be Americans. Malcolm, Martin, JFK and RFK's assassinations. There is also 3/5ths of a human being in the U.S. Constitution, The Dred Scott "Niggers don't have no Rights" continuing Canon of U.S. social organization, the Fugitive Slave Act, the Slave Auctions, nigger dogs and "paterrollers" slashing through the Black southern nights looking for "yo' boy," the cotton, the 18 to 25 life span of the mature slave, the splitting of families, the daylight enemies of "race mixing" who are the great race mixers of the night.

But all this "White America" explains with a methodology that Josef Goebbels learned from. Just as Hitler's race codes were taken from the Southern "Black Codes" that helped destroy Reconstruction. Racist theories and fantasies, crackpot "White Supremacist" books, flicks and other maniacal propaganda and incredibly deformed lying anti-history. "White America" explains their supposed fellow citizens with "Nigger" and "Coon" and "Darky" and "Shine" and "Spear Chucker," "Woogie," "Inferior," "Jim Crow," "Boy" and "Girl" and "Uncle" and "Auntie" and dolls, minstrel shows, talk shows, Damon Wayans and "Living Color," and Tom Ass Clarences. Or Black Magic, Black Ball, Black Sheep, Black Heart, Black Humor, Black Thursday, Black Mail, Black Hat, Kinky, Wild and Wooly, Niggardly, Denigrate, like they say, things can look very Black.

In the 19th century, there was a "slave disease" called "Draptomania" where in some fit of malaise a once trusted slave would suddenly throw down "drap" his tools and run away from the plantation. It had to be a sickness otherwise why would a good darky want to leave their kindly massa and zoom off in the woods.

Now they explain us with the "Bell Curve" like Hitler's reasoning that Jesse Owens had an extra bone in his foot, that's why he could dust Superman at the '33 Olympics. Now we missing a critical bone in our head. "It's not that we don't want niggers to be equal American citizens, they just are not mentally capable. Don't blame "White America!"

The denigration and dehumanizing of the African people begins obviously with the slave trade, which is the denouement of the internal strife and degeneration of the African kingdoms themselves. The internal slave trade is what gives the catalyst to the European or Atlantic Slave Trade. And with the fall of Songhai, DuBois notes, the Africans would be plunged into centuries of tragedy and ignorance and lies. The deeper into slavery Africans were plunged the further away from Humanity they were pushed.

But two things should be mentioned, to be carried throughout any discourse on the subject. First, the Africans began the slave trade by enslaving themselves and selling themselves to the Europeans. Second, many people have been so whipped and demeaned, but when DuBois discussed this question as it existed in the 19th century, making these comparisons between the Black slave workers and the rest of the world's tortured masses, he adds, "but none of them was real estate"!

So that the plummeting humanity of the African reached its nadir in the U.S., with the yoke of Chattel Slavery. America is the society that still asks the question, "Can property become a citizen?" So far, the answer is a ringing "Nix!" Though, for sure, paper we have, mountains and mountains of paper. But, test the reality of the 13th, 14th and 15th Amendments to the constitution, the presumed passports of the Afro American people into America as equal citizens (the 13th says, slavery is abolished, except as a punishment for crime...is that why 1 out of every three Black Males is in the snare of the criminal injustice system? The "Due Process" of the 14th Amendment became a method to ensure that corporations have all the privileges of a citizen, but none of the responsibility. The 15th is for voting rights....Well even in fair New Jersey our present governor's (Christy Whitman) brother and campaign manager bragged that she was elected because they managed to repress the Black and Latino vote. They Gerrymander even in New York City.

Citizen? Well, check out "Forty Acres and a Mule," where that went. The basic provision for Black equality as small independent peasants after slavery was finally eliminated. Like the claim that the Afro American people would now be citizens of the U.S. with full citizenship rights. And after 40 acres, look to the new deal, the new frontier, the great society, civil rights, affirmative action, all gone, and now even talked bad about, just like the 40 acres. All of it talk, paper, bull doo doo of various varieties. But no equality. No citizenship. No democracy. No Self Determination. After the civil war, DuBois said this denigration and belittlement of Black people was part of a campaign to help oppose the Black thrust for equal rights and democracy. Chattel Slavery became national oppression with segregation and discrimination lynching and the rest, "separate but equal" they said in 1896, which be American Apartheid, again, way before South Africa. How innovative is "White America" around social questions!

But despite the hypocrisy, the endless Sisyphus Syndrome of Black Desire, pushing the huge boulder of struggle for democracy and full citizenship up the mountain of "White America" only to have it hurled back in our faces, believe it or not, Black people have not gone anywhere. In fact, there is continuous evidence of their presence in America. You could look underneath the paper hype of a Paul Whiteman "The King of Jazz" and find Louis Armstrong and The Hot Five and the real Kings of Jazz. You could turn Benny Goodman upside down so the pennies would fall out and maybe run into a Duke Ellington or Fletcher Henderson. You'd be much closer to a "King of Swing," certainly BG wasn't. You could frisk the Elvis pathology and find Big Joe Turner or Big Maybelle's phone number. You might even get to hear a real blues. I mean, listen through the door when they discuss Fred Astaire, and you might hear Bojangles mentioned or the Nicolas Brothers or Bunny Briggs. Or hold Buddy Rich and Gene Krupa records up to the light, you'll see Jo Jones and Max Roach's names written in invisible dis. We are routinely discovered. "Dissed" and "Covered." You want I should mention Al Jolson or "Rock and Roll" or "Cool" or "Fusion" or "Rockabilly" or American language, mores, life style, culture? Turn any of them upside down, so the other two pennies fall out (our two cents, which the 3/5th deprives us of), and you'll find the Afro American people, their culture, history and struggle in the U.S. Dissed and Covered and Hidden and Exploited.

Exploited? Well, say if Michael Jackson sold 93 million of his "Thriller" album and he gets a "good taste," say 20 percent. Where's the other 80 go? Whitney Houston and Michael Jordan, and the rest, how much is "White America" making from them? Most of the money made from those performers supports "White America" not Afro America. Such a thing as the entertainment industry, whether song, dance, sports or controversy. We are a people brought from Africa in Chains as slaves to do work for "White America," for hundreds of years, now accused by these same unrepentant slave masters of being lazy! Incredible!

For one thing, it is a gross understatement to say "White America" combines both ignorance and arrogance in one dumb package. So that they are the most fact-deprived people in the world, no matter the tons of dis and mis information they hurl around. "White America" kind of knows almost nothing about their history, their culture, nor the true history and culture of the real

America, which is multinational. "White America" is so twisted it's trying to stop Americans from speaking Spanish when most of the people in the Western hemisphere speak Latino Spanish. But "White America" demands to be illiterate. Most high school students in Texas don't even know where Mexico is, and they in it!

We have been talking about "White America" because that is the context in which the south exists, formally. Though the south was won for the Union by 200,000 Afro American soldiers, it was seized and annexed by "White America" and the Afro American people returned to slavery (with the destruction of the reconstruction). This, in direct violation to the last real treaty between emerging Afro America and the United States. Actually "White America" 's re-emergence was predicted by DuBois in the '30s when he said that now it takes 200,000 to elect a congressman in Michigan, only 30,000 to elect one in Dixie (because of the discrimination, Klan, poll tax, &c.,) but that, eventually, the rulers will turn all of this society into the south. (Witness Clinton, Ark; Gore, Ga; Helms, N.C.; Gingrich, Ga; and Dole from Kansas a border state, and the birthplace of the Republican party. The attacks on Civil Rights, &c.

So that there is a deep and antagonistic contradiction between Black history and the sham distortion "White America" mashes on the unsuspecting as history. His story alright, as in "lie," but no real persons. There is, likewise, a deep and violently antagonistic contradiction between Black life, history and culture and the racist social organization and neo-slavery consciousness of "White America." In essence, "White America" is an oppressor nation, and the Afro American Nation has been its constant victim and prey, since it came to exist, in the "Black Belt South" after Chattel Slavery was supposedly ended. This is the main dangerous secret the south is hiding, that after the Civil War, during which the Afro American people were supposedly freed by the government of the United States from the chattel slavery of the seceding Confederacy (and even told that they had the right to bear arms to defend this newly gained freedom) that Black people overthrew the confederacy by (1) A General strike, in which the slaves left the plantations wholesale, therefore destroying the economy and logistical and supply capacity of the Confederacy (2) Engaging in Armed Struggle, at the side of the Union, destroying the Plantation owners as a class, including their land and property.

Yet it is the daughters and sons of the slave owners and the overseers who are the governors, senators, presidents, big businessmen, while Black people are tortured as an Oppressed nation in the Black Belt South. How, a nation? Well, then what are we? There is no such thing as "Second Class Citizens." That's like saying someone is "almost alive"! Since Black people have never been allowed to integrate into the U.S. as full citizens. By 1896, "Separate But Evil" was the law of the land. By 1915, Blacks could not vote anywhere in the South and always had trouble everywhere else in the country. The Afro American people are a nation, a nation by virtue of being a "historically constituted, stable community of people, formed on the basis of a common language, territory, economic life and psychological make-up manifested in a common culture." (A dude named Joe, from Georgia, gave me that scientific definition.)

The Afro American people are also an oppressed nation. An oppressed nation is one that suffers robbery, denial of rights, super exploitation and repression of democracy from an imperialist power. Face it, as the good Dr. (DuBois) said, the U.S. has never been a democracy and Black people have never been citizens! Though Social Democrats try to make "Racism" the main and only problem Afro Americans suffer at the hands of "White America." The racism, which is oppression because of physical characteristics, just adds a further ugly, a constant ubiquitous torture, because we don't have to have yellow stars put on our arms, like Stevie Wonder said, we wear our identification as oppressed people, those who it is alright to slander, lockup, beat up and murder, on our faces.

Say all that to say, that despite the chattel slavery, American apartheid, oppression, super exploitation, Black people, like I said, have not gone "enty" (to quote Al Hibbler) where. We are here. We have been here before most of the other "White Americans" (given the sobriquet "White" so as to remedy the harassment and exploitation of their period of immigration with a passport to supremacy over at least niggers.) Not only have we been here in the U.S. spread through most of it, but concentrated largely in the south, some 60 percent of us, still there at the scene of the crime, but that factor of a Psychological development manifested in a common culture" is spread through and over and inside the U.S. and even "White America" like the subconsciously retained combination to the family safe.

What is critical to understand is that this Afro American Nation, because it is oppressed, has the right to Self Determination. That is, there is nothing in Heaven, Hell or Earth that says Black people must stand by and be tortured and super exploited by a historically confirmed oppressor nation and wait for the Godly light of enlightenment to transform their oppressors into fellow citizens. But also, the Afro American Nation, is not Racial. Though racism, for sure, makes the general underdevelopment of the South, for instance, even more withering and destructive, for Afro Americans, obviously. But the Black Liberation Movement, in the south or anywhere else in the U.S. is struggling for Democracy and Self Determination, and in the areas of our majority and concentration, Self Determination is the democratic reform which unlocks the process whereby equality comes.

But the Black South (look at the map, cost a dollar from the Dept of the Interior), those areas where Black people are concentrated as a majority or in large plurality, demand Self Determination, just as those Black people inside the rest of "White America" demand Democracy. They are the same demand, two sides of the same coin. The fact that a nation is not "racial," but a community of people, is important to this exhibition, even though there are only the self taught Afro American artists showing here. But this is only because of the historic and continuous segregation, discrimination and exclusion of Black people from almost every facet of American life.

Great parts of the south itself, The Afro American Nation, is a historically constituted community of people, made up of Black people, Native Americans, Mulattoes, and even an Anglo American national minority (white folks). We know minority rights has never been a hot issue in the U.S., but watch that change now that South Africa, for instance, has to wrestle with that bad boy. I emphasize all these things because what these self taught Afro American artists are bringing is not a Racial art but a National art. That is, if we understand the actual national character of the "lower south" which I refer to as the Afro-American Nation, Afro America, if you will, then what I am saying will be clearer, agreed with or not.

Since I am referring to the areas of Black concentration, the majority there are Black, but the nation itself is multinational. But it is a separate place from the U.S. though part of its state suzerainty. Hence, the Black Belt culture, though indelibly shaped by the Afro

American experience and Afro American culture, is, even with that recognition, multi-national and as a whole, is the congregating organism, historically, of Native Americans, Mulattoes, Whites as well as Black people. So that whether we are talking about Elvis Presley or Jerry Lee Lewis or Dr. John, or Charlie Pride, we are still talking about the expression of a culture, that while obviously heavily influenced by Black people, still is drawn from and shapes all who are the products of its historical material, social, psychological, hence, aesthetic nurture.

What is "Racial Art" and Racialism, in general, is the expressed confirmation of Black national oppression. As such, of course, the whole of "White America" and the domestic nations it oppresses, Afro America, Mexican America, the Native Nations (not mentioning here the multiple oppressed nationalities who are not nations) are stamped with the affliction of "racialism," which is one aspect of the national oppression. And this is not endemic merely to the U.S., in the era of imperialism, in general, that is one of the essential characteristics of international relations that most nations of the world (the so called "3d world") are victims of oppression, exploitation, annexation, colonialism now neo-colonialism at the hands of a handful of European and with them U.S. and Japanese industrial states. What is "racial art" is the expression of the exclusion, rejection, caricature of all people except the "chosen" insect: the Wasp. From its twisted lying "story," God, creation, and everything of any value is about, created by and for Whites. Art is white. Scholarship is white. Beauty is white. History is white. All good things are white. Intelligence is white.

Even on a football field, there are rules now making displays of Afro American culture (particularly that directly derived from Africa) illegal! But from watching the box, there doesn't seem to be much chance of that really getting over. Check the next touchdown Djeli ya in the end zone. Dion Saunders starts his a few yards before crossing the goal. And even when the Lords of Measure (appropriately dressed in Black and white stripes...jails and segregation) sometimes temporarily think they have brought a presumed nix to these dances, gyrations, twists and shouts and stepshows, these momentary expressions of the funk still get over, like syncretistic bundles of any oppressed people's culture gets smuggled in, they use a trick that is even more slick. Like my man, scored, and froze there, unmoving, in the ancient "attitude," a la

James Br own, standing stock still, shivering with the acknowledgement of the spirit rhythm.

To dance or gesture, "signify" after a score is opposed by law! In ancient Africa, War was an athletic contest of strategy, tactics, courage and toughness, but it was, literally, a game, acted out with wooden weapons. The coming of iron, the Ogun spirit, changed all that. Ogun as in Goon. So the language was part of that game-war. What they now call "trash talking" which was originally "talking shit" then "talking trash " (In polite society). What was called "The Dozens" i.e., "The Songs of Recrimination" are acted out each night in the National Basketball League, but it is thought vulgar and superfluous. In fact, the mouth, is from ancient reference, one of the most virulent aspects of defense or offense, for that matter. The "RARARA" calling on the great Being, The Sun, itself, to lend your people its magnanimous creativity. Who Ra?

Ditto, the Drum Majors with their African Lion Manes, still the headdress of accomplishment, challenge and victory. The Baton, being twirled, the high steps and please dig the boom boom -boom boom boom, and those charging beats from way cross the water and the mists of history carried like watermelon seeds under the decks of doom. American culture itself is partially Black, partially of African heritage. Music, Dance, Speech, Theater, (musicals or minstrels), Athletics, Fashions, Cuisine, its all there, from the old Djali (the lead laughers, the Song Chiefs, the historian poets) until the contemporary "Black face" of Rock and Roll. The culture of the Afro American nation in its land base the south is the font of Black culture throughout the U.S.; it is also the chocolate at the bottom of the glass of milk that makes the whole thing....well, check it out! But that culture is composed also of Native American and European aspects. It is a composite of these. In fact, the general culture of the Western Hemisphere is the same African, European, Native American mixture, a mestizo culture despite the mindless denial of "White America" in favor of the non existent "purity" of Adolph and the Bad People—a kind of tribal supremacy of isolated barbarians.

But it is a class distinction, finally, that constitutes the measure, the "bottom line" of value. That is, the Afro American and the Native American (including the various Latino) cultures are those of oppressed nations and peoples. The culture of chattel slaves and the colonized and subjugated peoples. This makes them, materially, and in the psyches of the "White American," "lower class." This even marks the "White American" imitations of them as "vulgar," "gangster," &c.

"White America" still suffers from a colonial consciousness itself, the intellectualized self devaluation of all that is American on the deep side, in favor of the antiquated or removed culture of Europe. The problem is that much of contemporary European life has been shaped by its association with "White America" and even real U.S. culture. The bistros and clubs of European metropolis are more consistently characterized by Blues and Jazz or Rock or R&B or some other variety of American popular culture, Mozart and them are not even the popular culture of Europe! Which is usually more derivative of the mestizo flavor of U.S. popular culture, particularly the Afro American.

In class and political terms, European culture is glorified and imposed as the intellectual and aesthetic measure by Imperialism to justify its oppression and super exploitation of the world's people. The "Superior Race" or "The Chosen," wherever you bees in the soi-disant "Judeo-Xtian" calumny, has the right to steal kill exploit oppress rape lie and rip off anything in the world because it is superior. Like the English used to(?) say about the Irish. "What're they gonna do with a bathtub except put coal in it."

The Black Belt south, is not only the site of the Afro American nation, it is also the scene of the horrific crime of slavery. In the Slave trade 100,000,000 Africans lost, murdered, drowned, otherwise wasted, and the sad demonic vector of this middle passage to chattel to oppressed nationality historic material life is still very much with us or haven't you seen the Rodney King video. I disagree with the Black Nationalists who talk about the "African Holocaust," we do not need to borrow from anyone else to describe our plight. Our enslavement and continuing torture is not a religious curse, it is the result of the European Slave Trade. And it continues.

So from within the oppressed nation inside the underdeveloped "White American" south, there has been a constant humming, cries, screams, rhythm of weird gravity, messages, prayers, denunciations, oaths of resistance, and likewise, a continuous stream of reflection on what it all is. But we are "twinned" by our Americaness and our Africaness, to paraphrase DuBois. If we cannot handle this "twoness" it crumbles our minds and our hearts into self hate and false consciousness and the dead end submissive slave psycho suicide of the "Negro," the Black who remains the slave master's property… still.

What characterizes the essence of the national art of the Afro American nation is the directness of its reflection of its real life. From the African, the Afro American, even as they developed into another people, a western people, maintained a sensibility that maximizes its experience as the most powerful expression of the world. Not that that experience is always rendered as naturalism or realism &c. But the emotional impact and significance, what it meant, as a tale and tail of instruction, revelation in the human world. For Afro American culture, life itself is a complex matter, always in motion, the intellectual component of which is the equivalent of anything's actuality. The world is always hipper than we know. The most ignorant of us then is anyone who professes to know all about anything?

Beauty is basically revelation, the halo of the existent. If we can dig it there glowing around everything. "Natural Evidence" I termed it in *Blues People*. That is, proof of nature and ourselves as nature digging ourselves, and digging ourselves digging our selves. (The "Attitude," like the Blood, Boddiharma, brought to the East. James Brown shuddering in the funk vibe, the spirit, the big Eye, relayed to whoever has eyes or

feelings. The spiritual aspect of Black culture goes back to Africa and has remained, whether religious or secular in form. The Africans said "The spirit cannot descend without song." The life of the most high. The most advanced. The creative is ness of what are.

The ancient Africans thought that everything was hip if we were hip enough to dig that. That everything was, in fact, one thing. Not the later self empowering "monotheism" of the sedentary Pharaohs. There was no such "thing" as God. There was Goodness ie Aliveness, which everything shared and displayed to the extent it did. It was the powers, the elementals, the forces, which were "divine," i.e., which allowed one, with careful study, to predict the course of things. The ancients, for instance, built the city of On at a point where the ultimate life giver could be observed and human life charted according to the great fiery beings' nature.

How mysterious are the ways of the world (the whirl) that now the descendants of The Children of The Sun, are still chained to the madness of Heathens even today. A cold punishment indeed for getting so backward as to innovate slavery. To be plagued with it

394

for centuries, like the dude say, "Jacoub, you sure you know what you doing?" The U.S. north and south are still distant reflections of an ancient contradiction between the north and the south of the world. Which formed when the sun woke up the dead glacial world of the far north and the floods split the world with a mouth that began with a smile and rose in its northern arc into a frown. Happy Niggers versus Serious White folk.

There is no doubt that the Djali rather than the Griot more truthfully expresses the accreted sensibility of the African and what is laid over in the Afro American and the American in many ways. We love to laugh. "Getting Happy" is what the Black Belt folk do in church, even transported into the various northern ghettoes whose national Afro American culture is more tightly held because of segregation.

Sterling Brown told about how under the neo fascist "Jim Crow" south, there was a phone booth in this one town that was the designated darky laughing booth. That is, if Negroes had to laugh, they better not let white folks catch them. So they had to, if their funny bone was so engaged, dash into the phone booth, so the laughter would be harmlessly hidden. The essential class nature of the Afro American national question, because of the racial aspect also puts you in mind of the torturous Hindu caste system and its socio fascist religious dicta, where, by statute, it is against the law for an "Untouchable" to blunder into the eyesight of a Brahmin. What is true about any apocryphal aspect of Brown's poem is that there has had to be a great deal of indirectness about the Afro American aesthetic "directness" which is accomplished by "laying on symbol," i.e., to sneak the insight in without endangering oneself to the brutal celebration of "White American" supremacy... i.e., assault, jail, murder, &c.

For a true history of Black people to be expressed absolutely freely, particularly the life and culture of the slaves and the life of oppression in its various forms. To speak of their real lives, feelings and authentic persona these slaves could not be slaves. Oppression and Segregation always hid and covered Black people and their real lives. They had to be dismissed, ignored, covered or lied about, so that the backward social consciousness of the oppressor nation could be maintained. Any attempt to break out of that national oppression, colonialism e.g., the revolutionary democratic demands of the '20s, '30s, '40s, '50s, '60s, once smashed, must then be disenfranchised ridiculed, distorted, lied about, so that the consciousness of the racial-fascist slave master colonial imperialist is restored. Why? So that the rulers of "White America" can continue to make mega-billions from their super exploitation, not only of Black people, but of most people around the world.

But the distance between the northern and southern aesthetic began long before there was America or an Atlantic slave trade. These have merely taken this distance all the way out to the point of violent antagonism. The ancient African, proceeding from the spiritual center of Music, Call (priest) and Response (congregation), and the Going Outness, i.e., "The Frenzy" or Trance. The other fundamental center of that culture was that it was anciently communal. The very world view that held that the world was one thing indissoluble and inseparable was the basis for the communal philosophical view, but from the material lives of people who must cooperate to obtain food, clothing and shelter the bottom line to all life. The expression of all the forces of the one operating simultaneously and moving in and out of each other in the dialectic of going through changes is how the philosophical stance shapes the aesthetic, both drawn from the real social life and structure of the people.

The polyphonic character of Black music, polyrhythmic and percussively centered remain until this day. The ancient pentatonic scale of African and Afro American music is found in many European "Folk cultures" confirms the oldness of the scale and that it predates the Diatonic (7 tone "tempered" European scale that arose in the 16th century). This aesthetic is expressed in graphics by the polychromatic surfaces of African and Afro American art. The love and intense self conscious use of color. Pythagoras brought the system of number, color, sound correlatives, he learned in Africa, back to Greece. Sun Ra brought them to Afro American jazz, where the Rockers copped the "light show."

The use of color as simultaneous expressions of self are again rooted in the communist aesthetic of African Art. As Max Roach, the great drummer says, "our music is essentially democratic even communist, in essence. It frees the players to be equal parts of the expression. European music is, in its symphonic forms, imperialistic. The Composer is the dictator, the conductor the general. Both have to see that only what is on the written page is played." The improvisational center of Afro American music is its expressive tour de force, although there is much of this music that is written, witness Duke Ellington's 2000 registered works of composition, or the great writing of Thelonius Monk, Jelly Roll Morton, Billy Strayhorn, &c.

In reading Olaudah Equiano, an early writer of his life as a slave, he tells of the traditional socialization of the West African around music and poetry like the American is socialized around sports. He says, "We are a nation of musicians and poets..." The traditional dress, by the way, was Guinea Blue, but with the Transformation the middle passage and chattel slavery wrought, that ancient homey blue was transformed as well as an image, a memory strained through sadness. The Blues. Our history says when we were free we were in Blue, but we blew and now we got the blues. And if you were listening to the brother or sister there, that's what they just blew.

The "natural evidence" means that whatever is there with "me," available to be expressed as evidence (yes) of my life as feeling, is ripe material for Art. Finally Art is presence, the being that I carry to register who and what I am to myself (and my other selves of which the world is composed and by) that quality and function, protect me (us) from non-being. Slavery, colonialism, &c., seek, fundamentally to reduce its victims to non-being. Cabral said, the oppressed people are removed from history by the oppressor. And only revolution restores them to history. He also said (in *Return To The Source*) that the people, ultimately, were the repositories of culture and by that fact, resistance.

So that the "collective improvisation" of classical Afro American music is by form and content antithetical to the monopoly capitalist reality and "rugged individualist" hype of "White America." And this is not solely as the lingering pre Columbian world view, but that certainly is in it, but also because here in the West, it was and is the whole of the Afro American, the whole of Black people throughout the western hemisphere and in most parts of the world who are chained to the idle worship, greed and fake civilization of the Euro-American imperialists. That torture is collective, so that the very grounds upon which the social solipsism of such "individualism" barely exists among Black people. The uniqueness the Black artist seeks is to bring a distinct voice as part of the whole. Not alienated from that whole, but a "new" contribution which continues the tradition of newness ie, as some wags have said, "The sound of surprise." The aesthetic is thrust from material conditions of real life and history.

The south, as I have tried to show, is anchored at its bottom and middle by an oppressed Afro American nation. A nation that arose as capitalism penetrated the south, as the feudal slave became a capitalist slave. Consolidated when the US democratic revolution the civil war was supposed to be was aborted by betrayal and replaced with American Apartheid and proto fascism of the Black Codes, enforced by the proto storm troops of the Ku Klux Klan. Read Richard Wright's vivid short stories, *Uncle Tom's Children* about the south during the '20s and '30s: the chilling fascist aura of the place Wright evokes. Or *Black Boy*. The dangerous tension of day to day life is a grey terror that hangs across every person, gesture and word like the Black and White subaural screaming just beneath the portrayals of Nazi rule you felt in the films about occupied Europe during WWII.

Yet in this slave ship of the south, the betrayal of the Afro Americans is one dimension along with the attempted genocide and subsequent betrayal of treaties, of the Native Americans and the robbery and exploitation of the white workers, particularly the rural poor, e.g., in Appalachia, is the aggressive shaper of the Afro American nation, the whole south and the U.S. nation itself. Another useful metaphor for this is the slave ship in its northern version, the whaling vessel. Herman Melville, one of the greatest of U.S. writers was attacked continuously for the grim truth of his revelation about the American nation, which like the mad Captain of the Pequod (named for a native nation in the U.S. wasted by White American genocide, also it means a small example of what is) driven by its master's sworn dedication to evil plunges across the ocean in search of the evil being that has wounded him and with that made him crazy.

Ahab, the doomed king in the Bible, is the captain. He is the instrument of the big owners, an employee, for all his grand insanity, hired to search out and kill whales for profit. But he has been psychologically and philosophically altered by his sojourn as overseer of the murder vessel. He has been attacked and altered by his supernatural prey. By a devil of whiteness. Like Ahab, a being roaming the seas to kill and destroy and terrorize. Actually, the whole world has been made into a slave ship. From the genocide of the native peoples to the slavery of Africans, which turns back on Europe itself with the World Wars and the fascist attempt at the genocide of the Jews. The racialism has revealed its true class nature in the modern world, as the primitive accumulation of colonialism and early capitalism, gained from stealing the primitive peoples lands and exterminating them, to the taking of Black slaves, to the development of European fascism, now express themselves in outrageous apotheosis in the world wide terror of imperialism.

The Pequod, which is multinational, like the world, like the real America, is ruled by a mad man in search of the diabolical figure of his own evil. The whiteness of the whale is the hype of murderousness which renders its evil mystical. Like white supremacy, in its inquisition ghost cannibal outfits, KKK. Ahab, the symbol of white murderous imperialism is himself maddened by it and seeks to murder the murderer, the biggest whitey of all. The Captain, the navigator, the bribed mates of the crew head for disaster death, deluded into chasing the manifest evil of the ghostly monster, created by slavery now passing as wage slavery and rising colonialism. The animal devil, the Sea Frankenstein of Imperial Europe and the U.S., whose ship this is and who are themselves the animus of the creature.

Seafaring murderers here in the real, searching the world for profit led by a prophet of evil The Devil as an actual being, a global predator. The predator of the "individual" alienated from human life to imprison and slaughter it. As Milton's Satan says, "Better to rule in Hell than serve in Heaven." The south is the hold of the same slave ship reformed as whaling vessel—created by genocide and chattel slavery and its diabolical conquest and mastery of North America and now the world. The south, which fought defiantly to remain an independent galley, has been made the hold of the larger slave vessel, the prison of slaves chained below the decks. The indentured and poor whites have become overseers in wage slavery, elevated in the artificial posture of "freedom. "White supremacy chains them to the master murderers with delusion—fool's gold.

The Whaling vessel seeks Whales to kill for their oil and flesh—like they were the big floating Iraqs of the 18th and 19th century, the savage "red skins " of the sea. They killed for oil, just like Bush did, for the same reasons. The art of the Black Belt is national, but it is also authentically American. National as it reflects and expresses the life and culture of that people, but as a raw material and the historic connection, for super profits, as part of and "a part from" the U.S. to the extent the slave is part of the plantation.

It also expresses an America realer than White America," whose bitter creation Satan uttered while falling among us. The ruler of Hell, Dis. Like Columbus discovering "India." Yeh. Dis & Cover.

But that's why "White America" thought Jazz was "about them," as Albert Ayler used to say. Mad Ahab chasing himself, yet whose closest "companion," though he cannot understand or have real feeling for him, is Pip, the Black cabin boy. Dig that, like *Uncle Tom's Cabin*. The Black Belt is a space occupied by oppressed and oppressor who are extremely contradictory, yet objectively "embraced" by the madness of mutual alienation from the rest of the crew. One with the madness of the demoniacal overseer, one with the madness of the prophet. The Fool and The Hanged Man, both doomed by the genocidal vessel on the course of destruction by delusion and evil. But the Black Pip is a "Pip" as well. (The dictionary meaning of Pip, is a Black spot on a playing card, but also, a name for someone defeated, and a dark spot on a fabric that appears to dance before the eyes.) The cabin boy was one of Gladys Knight and their ancestors. "I heard it through the grapevine," she and the Pips told us.

Black Pip is not a sinner King slain in the Prophet's vision, which is reality. Because "That's a pip!" like "Bad" or "terrible" or those recent terms, "Dope" or even "Stupid" terms of the Black Nation's struggling majority, whose language "White America" says is "the same" as "White America's" only because to admit the full dimension of its autonomy in syntax, definition and metaphor, would be like admitting that the slave and the slave owner share nothing except their objective connection as owner and owned. Art is "exist," are, R, (the sun's symbolic I/Eye). The artist brings worlds into existence through his creativity. His emulation of the sun. He holds a "mirror up to nature," as the Bard said. For those artists of the Afro American nation, this their surest technique. For Afro American art, generally, in the main, historically, reality had to be addressed, reflected, struggled against, changed, because they were slaves, in reality. This is the "ideological reflection" of the world," Mao spoke of.

It is no accident that some of the greatest American art has come out of the Black south. Whether, music, known and imitated across the world, dance, poetry, cuisine, style, Bruce Franklin tells us there is no American culture without Afro American culture, likewise, there is no Afro American culture without America. But

"White America" denies the existence of Black people except as "real estate." Freed from privately owned chattel slavery to become "slaves of the whole (white) nation" And now, with the murderer of Richard Kemble's wife reputed to be prominent in the U.S. Senate and a drunken lizard as speaker of the house, the 3rd Reconstruction has been destroyed, the big rock of disenfranchisement, robbery, denial of rights, comes plummeting back down on Black heads. Pip and Ahab, though still in the same space, have their backs against opposite walls, railing at each other. What do the torturer and the tortured scream at each other? The nature of the universe, of course, the divinity of Good vs. the demonism of Evil. (God & The Devil are both here with us, both live on credit, both belong to the same church.)

When I went, with a group of scholars and writers, on a tour to visit these artists, we 1st gathered in Atlanta. And from there went to Birmingham, Bessemer, in Georgia, and then to Fayette, Alabama to Oxford, Miss and then to Memphis, Tennessee. It raised a swarm of perceptions. Beginning with hip Atlanta, victorious Wall Street's main branch bank and headquarters in the newly conquered south. The doorway for carpet baggers, scalawags and compradors. And, like shadows, those same, variously found among the newly rising Black Bourgeoisie after the civil war. Atlanta is also their capital. (Does it seem strange that capitalists would call the center of their dominion, The Capital?) Segregation was the extent of the Black Bourgeoisie's autonomy. Rejection was the extent of their self-determination. Atlanta, where DuBois tried to build a collective Black education paradigm and did the most advanced scholarship on the Black Belt. He likened Atlanta to the fabled Atalanta of Greek mythology, who, in the big race, loses sight of the prize, stooping to pick up the gold, forgets the goal, and is in the process of selling her soul.

Atlanta, where Booker T made his compromise, the illusion of the small proprietor, who is actually, the mascot of rising monopoly, the emerging comprador listening to the Victor, money, "His Master's Voice." Atlanta, where "I Am Somebody" became, at the 1988 Democratic convention, the house slave's declaration of pride in his liveried submission to "White America." Atlanta, of the National Black Arts Festival, and now the Olympics, where Martin Luther King was born, the capital of the Afro American Nation. Naturally, it was a call from Atlanta that got me into the orbit of this revelation. Bill Arnett, of the Anglo American minority, has wrestled with the Abominable Snowman (Moby Dick, on shore) to get this art recognized and understood, for what it is, part of the national art of The Afro American Nation and one of the bright vectors of creativity of the entire U.S. society.

The art is national because it is the expression of a national psyche a reflection of it's material life projecting its' spiritual being as well. A living image of it's human experience and consciousness. The art of the oppressed is always "inferior" to the art of the oppressor. This is confirmed by guns and money. By the power to define the slave by the extent of his subjugation and "real" value as a commodity, by his owner As fixed capital to the owner of money, part of the means of production to the slave master. Art? Incredible. (From Blacks?) say the Klan of "White America" Nazi sycophants disguised as curators and art critics. Yet, there is nothing of value to the progress of human society, its understanding or belief, created by the demented greedies who offer such judgment about Afro American people and culture. Except, imagine the mind that can find a reason for self adulation, to the point of universal solipsism, in reducing the world to what it is: Hell. No matter who they say, if all the people and nations on the planet and perhaps the next, depending on where most of you (population and "pieces," end up), we all must concur that the "white" rulers, historically and right this f'ing minute, are the most brutal, violent, crazy, evil, dangerously ignorant, claimers of "humanity" we know. Take a poll of the people of the world. The majority of whom are treated like niggers.

Yet, from such a historical concrete material life, confirmed by the people and each nation's actual lives, to claim such absolute superiority over every other human in the world is like the hideous cry of an alien predator. A near human. The snow slows change, but spurs busyness. With what furious energies did the have nots of a "natural economy" sail out and around the world to fulfill their psycho-physical needs. The bleak winter, part of the separation of the middle of the earth by Glaciers and endless winter. The frowning North, here theft was high art and a characteristic even of the northern Gods & Heroes. There, the retrograde African paradigm of slavery would find its fruition in class structure unmitigated by a continuing collectivism (as in most of the south) and so provide the time, place and condition for the consolidation of capitalism.

Why claim anything but truth? For who would do that?

Criminals, the Insane, Demagogues, and those for whom any actual living heaven is as impossible as stuffing Jesse Helms through the eye of a needle. Interesting, that Mr. Are Net, or R-Net, is some agency able to catch some of the Ra, the sun. (Names are not metaphysical, they are descriptions which, if originating in material life and representing some quality possessed by or influencing the named, can certainly, at some point, characterize the bearer, in some way. E.g, we can grow into our names, as a kind of mantra of possibility or desire, &c.)

The very relevant and operating quality of this R Net is that he has gathered some of the Shine and the Sun, in a dazzling reflection of we feeling, we knowing, we wanting. This exhibit is all of that, in capsule, from the beating heart of Black us, who are the Africans, betrayed by Black Kings and Queens, into the chains, the yoke, the bloody march, the slave ship, the middle passage, sold to cannibal ghosts! Lucky us! Lucky we, us, i. to have been sold by soul-sellers to the soul buyers. To be enslaved by Adam's children, Kings of the northern cradle, and transported and transformed. Was Africa, but that was all that was left of our past the Af-, the before...and then the roaming seizers turned us Ro (Roe-reborn by Row, a boat, stacked underneath in rows, by slave ship, under whose deck we are bound. There is no "A" (Am-Self, Ame-Love) on we "merica, it is simply "merica, where we have sent our lower selves (our higher selves) into slavery, to submit to the children of them naked people the old folks ran out of Eden. Great imitators, they call their land The Gotten of Eating, like the old Roman God of War Ate.

The Afro American, Africans transformed by a baptism into chattel slaves of the planter land owner class in the "White America" of the south. Who went through changes from Africa slaves to American slaves. From feudal slaves held to the land as part of the production. But the real blues bided its time till slavery was spent, at least on paper. And here it come, like walking away from the plantation. Not running, but "hatting" in a steady rumbilin beat. A yeh, "good bye low crackers/ I'ma harvest me a life of my own."

When the deal went down, we had got away from that there and made it as far as this here. It turned from country and went to the city. Still blue, it carried both proof and evidence. As memory and the poem of being. We was always our own instruments. We could use our hands and turn dead trees to long distance telephones. Ancient blue rappers that made the forests talk and sing. Could Michael Jackson look up in the air and see the Moon Walk?

But our blues was always with us. Turn your hat around or not. It was something ya walked with, something carried. The expression of We — Us — I, Black and what–up-Blue? It could be in a hallway, fire from the cold, the dead slate industrial big city streets. The beat would stir up some heat. Some light. Some of that old time brightness would come. No matter we be hittin, some times, some hard ass things. Life, when it move you to sing, has made an impression. It didn't just pass by anonymous.

But when the blues come in with "freedom." It was still not free. The grey cavernous concrete and shadow cities. Blood be blood. Blood turn into blood. Your hands so cold, with nuthin in em. You must make a fist just to keep warm.

(2006)

Emilio

Say I knew Emilio Cruz over forty years. That seems right. Maybe more, I don't want us to sound too old. But then to be really on it, specific, I'd say I knew Emilio best when I lived down here among the Dangs. And saw, him every other day or so, Him, William White, Bob Thompson and I'd have to throw in Joe Overstreet. Notice I sd Throw. We was most tight. My man, Vincent Smith, I'd known longer than any of these dudes except White, But vision this bunch as the Arty Bloods I was closest too. Some of yall knew this little knot of talking talking cussing cussing signifying signifying, laughing, yeh laughing laughin laughin Negroes. Yeh we used to laugh. At any and every, why cause think about it like this, if we wasn't gonna laugh, we wdda had to kill a buncha folks, I mean daily.

Of this group Emilio had the most violent, or say the most artistic disposition. Some Negroes wanted to shoot dope, some wanted to get drunk or suck they knuckles, some wanted to wheez when they was laughing and take the nut line in any conversation. And some just wanted to knock somebody out. Not just fight, but knock em out. Emilio and I were athletes. The rest of them dudes cdnt play nuthing but they mouth, and that smoking Art they were turning out. But me and Emilio styled ourselves fantasy Olympians. Me, I could play anything. Hear that. But where me and Emilio used to get down was playing baseball or softball.

Every Sunday we would go to some field somewhere in the West Village, with a bunch of other painters and poets and play at least one nine inning game of soft ball. Then go somewhere and admire ourselves with drink. And Emilio could play. He was a short stop most times. Fast, slick, not as slick as he thought he was, but slicker than most of us. He'd stick that apple wheel around and fling it to first base, then pop his fist in the glove, wham. Dig that. Got that somebitch, you dig! Yeh, we'd shout. But the one thing about Emilio that I'd never forget and if you know his work, his art, you probably can sense it. Maybe. But Emilio had the worst, or the quickest, and the most consistently explosive temper of any creature in Christendom. In fact, part of my weekly gig was pulling Emilio off some ill-fated lame who had ventured an opinion Emilio took as too ignorant to be accidental, or some affront (real, imagined, or unspoken,) and boomaloom.

Emilio wd be on them like Lon Chaney, Jr, Full Moon style. See, a lot of you folks didn't know one of my early gigs was as Kofi Anan of the Lower East Side. And people used to wonder why Emilio was so quickly, urgently violent. Some people used to wonder that about me, as drawn to peace as I was. The under theme is that the violence, in word and deed, was as an honest replication, a forthright reflection of the place itself. Remember, all this is pre-Malcolm. This is right around the time Dr King and them walked that walk in Montgomery, a minute or so before Fidel Castro y Los Barbudos lit up Havana with the light of self-determination. And all of us, at least the folks I valued most, were leaning into that rhythm, were feeling those vibes even then. We was being whatever skewed version of the near future we could pick up there, here in the craziness jungle of lower east side Greenwich Village U.S.A.

Even much later when I wd check Emilio's violently striking work, human beings assaulted absorbed by animals, truncated into inanimate subjects, or having their heads and bodies punctured by giant nails, it confirmed for me the negotiated rhythms by which we moved and lived among the so called great artists and intellectuals of the planet. Whether it came out of our mouths, on our canvases, in our scripts, or right there on the baseball field or Cedar tavern, where ever we might be accosted by the foolishness of illegitimate domination.

But then I remember next, and actually deepest, Emilio's howling laugh, like an all-clear signal after an airraid. Especially that was something among the talking talking talking, arting arting arting, laughing laughing dudes that we was. That was daylight confirmation of our intelligence and love for each other and all that was worthwhile, to us, in the world. So the idea that now them is only Overstreet and Me from that bunch makes me need to hear Emilio laugh again. Makes me understand very very clearly the huge nails stuck in the Black dude's skull. The head poking out from under some phantasmagorically outsized thumb. What we were prefaces too was our own growth, & the past which remains alive as a confirmation we understand ourselves. In that craven haven of the informally insane, we had to thrive, to stay alive, and so we used our selves in ways that were like our souls demanding, yet to breathe, no matter the ghost who clutched at us always was wholly un—.

For my man, & from the underseen trap door of our immortal nexus, we were taught on the street, with our hearts and by what we loved, to be always the opposite of silly silent Negro Nuts. Our nuts was from stuff in the sky. They was them. We was not brilliant, we became more than that & so like our best Fathers, could still Shine! Now when they wants to go off & check unseen, it makes it difficult to make young whip snappers believe you know what u talking about! How that funny laugh! In these scramble of words, we was the movement becoming itself as whatever aspect of itself it could then muster. Even your Eulogist has some parable of rep for quick draw mouth & tong & hammer. To be ourselves before we cd, as we were becoming, past that where but on it, going to it and so to see Emilio's mature work was pre-understood by us from his projection of himself way back. Dig? A person's life, said Keats, "is an allegory." Later.

What some folks, whom others cd rightfully claim were "brilliant," miss is that Emilio was not harsh, he was intolerant with misunderstanding of the obvious. And this trait endeared him to me and me to him. We wd thrust into your "discourse" from reality whether you have a value for it or not. This could cause an indiscretion of a fantasy or naïve politic. Plus there was nor is no conceit too great for us to challenge with the measure of our own emotionally held intellectual winnower of bullshit, our then still developing, later more fully constructed organic, instant disperser of jive And the lames (presidents and/or worlds) which used that to travel.

See you later, man....in a minute, actually!
(2004)

Rhythm & Rime

Rhythm (which is preWrit Them....signifying change of epoch, from verbal to paper) is the registering livingness of matter, nature, everything that exists. And "alive" is in contention, actually in terms of the ancient measure of the Animists who said EVERYTHING IS ALIVE to varying degrees. It was not One God, they referred to, but that EVERYTHING WAS ONE THING. In fact, Matter means Mother, e.g., Mother Nature, of which, Hello Out There, we are also part of. As the abuse of the environment should show even the Abusers of same, more and more each day. Matter, the Mother, Alive. And without End. The shallowness of what passes as modern institutional religion (i.e., since the seizure of armed hegemony over such by the same forces who murdered the anti-imperialist, Jesus Christ. So that the actually recent "trinity" of the world rulers not only excludes the woman (to reflect the world wide overthrow of mother right and the emergence of ancient slavery which followed ancient communalism), but replaces Spirit with a Ghost.

In this same revisionist telling, done to affirm the divinity of the newly defining authority, its political-economic base and its social and cultural requirements. So that now the mythology is not used to explain nature but to oppose it. For instance, by saying Adam gave birth to Eve, when Adam means to add on and Eve means before. Again, to give divine origins to the enslavement of women. And with the emphasis on the Father and The Son, to reaffirm the new order of inheritance. So that mystical Adultery as a Holy Royal Prerogative and the Succession of Wealth and Death are what is given us. The new church took the ancient name, Nun, which meant the Sky and transformed it into NONE, and raised polygamy and the Greek rulers degeneration to Boy Love, to divine vocations. The world in its ceaseless motion and movement, still maintains that slavery, as my wife points out, the male vs. female was the first class struggle. The overthrow of ancient Communalism to be replaced by Slavery, the results of that world wide defeat of Women.

If we can presume to rationalize the motion of the world as metaphor, the real world, as a constant pulse reflected in all existent things. Like the heart, coming and going out, like the breath, then we can make an aural and visual paradigm of the world rhythm as well as its rime. For certain, what has no rhythm cannot exist. Even our dreams have been charted and characterized by their changing rhythms. Our breathing, our heart beat and pulse, clearly reflect our physical and emotional states. So it is with all things. The days, weeks, months, years, seasons, the tides are all measured according to their rhythmic reoccurrence. But if you look at the phenomenon of rhythm, you find that the beat consists of sound and not sound, being and not being. The Be & the At. The pulse of everything. Go. Stop. Yet the Stop is part of the Go. Dialectical as everything else. No hot without cold. No up without down. No slow without Fast.

Another characteristic of rhythm is its thorough going impact on everything heard or unheard, felt or unfelt, as well as by the absolute totality of its omnipresence. It is not a reach to characterize Human life and history by its rhythm, almost literally. But if we understand the rhythm of life itself, we must also understand that it is shaped also by the quality and form of its living motion. And those are recognized in the absoluteness of their appearance, as CHANGE, which is what the motion of matter exists as. CHANGE, which is absolute. So that the rhythm of everything corresponds to a beat, a pulse, the constant waves reflected in the sea, by the rays of light which give us color, and to the very changes in human life and society themselves. But these aspects of existence correspond exactly to all of nature, and can be understood ultimately by our sense organs if we persist in our investigation and analysis. For instance, water, moving at a regular rhythm, up or down the scale of measured temperature, will proceed in either direction, then at one point it makes a leap. It changes from merely quantitative changes to the leap which brings qualitative changes. That is, the water will either leap upwards and become steam or downwards and become ice. As it is natural science it is with human society. It is just that would-be owners of the world obscure the obvious like store keepers do wholesale prices.

That is why when we speak of the motion of history, and understand how human society has gone through changes. That there have been periods of steady rhythm, a stability, a unity of social forces, what the politicians call Peace when there has been no such boogie man. And there never will be as long as very few people can live like human beings and the majority of the world is in chains. But after these periods of so called Peace, then All Hell breaks out again, that is the quantitative periods of stability and regular rhythm are replaced sharply by great leaps in society where all things including humans are thrown into violent displacement of their former stability, and the social relations and very nature of human society are changed. Sometimes for the better, many times for worse. But these leaps are the change from evolution, which is constant and relatively stable, to Revolution, where, as the word indicates, everything is overturned. As the Bible said, when there is a human advance, it means that "the last shall be first."

Rime, in the ancient spelling, is a concordance of elements, here words, so that a unity of sound, sometimes meaning, is reached. As verse, it means there is a regular turning, that is ending and new beginning, signified in some classic poetry by the Rime. The insertion of the H in the words, usually after the 16th century, signifies the 1st translations of the bible into English (Tynsdale) and the contention of the English Church with the Roman. The H in the ancient glyphs is a symbol of building, a tower, like Babel, (To Where? the people shouted). The I is the eye of Ra, the sun, the oneness of everything.) 1611 is the publication of the King James Bible, two years after we arrived on this side in the bottom of the slave ships, the first called, "The Good Ship Jesus." In human history, the largest leaps, revolutions, have been marked by their deep impact on human life and society. The leap from Ancient communalism to slavery, the leaps from slavery to feudalism, the leap from feudalism to capitalism. And in each human society these revolutions touched, we would see a similar evolutionary motion, and life there within that framework of collective social life and then we would see the torrent of change to that society these revolutions made.

For the African people, the leap from communalism and the early domination then equality of women afterwards, brought the revolution of internal slavery, which ultimately led to the selling of ourselves to Europeans and Arabs. Before that the societies of the interior of Africa and the South were dominated by mighty Egypt, in which at least one historical proletarian revolution was fought and won (Slavery built the pyramids, and the slaves revolted driving the rulers out of power, but like the Civil Rights Movement, the Sisyphus Syndrome set in, and what was thought to be vanquished like Black national oppression, crept quickly back into place.) The Fall of Egypt, The Fall of Mali, The Fall of Moorish Spain, these were revolutions which finally got us here. The Revolutionary War, the Haitian Revolution, The Civil War, were likewise, leaps, sharpening and changing the rhythm, a new form of motion emerging. The social order changed, unfortunately, not to the extent we desire.

Just as the seeming Rime, the confluence and conjunction of desire and reality, the Civil War and proposed Reconstruction made, by 1876 the whole text of our lives was in retrograde, another leap, but as DuBois shows in *Black Reconstruction*, it was a backward leap, where instead of Chattel Slavery, the Afro American people were given a more modern set of chains, but by the end of the century we could not vote anywhere in the South. The Civil Rights Movement was likewise, a sharp change of rhythm, a leap, a different form of motion emerging, but as well, with the headlong plunge into a fake welcome into full citizenship that the entire force of the Black Liberation Movement proposed, and the nation, with its Voting Rights and Civil Rights Bills and Affirmative Action seemed to confirm, the Sisyphus rhythm reemerged, the retard its called in musical terms, and today Negroes who rose upon the steady beat of our insurgent rhythms and marching feet, are the very mouths out of which the confirmation of yet a new backward roll down the Sisyphus mountain, retard style, is given.

What is clear is that our rhythm must be felt and understood by us, as what DuBois described as a "true self consciousness." We must not let that rhythm, which is linked to Self-Determination, Self-Reliance, Self-Respect and Self-Defense be covered by alligators, as Garvey called them, disguised as friends. We must not let that self determined rhythm be coopted and copped. Dissed and Covered, like they say, discovered. We must not let that rhythm be denigrated

411

as oppressive, utopian, old hat, or unfair. It is our rhythm, which can only fully emerge from the paradigm of our music. That is, collective, with both improvisation and composition, and syncopated as we know how, and funky as the world we trying to change. It will be a multi rhythmic thrust, what they call polyrhythm, with many individual rhythms, harmonically joined in that collective forwarding, which is the oldest African form, polyrhythmic, dressed under or over with the blues, (which is our memory and our expression of the whole self and history of us.)

Like Cesaire said in his great poem "Return To My Native Land," they have already done everything, called us everything, told all the lies and committed more murders against us, who were not the greatest sufferers, but who were singly real estate. Now with some 447 billion dollars as our Afro American Commonwealth, concentrated in those twenty-seven cities throughout this nation that we live. The question is when will we dig the one, as musicians say, the beat, the funk. When will we dig OUR own sweet One. Who we BE and where we at. Our beat. That is the rhythm that will transform our future, and the millennium. Keep on walking and keep on talking, but now organizing, setting our own program, and fighting for a people's democracy, a human world. Just like the music, call and response and The going out frenzy of digging the entire universe of our being. Like John Coltrane talking about, you knew it, FREEDOM!
(1990s)

MX Impact on Culture

Malcolm X was and remains the most influential Black Revolutionary of our age. It was Malcolm who clearly identified for our generation the fact that the Afro American People were an oppressed nation, with the right of self-determination, up to and including separation. By the end of his life he had made the transition from a cultural and religious nationalist, stripping himself of a great deal of the bourgeois metaphysics of the Nation of Islam and focusing on the political agenda of Black revolutionary anti imperialism: he laid out that fundamental requirements for the Black nation were (1) Self-Determination, (2) Self-Respect, and (3) Self- Defense.

He began to build the Black united front still tragically missing from the Afro American people, the OAAU, separated it from his religion, and he had also embraced the African and Third World Anti Imperialist agenda. He even began to sound off specifically against capitalism as a "blood sucker." Malcolm's classic cry of "The Ballot or The Bullet," and his Afro-American class analysis of the house Negro vs. the field Negro are still critically important links of understanding for the Black liberation movement. That is, that either Black people will be admitted into America on the basis of democracy (to paraphrase DuBois) or America will cease to exist. It is no wonder that as the Bourgeoisie had almost totally coopted the petty bourgeois democracy of MLK, with the holiday, and the embrace by even straight out fascists, witness Powell's showing for MLK's birthday celebration in Atlanta right after destroying Iraq, as if this was part of King's Legacy.

It is no wonder then that they would come after Malcolm, with Spike Lee's mindless vendor rip-offs, Bruce Perry with his Malcolm as a pathological white man, the Nation of Islam's various statements, and virtually every Negro who never and wouldn't ever have anything to do with revolution and certainly not Malcolm, the revolutionary, being commissioned, from operas to documentaries to picture books, to anthologies of articles edited and filled with buppies and the retrograde Negro trend, distorting, coopting Malcolm, in the end simply to say as the house Negro always says, this is the best of all houses, where wd we go if we leave the master's.

For the retrograde, the Playthell Benjamins, Stanley Crouches, Sowells, Lees, Skip-along Gates, the Civil Rights movement is over, and they have benefited so what are the rest of you crying about? You ain't got nothing cause you still niggers, and niggers, as any newspaper can tell you, are a criminal class. It is they who are spoiling jack crackers. There never was a democracy. We never been citizens, America — welfare, crime, corruption, laziness, drugs, bad youth — you name it.

And this is just the replay, the rerun, of the post reconstruction 1890s, so neatly numbered because it represents simply an economic and political cycle of Imperialism and its crises. To get in on the spoils of the 19th century post slavery, post Paris Commune, '90s, the resources necessary for Black democracy had to be stolen. by Rockefeller, the banks, the railroads, the insurance companies, Morgan, Dupont. the robber barons to cop Puerto Rico, Cuba, Philippines. When they withdrew the resources and made Black people recycled chattel, they then, to paraphrase *Black Reconstruction*, went on a campaign to vilify the Afro American people to prove that the reason we could not be citizens, the reason we still lived like slaves even after the emancipation, was that we were inferior to begin with.

The books like *Cannibals All,* or *White Supremacy and Black Inferiority*, were like the *Bell Curve* and the Bob Grants of today. *Birth of A Nation* was necessary, said Woodrow Wilson, to preserve American culture. Dig that. Plus the kicker was, since it was the almost 200,000 Afro American troops in union blue who liberated the south, who were finally set loose to race across the south destroying everything in sight, and, this is important,

414

ELIMINATING THE SLAVE OWNERS AS A CLASS, this image, like the '60s militant had to be caricatured, made fun of. The Stepin Fetchits, and Sambos had to replace Nat Turner and Fred Douglass. Just as the Spike Lee images, and the new garbage readied for us about the Panthers, will seek to replace the revolutionary image with the put down pathetic distortions of the retrograde, (this is why they are being paid, this is why they are so necessary) for the entire reactionary armed forces of the imperialist super structure. This is why it is so important that we intellectuals and artists intensify our resistance and fight the onslaught of frankly fascist cultural attacks with all the weapons at our disposal.

The New World Order is simply international fascism, a world completely dominated by international corporations. In The U.S. the imperialist bureaucracy and militarist sector of the state combined with the Lords of finance capital. The military-industrial complex as the operation officers of international finance capital. World Banks, in order for the U.S. imperialism to get in on the new markets made available by the fall of Soviet Social Imperialism and Chinese mounting revisionism, and the cooptation of the liberation movements all over the world such as ANC: they must withdraw the resources from the U.S. itself, so that with the mystical rubric of "budget cuts," they transform the U.S. itself into one of the third world countries they are stealing our money to exploit. For the Afro American people, this is accompanied by cant of welfare, corruption, anti big govt, the free market, selling off of public communications, elimination of the public sector itself. As the entire nation, and the world, Blacks in the U.S. and the rest of the 3rd world 1st, are privatized. Remember John Hawkins was a privateer. His flag was a skull and cross bones. Culture is the operative form of our lives and our social political economic and super-structural relationship with the world. Malcolm X was a propagandist for Black Self-Determination as the fundamental human right of an oppressed nation, that even had the right to separate if this was the will of the people. Lenin and the Comintern and even the then revolutionary CPUSA had put forward these things thirty years before Malcolm. Just as the RNA, APP, RCL, had in the '60s and Elijah Muhammad before all, which is where Malcolm got it.

But the oppressed Black nation is a concept still connected to Black nationalism, rather than seen as the democratic right of an oppressed people. Malcolm brought cultural revolution to the U.S.

by way of the Afro American people. He forced us and the world to look again at the plight, the history of the Afro American people. Malcolm altered the thought process of Black people, he gave them new more militant references with which to measure their lives, and for the artists and intellectuals whom he genuinely touched, moved us to join him and the advanced sector of the Afro American community and call for Self Determination, Self Respect and Self Defense for the Oppressed Afro American nation.

The retrogrades and the imperialists themselves want to squash that image, hence every fool from Damon Wayans to Clarence Thomas. They want to pretend we are integrated into America, but at the same time say that if we are living like sub Americans, it's because of our inherent inferiority and incapacity. But here is where the revolutionary intellectuals, artists and cultural workers must focus. We must use Malcolm's lines on Self-Determination, Self-Respect and Self-Defense to focus a new and more fierce counter attack against the new fascist world order.

First we must value and practice Self Determination. Self Determination is the 1st step. Even for those people who see the final place of the Afro American people as citizens of a democratic U.S., obviously it will not come from just the wish. Even democracy in the U.S. cannot be brought about except by self determination. That we initiate and determine our own struggles. In the arts and scholarship then, we must flood the country with forums and poetry readings, and $2.00 books $100.00 movies, defining, redefining our struggle. We cannot wait to be published or produced by our fuehrer and wd be gas oven attendants.

We must give plays in our living room (discussions in our basement or backyard). Urge the people in our circle or community to give parties where serious matters are the parties' focus. Like what should be the relationship of the Afro American people to the USA. Or what is self determination. Invite the poets, musicians, dancers, rappers, performers, talkers, scholars, athletes of all kinds to participate. It's time to pull out the RAZOR. Revolutionary Art delivered in a revolutionary method. Self Determination means we cannot be stopped by our enemies. We cannot complain about not getting published or produced or getting tenure. Where are your neighborhood lectures on communism for the advanced in the community? Where is your garage art gallery.

Instead of merely criticizing imperialism, cultural workers

need to be producing a cultural revolution, using revolutionary art and counterattacking against the pro/fascist B lack caricature culture. Thats why we must counter the Martin Lawrences and Wayans and Def Jams and Living Color and Beverly Hills Rappers, with The Revolutionary Afro American Tradition. With the Douglasses, DuBois's, Turners, Tubmans, Their lives. Films. Stories. Paintings. Every city where we live is a Motown. A Motown Collective for the production of revolutionary art for cultural revolution. These entire cities must be transformed into revolutionary cultural garrisons, armed collectives of revolutionary art and scholarship for self-reliance and social development. They have all but coopted rap and made it into a sinister form attacking our people, our mothers and wives and sisters and daughters. We must re-arm rap, organize a progressive youth culture. Teach the classics and revolution: the democratic and socialist essence of all national cultures. Don't just criticize the media, counter attack!

That's why they have taken the music out of the community. Now instead of other folks riding caravans into the various Harlems of North America to hear the music, we have to go to the high rent districts to see our own advanced artists. This is cultural aggression, and we must counter it. Where are our community lectures and concerts on Duke Ellington, Trane, Tatum, Billie Holiday, Monk, Bessie Smith? All here should demand, send a letter to the Black Arts Festival in Atlanta, so that next year a summit of cultural workers and progressive Afro American intellectuals is held to do practical work on self reliance, the organization of cultural institutions in the Afro American nation. Self-respect, the rebuilding of the revolutionary Afro American consciousness, which is what Malcolm did, create a revolutionary consciousness among the people. This is his legacy and this is our task. The only thing Black people have any control at all over is our culture. Did you see the stock market jump when Michael Jordan came back? One Black dude with a basketball. Did you know Michael Jackson sold 93 million copies of his last album? Did you know there were 1 million Black people last year in Atlanta for the Black Arts Festival? The culture is ours, it must be given a new insight into its own revolutionary history. Revolutionary art is the main ingredient in contemporary education. The schools have been turned into traps and storage centers for later concentration camps. The crime bill is the new black codes, the "contract with America" the new separate but evil. We have never been citizens and the U.S. has never been a democracy. The act of self-determination in the culture, led by revolutionary art and the reintroduction of the revolutionary history of the Afro-American people, is what we need not only to transform the consciousness and arm us against rising fascism, but to begin to create a self-reliance a self production of our artistic and intellectual culture.

The artists and intellectuals must work with the whole people to direct, control and make the culture self-reliant; able not only to teach and inspire but finally to employ and expand. These vacant lots, playgrounds, schools, churches, bars and restaurants in our community should be our venues. These should be our local and nationwide networks for the circulation of the revolutionary art and spread of cultural revolution. We must stop fascism.

Where we live is critical. Where we actually live. We are focused on the nation and the international. But what is the cultural level of our own community? Are there bookstores, theaters, art, movies, publishing companies, concert halls, (even as large as 50 people in a basement). These great discussions we have in places like this must be brought back to the communities. We must create youth organizations and schools based on the self reliance possible through control and utilization of our own Afro American culture, neutralizing the fascist onslaught with hot syncopated anti imperialist laser funk. The history. The ideas. The struggle. The information. The directions.

We should stop lamenting the obvious cultural death of the U.S. and bring our own revolutionary culture back to life. Self-Defense was Malcolm's last dictum. Speech to articulate our lives is the 1st line and our mouths are in somebody else's pocket. Our artists stand in line waiting to be produced by slave masters and overseers. Awards are given to the Negroes who agree with them the best.

Publish that book, that pamphlet. Put that mural on the side of an abandoned house. Give the concert in yr basement. We should also at the BAF put together a national council to give awards to our own people in the name of the Douglasses, and Margaret Walkers, and DuBois and Robesons. Instead of lamenting the book awards and genius awards to hanging Negroes, we should be putting out our own. This is basic self-defense. The next line is the united front for AA self determination, part of the uf against imperialism. The

next line is the anti fascist electoral party a democratic workers party to fight the democrats and republicans and the cooptation of the Negro compradors and trade union bureaucrats. Revolutionary Art Cultural Revolution. This is The RAZOR. And we are the Blood, and everybody know all Bloods carry razors.
(1993)

Askia Toure:
My Brother, The Revolutionary Artist

I've written this before, in my partial Autobiography and in the brief exposition on The Black Arts Movement. As a matter, of fact, just recently in Chicago, where some folks projected a Black Literary Hall of Fame, I said these same things, though, unfortunately there, and among people who should know better, I said them as a somewhat acid footnote on the somewhat skewed program and "enstoolment" that was going on.

Of the many poets, writers, cultural workers, artists, &c., I know and have known, Askia Toure is, in my experience, one of the most consistent and openly revolutionary democratic artist-activists I know. This is so important these days, because all over the place, small things crawl out of smaller holes whimpering distorted half prevarications about the world, Black people, politics, art and whatever there is that can be lied about.

DuBois told us that the Black National Revolutionary Democratic Movement suffered from the Sisyphus Sydrome, ie, just as soon as we roll the rock of our National Oppression up to some new stage of progress, our enemies ("The Gods") roll it back down on our heads. So that now the gains of the '60s are hurled down the slope of resurgent imperialism and re-incarnated Negrossity. As Mao used to call it, our enemies are trying desperately to "reverse correct verdicts." That is, to turn back whatever actual progress the oppressed people of the world made in the '60s when "Revolution Was The Main Trend!" and what they actually haven't turned around yet, they lie about. Revisionist history is a growth industry these days. One has but to witness the newly molted hordes of Negro ho's ubiquitously kneeling and preying all over the place, selling us, along with their own a hinds and b hinds.

That's why we should value this brother and revolutionary comrade, Askia Toure, because no matter the sell-outs, betrayals, newly outfitted house slaves, neo-con traitor coons, Negro skin merchants posing as "non political" straight men for the Beast (Askia's favorite word, right out the Bible)...Askia has remained true to the deepest principles of the Black Liberation and Revolutionary Democratic Movement, that we destroy our own National Oppression and with that, imperialism itself.

Askia is that revolutionary intellectual that all oppressed peoples must have and who are inspired and called by the people themselves, to step forward to lend the total dynamic of their minds and their lives to this struggle for democracy and self determination, who have been, no matter what they called themselves, anti-imperialist agitators and propagandists almost from the jump.

I met Askia, like Larry Neal, in the midst of the Black Liberation Movement, in the whirlwind of the struggle itself. We met each other as comrades in struggle, even before we knew each other as artists! Because, even though we are writers, artists, cultural workers, the very essence of our art, the very soul of Askia's poetry, is the will to struggle for our freedom and the oppressed peoples of the world.

And for this, he, like many of us, has had to take the hit, i.e., to be dissed and covered, passed over, character assassinated and lied about, dismissed as an artist, demeaned as an intellectual, deprived of all but barest means of survival. WHY? Because, like too few of us artists, as we bent and were bent to harvest other peoples' profits we had to become our own prophets.
(2003)

The Beatitude of BomKauf

See, Bob and I were in that mix of late '50s early '60s milieu of poets and media hype, as the colored guys. We and Ted Joans. A few others, on the quieter side, until the new music roared in and another side of the joint got rightly hurled into the light. And we went wherever, B & I, behind or despite that.

Earlier, he came to the lower east side with wife and Parker, his son, Bird named. And we talked, dug each other, I remember. Not out of some clearly "Black" thing, because, to tell the truth, neither one of us was animated by that then (58 or so.) Bob was something because he had come out of what became the earliest interior hype of all that. Like he said; "That Beat Shit." Bob then was publishing his fugitive Beatitudes, before the Mediacracy got hold of the "idea," long before they copped the. artifact as further proof of their omniscient larceny. Beatitudes and Bob's comic strip narrative poems/manifestoes on Abomunism, were the outest then. E.g., The ABOMUNIST MANIFESTO. He was a sho (nuff) real BOHEMIAN SURREALIST WAYGONESPHERIC dude, before, and always, further, than any of the soon to be touted up a storm.

Am I saying that Bob was Chuck Berry, before the Beatles copped, then happily claimed, "That's where we got our stuff..." Naw, ain't saying that. Could. But ain't. Bob, was always, BomKauf, the other, the brother, out there doing what ever it was, and reporting back from the front lines of absolute out to lunchism. When most people was still talking about Crazy and Wild! &c. Out to Lunch hadn't even come from Breakfast.

That stream of Be atitudes, Abomunist Manifestoes, "Abomunists live off peanut butter and frink," had already turned on the non network Outvision sets. And dig, who yet, completely understands, except THE OTHERS and myself, what Frink is Frinking? For that matter who yet understands what "Shifafa" is except Nat Cole, THE OTHERS and me?

I knew that the Abomunists were domestic Purples (which is Read as opposed to Red). THE OTHERS thought they were funny too, but I knew, later, that Abomunists had no future in America, as long as it was run by the ones that didn't get up in the tree, smash they monkey toe into thumbs and think up language.

Bob and I, as I remember, would laugh throughout our conversation, about, what else....all those who wasn't THE OTHERS or ourselves. We talked about Bird, and Parker. And I remember, in that grey freeze of the Lower East Side, people were looking for Bob, his wife naturally, looking for Bob, and Bob would show up, later, laughing.

For those who could dig that Bob was a Sho!realist (as in Sho! Or Sho Nuff Or like Barry White, "Sho you right!" instead of "Sure") Because that half of him rendered to surrender him to poverty, was still syncopating his patter, and unlike the half of him that was celebrated by the alligators at their convention when they voted that, "Hell let the motherfucker starve anyway, half of that shit is a nigger!!}

Are you making some terrible statement about San Francisco avant-garde anarchist Buddhist store keeper mother fuckers? Hey? Would I do something like that? After all, Bob was published by CITY LIGHTS, the same publisher brought A.G. out of inner into the light of green. My man, anywayz, "so what?" as Miles wd say.

No, I'm saying that I watched Bob Kaufman starve to death. From lack of all the things we need to unstarve and be somewhat healthy, even in Dis. Bob, for instance, when he returned, into the presumably more profitable hype of what it was he had thunk up , as social movement, not as just a Poem. There was only his myth to take him in, and clothe him in visibility. No Bread. And we know, Hey, wait a minute, Roi, I mean Baraka, we gave Bob a lot of money and he spent it on Drugs.

And just because the officials say the same thing about Van Gogh and his frigging ear doesn't mean we were cruel to Bob. We were not cruel to Bob, do you understand? So put that in your pigmentation and turn to another station. No, starvation is not just lack of cash. Though we can go to the crooks' books and see what was took. Who got took. And we know Bob was, whats the were'd, incorrigible. Always fighting with the cops. Always getting beat up. Jeez, what were we supposed to do?

To good questions like this, like my granddaddy, the good Dr. said, "I answered not a word..." But I remember, my wife, Amina and I, saw Bob, the last time, in S.F. at some outside big time poetry reading. Jayne Cortez could probably speak on it, I know Ted Joans can. And there was Bob, completely disoriented, physically beaten into a literary myth colored guy, stammering and letting us know, in the half cracked stutter of barely understood syllables, that he was going to die. While "around him" (McKay), pill pushers were pushing but crying that he shouldn't, and the making- money- from -poetry- guys were not giving him readings or the hype of the instantly recognized. Saying, "Isn't it too bad, we're letting this half nigger motherfucker die like this."

And yr boy, yr correspondent here, got visibly niggerish, saying all kinds of loud things to the assembled, about how they were some low down scummy Cookies, for doing this. "But he brought it on himself," they fled. So the world tells us through whoever got the microphone and a million cruise missiles.

Sho, he brought it on himself. Like we all did, standing somewhere where somebody cd put a bag over our heads, drop us in the bottom of a boat, and Voila, we wake up in Charleston, waiting for our new neighborhood to get famous and become a dance craze for F. Scott Fitzgerald.

Beatitude, Abomunism, they errors was that they were real. They were reporting from outside of the nuthouse, saying. Yall a bunch a nutty motherfuckers, all right. But not nutty as me, who you done made nuts and, dig, HALF Black, look at me, with curly hair and shit. And who gonna put up with dull ass torture, wd be different if you motherfuckers could make me laugh. But now I got to listen to Brahms and cant even smear him on a Ritz cracker.

Bob was talking about our real lives. To be fixed by the torture of this whole ugly and to see it and understand it and demand that it understand its inhumanity. Like its funny. Its out. Its weird. But then, you got to come out the idea, come out the righteous fist of perception and rationalization and figure out of what use is all this rottenness, so we can, at least, live and laugh at

this shit. Dizzy understood clearly, that Squares are armed and dangerous and that laughter is hot as the volcano in our heart, and a bulletproof vest, if you get it on right.
(1996)

Art & the Political Crisis

The main political crisis in the world today for Pan African peoples is the lack of Democracy and Self-Determination. Whether we are oppressed nations as in U.S. Colonized under apartheid as in South Africa, or neo-colonized new subjects under new look just like our selves rulers, as in most of the 3rd world, or in whatever mode, we have the same fundamental problem, lack of Democracy and Self Determination.

This has been our main political crisis for four centuries now—a protracted historical drag. Nothing else can be more of a crisis or contribute more to that crisis for us than that—lack of Self Determination, lack of Democracy, and because of these, lack of self respect as shown in our lack of institutions as well as lack of self defense.

Today this main problem is exacerbated by the right wing motion of Imperialism toward its ultimate denouement Fascism all over the world. The Reagan years have been characterized by sharp rightward movement and destruction of all but remnants of the '60s mid-70s anti imperialist political movements including the sharp upward surge of the Black Liberation Movement in its Pan African manifestation.

Linked to the outright fascist regimes of South Africa in the south and Israel in the north, both serving as oppressor caps on the African continent, Imperialism has tried for the last twenty years to reverse the progress made by the peoples movements of the '60s all over the world. They have smashed Peoples governments from inside and outside, assassinated leaders, destroyed programs and institutions, destroyed organizations. They have demonstrated the Sisyphus Syndrome where we roll the rock up the mountain with our liberation movements only to have imperialism roll these huge boulders half way back down, hoping to crush us.

For the Black Liberation Movement, internal contradictions, lack of scientific organization, lack of independent legal/electoral organizations, attacks by the state were the key elements stalling our forward motion.

Art is relevant to these struggles if that art is 1st creation not imitation. Art not Aren't. All that human beings create is art (good or bad art). Art cannot be separated from the world. The world creates it. We need art of Self Determination, Art of Democracy, Art of Independent Realization.

Art that opposes reaction and fascism. Art that exposes imperialism. Art that makes us think past imperialism. Art that jumps at the Klan's throat. Art that educates us for Self Determination. Art for Self Defense. Art is relevant to the political Crisis of lack of Democracy and Self Determination if it mobilizes the Pan African people and others to fight against it. Art is relevant if it focuses the Pan African people and others to fight for Democracy.

Art is a creating, it implies a visualization, an imagistic re-appropriation of the world in terms the artist *does* control. Art is relevant if it is a creation we need! Most of the state and corporate sponsored art is negative, no matter the medium, books, tv, broadway, films, because it confirms and means to keep the status quo. Most commercial literature is negative because it likewise is status quo oriented.

The official prize gathering art of U.S. and Imperialist world is status quo oriented. White supremacy oriented. Most abstract art, for instance, is cool now that the bourgeoisie is oriented to it, because as Brecht says it challenges no one, except the masses who believe a Jackson Pollack would make a great sport shirt—but worship it, Hell No!

Abstraction is a methodology not a goal, what it says is technical and formal. Its content principally quantitative rather than qualitative. Education cannot exist without Art. Education is Art. Science and Education are the essence of Art.

What is key is that we oppose imperialist art w/ peoples'

art. Our peoples' problems are legitimatized by imperialist art. According to imperialist art Black people's problems were created by them. *Birth of A Nation* or TV melodramas 89 all say we are not worthy of self determination. We are sub human. We have created nothing. Exactly what Bloom's closed *American Mind* says.

This is the art our children are suffocated under — that tells them these things, and in a very boring way. Education is Self Consciousness (True Self Consciousness DuBois said) for social development. Self Awareness of one's own experience so that we alter our patterns extend, reorient, continue, &c of our lives — social development.

Toni Morrison says Bloom's canon (ie, Aristotle and the official white supremacist catechism) comes after they conquer with the cannons! The mental mold necessary for slavery is given us in art — whether seemingly innocent song or curriculum of study.

Art shows, teaches, makes analogy. Its beauty is in its "preciseness" of feeling, its emotional exactness. Art moves us because of the moving it is to tell the truth. Truth and Beauty. Truth is Beauty. No matter how ugly. Truth's affirmation is Beauty.

Part of the struggle of the Pan African peoples must be in opposing the teaching of the goodness the correctness of slavery. Black art Pan African art is powerful. It is opposed as seriously as Pan African people. And by the same forces. Because if the art emerges, if the art is allowed to live free, the people soon will. That's why the drums were banned. That's why our most serious music is kept off radio and out of schools. Music is not abstract actually and it is very powerful. No lyrics necessary, sound carries ideas!

It is necessary to reorganize an international Black Arts Movement like the '20s Renaissance, Harlem Renaissance, Negritude, Negrissmo, Indigisme roaring in all parts of the Pan African world, which given our dispersal is the whole world. An international cultural revolution, if you will, with the force and focus of the '60s Black Arts Movement or the 19th century Black Convention and Slave Narrative Anti Slavery outbursts. Art carries peoples lives, history, present and projects their future. If the art is allowed to live be exposed and influence, then more and more people are molded by it. And what the art wants the people see and feel and want. Art valorizes and glorifies our lives. The creators. That's why it's so dangerous.

Who would oppress Duke Ellington or Art Tatum? Could

anyone believe anyone saying Sun Ra or Coltrane is inferior? You would have to believe Tawana Brawley if you heard Billie Holiday sing "Strange Fruit." You would also understand the tremendous historical weight and circumstance that faces us, against which we struggle, that awful roar, if you read Fred Douglass or heard "Black, Brown and Beige."

The emotions, the mind set and aesthetic are also a root of political perception and rationale. It is the fundamental task or Pan African artists to reconstruct as art a world we can live in, the world we live in now, precisely. We must aggressively reconstruct the world through art. Not abstractly but in reality; not for its own sake but for most of our own sakes, for liberation's sake. For our future's sake.

Art is a struggle parallel to the struggle Fred called for, it is the same struggle. Class struggle. Struggle between contradictory groups and their ideas. There are two cultures in every nation. Oppressed and Oppressor. Always that struggle goes on. Slaves vs. Slave Masters.

We must intensify this struggle and struggle to transform this stuggle's nature. We must create our language and images as ubiquitous and accessible. We must consciously seek to network and combine internationally. Whatever discipline. With Africa as our international base, not as a means of ignoring our own national histories, where ever we are in the diaspora, because it is only history that confirms that where ever we are we are part of the Pan African peoples. We must create art structures which put out ideas images and increase resources.

Cultural revolution Mao created to continue revolution, oppose hidden bourgeois/ imperialist cooptation (such as is going on now). When China denounced cultural revolution after Mao's death we knew we (and they) was in trouble!

Art is the proof or our lives! The best use and paradigm for our lives. Government is art. Creation. Social system is art. What Humans create; at best is science and art. Knowing and Doing! For an artist to say art is irrelevant to politics is to support slavery and imperialism. To give over our lives to those whose art is slavery and concentration camps — whose art is imperialism.

When we say Pan African people we mean of course Black people world wide. All dependent, unfree, neocolonized, lacking self determination self respect self defense. The slave trade left us everywhere in the world. Africa was even partially depopulated by slavery. It is our holocaust and it is still going on. But unlike other holocausts we cannot see ours on television every night even during black history month! If we could that holocaust would soon be over!

We Pan African Artists must seek to reconnect our world mind, no matter we are distributed every where by slavery. Because such distribution, outside the Mother, Africa can be transformed into strength from weakness. Our world wide distribution means we can be influential in many lands, strengthened by a self organization of ourselves consciously to net work for Self Determination!

But not only Self Determination where we are and for the whole of the Pan African people, but we must consciously work for a unified independent socialist African state.

Because, ultimately the recreation of our Mother, Africa, as a unified socialist state, not the many existing balkanized self contradictory dependent neo colonial states would help insure Self-Determination for the Pan African Peoples internationally.

The networking, institutionalization of our arts, that is our creation as focus for our whole development. International networking of African mind and focus. These are the creations consolidation as resources of liberation.

Because in our art is the spirit of liberation. Jake Lawrence, Coltrane, Jimmy Baldwin, Public Enemy, Billie Holiday, or Achebe, Ngugi, Pbitek, Sembene, Marley, Smith, Braithwaite, and all of us res', you know. Filled with that spirit we become self conscious truly self conscious not double conscious (i.e., seeing ourselves, not ourselves through the eyes of those who hate us.) We bring our gifts as WEB Sd, the gift of labor, the gift of song and story and the gift of spirit!)

What remains is the work: We need five zones of networking, Africa, U.S., Caribbean and South America, Europe, Asia. And from these zones based on periodic meetings must come Offices, Newspapers, Magazines, Performance Sites and Theaters, Art Galleries, Production Capacities. Annual International Meetings, Bi Annual Conferences, Regional Meetings, Programs & Productions, Seminars and Training Programs, Money and Resources, and the building of black cultural districts which could be the material consolidation of Arts Festivals. One project on the drawing board in this motion is the production of an annual Pan

African Festival of Poets and Musicians on Goree Island, Senegal. We hope that very soon the 1st such annual arts festival will have as its theme An International Gathering of Pan African Poets & Musicians to Mobilize for the Elimination of Slavery on The Planet Earth For Ever. DEATH TO APARTHEID!!! It is a good beginning, but there is much to be done.

(1990)

Emory Douglas:
A "Good" Brother, A "Bad" Artist

EMORY AND I GO BACK, not just "a minute" but "a few minutes," We first met in San Francisco, I guess, early 1967 when I'd come out to San Francisco State University as Visiting Professor, with my wife Amina, plus our oldest son, Obalaji, still in the hangar. At that time we had started the Spirit House, and lived on the third floor, The theater was downstairs which was the performance space for the Spirit House Movers, poetry, dance, films, forums & later, the Afrikan Free School.

Jimmy Garrett, the Chairman of the Black Student Union at San Francisco State, had come out to Newark, late 1966. Ron Karenga, the Chairman of the newly formed **Us** Organization had come by unannounced about the same time, for one thing, because the 2nd Black Power Conference was scheduled summer of 67 in Newark. That was the first time I'd met either one, but it was characteristic of what was happening during that period.

Both had invited us to come out to the West Coast. Karenga came also, perhaps, to debate me casually on whether the Blues was heroic as I suggested in my book, *Blues People*, or was it, as he said, "submissive." Garrett, on the other hand, came with a specific invitation, to come out to San Francisco State, as a Visiting Professor, and actually, as I understood, to begin the movement for the first collegiate Black Studies Program. Sonia Sanchez was also invited.

One often reads or hears about "the Sixties" and the images provided to give flesh to the phrase differ very widely according to the describer, By now, for some parts of the mainstream, It means the Beats, flower children, the Beatles, Elvis Presley. But at the base of that turbulent period was the Civil Rights and Black Liberation Movements here in the U.S., as part of the worldwide Anti-Imperialist upsurge. That period when Mao Zedong declared, "Countries want Independence, Nations want Liberation, People want Revolution," which he characterized by trumpeting, "Revolution Is The Main Trend In The World Today." And millions of people around that world were the exemplary paradigm confirming Mao's wisdom.

At State I proposed to the student union that my residency be used to organize and carry out a "Black Communications Project," utilizing willing volunteers from the Black student body and Black activists from the area (San Francisco Oakland, &c.) to bring programs of Black culture (e.g., theater, poetry, music) to the various campuses in the area, and to other venues we might develop.

Using the campus facilities at State and actually headquartered in the Black House, a venue sprung out of the Black Arts renaissance in San Francisco's Black Fillmore District, we began to organize the Black Communications Project. That "We," the core of the project, was Sonia Sanchez, Nathan Hare & as soon as we arrived, writer-activists Ed Bullins, Marvin X, Duncan Barber, Hilary Broadus, Rosita Broadus, Carl Boissiere (who had just formed Black Arts West), along with my soon to be bride, Sylvia Jones (a little later, Amina Baraka). Indispensable was the energetic Black student leadership headed up by Jimmy Garrett, which Included George Murray who was the first minister in Ben Caldwell's "The First Militant Preacher" as we called it (the official title is *Prayer Meeting, or the First Militant Minister*). Murray later became the Black Panther Party's Minister of Education. Emory Douglas became our resident set designer, later the Minister of Culture and primary artist (or "Revolutionary Artist") for the Black Panther Party newspaper.

The cutting edge of the Black Communications Project was the plays we toured with, Bullins's *How Do You Do* & *The Electronic Nigger*; Marvin X's *Flowers for The Trashman*; Caldwell's *The First Militant Minister*; *Papa's Daughter* (with Danny Glover as Papa) by Dorothy Ahmad, Jimmy Garrett's *We Own The Night* (which premiered at a Black Panther Benefit in San Francisco at which Ike & Tina Turner also performed) and my own, *Madheart*. We performed these plays plus the poetry readings, African dancers, singers at State, at the Black House, at several outdoor venues, at colleges like Laney and Merritt and other places up and down the coast. The sets were always Emory's, though sometimes scaled down, by his design, to a practical minimalism, depending on the requirements of the different venues.

The Inspiration for the Black Communications Project was the work we had done in Harlem in the summer of 1965 with the Black Arts Repertory Theater School (BARTS). The theater had opened that spring, and after Malcolm's murder, ignited the national Black Arts Movement.

That summer of 1965 we had outfitted four trucks with stages made from banquet tables, created by painter Joe Overstreet, microphones, easels, paintings, musicians, poets, dancers, actors and sent them all over Harlem, to do drama at one site, poetry at another, the music somewhere else, and an exhibition of Black graphic arts at another. All of it under a black-and-gold flag heralding the Black Arts Repertory Theater School, created by painter, William White.

The most important things we wanted to do were: (1) Create an art that was "Black" in form, feeling, and content. (2) We wanted to bring that art "into the streets." We wanted a "mass art," out of the little elitist dens of ambiguity. And so we performed in parks, on the streets and on the sidewalks (literally), in vacant lots, housing projects, playgrounds, in front of bars and supermarkets. The most important point (3) We wanted a Revolutionary Art, not Just skin flicks. We were Malcolm's Children, and we wanted a Malcolm Art! One that was itself an example of Malcolm X's call for Black Self Determination, Self-Respect and Self-Defense plus W.E.B. DuBois's "True Self-Consciousness." So that the practical paradigm BARTS provided, though limited, was vital enough to ignite Black intellectual and artistic minds around the world. In much the same way, I can presume, the Harlem Renaissance in the '20s set off Negritude in the West Indies and Africa, Indigisme in Haiti, and Negrismo in the Latin-speaking Caribbean.

However, at base, it is the very motion of the people themselves that creates the initial shock wave that the most sensitve artists and Intellectuals respond to. Although BARTS lasted as an organization a little over a year, destroyed by internal ideological and political struggle that grew antagonistic, more than likely intensified by some variation of the U.S. government's COINTEL program, one of its operations was called Operation KAOS.

But this short-lived organization (which should have been nurtured into a permanent institution) sparked a series of like organizations across the country, creating what was called the Black Arts Movement. One of the most energetic aspects of that movement was theater. Similar groups began to operate very soon in Detroit, Chicago, San Francisco, Philadelphia, Atlanta, New Orleans, Pittsburgh, the number continuously rising until the '80s when like the rest of the Black National Movement for equal rights and self-determination, it suffered from what DuBois called "the Sisyphus Syndrome," where having been punished by the "Gods" for refusing to die, we are fated to roll the huge boulder of our struggle up the great mountain of real life only to have it rolled back down on us. This is supposed to go on forever, at least that's what the people who taught us that myth said.

When BARTS split apart, I went back to Newark and opened the Spirit House, where the Black Arts could move, influence and teach Black people. What continued that Influence, kindled by the very heat and motion of the times themselves, the Spirit House Movers, began to travel and bring Black theater to cities and institutions, sponsored in the main by liberation & civil rights organizations and student groups. We also performed in the streets and school auditoriums and even in people's apartments.

Going to San Francisco State was part of that burgeoning movement. And in some ways the forces we encountered there were thematic characteristics of much of the movement itself. The Communications Project combined the Black Student Union and the full up energy of a student movement fueled by notions of actual revolution, The Black Panther Party for Self-Defense was in its initial stages, militant young Intellectuals (Huey Newton was a law student, Bobby Seale a standup comedian), and a sampling of a cross-class spectrum of the "national movement" though its developing political line drew a large sector of Black working class youth, and with the addition of Eldridge Cleaver, began to attract, like himself, the lumpen, That "dangerous class," as Marx described them, those he described as "already broken by capitalism," but Cleaver made this group a focus of his propaganda, in parts dipping into the rhetoric of the Russian Anarchists, Kropotkin and Bakunin.

When Huey Newton and Bobby Seale and some others

created the Black Panther Party for Self-Defense, it was like many of us, as the children of Malcolm X. For the young intellectuals of my generation It was Malcolm who literally moved us. From wherever we were to wherever our listening to him told us we needed to be. Myself. as a bohemian writer in New York's Greenwich Village to Harlem, Huey and other young folks in the Bay Area from places like Laney Jr. College, Merritt and San Francisco State, from undergraduates to soldiers in the Black liberation Movement. Emory Douglas was one of those actually very courageous young folks.

I say this because I remember first meeting Bobby Seale some years before when he came to me to get an autograph on *Blues People*. He was doing a gig as a standup comedian. George Murray, another San Francisco State student, a mild-mannered history major, the Communications Project cast him as the first militant preacher, in Ben Caldwell's work. Emory Douglas made a similar initial transition when he became the set designer for the Black Communications Project. Before that project was completed, the Black Panthers had grown significantly because of their take no b.s. new style militance. Word that Huey Newton and the new organization were actually intervening in police harassment, Huey pulling out a law book and deconstructing their would-be charges, as illegal and fundamentally racist, ran through the Bay Area, and indeed began to burn across the country. So some who had made the initial leap from student to Black Militant Actor, began to want to really act upon the reality of our time.

Not only the students were moved with the continuing spirit of Malcolm X now being hoisted in sharp continuum by these new Black Panthers, but more and more Black people, as the word spread, and certainly even a significant number of Whites and others, even finally across the world.

Remember, this was a period when the image of people struggling was heroic, "Revolution Is The Main Trend in The World Today'" When I could dialogue with a young brother who used to stand outside our rehearsal site, who admittedly was standing there just so he "could dig the babes," and without harangue get him to come into the place by asking, "Didn't he want to do something for the people?" So that Danny Glover, became an actor by wanting to "do something for the people."

When analyzing anything the Marxist teachers tell us we

must always use "time, place & condition." So the many revolutionary movements, organizations, formations, events, actions, people throughout the world were part of the whole of that revolutionary time, place, and condition. During such periods, Lenin said, things that ordinarily take quite a long time to develop would come to fruition in a short time. Everything is speeded up, hyped, exaggerated, exploding, minimally sizzling with dynamic prognosis.

The B lack Communications Project was born of that combination of elements running straight up the revolutionary Richter scale. The Black Panther Party for Self-Defense was born in Oct 66, a year after Malcolm's murder and the Watts Rebellion. A year later Detroit and Newark would go up in smoke. A month after we got to San Francisco, in May 67, Emory went with Bobby Seale and a group of Panthers to the California state legislature in Sacramento. They were carrying weapons (which were then legal) and read a statement to protest the state assembly's preparing to pass a law saying the carrying of guns was illegal.

On the way out of town they were all arrested but the publicity from the event made the Black Panthers known worldwide. It seemed to me that that was, like they say, the denouement, climax of one period and the beginning of another. Emory had been doing sets, actually flats that could be put up and taken down very quickly and without too much fuss. They had to be moved by small truck and auto. Plus the sets had to be transformational, to serve for a play like Bullins's *How Do You Do* and Caldwell's The First Militant Minister or my Madheart, Plays, that while they had some general theme of Black liberation, minimally freeing one's mind from dupery, they had dissimilar settings, though come to think about it, the main thrust was the text, the sets Emory managed to create a one (almost) fits all design.

Emory was very dutiful as set designer, full of ideas, innovative, and more art than construction. Plus there was no strife between us because having discussed the plays and given him the scripts, there was little else to be done since he cheerfully gave us what we thought we wanted. Add to this that the kind of gypsy company we put together was not the usual drama group, so that it was all somewhat new. Interestingly, I learned years later, when my wife and I traveled to his birthplace, that Garcia Lorca's traveling drama group, which moved about Spain in an old bus, was called "Baraka."

When we first put together the B lack Communications Project, and performed at the Black House, the early Panthers stood security for us. I remember "Little Bobby" Hutton as one of those pulling security for a poetry reading at the Black House, he even got into discussion with my wife, Amina, about the uses of poetry, &c. in a revolution.

But certainly while there was an overt consciousness of our differences, contrasting to the earlier days during the Black Arts Repertory Theater School, when "Black" was supposed to be an ideology, there was none of the fierce contention that seemed to have developed in the Cleaver era, which emerged when both Huey Newton and Bobby Seale were in jail, 1967 was also the year Rap Brown and I went to Jail.

This context is so important because brothers like Emory Douglas, who were themselves artists, like those of us in the Black Communications Project, Spirit House, and indeed the other Black arts organizations that sprung up during the period, thought of ourselves as revolutionaries. The brothers and sisters who had recently formed Black Arts West, Ed Bullins, Marvin X, Hilary Broadus, Duncan Barber, Carl Boissiere certainly considered themselves revolutionaries, even the leading students in the Jimmy Garrett-led Black Student Union of San Francisco State. The latter was the broad coalition of forces that Emory Douglas came out of and where some of his revolutionary zeal was intensified.

We did fundraisers with the Panthers in San Francisco and in New York before that. The historic San Francisco gathering, at the old Fillmore auditorium was when the Panthers drafted Rap Brown and Stokely Carmichael as Minister of Justice and Prime Minister (of "Colonized America"). Ike and Tina Turner were on that program (Ike, in his flower-child haircut, made a fool of himself lurching back and forward backstage haranguing the Panthers about "his money"). The Black Communications Project put on Jimmy Garrett's explosive one-act play *We Own The Night*. The title was taken from a poem of mine (from *Home*). I was the director and Emory Douglas the set designer. The set a slice of the ghetto in the midst of a Black uprising!

A year after Emory and I were no longer working together, he wrote, "Besides fighting the enemy, the Black Panther Party is doing propaganda among the masses of black people, "The form of propaganda I'm about to refer to is called art..." The Black Panther

Party calls it revolutionary art—this kind of art enlightens the party to continue its vigorous attack against the enemy, as well as educate the masses of black people. "We, the Black Panther artists, draw deadly pictures of the enemy—pictures that show him at his death door or dead—his bridges are blown up in our pictures—his institutions destroyed—and in the end he is lifeless."

This statement titled "REVOLUTIONARY ART/BLACK LIBERATION" (The Black Panther, May 18, 1968." the day before Malcolm X's birthday) could be a statement by any of the Black arts organizations, certainly those coming after BARTS, because those were our intentions exactly. Emory even quotes from a poem of mine popular during the period "Who will Survive America?" Black people will survive. To show the nature of the objective united front that existed to a certain extent in the BLM then, Emory also quotes from Carmichael, talking about "undying love for the people" and Rap's "We shall conquer without a doubt." Emory's posters showed this alliance of struggle he describes, "Minister of Justice H. Rap Brown burning America down." Prime Minister Stokely Carmichael with hand grenade in hand pointed at the Statue of Liberty." Minister of Defense Huey P. Newton defending the Black community."

The quote of mine was associated with the drawing on the poster Emory did of me, which ironically enough became the cover, years later, for the first version of the poem, "Somebody Blew Up America!" The Black Panther newspaper, Indeed all its propaganda that utilized Emory's art was always dynamically effective. He gives paradigms for the kind of work he and other revolutionary artists should be doing, in this same manifesto "We draw pictures that show Standard Oil in milk bottles launched at Rockefeller with the wicks made of cloth from I Magnin...pictures of pigs hanging by their tongues wrapped with barbed wire connected to your local power plant. This is revolutionary art-pigs lying in alley ways of the colony dead with their eyes gouged out-autopsy showing cause of death. They fail to see that majority rules."

Emory's art was a combination of expressionist agitprop and homeboy familiarity. I always felt that Emory's work functioned as if you were in the middle of a rumble and somebody tossed you a machine pistol. It armed your mind and demeanor. Ruthlessly funny, but at the same time functional as the .45 slugs pouring out of that weapon.

A drawing like "Revolution In Our lifetime" (p. 17 *The Black Panthers Speak*, P. Foner, ed. Lipincott, 1970) is so effective because it looks like it comes from the revolutionaries themselves, that they actually have drawn pictures of themselves!

The signature image that Emory created was, of course, "The Pig," the Panthers' term for the killer police force 'occupying" the Black ghettoes of America. In May '67, a very early issue of the newspaper (first published April 25, 1967, which screamed headlines about the murder of Denzil Dowell) gives this definition of a pig, "a pig is an ill-natured beast who has no respect for law and order, a fool traducer who's usually found masquerading as a victim of an unprovoked attack."

Emory's "pig' was a nasty scrawny filthy creature with the projected sensibility that was mostly slime lover and animal slacker. If you will. The bravura touch was the flies that always circled the creature's nasty self. Whatever one thought of the Panther philosophy as a whole, I did not meet anyone among any sector of the Movement that did not dig that pig, just looking at it would crack you up in a mixture of merriment and contempt!

Of the two artists I most Identify with the hottest revolutionary images used in Black liberation Movement journals, Emory Douglas and the Nation of Islam's Gerald 2X, with his ubiquitous "devil' in Muhammad Speaks, with fangs hanging out of each side of his George Bush-like mouth, as I said in a poem, "used for sucking oil and blood," plus the little "Devil" tail sticking out his hiney, Emory together with Gerald 2X were, without a doubt the baddest political graphic artists in journalism. As seemingly contradictory as their ideologies were (are) they were the substance of the goodness of a national liberation united front. A double-barreled art gun.

That "homeboy' quality of Emory's art makes it harder to ignore, since it is not delivered with the customary art-gallery panache, these come on like drawings, straight out of the hood. Emory's International hands choking the pig out of shape even while his gaggle of flies still circulate around his snout, and dollar bills fly out of his pocket, the hands of all colors, squeeze and choke the pig, with his American flag stars coat, and written on the strangling hands "Get Out of The Ghetto," "Get Out of Africa," Get Out of Asia," "Get Out of Latin America," squeezing tears out of his terrorized shut eyes, Juice out of his choking snout and mouth. and the ill-gotten super profits out his pockets. This is an international cry against U.S. imperialism.

As Emory stated, this is the function of Revolutionary Art, to expose the lies and oppression of the enemy, and in so doing win the minds of the people. That's what Mao's Cultural Revolution was, actually an extension of what Lenin called for seeing the lack of revolutionary culture as one chief obstruction to carrying out the complete mandate of the Bolshevik revolution. That was why the Harlem Renaissance and the Black Arts Movement were important. That's why in such a retrograde period as we are in, when the huge Sisyphus rock we rolled up the mountain of our struggle in "the '60s" for Equal Citizenship rights and Self-Determination" i.e., a People's Democracy, a necessary stage before socialism, has been, like the Greek myth DuBois likened to the National Black Struggle, rolled back down on our heads. A new renaissance of Revolutionary Art to help roll that rock up the mountain, one (we hope) more 'gin is absolutely necessary. We know that digging Emory Douglas's "Badness" Indeed his 'Terribleness" will help in that struggle. *(2006)*

Slo' Dance by Ted Wilson
An Introduction

If this is a first book, it is only in the literal sense. Meaning, the presence the book projects is deep with accreted experience and its perception, rationales and use of poetry reaches much deeper into the author and the reader than most firsts. The work tells us Wilson has been around the whole construct of art, writing and political commitment, and has even penetrated, with his knowing, the "hard heads and soft behinds" of both the aesthetic and social base of what he has witnessed: as living consciousness, in the day to day wasteland of Dis and concomitantly as an artist.

But to be an artist, a term so bitten by opportunism and dissembling distortion, one must re-remember constantly what it does mean. To Create, from the only essence that the goodness of the infinite creating comes from.....Truth and Beauty (Dig Keats, DuBois) the candidate must, it seems, regard his own consciousness as capable of generating those qualities with as much materiality and certainty as the existing world.

So that when the work is somehow collected and presented, it must be the result of a sharp focus on the external and the internal. With such willful determination that it is the real we come away with, not just the banter of yet another subjective, usually privileged, but many times near tragic "notness."

We carry what we are as who these experiences, as the context of our motion through life, make us. It is in the main environment, and our perception, clear or unclear rationale or

442

explanation of what is perceived, and then our *use*. Where we are and how we know and who we want to understand we are to become is material life, as culture, consciousness and the fundamental social life as we scramble for food clothing and shelter and the context of that.

Wilson I met in the 60's Black Arts eruption of mass and individual development. The period when "Revolution" was "The main Trend in the World Today." Specifically as a mover characterized by the sometimes frantic but ultimately profound upsurge of the Afro-American people to redefine themselves, as an aggressive act of Self Determination. Malcolm X, Martin Luther King, Fidel Castro, The Black Panther Party, the Liberation of the African Nations from straight out colonialism, these were some of the dimensions of our growing, and Ted Wilson was an active and conscious player in that revolutionary motion. A cadre of the movement, however defined, that left much of the world with new understanding and a new era of multidimensional struggle.

So that Wilson is shaped by some of those concerns and has come to this place from that earlier place through a ubiquitous and formidable complex of events, processes, trends, ideas, reflections, reunderstandings, commitments. We are shaped by our lives as our lives and this is the self that reflects and recalls and thinks, creates and destroys.

The Black Arts Movement in Harlem in the 1960s was the social and aesthetic force that produced these affirmations:

1. We wanted an art, a poetry that was BLACK, i.e., Afro-American in form and content, as recognizable as such as Petey Wheatstraw or Lady Day.

2. We wanted an art, a poetry that came out of those close circuits of maledict, out of tidy impotent classrooms and holy quarks of the IN. That would leave the alabaster whatnots of the Ain't and dance in the street so what thy bee'd cd really be see'd. We wanted poetry that would mean something to the great masses of people, particularly, we wanted to animate the lives of Black people and be animated by the whole of our mass selves.

3. We wanted most a Revolutionary Art, an art that would

help liberate Black people, an art that would help tear this whole playhouse of national oppression and racism rat down!

Sometimes, e.g., the story *Willie*, the surface can easily be seen in the light of the first two aspects of the rubric, but here the heart of the narrative is like an outline of consciousness acquired. An archetype, which describes the dimensions of a particular culture, a particular time place and condition, and like the novel of youth growing to adulthood, is heaviest as a paradigmatic recall of that.

The poetry as well carries a specific history, even its speech and reference characterize a path a maintenance, a reconfirmation of a certain social consciousness that is easily related from the natural context of its author's understanding. He is telling us, but initially re-telling himself.

He says, "we are not writing for us but to us." Though the "to us" is in practice initially....emotionally and intellectually, "for us," particularly if its effect is to lift us reacquaint us with our strengths and weaknesses. It is the directness of its Use as literature..."like the music we play...ya dig?" that reaches beyond the page into our own becoming.

There are many contradictory reflections: "Black as my heart the night grows whiter," even a continuous undercurrent of agnostic indecision...as to what is real or the real real or the unreal...but it grows incisive... "a narrow passageway / a window of despair," positing that, that is how the real gets known!

Dance is full of colliding Yeses and No's as when he says "no blues...a wheel of fortune..." but the book, if it is anything, is one material meaning of the blues. And the trail of how that word-presence, BLUE has changed with the middle passage from "our favorite color" to such deep tragedy it haunts us all, even sweet even pretty, you funky... "...blues be good, be good be good..." at the margins of our consciousness "a night song."

The poet says he is "a passenger"...in what vehicle we wonder. Perhaps like Sun Ra's telling... "You on the spaceship Earth and you outward bound, destination unknown. But you haven't met the Captain of the spaceship yet!"

That is the essence of the contradictory stances, except he is a passenger in and as his own self. The coming consciousness of

444

the reality of the personal vehicle and the larger vehicle given to him by his sense-world, that is real and his own reflection which is the poetry.

"We come here from Goree"...deep recall... "Space is the place...sorry but I can't take you..." Ra, direct, Matter and its dissociative reflection. The whole spectrum of digging not yet clearly resolved, so there is a constant reverberation as to what is believed, known, thought, and actual.

Speech itself, the elder registration, precise in its twisting and specific touching— "Dap daddy smiled a beaming smile / all the while growling." If we recognize what is "Dap" who and where for is "Daddy," we know at once for the complete image, just exactly why he smile and be at same time, inside wild. Yes, indeed.

The cultural motif like speech is observation and history, registration and description. "The night was a flatted fifth," evoking a whole passion, period, and way of looking at the world, place, and art. We are swept with the familiar, but always renewed by the power of a precise digging, a reawakened feeling.

Wilson's title, as many of the pieces, is political upfront and down under. Liberation is more than a statement: it is an emotional commitment. Hence, poems to people like the popular Pan-Africanist Elombe Brath, his name something to conjure with, and the work draws someone not familiar with the person into the practice that is that person.

Mao sd, we must create art that is artistically powerful and politically revolutionary at the same time. It is a life's work to bring the two modes of seeing which are actually inextricable in reality, to the conjunction of our own rationale and use. Wilson is beginning, not as a persona, but as a public cultural worker, artist, to go to that awesome space around and within himself.
(2004)

My Man, Claude Brown

Claude and I grew to Self Consciousness in the anxiety & explosive eruption of the '60s, became more universal through experience, deepened by the confirmation, no matter how tragic, of our continuing passions.

It was an emotional up, to talk to Claude, someone who after a few minutes became "yo man." Certainly now that he was just Man the child no where in sight.

He came to Newark to go to Law school. But it was, to quote Claude, "too jive," though he persisted as much as he insisted, it was "too jive." And, after all, Claude was, by now, a recognized literary figure. And began to act as if he knew all that regular American defined profundity any way. Plus, he didn't even dig it. Like he said, it was "too jive!"

Claude reminded me of some of the dudes I used to hang with on the Hill, Hillside Place growing up in my teenage Newark. Slightly acerbic, but pithy as the folk and whatever the topic, an obvious can't-help-it grinning would make whatever it was slightly funny. Claude was really a low-key Counselor and what he counseled always ended with his eyes rolling up, his arm on your shoulder, "You dig? Hey man!"

Claude's *Manchild* was in the mainstream of Afro-American literary tradition. Autobiography, his own hard as truth life, as clear as them Harlem tenements, as revealing and as revelatory as Fred Douglass' *Narrative*. In fact, was Claude's version of "…Narrative of a Slave, Written by Himself."

In 1965, *Manchild*, like Malcolm's Autobiography, was the revelational tales that objectively reflected the recriminations of fire that expressed and explained the hundreds of rebellions that torched American cities across the nation that entire decade. These life spun shocking tales were the "mea culpa" histories of Black rebellion, the boiling self consciousness that could be heard if one could understand the language of Fire!

The straight out open clarity and hope-to-die authenticity of a Douglass, a Malcolm, a *Manchild*, spoke as the slave could not, but in his voice and from his experience, and the essence of that truth was empowered as a mass social and political force that wrung change even here in Hell!

I guess Claude stayed in Newark because you cd be in the City quicker than coming from Queens or Long Island. Plus our city is mostly Black and Claude appreciated the demography as well as the self-determination which had put Black faces, at least formally, atop the municipal machine. So it was dark as Harlem, but a ratch or two less frenetic. Black country folk, 12 miles from the Apple.

My wife, Amina and I, entertained and were entertained by Claude dozens of times throughout the years, whether at the many parties my wife organized like works of art, or as a guest artist reading from his works at our Last Sat of the Month programs of Revolutionary Art for Cultural Revolution in our basement arts space theater, Kimako's "Blues People."

What always surprises me is how pain is a slow moving Negro who gets there just when you think it can't. Sadness too, like that same dude, dragging through at an even more sodden pace, wrapping its dusty arms around you suddenly so tight it's hard to breathe. And it is that funky grip that squeezes tears, blue grinning tears, right out yr heart.

I didn't think Claude wd just get his hat without at least calling. But he did call. For the last few months, he called me regularly trying to get some biographical material from me, he sd, so he could send it to some foundation to get me a grant. With that recently Miles Davis, Louis Armstrong timbre to his twinkling self.

"Yeh, man," he'd rasp, "send me all that stuff that tells all the stuff you been into for all this time. You need to get a grant!"

So, all I can say is "Hey Claude, Yo my man, tell me your new address. I'll get it over there in a minute!"

"Ok, Man, Later!"
Then he'd be gone!
(2/6/2002)

Goodness Disappearing
or On Hold
Another Man Done Gone

Ron, it's so cold, so cold. That our whole young phalanx of resisters insisters, militants, insurgents, revolutionaries, the Black Intellectuals who rose mid sixties to challenge the entire intellectual, psychological cultural basis of White Supremacy Slave Owning America has gradually been depleted — with an eerie repetitious militancy. Like drums or gunshots from some kind of infinity with the finite mock of sadness.

So the death of a close comrade in the Black Arts sets me into a frame of grief and daunting apprehension. Ron who came up with me, like we say: when the Black Arts Repertory Theatre proclaimed the Black Arts Movement. The mid 60's commitment of the most advanced Black Artists to use their work to raise the consciousness and level of struggle of the Afro-American People. To use that art as a weapon, to make a Malcolm X, Art of National Struggle. To create A Revolutionary Art!

An art that would be Afro-American in form and feeling in the focus of its content, as Black as the Blues, The Sorrow Songs, as Black as Blind Lemon or Bessie Smith, as deep as Billie Holiday, Duke Ellington or John Coltrane, as wonderful as Sarah Vaughan or Louis Armstrong. An Art that would come out of the narrow places of elite regard and hit the street, a mass aimed art, aimed at Black People, to move and empower, and mobilize and help organize Black People.

And almost as soon as word hit the high and low ways, we heard that Woodie King and Ron Milner in Detroit, responded with Black Arts Midwest, and soon we would dig Ron's *Whose Got His Own* and *What the Wine Sellers Buy* as the first shots fired in his expressive and constantly expanding repertory. Because Ron was a consummate professional, and openly confirmed rationalist, he knew what he wanted to do and relied on his mind and heart, not mysterious inspiration to supply the kazi to turn it out. *Jazz-Set, Checkmates.*

Plus Ron, unlike some of us, was not want to zip off into the abstract and turgid waygonesphere. He wrote about Black People, working people, their lives and conflicts, their passions and loves and tragedies. He wrote about the real life he had experienced and witnessed, analyzed and summed up. We would talk often about that: what is a play, what is relevant to our people, our struggle. How do we create a theatre of The known to make the unknown familiar and useable. And as always, the great Woodie King was likely to be our engine.

Whenever I came to Detroit, naturally Ron and I would hang, I mean hang on out, day and night long passionate, not conversations, they were too full of everything we knew remembered and desired to be framed as such, they were more like open ended discussions or intimate one-on-one funny time seminars, or it didn't matter, other folks could be present and wave at the words as they sailed back and forth between us.

We would stay up half the night laughing at each other's peculiarities and recalling whatever we liked or didn't. We cd talk about The Black Quartet, with Ed Bullins and Ben Caldwell, produced in NYC by Woodie, of course, or nuttiness observed at would-be Black Arts or Black Drama Festivals or certain Hip or very Unhip Negroes, the state of the United Snakes. Anything. And in the end we would fill each other with a kind of wonderful joviality and compassionate comradeship. Like we dug we were Brothers, Artists, Comrades in the service of the People. What ever that brought or took away from our lives. Our deepest bond is that we knew we were both down for the whole number, the protracted struggle. And that felt good and we dug each other for that.

Will I miss Ron, Ho! Like somebody stole a few thousand words out of my brain. Like I'd miss part of my self and spent the rest of my life half sad, half pissed off about it, every time it came to my mind. Yes, I'll miss him. In fact, I aint ready to believe it. Probably never will be.

*****

WE SHOULD PONDER THE DWINDLING RESOURCES OF OUR CULTURAL REVOLUTION AND RE-IGNITE THAT SPARK THAT'S LEFT

Some Black Revolutionary Artists of the *Black Arts Movement* and Environs not many knew. The amazing *Henry Dumas* left too early, some fiend in the subway station murdered him for, they said, jumping a turnstile. That was not believable but it shot through us at the rising height of our rebellious frenzy (68).

Then *Larry Neal*, straight out of his poem "till the butcher cut me down." That was deadly, both, a double deadly slice at our vital production and a reduction of ammunition for the struggles to come. And they are here.

Some others disappeared. We heard no more from Cleveland's *Rudy B. Graham, Norman Jordan* vanished somewhere into infinity. Norman, some sd, obsessed with ritual nudity. *Mae Jackson*, I heard from a few ticks ago. She must be summoned to re-ignite.

Ray Johnson, L. Goodwin, Ahmed Alhamisi, DL Graham, Jacques Wakefield, Kuwasi Balagon, where, doing what? We need their words. *Sam Cornish*, is he still in Maryland?

Bob Bennett, Al Haynes in Boston...*A.B. Spellman, Charlie Cobb* with *Walt Delegall* in DC, we need to hear their voices! Where is *Bill Mahoney? Joe Goncalves*, who was the provocateur of *Black Poetry Journal*, another heavy thinker he writes from Atlanta. And where the wonderful *Welton Smith*? He said it "They want to be White Women" an ugly prophecy hammered down now with "White Chicks," yes, played by Negro men.

Can someone summon *Lindsay Barrett* who left Jamaica for Nigeria, who erupted with a scarlet beauty? *Charles Anderson, Richard Thomas, QR Hand, Lethonia Gee, Ron Welburn*, (the brilliant analyst of The Music who the demons removed when they felt the shift to passivity had come and so they sent all our writers on the Music to Sports, and now not a one speaks from those big mags and the theft rises almost unopposed, even Stanley *Crouch*, the most famous "defector," has been mugged.) *James Danner, Barbara Simmons*. We have not heard from *Lefty Sims*, straight off the Harlem prairie, Lebert Bethune (in the islands they say). What about the two missing in action in Chicago, Amus Mor and Carolyn Rodgers. Mor's "Poem to the Hip Generation" exited our whole generation with its use of the Music and the mytho-biographical narrative of person and place. His reading on Woodie King's Motown issued poorly distributed *Black Spirits* remains an awesome example of the artistic and political power generated by the BAM. Rodgers was reputed to have gone into the church on the heavy side. She made the Chi Hood a place of living struggle and revelation.

Where are they all? Let them reappear and tell us help us give us a missing strength and power. They are some of the forces of the Black Arts Cultural Revolution. We are pressed now against the wall of erased truth and newly neoned lies and dishonour.

We had already lost a great innovator, *Lorraine Hansberry*, who flexed the breath we did not even know we had. And she, for all the ink about *Raisin*, is still not fully known for the power that followed. "The Drinking Gourd" Whites in Harlem do Genet's "The Blacks" but no one seems willing to do Lorraine's power answer "Les Blancs." How many years before all of her is known?

And *Jimmy Baldwin* too, the other explosive paradigm, who helped set the tone, the direction of the Black Arts Cultural Revolution with all of his searching works evaluating sorry America. *Blues for Mr. Charlie* presented the choice, the gun or the bible. He said, one of them gonna work! And so he was removed from the pantheon of the *Colored, OK to read. No Name, In the Street,* or *Evidence* makes it all abundantly clear of our protracted struggle as well as the wooden Negroes barb wiring our path!

Margaret Walker the grand dame of Black American poetry also passed a few months ago. That was as debilitating culturally as Langston's exit. Add (really subtract) *Gwendolyn Brooks*, our first Pulitzer poet or *Dudley Randall*, long time publisher of the nervy and adventurous *Broadside Press* or *Black World* editor, Hoyt Fuller.

And then, so soon too many of those who their baton was intended *Stokely*, that energy and commitment to organizing plus that love for the people is dead, and Detroit's revolutionary theorist, *James Boggs, John Henrk Clarke*, our towering Historian, likewise to the spirit world. *Calvin Hernton, James Stewart, David Llorens.* The Great visionary of sound and thought, *Sun Ra* probably on Saturn reaching us when he can. *Hart LeRoi Bibbs* to Paris to eternity. My main man, Actor, Activist, *Yusef Iman*, a vacuum where he pummeled the air. (Remember the LP's "Black & Beautiful," "Nation Time" or "Black Mass" w/Sun Ra) the troubled but lyrical insistence of Harlem's *Clarence Reed* long dead, still unknown. The lovely irony of *Tony Cade Bambara* that too removed from us. Big hearted, Big voiced, *Lance Jeffers,*

Jamaica's *Mikey Smith* the thrilling "Dub" incendiary murdered in Jamaica by "Blindaga's perverts. Though Linton Kwesi Johnson, Kamau Braithwaite, Oku Onuora, Mutabaruka remain & yet cook! *Ngugi wa Thiongo* had to escape from Kenya's government murderers. The still unknown but important Ugandan *Okot p'Bitek* suicided by frustration. We could add *Martin Carter* and *Walter Rodney* as part of our United Front as well as the so called "Black Beats," *Bob Kaufman* and *Ted Joans* with their uncategorized assaults on the Ignorant, the Arrogant and the Greedy.

Except we shd know that all those works must be brought back, republished, that spirit and those lives of fire and hope re-presented to the world! That is a concrete critical task. These are works that can reignite our Cultural Revolution, in the face of Imperialism murderers, liars, deceivers, white supremacists and wooden Negro apprentices and compradors.

We are still bowed with grief and longing for, one of our closest bad bard comrades in struggle, *Gaston Neal*, who has still to have his sizzling book appear. Bobb Hamilton. My sister Kimako, who fought the ignorant saboteurs with us at the *Black Arts Repertory Theatre School* who created *The Kuumba Theatre* and *Kimako's* to raise the life spirit and cultural understanding of Harlem. She and *Arthur Mitchell* had a mid-town Ballet theatre before and after the Black Arts.

And just this year, *Nina Simone, Benny Carter, Vincent Smith, Tom Feelings, Jeff Cobb, Ray Charles*, the truth, beauty and power of some who gave full dimension to the grandness of contemporary Afro-American Arts and Culture. Or the rebellious colorists, *William White, Bob Thompson*, gone long before them. The ingenious *Bob Blackburn.*

Certainly from the specific pledge of understanding and commitment to Black American Political and Cultural Insurrection the Black Arts Movement itself proclaimed, we must look back and review as we go forward. And since then dwell a moment on the Monumental subtraction of our force the Coltrane, Clifford Browns,

Duke Ellington, Billie Holiday, Olatunji, Albert Ailey, Thelonius Monk, Albert Ayler, Sarah Vaughan, Marvin Gaye, Miles Davis, Elvin Jones, Eddie Blackwell, Julius Hemphill, Don Cherry, Lester Bowie, Don Pullen, in addition to Huey Newton, Martin Luther King, Malcolm X. It should be hurtfully clear how much we are in need of a regrouping a repositioning, a reaffirmation, remobilization of the Afro American Artistic Culture.

So from the specific parameters of the Black Arts Movement, we know that *Ed Bullins, Ben Caldwell, Woodie King, Marvin X, Amiri Baraka, Sonia Sanchez, David Henderson, Ted Wilson, Carol Freeman, Ojijiko, Askia Toure,* (Rolland Snellings), *Willie Kgostisile* (in South Africa), *Ed Spriggs* (the spark that built the now enemy-occupied Studio Museum of Harlem), *Reggie Lockett, Sam Anderson, Clarence Franklin, Jay Wright, Yusef Rahman, Lorenzo Thomas, Joe White, Charles Fuller, Haki Madhubuti, Sterling Plumpp, Jimmie Garrett, Gylan Kain* (in Netherlands), The other *Last Poets: Felipe Luciano, Daveed Nelson, Umar Abiodun,* I know they alive and well. Nikki Giovanni, Mari Evans, Johari Amini, they around.

Victor Hernandez Cruz (in Puerto Rico?) was in "Black Fire," though we have also lost our Latin brothers, *Mikey Pinero,* the great *Pedro Pietri.* But *Miguel Algarin, Sandra Esteves, Papaleto, Piri Thomas,* are on the scene. And Miguel's NuYorican Poets Theatre still stands and delivers. Just as *John Watusi Branch's African Poetry Theatre* in Queens holds fast. Marvelous *Woodie King* still kicks out new drama monthly at the *New Federal Theatre* in NYC.

Marvin X's Recovery Theatre in Oakland is still producing. *Amina & Amiri Baraka's Kimako's Blues People* has functioned for the last 15 years in their basement, in Newark. Closed for the last year by the obscene tragedy of our youngest daughter Shani's murder. They are planning to reopen it later in '04.

Haki Madhubuti's Third World Press is a powerful institution of confrontation with ignorance and ugliness. Baraka has begun publication of the newspaper *Unity & Struggle* (June 04) and is calling for allies in initiating a journal and publishing entity called *RAZOR. Sonia Sanchez* and her son, *Morani* are filming a series of interviews with BAM activists, which is something now critically needed.

All this together suggests though we are now near bottom of the Sisyphus Syndrome, as Dubois termed the up and down motion of the BLM, the Afro-American struggle for Democracy & Self-

454

Determination! We still have a great many resources needing only to be re-mobilized. Plus we must begin to re-produce and re-present the important works in the huge treasure chest of the Afro American Artistic and Political culture! And as well, re-introduce those revolutionary figures who have contributed the power, the truth and beauty of Black American Culture.
(2004)

Lift Every Voice & Sing!
A Cultural Paradigm of Afro-American Self Determination & Creativity

Lift Every Voice...was part of my growing up. Very early in my expanding perception I understood that at certain programs my parents took me to, the Negro National Anthem would be sung: The National Association of Postal Employees gatherings, dances, conventions, meetings, &c. When we went down to Tuskegee where my mother had attended "Normal" school, and I saw a statue of Booker T. Washington pulling the cover of ignorance off the prototype slave, there was the anthem loud and heartfelt.

At a few gatherings in Newark, at Bethany Baptist and some other churches (for special programs, e.g., Roland Hayes, Philippa Schuyler), the Howard University Alumni House, The Colored YMCA's, The Terrace Ballroom, my mother's various clubs (e.g. The Girl Friends') programs, soirees. It might be a benefit for the NAACP or Urban League, or the Black Community Hospital, or my grandfather's Black Republican meetings, my grandmother's American Woodsmen sets (an Afro American insurance company) and Poro(!) programs of Black beauticians, the anthem usually ended the programs.

When we went down to Tennessee, to visit Fisk, where she'd gone to college, where there were also those dynamite murals by Aaron Douglass, I remembered all my life, *Lift Every Voice*, was sung, further animating that gathering with the heap of heavy vibrations from the folks I saw and, I felt, Black angels hovering invisibly, rah rah ing the proceedings.

At gatherings like this, I was reached deep down throughout my self. A feeling of, some still not completely identified, "We-ness"...that we B lack folks were actually *real* and had desires independent of the craziness and lunacy of the vicious racist white folks I was told about every few evenings at the dinner table. Tales, events, ongoing commentary on the bestiality of American Apartheid and the struggle and travails, including lynching present and past, remembered and talked about, of the Afro-American people.

As a child, certainly, I took all this in. And it bottomed in me as a kind of base, a foundation of humanity sought. A map and diagram, a historic journey laid out from which I would draw on always. So I had deepness given to me, throughout my childhood, that we were "colored people," that we were suffering unjust, uncivilized, unchristian, even maniacal treatment by ignorant, evil, "jealous crackers." The last, my grandmother always ended with, in memory of my grandfather's two burned up grocery stores and threatened funeral parlor in Dothan, Alabama. Where my family finally had to flee, terrorized by Klan like forces who threatened to kill them all, for the crime of self-determination, an openly strived for socio-economic advance and stubbornly husbanded dignity.

When we went back to Dothan, on the Tuskegee trip, I heard about the past from some old near dead red faced mummies sitting in a grocery store, who opinioned that I "talked too clear" at age 7 or 8. I'm sure the older Jones's took my almost falling into a well, after the dead people's "playback," as an omen of the death threat still hanging over the place.

No doubt the bitterness of the small Black petty bourgeoisie, driven from the Black Belt to Beaver Falls (near Pittsburgh) and finally to open a store in Newark, N.J. where shortly after, the depression put him out of business...was also part of my socialization and slowly crystallizing consciousness. Hearing *Lift Every Voice*, seemed always to give me a sweeping "recall" of everything I'd been told and even witnessed (the dirty colored car of the segregated trains to the south, the balcony colored section, reached by rickety side stairs of the movie, the crazed reaction to my seven year old speech, my mother, one day, in Newark, cussing out a white store keeper for calling the nuts she was buying "Nigger Toes"..."Those are Brazil Nuts, Lady!" Then stalking off, whipping little me behind her as she exited on fire.

But the song had a blossoming beauty to it. The words began to deepen in me over the years. What my consciousness had grasped as literal meaning was also given a heavier gravity by the emotional opening the words carried with them. A direct access to the "true self consciousness" Du Bois speaks of. That there was a beauty to us there, a dignity, a strength, untouched by the acknowledged Ugly of American national oppression, its robbery, denial of rights, slander, repression, violence, murder — That we existed independent of that, somehow, that our "humanity" was as real as we were and *could not* be damaged by the devil himself.

Even today that feeling remains, every time I hear the anthem. It's why I included it in a "Word Music" work my wife, Amina and our group, Blue Ark, do often called FUNK LORE: BLACK HISTORY MUSIC, where we perform a ninety minute overview of Afro-American History and the music that is its cultural chronology, from the Middle Passage to Malcolm, ending with my wife's great poem about Malcolm X, backed by the Anthem. It provides a stunning denouement. Summing up Black history as a living being, still struggling for Self Determination, Equal Citizenship Rights and Democracy!

Lift Every Voice must be acknowledged as James Weldon and Rosamond Johnson's greatest work (albeit, "Black and Unknown Bards" and "The Creation") because not only is it exquisite poetry, but a lyric whose aesthetic dialectic uncovers and releases deep historic and ennobling experience from within itself, swinging joyously into ourselves, triggered by our singing. (In this sense, it is truly the highest form of a **People's Poetry**!). As if our voices were the only necessary ingredient to be added so that we can actually rise, soar and become, for that expression's duration, that "band of *angels*" in the chariot, *ourselves*, and when returned to earth, more strongly aware that our task is to carry ourselves "home," that is, to continue the historic revolutionary democratic struggle to transform this Heathen Hell into a dwelling fit for evolving Humanity. *(12/1999)*

Preface to the Reader

The first book I published was called "Preface..." Now, some thirty years later, another Preface, now more clearly as both "anchor" (as in relay races) to one motion and as "1st leg" to another, further motion.

This Reader should give some description of my own changing and diverse motion, of where I been and why, and how I got to where I was when next I "appeared" or was heard from. It has always been in the literary sense somewhat difficult to "appear" or be heard from, (sometimes more difficult than others). For instance, in the last decade, it has been extremely difficult for me to "appear" or be heard from, except if you could actually hear me talking.

The general media typology that lists my ideological changes and so forth as "Beat-Black Nationalist-Communist" has brevity going for it, and there's something to be said for that, but then there is the complexity of real life, like notating Monk.

"You mean that's not accurate?" Dick or Dixie Dugan wd counter.

"Well, yes and no," I'd drawl. Acknowledging with an easy dismissal any mental disclaimer needed, to sound so Zennish.

But the truth in that is this: going toward and away from some name, some identifiable "headline" of one's life includes steps that have names too, but we aint that precise yet—though many try. We go from 1 to 2 and the crushed breath away from the "given" remains unknown, swallowed by its profile as to what makes the distance. But there is real life between 1 and 2. There is the life of the speed, the time it takes, the life there in, in the middle of, the revelation, like perception, rationale and use. To go from any where to any there.

Hopefully, there is enough motion, movement, in these works to show not only the letter increments identifying change but the minute organic calibration breaths go going gone been gone, contain. From here to there and the how you gots in the middle.

What does need hammering away at is the reason that I have not been on the scene recently. As a young person confused by definite energy and perception, I could publish like a scatter gun of quasi-defined sensitivity, though some times even at odds with my self. The bohemian rootlessness and quick draw aspect (actually the safety net for the Castle dwellers, who can see no matter how loud you get, you still don't know the whole story) would give way more and more to what was at first I thought the shadow of an earlier life, but it was the dimension of myself I had to learn, to complete the rationale. The explanation.

Black Nationalism, was an emotional historical fulfillment. Like that shadow, it was the rest of myself I had yet to get together, and so used in the way one does a whole telling of that, the whole memory, begets a wholer self. Malcolm X, Robert Williams, Cuba, The Black Arts were fire burning the stone, giving up the living touching heart of me, to myself. And to who ever was out there. The rush of feelings held in by education, socialization, but that was real and could be touched. And so it rushed out, armed with the seen, the understood, the resisted ugliness of all they stack around our hearts hoping to stifle the funk.

And so struggle, change, struggle, unity, change, move, and more of the movement, the motion. The work reflects my life and ideas of that. All of it a whole realized or half realized or some way station.

When we said at the Black Arts: (1) An Art that is recognizably Afro American (2) An Art that is mass oriented, that will come out the libraries and stomp. (3) An Art that is revolutionary, that will be with Malcolm and Rob Williams, that will conk klansmen and erase racists, we meant that not only with the fervor and new fire of youth, but with the certainty and necessity of our realest history. This remains today.

I became a Communist through struggle, the intensity of

realized passion, understood, but now finally stood under, as a force, your own ideological clarity, like a jet stream, a nuclear force of reason, from way back, birth black, history fueled experience directed. Until finally you understand that hate whitey is accurate since the only whitey is system and ideology, that whites is a class and the devil that do evil. Though, for sure "white" peepas (and what is that "white" — when everybody's mama is Black?) has been socialized to be hierarchical monsters, and rainbow smaller b's and petty b's have had the likewise "classic" "judeo-xtian" "greco-roman" "intelligent (like Larry Byrd)" "upscale" "straight (as opposed to kinky)" gibberish degreed in their caps and tattooed in their feeling skins like gowns.

But still it was easier to be heard from with hate whitey than hate imperialism! The retrograde trend of ideology meant to tell us struggle is old hat, Black is old hat, communism is dead, and nothing matters but greed does not need consistent objection and analysis of its changing same ol' ugliness. To grow a younger set of weasels, the old weasels do not need our resistance. They go back in history to erase us, imperialism must be Elvis Presley to our Big Mama Thornton's Dis'd and Covered (they call it Discovered!).

October 1990 we are poised on the brink of a war that Robert Redford told us about several years ago in the last minutes of "Three Days of the Condor" e.g., "it's about oil, isn't it?"
(The villain nods, once, now terrified)
"Are we planning to invade the middle east?"
(Again the same single head shake up and down)

American people roll the huge stone of slavery up off them through consistent struggle but also with continuous revolutionary outbursts. Then at another point the villains conspire to push it back down upon us. Hopefully, never as far down as before. We are in the down the slope motion now. The Supreme court is now peopled largely with "ugs" wearing cellophane klan lids. Since the death of the Kennedys, the U.S. has been in the slowly tightening grip of would be creators of the new international corporate state. What we struggled for they have attacked, undermined, ridiculed, and even grown blackus retrogradus to oppose (from soul to sowell so the speak) our self determination and a U.S. peoples democracy.

My writing reflects my own growth and expansion, and at the same time the society in which I have existed, throughout this

longish confrontation. Whether it is politics, magic, literature, or the origins of language, there is a historical and time place condition reference that will always try to explain exactly why I was saying both how and for what.
(10/6/1990)

Newark, My Newark

I was born in this town, this old brick city of sidewalks and gray steel winter shadows. A depression baby, at Kenney Hospital (named for a Black doctor) on West Kinney Street. It's now another church. One thing we got here is churches. Churches and taverns.

I live in Newark, first, because it is my home. Where I grew up and met my wife and raised a family. It is a place where I can still walk down the street on any day and greet people I went to elementary school or high school or college or played basketball or hung out listening to the sounds with. Newark is still the measure of my understanding of social life and political and cultural struggle worldwide. Here is where we are struggling to see practical roots put down as part of a worldwide struggle for democracy.

But for me, this city — originally, if you look at its charter, New Ark — has always been the measure of everything else. The future, the past, the roaring silence we think of as Now. It has been, and is, a measure, a set of standards and life-influencing principles it carries with it, that I have always related to in one way or another, even far away from Home. Because there is a depth, a realness, a harsh confirmation that wherever I might go and whatever I might do, no matter how it was rendered glitter and dazzle or transcendent revelation or even triumph, there was a link of tether, a chain of brick, a rein of concrete that held me to the early perception and subsequent rationale I got walking these mumbling streets — that the American Dream was only a dream, and a bitterly corny one at that.

I was always cared for enough and talked to enough and educated enough (even before, between, and independent of schools) to understand the hard truths given to me by the place. I learned more about American social mores and history at the dinner table than from any formal education. Likewise, I understood and was given more deep understanding of who I was, among the many faces and names and lifelong friends, than in my extensive travels and experiences across the world.

No, I have no "poor stories," as my wife, Amina, has labeled so many of the current obligatory rags-to-riches tales of the recently prosperous. My people, like most Black people, came from the South. Father from South Carolina, mother from Alabama. I was a child of civil servants — father a postman, mother, for many years, a social worker for the housing authority.

At Barringer High, I was a member of the cross-country team and won my first letter for the two-and-a half mile. Then letters for the hurdles, half mile. I placed fourth in the city in 1950 when Barringer won the city championship.

I know most of the older officers in the Newark Police Department who went to Barringer. Just a few months ago, at the site of the shooting of Dannette Daniels by a policeman, when I stepped forward to speak with the police director, who was at his side but an old Barringer schoolmate, a football lineman, Louis Dell Ermo — We shook hands, laughed, and lied about our school days. On the other hand, in 1967, during the Newark Rebellions, it was a Barringer schoolmate who first busted my head open with his pistol.

I walked these streets with other young men, searching for the hip sounds of our day, trying to be hip walking across High Street with a trumpet, wanting to play like Miles Davis, hanging out at the Masonic on Belmont, and digging Illinois Jacquet, Ruth Brown, Little Esther, plus the Nat Phipps Band, who brought the latest Bop sounds to us every week, at the teenage canteens, the Court Street Y, Wideway Hall, The Terrace, Lloyds Manor, Club Harold.

I hung out with the Shorters, Wayne and Alan, when Wayne was with the Phipps and Bland bands. I used to try to stand close to Little Jimmy Scott, hanging out on Hillside Place, when I lived right around the corner and ran with the Hillside Place crowd, with my green Tyrolean "sky" and "swag" checked overcoat, in a gray-flannel suit with 22-inch cuffs, purchased where the hip got their "vines," at Wolmuth's on Market Street.

Newark has always been that deeper experience of my development. I was no "street tough," not in anybody's eyes, least of all my own. The hardest dudes I ran with would take off their hats in each other's houses if their parents were home and sit respectfully, maybe signifying to each other with barely stifled giggles if somebody's "fiiiiine sister" ripped through.

I left Rutgers-Newark (when there were about five Blacks in the whole joint) because Barringer had worn me out with marginalization, like the band instructor who called the Black kids "Sambo" (except me, I guess because I had the horn held in my hand like a bludgeon). So I got away, with my mother's urging and went off to Howard University, unconsciously swearing to be done with marginalization and non-being forever.

I returned to New Ark after college, the Air Force, Greenwich Village, Harlem, and took up my life here again at 30. It was with an experienced and educated and world-chastened perspective. I had become a fairly well-known writer, both celebrated and denigrated, perhaps with equal effect. I had left the Village to go to Harlem after Malcolm X was murdered: I was self-consciously and genuinely enraged. I had to be directly in the ranks of the people who most deeply loved me, the Afro-American people. For me, Malcolm's assassination was a simple declaration of WAR on Black people — on all democratic people—just as the murders of Martin Luther King Jr. and John F. Kennedy had been.

So I returned to do the "real" work, the day-to-day work of "making revolution." In Harlem I had founded the Black Arts Repertory Theater School, which became, though short-lived, a spark that set the Black Arts Movement sweeping across the country. In the BAM we used our art as a weapon of social transformation, not just to titillate the kindly liberals. This approach has, of course, brought tons of criticism from Richie Rich. Any critique of America, no matter in what form, will draw torrents of opposition not only from those who misunderstand but also from the prostitutes of the status quo. And I have not always helped my case, thundering often in those early years of my return in blind anger as a Black Nationalist, too many times condemning all white people, mistaking the normal ignorance of Americans with the class interest of the powerful.

When I returned I met a beautiful young artist, Sylvia Wilson (known as Amina), whom I fell in love with and who became my wife and who has remained, for the 30 years of our marriage, my closest comrade in struggle. And if it's one thing we do know about, it's struggle. Later, I opened the Spirit House, in an old building on Stirling Street. From the time Amina and I married, the Spirit House was the center of our many activities. We put on plays to a growing and highly enthusiastic audience. Amina first developed the African Free School there, and with our friends she began to teach the neighborhood children about Black History and found that many of these children could barely read.

I Started *Community Newspaper* and taught the youth how to work mimeograph machines. We circulated this modest little missile throughout our community, taking local polls on issues like "Do you think Newark needs a Black mayor?"

Soon Amina and I and a steadily growing group of activists drawn to the Spirit House got into struggles around "controversial" issues and were increasingly harassed by the police. Yet, even with the African Free School we fought for "thorough and efficient" public education, particularly affecting the closest school, Robert Treat, whose name we changed later to Marcus Garvey. We became active in many of Newark's raging controversies, but we still maintained our commitment and activity around the arts.

When the '67 Rebellions shook Newark, as the predictable denouement of the vicious racism and segregation that openly marked the city then, I was thrown in jail the first night, head split open, all my bottom teeth loosened, until they came out 25 years later. From that time, we became more organizationally conscious. I joined with a group of young men, the United Brothers, interested in Black Power via the electoral system.

Amina formed a women's division. Her work in education, social development, and Pan-African cultural innovation incorporated traditional African customs and practices. She innovated the African-based hairstyles and traditional "bubbas and lappas" and jewelry now seen ubiquitously throughout the country, as we brought together the Committee for United Newark. This group spearheaded the organization of the Black community and in alliance with the progressive forces in the Puerto Rican Community,

466

mobilized a broad coalition of democratic forces in Newark to elect the city's first Black mayor, Kenneth Gibson.

Many of us believed that simply replacing white faces with black faces in high places was not the solution — though the question of Black self-determination, at the root of our concern, remains an unresolved question nationwide. The elevation of many of our old associates to positions of actual power in the city taught us the brutal lesson of class struggle. Because too often the most visible sector of the Black middle class runs as swiftly away from the real problems crippling the Black community as does its white counterpart. The most backward sectors of the Black bourgeoisie were militant only to the extent that they could get into power or use the Black masses as their mules. So as we struggled against Black national oppression and now against many of these Black faces in high places (many of whom we had worked to put there), the relevance of class struggle brought Amina and me and quite a few other folks into Marxism.

Amina and I have co-produced and raised five children here in this Brick City. Obalaji, our oldest boy, an All-City athlete in football, basketball, and baseball at Malcolm X Shabazz High School; Ras, the next, who has already run for mayor and is deeply rooted in political struggle, like his parents; Shani, the little All-American basketball point guard, our only girl, now teaching and coaching at University High School; "Little Amiri," my namesake, who is part of a rising and highly innovative Rap Group called One Step Beyond (watch for them!); and Ahi, the youngest, who has already gone through more hell in his life than most adults have.

In June 1992, Amina and I gave a Father's Day gathering at our home and brought together close friends and their children with music and poetry and rounds of good feeling and pledges of recommitment to the family. After the gathering, our son Amiri was taking a group of girls home when, at a traffic stop, a group of youths approached the car and pulled him out, robbed him, and took the car keys. Amiri, outraged, ran into one of his older brother's friends, who got the money and keys returned. But Amiri, still fuming, came home and got his younger brother and some of his pals to go back. They didn't realize that these boys were drug dealers, and when the car our boys were in approached the spot where Amiri had been victimized, shots rang out from a .357 magnum handgun. The huge slug tore through the car door, and even though Ahi ducked, the bullet struck him at an angle on the side of his head and whipped around, still under his skin, until it stopped, bulging horribly out over his eye! The bullet did not, thank whatever, penetrate his skull, and this is the only good luck we claim.

Even though the bullet was removed and Ahi lay in therapy for months, he was visibly damaged by that hideous crime. The boy who did the shooting was captured and jailed and later, when he got out, shot down, presumably by some competitors in the same business. But Ahi's speech is impaired, and the effects of his injury are protracted if not permanent.

At my insistence, we put him back in University High and, when he graduated, sent him, like Ras and Amiri Jr., to my alma mater, Howard University in Washington, D.C. But the effects of that grim experience did not vanish. It seemed to us that, from that collision with madness, Ahi was determined never to be so victimized again, and so his entire perspective and relationship with the community was altered.

At this writing, he sits in a halfway house in Newark, run by Kintock Group, part of Governor Whitman's privatized empire of penal institutions, where he waits to be released, even though he was due to be paroled a month ago. At the time of his arrest, Ahi had finished his sophomore year at Howard and had come home for summer vacation. He was arrested with a youth he had grown up with, who had remained on the streets while Ahi went off to college.

There is a lesson in this that must be grasped by any of us seeking to change not only this Ark of Brick, but the entire society. We cannot leave some of the children on the streets while others go off to college. We cannot change our city until we make their public school education the fundamental requirement for employment in every public and municipal office. We cannot change the city or the country until we have open admission in all public universities, particularly those in inner cities. Until we can use our tax money to repair the cities where we live, to see that all citizens are properly fed, educated, employed, and provided with cultural experiences and recreational activities that they actually can participate in, we all lose. Newark is a gold mine of social, cultural, and commercial development, but the people's needs must be satisfied by

transforming the city from a warehouse of absentee wealth and profit to a vital center of collective self-development. No city of almost 300,000 people is really poor!
(01/1998)